Railw
Resto
2004

Edited by Alan C. Butcher

PLATFORM
5

41312

75
F

Ian Allan PUBLISHING

Contents

Front cover: National Railway Museum-owned No 30587 is seen in action on the Bodmin & Wenford Railway soon after restoration. *Alan Barnes*

Back cover: Isabel seen hauling a demonstration goods train on the Amerton Railway in September 2003. *Alan Barnes*

Previous page: Visiting the Bluebell Railway from the Mid Hants line No 41312 stands at Horsted Keynes. *Alan Barnes*

Right: The driver hitches a ride as *Polar Bear* runs round its train at Amberley Working Museum during 2003's Railway Gala Weekend. *ACB*

First published 1980
Twenty fifth edition 2004

ISBN 0 7110 2933 4

Published by Ian Allan Publishing

an imprint of Ian Allan Publishing Ltd, Hersham, Surrey KT12 4RG
Printed by Ian Allan Printing Ltd, Hersham, Surrey KT12 4RG

Code: 0403/C3

RAIL BICENTENARY

National Railway Heritage Awards

2004 marks the 200th anniversary of the first steam locomotive to run on rails — Richard Trevithick's locomotive at the Pen Y Darren Ironworks. 2004 also marks the centenary of *City of Truro* reaching a speed of 100mph. It is also 400 years since the first recorded existence of rail track in Britain.

These important milestones will see a variety of celebrations, marking the history as well as highlighting the achievements of today and looking forward to the future of rail travel. Events will range from a major public Bicentennial Rail Celebration run by the National Railway Museum at York (29 May to 6 June) along with smaller-scale activities around the country's heritage railways and museums.

Details of most special events and open days can be found within the pages of *Railways Restored* and 'Rail 200' events at http://www.rail200.com on the the internet.

'Rail 200' is supported by a wide range of organisations associated with Britain's railways, including the Strategic Rail Authority, The Association of Train Operating Companies, The Railway Forum, the Heritage Rail Association and a number of other companies well-known within the railway field.

The Awards have been made annually since 1979 with the object of encouraging high standards of structural restoration and environmental care, thereby promoting public recognition and awareness of historic railway structures and their place in the environment. We aim to promote careful design and quality workmanship in restoration, modernisation and maintenance, after taking full account of all relevant factors, particularly, of course, manpower and finance. In this way, we encourage both public and private railways to present their operational premises as an attractive 'shop window', while occupiers of former railway buildings now used for other purposes are similarly encouraged to retain as much as possible of the original character.

The organisers are the HRA and the main sponsors are Ian Allan Publishing Ltd, together with the Railway Heritage Trust, Westinghouse Rail Systems and the Association of Train Operating Companies. Judging is done from the beginning of May through to the end of August and those short listed are notified at the beginning of October. The Awards are presented in early December at a prestigious location by a well-known public figure, with full media coverage.

1992 saw the inclusion of Ireland in the Awards initially with the addition of a special Premier Award and up to three Certificates of Commendation in each sector.

WHAT IS ELIGIBLE?
1 Any present or former railway structure such as a station, warehouse, bridge, viaduct, tunnel or signalling installation, that has been sympathetically restored for whatever purpose.
2 A replica structure intended to re-create or augment some aspect of the railway heritage.
3 A new structure designed in traditional style in order to blend with or complement the local environment.

WHO CAN ENTER?
Any group in Great Britain and Ireland involved in railway preservation, whether as a private railway company or as a less formal organisation. Railtrack, Irish Rail, Northern Ireland Railways (NIR). Other public or commercial organisations. Private individuals.

The scheme is divided into:
(a) The Volunteer Sector for organisations run wholly or largely by volunteers.
(b) The Public & Commercial Sector. In cases of doubt, the awards committee decides which sector is appropriate.

For application forms apply to:
Robin Leleux
12 Bilsdale Way
Baildon
Shipley
West Yorkshire
BD17 5DG

Editor's Notes

On the following pages will be found a guide to the major preserved railways, railway museums and preservation centres in the British Isles. Information for visitors has been set out in tabular form for easy reference, together with a locomotive stocklist for most centres.

Many preservation centres and operating lines provide facilities for other groups and organisations to restore locomotives and equipment on their premises. It has not been possible to include full details of these groups, but organisations which own locomotives are shown under the centres at which they operate. In addition, a full list of member societies of the HRA is given elsewhere. In the case of most operating lines their length is given, but there is no guarantee that services are operated over the entire length.

Within the heading to each entry a heading block has been incorporated for easy reference as to what each site offers in the way of passenger service to visitors. These are as follows:

Timetable Service: Railways providing a passenger service between two or more stations with public access; eg West Somerset Railway.

Steam Centre: A railway or preservation site offering a passenger service on a short length of line, on a regular basis, with public access at only one point; eg Didcot Railway Centre.

Museum: A museum or site that does not offer a passenger service on a regular basis, if at all; eg London's Transport Museum. Some sites may however offer rides on miniature railways.

Railway Centre: A catch-all for those centres which do not fall clearly into any of the other brackets. Generally those offering rides over short distances using non-steam motive power.

Attraction: Where the railway is an addition to the main attraction of the location (eg Exbury Railway).

As well as a guide as to what to expect on each site, this year's *Railways Restored* shows what, if any, particular professional body the Companies or Societies belong to. These are:

HRA: Indicates that the organisation is a member of the Heritage Railway Association (HRA).

TT: Indicates that the organisation is a member of the Transport Trust (TT).

Membership of the HRA and TT is open to both organisations and private individuals. Private members are able to take advantage of concessions offered to them by the organisations that subscribe to these two bodies.

The concessions range from a discount on the admission price to free entry. The TT's Travel Back leaflet provides details.

Details given under **Access by public transport** should be checked beforehand to ensure services shown are operating. Unless the Heritage Railway, Steam Centre or Museum has identified the privatised train company operating the service, the phrase 'by rail', or 'main line', has been used to identify access by train.

Visitors wishing to see specific items of rolling stock or locomotives are advised to check before their visit that the exhibit is available for inspection. It should be stressed that not all items are usually available for inspection due to restoration, operating or other restrictions.

Editor's Comment

It seems only yesterday that the late Captain Peter Manisty, Chairman of the then Association of Railway Preservation Societies suggested that Ian Allan should take over publication of the ARPS yearbook, that this is the 25th edition of *Railways Restored* shows how quickly time passes. As the ARPS evolved into the Heritage Railway Assocation so has *Railways Restored* evolved; the first edition stretched to 96 pages and contained line diagrams and a good number of photographs to illustrate some 74 entries. This edition is 176 pages of editorial with over 170 places of railway interest, with, unfortunately, less in the way of illustrations.

This edition welcomes a number of new arrivals to its pages including the Lynton & Barnstaple Railway (revived at the original Woody Bay station); Royal Deeside Railway (whose stock includes the unique battery-electric multiple-unit that operated on the line before closure); the East Hayling Light Railway; the Wensleydale Railway and the new lines at Exbury Gardens and Evesham Light Railway. The former Timothy Hackworth Museum will be reopened as Shildon Railway Village in September as an out-station of the National Railway Museum. Ireland is not forgotten with the inclusion of the Giant's Causeway & Bushmills and Waterford & Suir Valley lines. One removal from the pages this year is the Museum of Army Transport at Beverley, sadly with mounting debts it could not survive; hopefully the exhibits will be on show elsewhere at a future date.

My thanks to those company officials and the many unpaid volunteers who contine to provide information to make *Railways Restored* the market leader. Hopefully the trend will continue with the 2005 edition with even more entries to show how healthy the railway heritage movement is.

Standard Abbreviations

AEC	Associated Equipment Co
AEG	Allgemeine Elektrizitaets Gesellschaft
A/Barclay	Andrew Barclay
A/Porter	Aveling & Porter Ltd
A/Whitworth	Armstrong Whitworth
B/Drewry	Baguley/Drewry
B/Peacock	Beyer Peacock & Co
B/Hawthorn	Black, Hawthorn & Co
BRCW	Birmingham Railway, Carriage & Wagon
BTH	British Thomson Houston
Buch	23 August Locomotive Works
D/Metcalfe	Davies & Metcalfe
E/Electric	English Electric Ltd
F/Jennings	Fletcher Jennings & Co
F/Walker	Fox Walker
G&S	G. & S. Light Engineering Co
G/England	George England & Co
GRCW	Gloucester Railway, Carriage & Wagon
H/Barclay	Hunslet Barclay
H/Clarke	Hudswell Clarke & Co Ltd
H/Hunslet	Hudson-Hunslet
H/Leslie	Hawthorn Leslie & Co
K/Stuart	Kerr Stuart & Co Ltd
L/Blackstone	Lister Blackstone
M/Cam	Metropolitan Cammell
M/Rail	Motor Rail Ltd
M/Vick	Metrovick (Metropolitan-Vickers)
M/Wardle	Manning Wardle & Co Ltd
N/British	North British Locomotive Co Ltd
N/Wilson	Nasmyth Wilson & Co Ltd
O&K	Orenstein & Koppel
P/Steel	Pressed Steel Co Ltd
RSH	Robert Stephenson & Hawthorn Ltd
R/Hornsby	Ruston Hornsby
R/Proctor	Ruston Proctor
S. F. Belge	Société Franco Belge
SMH	Simplex Mechanical Handling
YEC	Yorkshire Engine Co
W&M	Waggon & Maschinenbau
W/Rogers	Wingrove & Rogers

Company abbreviations

BR	British Railways
DB	German Federal Railway
DSB	Danish State Railways
GWR	Great Western Railway
JZ	Yugoslav Railways
LBSCR	London, Brighton & South Coast Railway
LMS	London, Midland & Scottish Railway
LNER	London & North Eastern Railway
LSWR	London & South Western Railway
MoS	Ministry of Supply
MR	Midland Railway
NLR	North London Railway
NSB	Norwegian State Railways
RR	Rhodesian Railways
S&DJR	Somerset & Dorset Joint Railway

SAR	South African Railways
SECR	South Eastern & Chatham Railway
SER	South Eastern Railway
SJ	Swedish Railways
SNCF	French National Railways
SR	Southern Railway
USATC	United States Army Transportation Corps
WD	War Department

Other abbreviations

BE	Battery-electric
DE	Diesel-electric
DH	Diesel-hydraulic
DM	Diesel-mechanical
DMU	Diesel multiple-unit
E	Overhead electric
EMU	Electric multiple-unit
F	Fireless
G	Geared
GH	Gas-hydraulic
IST	Inverted saddle tank
LRO	Light Railway Order
ParM	Paraffin-mechanical
PH	Petrol-hydraulic
PM	Petrol-mechanical
PT	Pannier tank
R	Railcar
ST	Saddle tank
STT	Saddle tank and tender
T	Side tank
VB	Vertical boiler
WT	Well tank
4w	Four-wheel

Multiple-unit Type abbreviations

B	Brake
C	Composite (First/Standard class seating)
D	Driving
F	First class
K	Corridor
LV	Luggage Van
M	Motor
O	Open (seating arrangement)
P	Pullman (ex-'Brighton Belle')
R	Restaurant
S	Standard ([or Second] class)
T	Trailer

Added together these give the vehicle designation, for example: DMBS — Driving Motor Brake Second.

The addition of an L indicates that the vehicle has a lavatory (may not be operational on some vehicles).

Some lines operate a Standard class only policy and the First class facility is downgraded. This may result in some vehicles having a different designation to that originally applied.

*Before a journey back in steam –
visit the preserved lines from your own armchair*

WATCH A ROBERT NEWLAND VIDEO PRODUCTION

A GLIMPSE OF STEAM No. 6

VHS £18.95

features the Great Central with:

- The Mail Exchange at Quorn.
- 60532 "Blue Peter" with a 14 coach express.
- V2 60800 on the Master Cutler and the S. Yorkshireman.
- 9F 92212 with 65 wagons – the longest freight in preservation.
- Double track steam: 04 63601 and Windcutters passing 8F 48305 on express goods.
  - And much more

A Recreation of Working Steam
A GLIMPSE OF STEAM No. 6
THE GREAT CENTRAL
A Scent of Steam Special

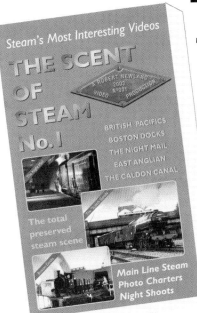

Steam's Most Interesting Videos
THE SCENT OF STEAM No. 1
BRITISH PACIFICS
BOSTON DOCKS
THE NIGHT MAIL
EAST ANGLIAN
THE CALDON CANAL
The total preserved steam scene
Main Line Steam
Photo Charters
Night Shoots

THE SCENT OF STEAM SERIES VISITS 5 or 6 PRESERVED LINES IN EACH PROGRAMME

- To travel narrow gauge try No. 3 (Llanfair) and No. 4 (Corris).
- For Victorian splendour admire Furness No. 20 and Midland No. 158A in No. 3.
- Visit the Great Western Branch Lines on No. 4 – Gwili (No. 8103) and Severn Valley (Nos. 85 and 5637).
- Watch the reflections in the Caldon Canal in No. 1 (44422, 80136, 48305 and 5197).

THE SCENT OF STEAM No. 1 to No. 5 £18.95 each
SAE for the lists of contents.   Cheque or PO

BEST BY FAR FOR NEWS & FEATURES

HERITAGE RAILWAY

The definitive magazine for all those interested in preserved railways

- Covers the entire preservation scene – steam, diesel, electric and horse drawn
- A five-year track record of bringing you the big exclusive stories
- Widest news coverage of all preserved railway and museum venues big and small, plus heritage traction on the main line
- Special features on new railway revival schemes
- Stunning photography from Britain's top lineside cameramen
- Monthly updates on locomotive restoration, running and movements
- Regular columns of carriage and wagon news, young volunteers, railwayana and the latest scale model releases
- Changeover Years flashback features on the late fifties and sixties
- Preservation's liveliest advertisement section

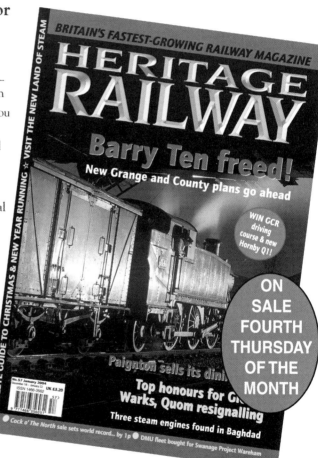

One of the many new entries in this year's *Railway Restored* is the East Hayling Light Railway, here *Jack* departs Beachlands with a train to Eastoke. *Phil Barnes*

England

Member: TT

Narrow gauge site railway (2ft gauge) formerly part of a sewage pumping station that now forms museum site. Railway relaid in concrete by MSC scheme during early 1980s to original track layout. New track layout as an extension to original laid with 35lb rail on wooden sleepers. All the railway system is now run by volunteers. Original Simplex locomotive kept on site in operational condition. Line originally used for transferring solid material from screens to tip (about 100yd). Demonstration skip wagon trains as well as passenger trains are run when the railway is operating

Location: Abbey Pumping Station, Corporation Road, off Abbey Lane, Leicester LE4 5XP

Operating group: Leicester City Council Museum, Arts & Records Service and Leicester Museums Technology Association

Telephone: 0116 299 5111

Fax: 0116 299 5125

Car park: Free on site

Access by public transport: Main line Leicester (London Road). First Bus route 54 from city centre (alight at Beaumont Leys Lane)

Length of line/gauge: About 300yd, 2ft gauge. Passenger

Industrial locomotives

Narrow gauge:

Name	No	Builder	Type	Built
Leonard	—	Bagnall (2087)	0-4-0ST	1919
—	—	Motor Rail (5260)	4wPM	1931
—	—	Hibberd (1776)	4wPM	1931
—	—	R/Hornsby (223700)	4wDM	1944
—	—	SMH (40SD515)	4wDM	1979

Stock

3 new passenger vehicles based on Leicester & Swannington coaches. 10 skip wagons, 2 mine tubs, 2 flats, bomb wagon, various miscellaneous. All locomotives are restored to working order except *Leonard* which is expected to be in use in 2004 when restoration work is completed

carrying on special event days and railway running days (small fare payable on Free-entry days)

Period of public opening: Daily to end March 10.00 to 16.00 Monday to Saturday and 13.00 to 16.00 Sunday; from 4 April, 10.00 to 17.00 Monday to Saturday and 13.00 to 17.00 Sunday

On site facilities: Museum/shop/toilets/car park. Refreshments only on Special Event Days

Facilities for disabled: Access to museum lower floor and grounds. Lift to Engine House and refreshments on event days. Wheelchair access to railway

Volunteer contact: Tony Kendal, c/o Abbey Pumping Station

Museum contact: Mr C. Stevens, c/o Abbey Pumping Station (Tel: 0116 299 5111)

Other attractions: Museum holds various transport, steam navvy, beam engines. Some items only viewable by appointment or on Special Event Days

Special events: Technology & Engineering — 4 April; Wartime Re-enactment — 23 May; Urban Rally — 26/27 June; Craft Day — 19 September; Xmas Steam — 5 December. Railway running days: 15 May, 5 June, 3 July, 7 August, 4 September, 2 October

Member: HRA, TT

Narrow Gauge & Industrial Railway Collection (incorporating the Brockham Museum of Narrow Gauge Railways)

The NG&IR Collection is part of an open air industrial museum set in 36 acres of the former Pepper & Co chalk pits. A 2ft gauge line has been constructed and this is used for carrying passengers in genuine workmen's vehicles

Museum Director: Howard Stenning

Location: Houghton Bridge, Amberley, West Sussex (3 miles north of Arundel) on B2139.

Locomotives
(2ft or 60cm unless otherwise indicated)

Name	No	Builder	Type	Built	
Polar Bear	—	Bagnall (1781)	2-4-0T	1905	
Peter	—	Bagnall (2067)	0-4-0ST	1918	
Townsend Hook	4	F/Jennings (172L)	0-4-0T	1880	(3ft 2.25in gauge)
Scaldwell	—	Peckett (1316)	0-6-0ST	1913	(3ft 0in gauge)
—	23†	Spence	0-4-0T	1921	(1ft 10in gauge)
—	—	Decauville (1126)	0-4-0T	1950	
—**	—	Baldwin (44656)	4-6-0T	1917	
Monty	(6)	O&K (7269)	4wDM	1936	(3ft 2.25in gauge)
The Major	(7)	O&K (7741)	4wDM	1937	
—	2	Ransomes & Rapier (80)	4wDM	1937	
—	—	Hudson-Hunslet (3097)	4wDM	1944	
—	2	R/Hornsby (166024)	4wDM	1933	
—	3101	M/Rail (Simplex) (1381) Armoured	4wPM	1918	
Peldon	—	John Fowler (21295)	4wDM	1936	
Redland	—	O&K (6193)	4wDM	1937	
—	—	Lister (35421)	4wPM	1949	
—	—	M/Rail (Simplex) (872)	4wPM	1918	
—	27	M/Rail (Simplex) (5863)	4wDM	1934	(2ft 11in gauge)
Ibstock	—	M/Rail (Simplex) (11001)	4wDM	1951	
Burt*	—	Simplex 9019))	4wDM	1959	
CCSW	—	Hibberd (1980)	4wDM	1936	
Thakeham Tiles	No 3	Hudson-Hunslet (2208)	4wDM	1941	
Thakeham Tiles	No 4	Hudson-Hunslet (3653)	4wDM	1948	
—	—	H/Clarke (DM686)	0-4-0DM	1948	
Star Construction	—††	Hudson-Hunslet	4wDm	c1941	
—	18	R/Hornsby (187081)	4wDM	1937	
—	—	Lister (33937)	4wDM	1949	
—	—	Hibberd 'Y-type Planet' (3627)	4wPM	1953	
—	WD 904	Wickham (3403/04)	2w-2PMR	1943	
—	2	Wingrove & Rogers (5031)	4wBE	1953	
—	—	Wingrove & Rogers (5034)	4wBE	1953	
—	—	Wingrove & Rogers (4998)	4wBE	1953	
—	—	Wingrove & Rogers (T8033)	0-4-0BE	1979	

†† not on site
** on loan to Leighton Buzzard Railway for restoration
* standard gauge
†includes hoist and 'haulage truck' for conversion to 5ft 3in gauge from Guinness Brewery

Stock
2 Penrhyn Quarry Railway 4-wheel coaches (2ft gauge, ex-1ft 10.75in gauge); RAF Fauld bogie coach (1940) (2ft gauge); Rye & Camber Tramway bogie (incomplete) (1895) (3ft gauge); Post Office Railway unit No 808 of 1930; 4 Groudle Glen Railway 4-wheel coaches (1896 and 1905) (2ft gauge); 60 other varied pieces of rolling stock of 12 different gauges ranging from 1ft 6in to 3ft 2.25in plus numerous miscellaneous exhibits including track, signals, etc

Adjacent to Amberley main line station
OS reference: TQ 030122
Operating society/organisation: Amberley Museum Trust, Amberley Museum, Houghton Bridge, Amberley, Arundel, West Sussex BN18 9LT
Telephone: Bury (01798) 831370 (Museum office)
Internet address: Web site: www.amberleymuseum.co.uk
e-mail (general museum enquiries): office@amberleymuseum.co.uk

e-mail (specific railway enquiries): gerryac@fastnet.co.uk
Car park: Adjacent to Amberley station
On site facilities: Shop, café, audio-visual show
Public opening: Wednesday to Sunday (inclusive) each week, and Bank Holiday Mondays, (open all week in school holidays) 10.00-last entry 17.00, 20 March-3 November
Special events: Railway Gala Weekend — 10/11 July; Miniature Steam & Model Weekend — 18/19

September. Please see press for details of further activities
Special Notes: Displays include working potter, blacksmith, boatbuilder and printer, stationary engines, historic radio collection and vintage Southdown garage and buses. A 2ft 0in gauge industrial railway system is demonstrated when possible, and a 3ft 2.25in gauge line is under construction. In addition, a 2ft 0in gauge 'main line' has been constructed. The 500yd line was officially opened by HRH

Prince Michael of Kent on 5 June 1984. The railway is operated every day the museum is open (subject to mechanical availability), with steam locomotive haulage on certain days — for details contact the museum office. Wheelchairs can normally be accommodated on the train. A Narrow Gauge & Industrial Railway Introductory Exhibition sets the scene for these and other set-piece display areas

Membership details: Friends of Amberley Museum, c/o above address
Membership journal: *Wheelbarrow* — bi-monthly

Steam Centre | Amerton Railway | Staffordshire

Following the restoration of Bagnall saddletank *Isabel*, construction started on the Amerton Railway on a 'greenfield' site in 1990. Passenger services commenced in 1992, but our volunteers have now completed the whole line which opened in 2002. The mile long line runs through the surrounding fields to a passing loop at Chartley Road, returning via two bridges over the Amerton brook. At Amerton station there is the locomotive shed, carriage shed and yard, the former GNR station building is now complete and being used as our museum and the Leek & Manifold Railway signalbox awaits the attention of our restoration team
Location: Amerton Railway, Amerton Farm, Stowe-by-Chartley, Stafford ST18 0LA (situated between Stafford and Uttoxeter, signposted off A51 at Weston)
Operating company: Staffordshire Narrow Gauge Railway Ltd, c/o above address
Telephone: (Railway only) (01785) 850965; Farm (01889) 270294
OS reference: SJ 993278
On site facilities: Car park at Working Farm. Museum under construction; licensed tea room and bakery (not operated by railway). Souvenir shop in railway ticket office. The railway is one of the

Industrial locomotives (2ft gauge)

Name	No	Builder	Type	Built
Isabel	—	Bagnall (1491)	0-4-0ST	1897
Lorna Doone	—	K/Stuart (4250)	0-4-0ST	1922
Pixie	—	K/Stuart (4260)	0-4-0ST	1922
—	526	Henschel (14019)	0-8-0T	1916
—	746	M/Rail (40SD501)	4wDM	1975
—	—	M/Rail (7471)	4wDM	1940
Golspie	—	Baguley (2085)	0-4-0DM/SO	1935
Dreadnought	—	Baguley (3024)	0-4-0DM/SO	1939
—	Yard No 70	R/Hornsby (221623)	4wDM	1943
—	—	R/Hornsby (506491)	4wDM	1964
Gordon	—	Hunslet (8561)	4wDH	1978

Rolling stock
4 toastrack coaches, 3 by Baguley, 1 ex-WHR, SNGRS-built passenger brake van and various wagons

Owner
Lorna Doone on loan from Birmingham Museum of Science & Industry
Pixie on loan from Leighton Buzzard Railway for 2004 season

main attractions at the farm, admission to most other attractions is free
Access by public transport: By rail to Stafford, then Stevenson's of Uttoxeter Ltd bus to Weston, then a mile walk to Amerton (no Sunday service)
Facilities for disabled: Wheelchairs can be accommodated in our 'Highland' coach where a wide door and access ramp is available
Period of public operation: Sundays from mid-March to end of

October. Saturdays from Easter until August Bank Holiday. Bank Holiday Mondays. Trains run 12.00 until 17.00. Subject to availability *Isabel* or *Pixie* will be in steam Sundays and Bank Holidays. Diesel haulage generally on Saturdays
Special events: Summer Steam Gala, with visiting locomotives — mid June (date to be confirmed); Santa Specials — December
Membership details: Membership Secretary, c/o above address
Membership journal: *Isabel Gazette*, quarterly

England

Member: HRA

Track has now been extended southwards to the first of three major crossings of the River Avon. The AVR's new platform 'Avon Riverside' was nearing completion at the time of going to press and, it is hoped, will be open for the start of the season at Easter. Once open, the new platform will offer the opportunity to combine a steam train ride with riverside walks, boat trips on the River Avon and links to the nearby Avon Valley Country Park

Headquarters: Avon Valley Railway Company Limited, Bitton Station, Bath Road, Bitton, Bristol BS30 6HD

Telephone: (0117) 932 7296 for timetable information. (0117) 932 5538 enquiries

Internet address: *Web site:* www.avonvalleyrailway.co.uk

Main station: Bitton

OS reference: ST 670705

Car park: Bitton

Access by public transport: Main line train service to Keynsham. Badgerline service No 332 (Bristol-Bath), No 558 (Bristol-North Common).

Access by bike: Bitton station is on the Bristol/Bath Railway Path (route 4 of the National Cycle Network)

Catering facilities: Buffet is able to provide hot and cold snacks, confectionery, hot and cold drinks and ice creams

On site facilities: Station buffet is open every day when the site is open, toilets, picnic area, children's play area close by

Public opening: Bitton station is now open daily for viewing its collection of locomotives and rolling stock, except for the period between Christmas and New Year for static viewing. Trains operate 21 March; 9-15, 17/18 April; 1-3, 8/9, 16, 22/23, 29-31 May; 1-3, 6, 4, 10/11, 18, 20-22, 24/25, 27-29 July; 1, 3-5, 7/8, 10-12, 14/15, 17-19, 21/22, 24-26, 28-30 August; 4/5, 12, 19, 26 September; 2/3, 10, 16/17, 24, 26-28, 30/31 October;

4-6, 11/12, 18/19, 22-24, 28 December; 1 January 2005

Special events: Mother's Day (meal option)— 21 March; Opening of Avon Riverside platform (subject to confirmation) — Easter; Railwayana Auction — 17 April; Day out with Thomas — 8/9 May; Teddy Bears' Picnic — 11 July; Art Exhibition — 28-30 August; Teddy Bears' Picnic — 19 September; Day out with Thomas — 2/3 October; Santa Specials — December;

Sherry and Mince Pie Specials 28 December/1 January 2005. Railway Experience Courses — (please contact for details)

Facilities for disabled: Coach converted for disabled use (no toilet facilities)

Membership details: Membership Secretary, c/o Bitton station

Membership journal: *Semaphore* — every 6 months; *Ground Signal* newsletter every 2 months

Locomotives

Name	No	Origin	Class	Type	Built
Sir Frederick Pile	34058	SR	BB	4-6-2	1947
—	41708	LMS	1F	0-6-0	1880
—	44123	LMS	4F	0-6-0	1925
—	48173	LMS	8F	2-8-0	1943
—	D2994	BR	07	0-6-0DE	1962
*—	51909	BR	108	DMBS	1958
*—	56271	BR	108	DTC	1958

*stored off-site

Locomotive notes: 41708 and D2994 in service

Industrial locomotives

Name	No	Builder	Type	Built
Edwin Hulse	2	Avonside (1798)	0-6-0ST	1918
Littleton No 5	—	M/Wardle (2018)	0-6-0ST	1922
Robert	7151	RSH (7151)	0-6-0T	1944
Meteor	—	RSH (7609)	0-6-0T	1950
Basil	—	R/Hornsby (235519)	4wDM	1945
Grumpy	WD70031	B/Drewry (2158)	0-4-0DM	1941
General				
Lord Robertson	610	Sentinel (10143)	0-8-0DH	1961
Kingswood	—	Barclay (446)	0-4-0DM	1959
Western Pride*	D1171	H/Clarke (D1171)	0-6-0DM	1951
Phoenix	70	H/Clarke (1464)	0-6-0T	1921
—*	Army 200	Barclay (358)	0-4-0DM	1941
—†*	—	R/Hornsby (252823)	4wDM	1947
—†*	—	R/Hornsby (210481)	4wDM	1941

*stored/undergoing restoration off-site
†chassis only

Locomotive notes: *Robert, General Lord Robertson, Pheonix* are in service

Stock

19 ex-BR Mk 1 coaches (10 stored off-site); 1 ex-BR Mk 1 Restaurant Coach; 1 ex-BR Mk 1 sleeper; 2 cranes; 1 Wickham trolley; numerous assorted wagons

Owners

44123 the London Midland Society
48173 the Bitton 8F Locomotive Group

Barrow Hill Roundhouse Railway Centre

Member: HRA

In 1839 the North Midland Railway devised an arrangement of stabling locomotives around a turntable within a polygonal building with a conical roof, hence roundhouse. In 1864 locomotives began to be housed in buildings of a square nature (retaining the name) and in 1870 Barrow Hill was built to this design. Retained following the end of steam, Barrow Hill remained in use until 1991. Saved from demolition at the 11th hour, the Grade 2 listed building is unique in Great Britain as the last surviving working roundhouse.

The roundhouse can accommodate up to 24 main line locomotives, and includes maintenance pits and ancillary services

Location/headquarters: Barrow Hill Roundhouse Engine Shed, Campbell Drive, Barrow Hill, Nr Staveley, Chesterfield, Derbyshire S43 2PR.

Situated near junctions 29/30 on M1

OS reference: SK 4175

Project manager: Mervyn Allcock

Contact address: Barrow Hill Engine Shed Society, address as above

Telephone: 01246 472450

Fax: 01246 472450

Internet address: *Web site:* www.barrowhill.org.uk

Car park: Adjacent to site

Access by public transport: Train to Chesterfield, Stagecoach bus Nos 80/90/56

On site facilities: Refreshments, souvenir shop and museum. Toilets

Refreshment facilities: Drinks and light refreshments

Public opening: Open most weekends — 4 major open weekends a year

Special events: Easter, summer, autumn and Christmas open weekends

Membership details: Martyn Brailsford, 18 Queen Street, Brimington, Chesterfield, Derbyshire S43 1HT

Society journal: *The Roundhouse* — three times a year

Locomotives

Name	No	Origin	Class	Type	Built
Kolhapur	45593	LMS	'Jubilee'	4-6-0	1934
—	2700	LMS	5P4F	2-6-0	1934
—	27505	NLR	2F	0-6-0T	1880
—	02003	BR	02	0-4-0DM	1960
—	03066	BR	03	0-6-0DM	1959
—	03094	BR	03	0-6-0DM	1960
—	D3000	BR	08	0-6-0DE	1952
—	08390	BR	08	0-6-0DE	1958
—	08869	BR	08	0-6-0DE	1960
—	D4092	BR	08	0-6-0DE	1962
—	08928	BR	08	0-6-0DE	1962
—	08936	BR	08	0-6-0DE	1962
—	D9500*	BR	14	0-6-0DH	1965
—	20056	BR	20	Bo-Bo	1961
—	20096	BR	20	Bo-Bo	1961
—	20168	BR	20	Bo-Bo	1966
—	25067	BR	25	Bo-Bo	1963
—	D5300	BR	26	Bo-Bo	1958
—	26011	BR	26	Bo-Bo	1959
—	31110	BR	31	A1A-A1A	1958
—	31524†	BR	31	A1A-A1A	1959
—	31407†	BR	31	A1A-A1A	1960
—	31411†	BR	31	A1A-A1A	1961
—	31412†	BR	31	A1A-A1A	1961
—	31417†	BR	31	A1A-A1A	1962
—	31433†	BR	31	A1A-A1A	1960
—	31460†	BR	31	A1A-A1A	1961
Spitfire	33035	BR	33	Bo-Bo	1960
—	33111	BR	33	Bo-Bo	1960
—	37072*	BR	37	Co-Co	1962
—	37079*	BR	37	Co-Co	1962
—	37201	BR	37	Co-Co	1963
—	37214*	BR	37	Co-Co	1964
—	37242*	BR	37	Co-Co	1962
—	37510*	BR	37	Co-Co	1963
—	37515*	BR	37	Co-Co	1962
Andania	40013	BR	40	1Co-Co1	1959
—	47053†	BR	47	Co-Co	1964
—	47229†	BR	47	Co-Co	1965
—	47245	BR	47	Co-Co	1966
—	47285	BR	47	Co-Co	1966
—	47375†	BR	47	Co-Co	1965
—	47628†	BR	47	Co-Co	1965
—	47707†	BR	47	Co-Co	1966
—	47712	BR	47	Co-Co	1966
—	47717	BR	47	Co-Co	1966
Sherwood Forester	45060	BR	45	1Co-Co1	1961
—	45105	BR	45	1Co-Co1	1961
Howe	50023	BR	50	Co-Co	1968
Alycidon	D9009	BR	55	Co-Co	1961
Tulyar	55015	BR	55	Co-Co	1961
Royal Highland Fusilier	55019	BR	55	Co-Co	1961
—	5800	BR	58	Co-Co	
—	73119	BR	73	Bo-Bo	1966
—	73138	BR	73	Bo-Bo	1966

16

Owners
*Harry Needle Railroad Co (for overhaul or stored)
†Fragonset Railways
§HSBC (stored)
2700 on loan from the National Railway Museum
27505 on loan from the Bluebell Railway
D3000 and D9500 Ian Goddard
03066, 03094, 20056 and 20096 Trevor Dean
33035, 45060 and 45105 the Pioneer Diesel Group
33111 the Class 33111 Group
55009 and 55019 the Deltic Preservation Society
73119, 73138, E3003, 82008, 83012 and 85101 the AC Loco Group
84001 the National Railway Museum

Name	No	Origin	Class	Type	Built
—	E3003	BR	81	Bo-Bo	1960
—	82008	BR	82	Bo-Bo	1961
—	83012	BR	83	Bo-Bo	1961
—	84001	BR	84	Bo-Bo	1960
Doncaster Plant150 1853-2003	85101	BR	85	Bo-Bo	1961
Lancashire Witch	86213§	BR	86	Bo-Bo	1961

Industrial locomotives

Name	No	Builder	Type	Built
Henry	—	H/Leslie (2491)	0-4-0ST	1901
The Welshman	—	M/Wardle (1207)	0-6-0ST	1890
—	9	YEC (2521)	0-4-0ST	1952
Marstons	—	— (2553)	0-4-0	—
—	—	Drewry (2589)	0-4-0	1956
—	—	YEC (2714)	0-6-0DE	—
—	NCB 20	Barclay	0-4-0DE	—
—	—	E/Electric (890445)	0-6-0DE	—
—	RMS 10	GEC	0-6-0DE	—
—	—	Planet	0-4-0DE	—
—	—	Hunslet (63000316)	0-4-0DE	—
—	4	Hunslet	0-4-0DE	—

Stock
1 ex-BR Mk 1 BSK coach, 2 ex-BR Mk 2 coach, 1 ex-MR brake van, 3 Tunny wagons, 3 Chub wagons, 2 ex-BR bogie vans, 1 dynamometer car, 2 ex-BR Lowmac, 1 ex-LMS brake van, 2 ex-BR brake van, 1 ex-SR brake van, 1 ex-GWR Toad brake van,

England

The Battlefield Line Railway

Member: HRA, TT

A quiet country railway operated by the Shackerstone Railway Society Ltd.

Headquarters: Shackerstone station (3 miles north of Market Bosworth in Leicestershire)

Address: Shackerstone Station, Shackerstone, Nuneaton CV13 6NW

Telephone: Timetable enquiries: (01827) 880754

Internet address: *Web site*: www.battlefield-line-railway.co.uk

Operating Manager: D. Weightman

Main station: Shackerstone

Other public station: Shenton

OS reference: SK 379066

Car park: Shackerstone (free), Shenton (council car park)

Access by public transport: Bus service from Nuneaton weekends only. Ring Traveline 0870 6082608 for details

Refreshment facilities: Tea rooms on Shackerstone station. Buffet/bar on most trains

Souvenir shop: Shackerstone

Museum: Shackerstone

Depot: Shackerstone

Length of line: 4.75 miles (8km)

Passenger trains: Shackerstone-Shenton

Period of public operation: Easter to October 2004

Special events: See leaflet and press for further details

Facilities for disabled: Special car park and toilets

Special notes: Family tickets available. Scenic countryside views including Ashby Canal. Shenton station is adjacent to Bosworth Battlefield (1485) Country Park. 20 minute walk along 'Battlefield Trail' to visitor centre, return by later train

Operating company/ preservation society contact: The Secretary, Shackerstone Railway Society, Shackerstone Station, Shackerstone, Nuneaton CV13 6NW

Membership journal: *Shackerstone News* — 2/3 times/year

Locomotives and multiple-units

Name	No	Origin	Class	Type	Built
Brush Veteran	D5518	BR	31	A1A-A1A	1958
Calder Hall Power Station	31130	BR	31	A1A-A1A	1959
Diane	D2867	BR	02	0-4-0DH	1961
—	03170	BR	03	0-6-0DM	1960
—	03180	BR	03	0-6-0DM	1962
—	11215	BR	04	0-6-0DM	1956
—	D2310	BR	04	0-6-0DM	1960
—	08818	BR	08	0-6-0DE	1960
—	12083	BR	11	0-6-0DE	1953
—	D9529	BR	14	0-6-0DE	1965
—	37227	BR	37	Co-Co	1964
—	47640	BR	47	Co-Co	1965
—	45015	BR	45	1Co-Co1	1960
—	51131	BR	116	DMBS	1958
—	51321	BRCW	116	DMS	1959
—	54289	P/Steel	121	DTS	1960
—	55005	GRCW	122	DMBS	1958
—	59496	P/Steel	117	TC(L)	1959
—	59522	P/Steel	117	TC(L)	1959

Industrial locomotives

Name	No	Builder	Type	Built
Linda	—	Bagnall (2648)	0-4-0ST	1941
Waleswood	—	H/Clarke (750)	0-4-0ST	1906
Sir Gomer	—	Peckett (1859)	0-6-0ST	1932
Dunlop No 7	—	Peckett (2130)	0-4-0ST	1951
Richard III	—	RSH (7537)	0-6-0T	1949
Lamport No 3	—	Bagnall (2670)	0-6-0ST	1942
William	—	Sentinel (9656)	4wVBT	1956
—	—	Barclay (422)	0-6-0DM	1958
—	—	E/Electric (8431)	0-4-0DH	1963
—	47	T/Hill (249V)	0-6-0DH	1974
—	—	R/Hornsby (263001)	4wDM	1949
—	44	Hunslet (6684)	0-6-0DH	1968
—	—	R/Royce (10254)	0-4-0DE	1966
—	—	Simplex (9921)	4wDM	1955

Stock

8 ex-BR Mk 1 coaches (including Griddle Car), 2 ex-BR Mk 2 coaches, 1 ex-BR Mk 3 sleeper; 5 passenger-rated vans; 1 rail mounted steam crane; 2 rail mounted diesel cranes; 35 wagons (inc 3 goods brake vans SR, MR,BR); 1 ex-London Transport Plasser & Theurer ballast tamper;

Owner

47640 Fragonset Railways

The railway station, signalbox and goods shed have been completely re-created along with the other exhibits to show a way of life long past. There are some very old locomotives in the collection.

Location: The North of England Open Air Museum, Beamish, County Durham DH9 0RG.

OS reference: NZ 214548

Telephone: 0191 370 4000

Fax: 0191 370 4001

Internet address: *e-mail:* museum@beamish.org.uk

Web site: www.beamish.org.uk

Car park: At museum

Access by public transport: Bus service from Eldon Square, Newcastle upon Tyne; bus service Nos 775 and 778 from Sunderland via Chester-le-Street; bus service 720 from Milburngate, Durham City

On site facilities: This 300-acre open air museum vividly re-creates life in the North of England in the early 1800s and 1900s. The Town has dentist's surgery, solicitor's office, Co-op shops, garage, sweet shop and bank. The Colliery Village has pit cottages, village school and chapel, 'drift' mine and pithead. Home Farm with farm house, livestock and exhibitions. Railway station complete with goods yard and signalbox, rolling stock on static display. Pockerley Manor illustrates the lifestyle of a yeoman farming family in the early 1800s.

Early Railways — opened in 1999, near Pockerley Manor, a large stone engine shed with displays illustrating the development of railways in the early 1800s. Visitors take a short ride in re-created carriages of the period pulled by the replica *Locomotion* or *Steam Elephant*

Public opening:
Summer (3 April-31 October 2004)
daily 10.00-17.00, last admission 15.00.
Winter (1 November-19 March 2005) 10.00-16.00, last admission 15.00, closed Mondays and Fridays. Also closed 13 December 2004 to 3 January 2005

NB: A winter visit to Beamish is centred on the Town and Tramway; other areas of the museum are closed and admission charges are, consequently, reduced

Length of line: 1-mile tramway — operational daily.

Pockerley Waggonway, 1/4-mile — operational daily in summer. Rebuilt NER station, colliery sidings

Facilities for disabled: Not ideal for wheelchairs. One carriage at 1825 Railway suitable for wheelchairs. Advanced notice for parties to Bookings Officer preferred

Locomotives

Name	No	Origin	Class	Type	Built
—¥	876	NER	C	0-6-0	1889
Locomotion	1*	—	—	0-4-0	1975

¥ undergoing overhaul off-site
*Rreplica

Industrial locomotives

Name	No	Builder	Type	Built
Twizell†	3	Stephenson (2730)	0-6-0T	1891
—††	14	H/Leslie (3056)	0-4-0ST	1914
South Durham				
Malleable††	No 5	Grange Ironworks	0-4-0ST	c1880
Coffee Pot§	—	Head Wrightson	0-4-0VB	1871
—††	E1	Black, Hawthorn (897)	2-4-0CT	1883
Hetton Loco	—	G. Stephenson	0-4-0	1851
Wellington	—	B/Hawthorn (266)	0-4-0ST	1873
Jacob§	680	McEwan Pratt	0-4-0P	1916
—**	18	Lewin (693)	0-4-0WT	1877
Steam Elephant	—*	Wallsend Colliery	0-6-0G	1815/2000
—§§	17	Head Wrightson (33)	0-4-0VB	1873

†on long-term loan to Tanfield   ††on static display
§under repair   **undergoing major rebuild
*replica
§§on loan from Darlington Museum

Locomotive notes: No 3 in working order. R/Hornsby not usually on display. Others usually on display

Owners

Hetton Loco on loan from National Railway Museum
Locomotion the Locomotion Trust
Wellington Eric Maxwell/Tanfield Railway

Note

Not all exhibits on display
Twizell on long-term loan to Tanfield Railway

Attraction | Bicton Woodland Railway | Devon

A passenger-carrying line of 18in gauge with stock mainly from the Woolwich Arsenal Railway and of World War 1 vintage
Location: Bicton Park, near Budleigh Salterton
OS reference: SY 074862
Operating society/organisation: Bicton Woodland Railway, Bicton Gardens, East Budleigh, Budleigh Salterton, Devon
Telephone: Colaton Raleigh (01395) 568465
Car park: On site
Access by public transport: Buses pass half-hourly from Exeter, Exmouth, Sidmouth in season

Locomotives

Name	No	Builder	Type	Built
Bicton	2	R/Hornsby (213839)	4wDM	1942
Clinton	4	H/Hunslet (2290)	0-4-0	1941
Sir Walter Raleigh	—	Keef	4wDM	2000

Stock
5 closed bogie coaches

On site facilities: Indoor and outdoor play areas, Glass Houses, Palm House, Grade 1 gardens, museum and restaurant
Length of line: 3,250yd
Public opening: Open all year, winter 10.00-17.00, summer 10.00-18.00
Trains operate: Winter 12.15 and 14.30, summer 6-8 trains a day
Facilities for disabled: Toilets, wheelchairs available. Special carriage for wheelchairs

---

Museum | Bideford Railway Museum | Devon

Member: HRA
Based at the former LSWR/SR station on the now closed Barnstaple-Torrington line, the site is undergoing restoration. The former signalbox has been rebuilt, double track laid throughout and signals erected. A growing collection of rolling stock is being gathered. Passenger railway rides returned to Bideford station during summer 2001 after a gap of 36 years. Long term aim of the Group is to reinstate the railway back to Barnstaple (9 miles)
Headquarters: Bideford Station, Railway Terrace, East-the-Water, Bideford, Devon EX39 4BB
Telephone: 07748 320562
Internet address: *Web site:* www.bidefordrailway.co.uk
OS reference: SS 456263
Operating society: Bideford & Instow Railway Group
Access by public transport: By train — Barnstaple 9 miles. Station is within walking distance of the town of Bideford and its bus stops

Industrial locomotives

Name	No	Builder	Type	Built
Kingsley	—	Hibberd (3832)	0-4-0DM	1957

Rolling stock
BR Mk 1 TSO No 4489, ex-SR Parcels Van No S2142, ex-BR brake van, ex-LMS closed box van, platelayers' trolley
2 18in gauge skip (ex Peters Marland Clay Works)

Owner
Kingsley the Torridge Diesel Loco Co Ltd

On site facilities: Museum, souvenir shop, book shop, refreshments, visitor centre, rolling stock under restoration
Period of public opening: Easter to end October — Sundays, Tuesdays, Thursdays and Bank Holidays 14.00-17.00; November to Easter — Sundays and Bank Holidays only
Special events: Annual open day — 8 August; Santa Specials — 11, 18 December
Disabled facilities: None
Membership details: Mr C. Fairchild, 4 Crichton Road, Carshalton Beeches, Surrey SM5 3LS
Membership journal: *Atlantic Coast Express* (quarterly)

Blackpool & Fleetwood Tramway

The Blackpool & Fleetwood Tramway is the sole surviving traditional street tramway system in the United Kingdom and attracts visitors from all over the country. During the autumn the streets are illuminated and tours are available by historic or illuminated tram.

Operating organisation:
Blackpool Transport Services Ltd, Rigby Road, Blackpool, Lancashire FY1 5DD

Telephone: (01253) 473001

Managing Director: Steve Burd

Operations Director: David Eaves

Customer Services Officer: Jean Cox

Length of line: 11.5 miles, standard gauge

Period of public operation: Daily throughout the year, except Christmas Day, Boxing Day and New Year's Day

Number of trams: 78 double and single-deck trams.

Trams

No	Trucks	Builder	Date
Boat Cars			
600	E/Electric	E/Electric	1930
602	E/Electric	E/Electric	1934
604	E/Electric	E/Electric	1934
605	E/Electric	E/Electric	1934
607	E/Electric	E/Electric	1934
Brush Cars			
621	EMB	Brush	1937
622	EMB	Brush	1937
623	EMB	Brush	1937
625	EMB	Brush	1937
626	EMB	Brush	1937
627	EMB	Brush	1937
630	EMB	Brush	1937
631	EMB	Brush	1937
632	EMB	Brush	1937
634	EMB	Brush	1937
636	EMB	Brush	1937
637	EMB	Brush	1937
Centenary Cars			
641	Blackpool	East Lancs	1984
642	Blackpool	East Lancs	1986
643	Blackpool	East Lancs	1986
644	Blackpool	East Lancs	1986
645	Blackpool	East Lancs	1987
646	Blackpool	East Lancs	1987
647	Blackpool	East Lancs	1988
648	Blackpool	East Lancs	1990
Towing Cars			
671	E/Electric	E/Electric / Blackpool	1960
672	E/Electric	E/Electric / Blackpool	1960
673	E/Electric	E/Electric / Blackpool	1961
674	E/Electric	E/Electric / Blackpool	1962
675	E/Electric	E/Electric / Blackpool	1958
676	E/Electric	E/Electric / Blackpool	1958
677	E/Electric	E/Electric / Blackpool	1960
Ex-Towing Railcoaches			
678	E/Electric	E/Electric / Blackpool	1961
679	E/Electric	E/Electric / Blackpool	1961
680	E/Electric	E/Electric / Blackpool	1960
Trailer Cars			
681	Maley & Taunton	MCW	1960
682	Maley & Taunton	MCW	1960
683	Maley & Taunton	MCW	1960
684	Maley & Taunton	MCW	1960
685	Maley & Taunton	MCW	1960
686	Maley & Taunton	MCW	1960
687	Maley & Taunton	MCW	1960
Balloon Cars			
700	E/Electric	E/Electric	1934
701	E/Electric	E/Electric	1934
702	E/Electric	E/Electric	1934
703	E/Electric	E/Electric	1934
704	E/Electric	E/Electric	1934
705	E/Electric	E/Electric	1934
706	E/Electric	E/Electric	1934

England

No	Trucks	Builder	Date
707	E/Electric	E/Electric	1934
708	E/Electric	E/Electric	1934
709	E/Electric	E/Electric	1934
710	E/Electric	E/Electric	1934
711	E/Electric	E/Electric	1934
712	E/Electric	E/Electric	1935
*713	E/Electric	E/Electric	1934
715	E/Electric	E/Electric	1935
*716	E/Electric	E/Electric	1935
717	E/Electric	E/Electric	1934
718	E/Electric	E/Electric	1934
719	E/Electric	E/Electric	1935
720	E/Electric	E/Electric	1935
721	E/Electric	E/Electric	1935
722	E/Electric	E/Electric	1935
723	E/Electric	E/Electric	1935
*724	E/Electric	E/Electric	1935
726	E/Electric	E/Electric	1935

Jubilee Cars

No	Trucks	Builder	Date
761	Blackpool	E/Electric / Blackpool	1979
762	Blackpool	E/Electric / Blackpool	1982

Illuminated Trams

No	Trucks	Builder	Date
*733	EMB	from Brush 633	2001
*734	E/Electric	from Pantograph 174	1962
*735	E/Electric	from Railcoach 222	1963
*736	E/Electric	from Pantograph 170	1965

Engineering Vehicles

No	Trucks	Builder	Date
259	EMB	Blackpool	1937
260	EMB	Blackpool	1973
750	MRCW	Blackpool	1907
752	MRCW	Blackpool	1928
754	E/Electric	Blackpool	1992

Preserved Trams

No	Trucks	Builder	Date
5	?	D/Kerr	1901
40	Preston McGuire	United Electric Co	1914
66	Brill	Electric Railway & Carriage	1901
147	Preston McGuire	Hurst Nelson	1924
304	Maley & Taunton	Hurst Nelson	1952
513	Maley & Taunton	Charles Roberts	1950
619	E/Electric	Bolton Trams	1987
660	Maley & Taunton	Charles Roberts	1953

*out of service

Owners
5 the Stockport 5 Trust
40 the Tramway Museum Society
66 the Bolton 66 Group
304 the Lancastrian Transport Trust
513 Beamish Open Air Museum

England

Bluebell Railway

Member: HRA, TT

This famous steam railway was the first standard gauge passenger line to be taken over by enthusiasts. It derives its name from the bluebells which proliferate in the woodlands adjoining the line. A strong Victorian atmosphere pervades this branch line which has a large collection of Southern and pre-Grouping locomotives and coaches.

Operations Manager: Mr Chris Knibbs

Headquarters: Bluebell Railway Preservation Society, Sheffield Park Station, Uckfield, East Sussex TN22 3QL

Telephone: Newick (01825) 722370 for travel information (24hr talking timetable); (01825) 720800 for general enquiries etc during office hours; (01825) 720801 – Golden Arrow Pullman (reservations and Catering Department)

Internet address: Web site: www.bluebell-railway.co.uk

Main station: Sheffield Park

Other public stations: Horsted Keynes and Kingscote

Car parks: Sheffield Park, Horsted Keynes

OS reference:
Sheffield Park TQ 403238,
Horsted Keynes TQ 372293

Access by public transport: Bus service 473 between main line East Grinstead and Kingscote (2 miles). See timetable brochure for details of operation

Refreshment facilities: Sheffield Park restaurant/bar/self-service; Horsted Keynes – Victorian bar/buffet. The line's 'Golden Arrow' Pullman operates a dinner service most Saturday evenings and Pullman luncheon service most Sundays.
 Telephone (01825) 720801 during normal office hours for details.

Souvenir shops: Sheffield Park, Horsted Keynes

Museum: Sheffield Park

Depots: Sheffield Park (locomotives), Horsted Keynes (stock)

Length of line: 9 miles

Passenger trains: Sheffield Park-

Locomotives and multiple-unit

Name	No	Origin	Class	Type	Built
Stepney	55	LBSCR	A1X	0-6-0T	1875
Fenchurch	72	LBSCR	A1X	0-6-0T	1872
Birch Grove	473	LBSCR	E4	0-6-2T	1898
—	27	SECR	P	0-6-0T	1910
—	65	SECR	O1	0-6-0	1896
—	263	SECR	H	0-4-4T	1905
—	323	SECR	P	0-6-0T	1910
—	592	SECR	C	0-6-0	1902
—	1178	SECR	P	0-6-0T	1910
—	96	LSWR	B4	0-4-0T	1893
—	120	LSWR	T9	4-4-0	1898
—	488	LSWR	0415	4-4-2T	1885
—	58850*	NLR	2F	0-6-0T	1880
Earl of Berkeley	9017	GWR	9000	4-4-0	1938
—	541	SR	Q	0-6-0	1939
—	847	SR	S15	4-6-0	1937
Stowe	928	SR	V	4-4-0	1934
—	1618	SR	U	2-6-0	1928
—	1638	SR	U	2-6-0	1931
—	30064	SR	USA	0-6-0T	1943
—	C1	SR	Q1	0-6-0	1942
Blackmoor Vale	21C123	SR	WC	4-6-2	1946
Sir Archibald Sinclair	34059	SR	BB	4-6-2	1947
Camelot	73082	BR	5MT	4-6-0	1955
—	75027	BR	4MT	4-6-0	1954
—	78059†	BR	2MT	2-6-0	1956
—	80064	BR	4MT	2-6-4T	1953
—	80100	BR	4MT	2-6-4T	1954
—	80151	BR	4MT	2-6-4T	1957
—	92240	BR	9F	2-10-0	1958
—	11201**	BR	4COR	DMBSO	1937

†purchased without tender, for conversion to tank engine, work in hand
*on loan to Barrow Hill Roundhouse Railway Centre
**on static display at Horsted Keynes

Industrial locomotives

Name	No	Builder	Type	Built
Baxter	3	F/Jennings (158)	0-4-0T	1877
†Stamford	24	Avonside (1972)	0-6-0ST	1927
Sharpthorn	4*	M/Wardle (641)	0-6-0ST	1877

*On static display
†On long-term loan to the Rutland Railway Museum

Stock

Substantial collection of pre-Nationalisation coaches including SECR, LSWR, Bulleid, Maunsell and Chesham vehicles. Also freight stock and engineers' vehicles plus 45-ton steam crane

Owners

592 the Wainwright C Class Preservation Society
541, 847, 928 and 1618 the Maunsell Locomotive Society Ltd
96 and 21C123 the Bulleid Society Ltd
263 the H Class Trust
73082 the Camelot Locomotive Society
C1 and 120 on loan from the National Railway Museum

England

Horsted Keynes-Kingscote
Period of public operation:
Weekends all year round; daily
16-20 February (half term); 5-16
April; 3 May to 30 September;
daily 25-29 October (half term);
daily 26-31 December. Museum,
locomotive sheds, buffet and shop
at Sheffield Park open daily except
Christmas Day
Special events: Goods Train Day
— 27 March; Collectors Fair — 25
April; Railway at War — 8/9 May;
Bluebell Music Festival — 12/13
June; Day out with Thomas School
Day — 18, 24/25 June; Day out
with Thomas Bedtime Trains — 18,

25 June; Day out with Thomas
Weekends — 19/20, 26/27 June;
Vintage Bus Day — 4 July; Toy &
Collectors Fair — 17/18 July;
Giants of Steam — 23/24 October;
Wizard/Halloween — 30/31
October. Further details of events
available on request
Facilities for disabled: All station
facilities are on the level and ramps
available for placing wheelchair

visitors into trains. Special toilets in
buffet at Sheffield Park and at
Kingscote, 'multi-purpose vehicle'
for use by groups, please telephone
to confirm availability
Membership details: Membership
Secretary, c/o above address
Membership journal: *Bluebell
News* — quarterly

Timetable Service	Bodmin & Wenford Railway	Cornwall

Member: HRA

The Bodmin & Wenford Railway
typifies the bygone branch railways
of Cornwall. The terminus, close to
Bodmin town centre, has an
interesting collection of small
standard gauge locomotives and
rolling stock, and the operating line
winds down to a junction with main
line rail services at Bodmin
Parkway. Passengers can alight at
the intermediate Colesloggett Halt
from where a footpath (not suitable
for wheelchairs or the infirm) leads
to Cardinham Woods (FC) with
waymarked trails, picnic areas and
a café. From the train there are
scenic views across the beautiful
valley of the River Fowey. A
second line circles Bodmin to
Boscarne Junction where it meets
the Camel Trail, a recreational path
for cyclists and walkers. A visit can
be made to the nearby Camel
Valley Vineyard (July and August
only). Most trains are steam-hauled
except Saturday

Location: Bodmin General station,
on B3268
General Manager: Mr R. Webster
Operating society/organisation:
Bodmin & Wenford Railway,
Bodmin General Station, Bodmin,
Cornwall PL31 1AQ
Telephone: All enquiries (01208)
73666
Internet address: *e-mail:*
enquiries@bodminandwenfordrail
way.co.uk

Locomotives and multiple-units

Name	No	Origin	Class	Type	Built
—	30587	LSWR	0298	2-4-0WT	1874
—	4612	GWR	5700	0-6-PT	1942
—	5552	GWR	4575	2-6-2T	1928
Wadebridge	34007	SR	WC	4-6-2	1945
Triumph	50042	BR	50	Co-Co	1968
River Fowey	20166	BR	20	Bo-Bo	1966
—	20197	BR	20	Bo-Bo	1967
—	33110	BR	33	Bo-Bo	1960
—	37142	BR	37	Co-Co	1963
—	D3452	BR	10	0-6-0DE	1957
—	D3559	BR	08	0-6-0DE	1958
—	51947	BR	108	DMBS	1960
—	52054	BR	108	DMCL	1960
—	53980	BR	108	DMBS	1960

Industrial locomotives

Name	No	Builder	Type	Built
—	—	Bagnall (2766)	0-6-0ST	1944
—	19	Bagnall (2962)	0-4-0ST	1950
Judy	—	Bagnall (2572)	0-4-0ST	1934
Alfred	—	Bagnall (3058)	0-4-0ST	1953
—	—	Bagnall (3121)	0-4-0F	1957
Peter	—	Fowler (22928)	0-4-0DM	1940
Progress	—	Fowler (4000001)	0-4-0DM	1945
Swiftsure	—	Hunslet (2857)	0-6-0ST	1943
Lec	—	R/Hornsby (443642)	4wDM	1960

Stock
9 BR Mk 1 coaches; 3 BR Mk 2 coaches; 1 Mk 3 Sleeper, 6-wheel 10-ton
steam crane, 4 GWR coaches; 2 GWR Siphon G; Various freight wagons

Owners
34007 the Wadebridge 34007 Ltd
30587 on loan from the National Railway Museum
37142 the B&W Main Line Diesel Group

England

Web site:
www.bodminandwenfordrailway.co.uk
Car park: Bodmin General and Bodmin Parkway
Access by public transport: Interchange at Bodmin Parkway arrivals by main line train; through tickets available from most stations. Local bus services to Bodmin
Refreshment facilities: Light refreshments at Bodmin General and bar on most trains
On site facilities: Railway shop, limited display of historic artefacts, toilets
Length of lines: 3.5 miles General-Parkway; 3 miles General-Boscarne
Passenger trains: 10, 17, 20/21, 24, 28, 31 March; 3-18, 20/21, 25, 27/28 April; 1-5, 9, 11/12, 16, 18/19, 23, 25/26, 29-31 May; daily — 1 June-30 September; 3, 5/6, 10, 12/13, 17, 19/20, 23-31 October; 3, 10 November.
Santa Specials 4/5, 11/12, 18/19, 22-24 December; Mince Pie Specials 26-31 December and 1 January 2005
Special events: Diesel Weekend — 21/21, March; Branch Line Weekend — 3/4 April; Easter 'Family Fun Weekend' — 9-12 April; Steam at War - 44 — 1-3 May; Steam & Diesel Weekend — 29-31 May; Day out with Thomas — 23 July to 2 August; Steam Gala — 4/5 September; Diesel Gala — 18/19 September; Ghost Night 31 October; Santa Specials — 4/5, 11/12, 18/19, 22-24 December.
Big Band; Steam & Beer Jazz

Murder Mystery; Vineyard specials — please enquire for dates or see leaflet
Driving experience courses: Courses held in spring and autumn. Please apply for details
Facilities for disabled: Level access to platform, shop and buffet. Disabled toilet. Disabled section on train. Registered disabled travel at child fare, carers conveyed *free*
Membership details: Mr C. Rennie, Bodmin Railway Preservation Society, c/o above address
Special notes: Reduced fares for families. Bicycles and dogs conveyed *free*
Membership journal: *Bodmin & Wenford News* — 3 issues/year

Steam Centre	Bowes Railway	County Durham

Member: HRA

The railway includes the only preserved rope-hauled standard gauge inclines, whose operation requires considerable skill and dexterity. You should not miss the opportunity of inspecting the inclines and winding house and haulage engine when you can. The Engineering Workshop has just been restored
Chairman: Phillip Dawe
Location: Bowes Railway, Springwell Village, near Gateshead, (on B1288)
OS reference: NZ 285589
Operating society/organisation: Bowes Railway Co Ltd
Telephone: Tyneside (0191) 416 1847
Internet address: *Web site:* www.bowesrailway.co.uk
Car park: Springwell
Access by public transport: Northern Buses services Nos 184 Washington/Birtley, 187/188 Gateshead Metro/Sunderland, 189 Washington (Brady Sq)-Gateshead 638 Ryton/Sunderland
On site facilities: Exhibition of Railway's history, wagon exhibition, workshop displays. On operating days — shop,

Industrial locomotives

Name	No	Builder	Type	Built
WST	—	Barclay (2361)	0-4-0ST	1954
—	22	Barclay (2274)	0-4-0ST	1949
—	20/110/709	Barclay (613)	0-6-0DH	1977
—	—	Hunslet (6263)	0-4-0DH	1964
—	503	Hunslet (6614)	0-6-0DH	1965
—	101	Planet (3922)	4wDM	1959
—	2207/456†	E/Electric (2476)	4wBE	1958
Victoria	2216/286†	H/Clarke (DM842)	0-6-0DMF	1954
BO3	20/122/514*	Hunslet (8515)	Bo-BoDMF	1981
—	—*	EIMCO (LD2163)	Rockershovel	1959

†2ft gauge
*2ft 6in gauge

Owners
WST on loan from British Gypsum Ltd
Barclay 0-6-0DH on loan from Mr P. Dawe

Stock
20 ordinary 10-ton wooden hopper wagons (Springwell built); 16 other wooden hopper wagons (of various pedigrees); 3 steel 14-ton hopper, 2 steel 16-ton hopper wagons; 7 wagons; 7 steel 21-ton hopper wagons; 1 reel bogie (for rope replacement); 1 drift bogie (for shunting by rope); 1 loco coal wagon; 7 material wagons; 2 tool vans; 4 brake vans; 4 flat wagons; 1 18-ton wooden hopper (ex-Ashington); 1 21-ton wooden hopper (ex-Seaham); 2 steel ballast Hopper Wagons; 1 tank wagon; 1 wooden side door coal wagon; 3 Londonderry Chaldron wagons, 2ft gauge 4-wheel manrider, 2ft 6in gauge R. B. Bolton-type bogie manrider, Easington Colliery weights wagon, 1 Pontop & Jarrow Railway flat bogie, 1 Dandy cart

Stationary haulage
Met-Vick/Wild, 300bhp electric (Blackham's Hill) 1950

refreshments and guided tours. One of the last operational Strowger mechanical telephone exchanges still in daily use. Steam-hauled brake van rides. Rope haulage demonstration trains. Tarmac car park available for helicopter visitors (prior permission required, phone site)

Public opening: Site open Mondays to Fridays for static viewing. Please contact for operating details during 2004. Santa specials week prior to Christmas. Disabled Children's Day — mid July. Guided tours Saturdays, out of season can be accommodated with prior notice (not trains)

Length of line: 1.25 miles of rope

BTH/Robey, 500bhp electric (Black Fell) 1950
Clarke Chapman, 22hp electric (Springwell Yard)
14ft diam, Gravity Dilly Wheel (Springwell)

haulage incline railway.
1.5 mile line used for passenger trains as the Wreckenton extension is now open

Special notes: Preserved section of the Pontop & Jarrow Railway; designed G. Stephenson; opened 1826; largest collection of colliery wagons in country, the only preserved standard gauge rope-hauled incline railway in the world; Railway's own historic workshops preserved, with examples of all of the Railway's wagon types

Facilities for disabled: Toilet and refreshment room
Membership details: Dr Peter Norman, Railway Secretary, c/o above address
Membership journal: *The Incline* — quarterly
Disclaimer: The Bowes Railway Co Ltd wish to point out that all advertised facilities are subject to alteration without prior notice. The company can therefore not be held responsible for any loss or expense incurred

---

Steam Centre	Bredgar & Wormshill Light Railway	Kent

Member: HRA

A short, 2ft gauge, private railway constructed and operated to a very high standard

Location/headquarters: The Bredgar & Wormshill Light Railway, The Warren, Bredgar, Nr Sittingbourne, Kent ME9 8AT
Contact: Bill Best, David Best
Telephone: (01622) 884254
Fax: (01622) 884668
Internet address: *Web site:* www.bwlr.co.uk
Access by public transport: Main line trains to Sittingbourne (5 miles) and Hollingbourne (3.5 miles). No taxis from Hollingbourne
OS reference: TQ 868579
Car park: On site (300 places)
On site facilities: Souvenir shop, museum, light refreshments, toilets,

Industrial locomotives
(2ft gauge)

Name	No	Builder	Type	Built
Bronhilde	1	Schwartzkopf (9124)	0-4-0WT	1927
Katie	2	Arn Jung (3872)	0-6-0WT	1931
Harrogate	3	Peckett (2050)	0-6-0ST	1944
Armistice	4	Bagnall (2088)	0-4-0ST	1919
Bredgar	5	B/Drewry (3775)	0-4-0DH	1983
Eigiau	6	O&K (5668)	0-4-0WT	1912
Victory	7	Decauville (246)	0-4-2ST	1897
—	8	O&K (12722)	0-4-0WT	1936
No 1	—	Hunslet (1429)	0-4-0ST	1922
—	—	Fowler (13573)	0-4-2T	1912
Limpopo	—	Fowler (18800)	0-6-0T	1930

(2ft 6in gauge)

—	6	La Meuse (3355)	0-4-0T	1929
—	105	Henschel (29582)	0-6-0WT	1956

Stock
3 bogie coaches, 1 four-wheel coach, 6 four-wheel wagons, 2 four-wheel tank wagon, 2 four-wheel works truck, 1 four-wheel guard's van, 1 open bogie coach

Bronhilde and train at Stony Shaw station. *Phil Barnes*

picnic sites, traction engines, 7.25in and 15in gauge model locomotives, working beam engine, model railway. Largest UK collection of Bean motor cars. Steam-hauled train rides from Warren Wood to Stony Shaw (1km).

Public opening: First Sunday in each month May to September (11.00-17.00). Also Easter Sunday. Admission: Adults £6, children £3
Special events: Steam locomotive driving courses, enthusiast day usually first Sunday in October

Facilities for disabled: Generally good including toilets
Note: A private site with no 'out of hours' access, but groups by arrangement

---

Steam Centre — Bressingham Steam Experience — Norfolk

Member: TT
Five miles of various gauges of railway running through extensive gardens, and a collection of well-maintained and impressive main line locomotives. All the fun of the fair, with something for everyone, a great day out for all the family
Location: Two miles west of Diss on the A1066
OS reference: TM 080806
Operating society/organisation: Bressingham Steam Preservation Co Ltd, Bressingham Hall, Diss, Norfolk IP22 2AB
Telephone: Bressingham (01379) 686900. Infoline (01379) 686907
Fax: (01379) 686907
Internet address: www.bressingham.co.uk
Car park: Steam Centre (free)
Access by public transport: Diss main line station (3 miles)
On site facilities: 10.25/15/24in and standard gauge lines, totalling nearly 5 miles. Museum, steam roundabout, souvenir shop and restaurant, extensive gardens and plant centre. 'Dad's Army' permanent exhibition open all year
Public opening: Open every day between Easter and end of October. Steam every day with narrow gauge rides and the Gallopers. 10.30-17.30. Christmas events in December (dates to be confirmed). Education services for schools are available with pre-booking in March-October period
Special events: Please telephone 01379 686900 for details
Facilities for disabled: Wheelchairs access to majority of site including toilets. Able to take wheelchairs on Nursery Line Railway and Waveney Line

Locomotives

Name	No	Origin	Class	Type	Built
Martello	662	LBSCR	A1X	0-6-0T	1875
Thundersley	80	LTSR	3P	4-4-2T	1909
Granville	102	LSWR	B4	0-4-0T	1893
—	490	GER	E4	2-4-0	1894
Henry Oakley	990	GNR	C2	4-4-2	1898
Royal Scot	6100	LMS	7P	4-6-0	1927
Oliver Cromwell	70013	BR	7MT	4-6-2	1951
Peer Gynt	5865	NSB	52	2-10-0	1944
King Haakon VII	377	NSB	21c	2-6-0	1919

Industrial locomotives

Name	No	Builder	Type	Built
Beckton	1	Neilson (4444)	0-4-0ST	1892
Beckton	25	Neilson (5087)	0-4-0ST	1896
William Francis	6841	B/Peacock (6841)	0-4-0+0-4-0T	1937
Millfield	—	RSH (7070)	0-4-0CT	1942
Bluebottle	—	Barclay (1472)	0-4-0F	1916
County School	GET 1	R/Hornsby (497753)	0-4-0DE	1963

2ft gauge locomotives

Name	No	Builder	Type	Built
Gwynedd	—	Hunslet (316)	0-4-0ST	1883
George Sholto	—	Hunslet (994)	0-4-0ST	1909
Bronllwyd	—	H/Clarke (1643)	0-6-0WT	1930
Toby	—	M/Rail (22120)	4wDM	1964

15in gauge locomotives

Name	No	Builder	Type	Built
Rosenkavalier	—	Krupp (1662)	4-6-2	1937
Mannertreu	—	Krupp (1663)	4-6-2	1937
Flying Scotsman	4472	W. Stewart (4472)	4-6-2	1976
Works Loco	—	Diss	0-4-0DM	1992
Replica	6353	—	Bo-Bo	—

10.25in gauge locomotives

Name	No	Builder	Type	Built
Alan Bloom	1	BSM	0-4-0ST	1995

Owner
80, 490, 990 and 70013 on loan from the National Railway Museum
GET 1 the Great Eastern Traction Group

Special notes: Reduced rates for coach parties. Prices on application

England

Steam Centre — Bristol Industrial Museum — Bristol

Member: HRA

The Museum houses machinery and vehicles associated with Bristol's industrial past, from horse-drawn vehicles to aircraft

Location: Princes Wharf, Bristol

OS reference: ST 585722

Operating society/organisation: Bristol Industrial Museum, Princes Wharf, Bristol BS1 4RN

Telephone: (0117) 925 1470

Fax: (0117) 929 7318

Car parks: Available nearby

Access by public transport: Buses to centre of city, 1km from Temple Meads station

Industrial locomotives

Name	No	Builder	Type	Built
Portbury	34	Avonside (1764)	0-6-0ST	1917
Henbury	—	Peckett (1940)	0-6-0ST	1937
—	3	F/Walker (242)	0-6-0ST	1874
—	—	R/Hornsby (418792)	0-4-0DM	1958

On site facilities: Shop

Length of line: Half-mile, extension of one-mile open on special occasions only

Public opening: Open all year Saturday to Wednesday 10.00-17.00

Facilities for disabled: Reasonable access

Special notes: Operation of railway on advertised weekends only, 11.30-17.00

Membership details: Officer in charge — D. Martin, Bristol Harbour Railway c/o above address

Steam Centre — Buckinghamshire Railway Centre — Bucks

Member: HRA

The Buckinghamshire Railway Centre is situated at Quainton Road on the freight-only Aylesbury-Calvert line, once part of the Metropolitan and Great Central line from London to Verney Junction. Quainton Road station is also the old junction for the Brill Tramway closed in 1935. The Centre is now home to the former LNWR Rewley Road station moved brick-by-brick from the centre of Oxford. Opened in 1851, this Grade 2* listed building is built in the same manner as the Crystal Palace Great Exhibition building of 1881 destroyed by fire in the 1930s. It is unique in its construction and provides a superb setting in which the pick of the Centre's locomotives and carriages are now displayed

Location: Adjacent to goods-only line to Aylesbury. Turn off A41 at Waddesdon 6 miles NW of Aylesbury, Bucks

OS reference: SP 738190

Operating society/organisation: Quainton Railway Society Ltd, The Railway Station, Quainton, Nr Aylesbury, Bucks HP22 4BY

Locomotives and multiple-units

Name	No	Origin	Class	Type	Built
—	1	Met Rly	E	0-4-4T	1898
—	0314	LSWR	0298	2-4-0WT	1874
Defiant	5080	GWR	'Castle'	4-6-0	1939
Wightwick Hall	6989	GWR	'Hall'	4-6-0	1948
—	7200	GWR	7200	2-8-2T	1934
—	7715	GWR	5700	0-6-0PT	1930
—	9466	GWR	9400	0-6-0PT	1952
—	41298	LMS	2MT	2-6-2T	1951
—	41313	LMS	2MT	2-6-2T	1952
—	46447	LMS	2MT	2-6-0	1950
—	D2298	BR	04	0-6-0DM	1960
—	3405*	SAR	25NC	4-8-4	1958
—	51886	BR	115	DMBS	1960
—	51899	BR	115	DMBS	1960
—	59761	BR	115	TCL	1960

*3ft 6in gauge

Industrial locomotives

Name	No	Builder	Type	Built
Blue Circle	—	A/Porter (9449)	2-2-0TG	1926
Scott	—	Bagnall (2469)	0-4-0ST	1932
—	—	Baguley (2161)	0-4-0DM	1941
Swanscombe	—	Barclay (699)	0-4-0ST	1891
—	—	GF3 Barclay (1477)	0-4-0F	1916
—	—	Barclay (2243)	0-4-0F	1948
Yvonne	—	Cockerill (2945)	0-4-0VBT	1920
Osram	—	Fowler (20067)	0-4-0DM	1933
—	3	H/Leslie (3717)	0-4-0ST	1928
Sir Thomas	—	H/Clarke (1334)	0-6-0T	1918
—	—	H/Clarke (1742)	0-4-0ST	1946

28

Telephone: Quainton (01296) 655450

Internet address:
Web site:
www.bucksrailcentre.org.uk

Car park: Quainton Road — Free parking

Access by public transport: Main line Aylesbury station. Local bus Monday-Saturday only

On site facilities: Souvenir bookshop, light refreshments, toilets, steam-hauled train rides. Museum of small relics, secondhand bookshop, miniature railway

Catering facilities: Hot snacks and light refreshments available

Length of line: Two half-mile demonstration lines

Public opening: Open Wednesday to Sunday inclusive from April to October. Steaming days each Sunday and Wednesday June-August.

Opening times: 10.30-16.30 as well as Bank Holidays

Special events: A series of special events are held throughout the year including Thomas the Tank Engine weekends

Facilities for disabled: Access to most of site including special toilets

Special notes: One of the largest collection of standard gauge locomotives, together with a most interesting collection of vintage coaching stock, much of which was built in the 19th century

General: The public area of the centre covers some 25 acres of land with views across the Buckinghamshire countryside. A picnic area is available at the miniature railway

Name	No	Builder	Type	Built
—	—	Hunslet (2067)	0-4-0DM	1940
Arthur	—	Hunslet (3782)	0-6-0ST	1953
Juno	—	Hunslet (3850)	0-6-0ST	1958
—	65	Hunslet (3889)	0-6-0ST	1964
—	66	Hunslet (3890)	0-6-0ST	1964
—	26	Hunslet (7016)	0-6-0DH	1971
Redland	—	K/Stuart (K4428)	0-4-0DM	1929
—	14	M/Wardle (1795)	0-4-0ST	1912
Coventry No 1	—	NBL (24564)	0-6-0ST	1939
—	—	Peckett (1900)	0-4-0T	1936
Gibraltar	—	Peckett (2087)	0-4-0ST	1948
—	—	Peckett (2104)	0-4-0ST	1948
—	—	Peckett (2105)	0-4-0ST	1948
—	T1	Hibberd (2102)	4wD	1937
Tarmac	—	Hibberd (3765)	0-4-0DM	1955
—	11	Sentinel (9366)	4wVBTG	1945
—	7	Sentinel (9376)	4wVBTG	1947
—	—	Sentinel (9537)	4wVBTG	1947
Chislet	9	Yorkshire (2498)	0-6-0ST	1951

Stock: *Coaches —*
1 LCDR 1st Class 4-wheeler; 1 MSLR 3rd Class 6-wheeler; 4 LNWR coach bodies; 2 GNR 6-wheelers; 3 LNWR; 3 LMSR; 1 BR(W) Hawksworth brake 3rd; 2 BR Mk 1; 1 BR Mk 2; 1 BR Suburban brake; 3 LNER; 1 LNWR full brake 6-wheeler; 1 LMSR passenger brake van; 1 GWR passenger brake van; 1 GCR Robinson brake third

Wagons —
A large and varied collection including 1 LNWR combination truck; 1 LSWR ventilated fruit van; 1 SR PMV; 1 BR(W) Siphon G; 1 BR horse box; 1 BR CCT

3 ex-London Underground coaches
1 2ft gauge post office mailbag car 803
Sentinel/Cammell 3-car steam railcar unit 5208 (ex-Egyptian National)
Numerous goods vehicles/wagons/vans

Owners
41298, 41313, 46447 and *Juno* the Ivatt Locomotive Trust
9466 the 9466 Group
Defiant on loan from Tyseley Locomotive Works

An unusual locomotive in the shape of gear-driven Aveling & Porter *Blue Circle*. Alan Barnes

England

29

Bure Valley Railway

Member: HRA, TT

Opened in 1990, the BVR runs over the old Great Eastern Wroxham-Aylsham line. It is paralleled throughout the entire 9 miles by the Bure Valley Walk and cycle path which offers excellent photographic opportunities

Headquarters: Bure Valley Railway (1991) Ltd, Aylsham Station, Norwich Road, Aylsham, Norfolk NR11 6BW

Chairman: Andrew Barnes

Telephone: (01263) 733858

Fax: (01263) 733814

Internet address: *e-mail:* info@bvrw.co.uk

Web site: www.bvrw.co.uk

Main public station: Aylsham (Norwich Road); Wroxham (Coltishall Road)

Other public stations: Coltishall, Brampton and Buxton

Car and coach parks: Aylsham and Wroxham

OS reference:

Aylsham — TG 195264

Wroxham — TG 303186

Access by public transport: By rail – Wroxham station is adjacent to main line Hoveton & Wroxham station (Norwich-Cromer/Sheringham line). By bus – Eastern Counties buses run between Norwich and Aylsham

Refreshment facilities: Restaurant at Aylsham with picnic area, light refreshments at Wroxham

Souvenir shops: Aylsham and Wroxham

Journey time: Approximately

Locomotives

Name	No	Builder	Type	Built
Wroxham Broad 2nd Air Division	1	G&S/Winson	2-6-4T	1992
USAAF	3	BVR	4w-4wDH	1989
—	4	H/Hunslet	0-4-0DH	1996
—	5	Lister	4wDM	
Blickling Hall	6	Winson*	2-6-2	1994
Spitfire	7	Winson*	2-6-2	1994
Thunder	8	BVR/Winson	2-6-2T	1997
Little Titan	9	Cheeseman	Steam crane	1975
Mark Timothy	10	Winson/Keef§	2-6-4T	2003
—	11	T. Turner†	2-8-0	—

*based on Indian Railways 2ft 6in gauge 'ZB' class

§based on Leek & Manifold Railway design

†under construction (as time permits) based on Great Central Railway locomotive

Stock

20 fully enclosed saloons, 2 fully enclosed compartment coaches, 1 fully enclosed brake saloon, 6 enclosed saloons designed to carry wheelchairs, 2 guard's vans, generator car, miscellaneous wagons including a rail-mounted flail and weedkilling unit and purpose-built p/way tool vehicle

45min each way plus turnround time

Length of line: 9 miles; 15in gauge

Passenger trains: Frequency depends on time of year, maximum frequency one per hour

Period of public operation: Daily 4 April to 26 September and 21-31 October

Facilities for disabled: Toilets at Aylsham and Wroxham, special rolling stock to carry wheelchairs; advance notice would be appreciated

Special events: Please contact for full details, Day out with Thomas — 29-31 May and 22, 26

September; Teddy Bears Day — 31 October; Santa Specials — 27/28 November, 1/2, 4/5, 8/9, 11/12, 15-24 December (advance booking essential); Mince Pie specials 28 December to 2 January 2005

Special notes: Steam locomotive driving courses. Group discounts available. Frequent Travellers Railcards. Children's Birthday Parties. Private charters by arrangement. Special combined train and Broads boat excursions run most days during the summer

Membership details: Friends of the Bure Valley Railway, Membership Secretary, c/o above address

---

Cadeby Light Railway

Member: HRA, TT

A new museum was opened in 1990, the 'Boston Collection', encompassing the lifetime collection of Teddy Boston and his family. The narrow gauge railway running in the grounds of the old rectory has been saved by Teddy Boston's enterprising widow and a

Narrow gauge locomotives

Name	No	Builder	Type	Built
Pixie	—	Bagnall (2090)	0-4-0ST	1919
—	—	Baguley (1695)	0-4-0PM	1928
—	—	Lister (4088)	4wPM	1931
—	—	O&K (4588)	4wPM	1932
—	—	Thakeham (4th)	4wPM	c1946
Delta	—	Deutz (10050)	0-4-0DM	1930
—	—	H/Clarke (D558)	4wDM	1930

small band of dedicated supporters in the face of considerable odds. Echoes of the *Titfield Thunderbolt* and Ancient and Modern. Their endeavours deserve your support
Location: 5.75 miles north of Hinckley on A447
OS reference: SK 426024
Operating society/organisation: Mrs J. A. Boston, The Old Rectory, Cadeby, Nuneaton CV13 0AS
Telephone: Market Bosworth (01455) 290462
Car park: Available
Access by public transport: Arriva 159 from Hinckley and Arriva Fox 153 from Leicester to Market Bosworth (1.25 miles away). Operator subject to change as this is a county council supported route
On site facilities: 2ft gauge railway, also traction engine, model railway, and a museum housing the 'Boston Collection'. Brass rubbing centre in church with over 70 replica brasses
Refreshment facilities: Light refreshments available
Public opening: 10 April, 8 May, 12 June, 14 August, 9 October, 6 November, 11, 26 December. Open

Name	No	Builder	Type	Built
—	—	Hibberd (2306)	4wDM	1940
—	—	M/Rail & T (1320)	4wDM	1918
—	87004	M/Rail & T (2197)	4wDM	1922
—	87009	M/Rail & T (4572)	4wDM	1929
—	—	M/Rail & T (5038)	4wPM	1930
—	—	M/Rail (5853)	4wDM	1934
—	42	M/Rail (7710)	4wDM	1939
—	20	M/Rail (8748)	4wDM	1942
—	—	O&K (3444)	4wDM	1930
—	87008	R/Hornsby (179870)	4wDM	1936
—	85051	R/Hornsby (404967)	4wDM	1957
—	—	SMH (104063G)	4wDM	1976
—	—	W&R (D6912)	4wBE	1964

Standard gauge

Name	No	Builder	Type	Built
—	V47	Peckett (2012)	0-4-0ST	1941

Stock
Penrhyn Quarryman's 'O' coach; Hudson open wagons, skip wagons, Cravens van fron RNAD Dean Hill, 2 slate wagons from Dinorwic Slate Quarries, flat trucks; brickcars and two vehicles from John Knowles (Wooden Box) Ltd

Also on site Aveling & Porter 10-ton steamrollers (7856/12) and a Foster traction engine (14593/27). Aveling & Porter 5163/03 is off site under repair

from 13.00. Please ring for further details. Admission free (donations requested)

Special notes: Party bookings by prior arrangement

Cambrian Railways Society

Member: HRA

The Gobowen to Blodwell line is some 8.25 miles long and is currently in an operational 'mothballed' state. The society are negotiating with Network Rail to lease this former Cambrian branch line with a view to restoring a heritage railway service between Gobowen and Llanyblodwell and eventually Llanymyned. The society have carried out much work towards this aim over the past 12 months and hope to re-open the first phase, Oswestry to Weston Wharf, by spring 2004.

Location: Oswestry station yard, Oswald Road, Oswestry, Shropshire SY11 1RE

OS reference: SJ 294297

Operating society/organisation: Cambrian Railways Society Ltd, Oswald Road, Oswestry, Shropshire SY11 1RE

Telephone: (01691) 671749

Car park: In Society's depot

Length of line: 400yd, opened 7 December 1996, the Light Railway Order having been granted

Public opening:
Daily 10.00-16.00.
Trains are expected to operate 11 April; 1/2, 30/31 May; 27 June; 17/18, 24/25, 31 July; 1, 7/8, 14/15, 21/22, 28-30 August; 4/5, 26 September; 31 October. Santa Specials 4, 11, 18/19, 31 December; 1 January 2005

On site facilities: Refreshment room — the 'Whistle Stop' (open on special days in former Llansantffraid signalbox) and picnic area

Special notes: Railwayana, artefacts and 20 bicycles, 17 motor cycles and 7 auto-cycles/mopeds on display. Peckett 2131 and Hunslet 3770 are on display inside the building. Group discount available. Also known as Oswestry Transport Museum

Industrial locomotives

Name	No	Builder	Type	Built
—	1	H/Clarke (D843)	0-4-0DM	1954
Adam	1	Peckett (1430)	0-4-0ST	1916
—	3	Hunslet (D3526)	0-6-0DM	1954
Oliver Velton	6	Peckett (2131)	0-4-0ST	1951
—	8	Barclay (885)	0-6-0ST	1900
—	322	Planet (3541)	4wDM	1952
Norma	3770	Hunslet (3770)	0-6-0ST	1952
—	No 3	Sentinel	0-4-0D	
—*	—	Hibberd (3057)	4wDM	1946
—	—	Planet	4wDM	1960

*mobile compressor

Stock

1 GWR auto-trailer; 1 GWR brake van; 1 LMS brake van; 2 tank wagons; 1 open wagon, 1 box van, 1 tank wagon (No 5), 2 tank wagon 4-wheel chassis (tanks removed) ex-Machynlleth Refuelling Depot, 1 GWR Syphon, Mess & Sleeping coach dating from 1911, 27-ton former TPO (now tool van), 4-wheel van, 12-ton box van, Warflat, bogie bolster, ex-S&M 10-ton box van.

Note: some of the above stock has since been removed from the site

---

Chasewater Railway

Member: HRA, TT

Founded in 1959 as the Railway Preservation Society (West Midlands District), the Chasewater Railway was re-formed in 1985 as a Registered Charity. The railway operates as 'The Colliery Line' to reflect its origins and location in the heart of the Cannock Chase coalfield. The railway operates a regular timetabled service between Brownhills West station and Chasetown (Church Street), with intermediate stations at Norton

Diesel locomotive and multiple-units

Name	No	Builder	Class	Type	Built
—	31203	BR	31	A1A-A1A	1960
—	W51370	Pressed Steel	117	DMBS	1960
—	W51372	Pressed Steel	117	DMBS	1960
—	W51412	Pressed Steel	117	DMS	1960
—	W59444	BR Derby	116	TS	1958
—	W59603	Pressed Steel	127	TSL	1959

Industrial locomotives

Name	No	Builder	Type	Built
Alfred Paget	11	Neilson (2937)	0-4-0ST	1882
Sheepbridge No 15	—	H/Clarke (431)	0-6-0T	1895
—	6	Peckett (917)	0-4-0ST	1902

England

Lakeside (which adjoins Chasewater's Wildfowl Reserve) and Chasewater Heaths.

Location: Chasewater Park, Brownhills (off A5 southbound, nr jct A452 Chester Road). Brown tourism signs are provided on A5

OS Reference: SK 034070

Operating society/organisation: Chasewater Light Railway & Museum Co

Telephone/Fax: 01543 452623

Internet address: *E-mail:* info@ChasewaterRailway.co.uk *Web site:* www.ChasewaterRailway.co.uk

Car park: Ample car parking within Chasewater Park

Access by public transport: *Nearest railway stations* — Walsall and Birmingham New Street. *Sunday bus services from Walsall Bus Station (St Paul's Street)* — 362 (Stand K) and 394A (Stand L) to Brownhills West (Rising Sun Inn). *Sunday bus services from Birmingham (Moor Street Queensway, adj Moor Street Station)* — Pete's Travel Service 156A to Brownhills West (Rising Sun Inn). Brownhills West station is approx 10min walk from the Rising Sun Inn. For timetable information and details of services, contact the Centro Hotline 0121 200 2700

On site facilities: Refreshments, shop, lakeside walks and large

Name	No	Builder	Type	Built
Asbestos	4	H/Leslie (2780)	0-4-0ST	1909
Colin McAndrew	3	Barclay (1223)	0-4-0ST	1911
Whit No 4		H/Clarke (1822)	0-6-0T	1949
Sentinel	5	Sentinel (9632)	4wVBT	1957
—	1	M/Rail (1947)	4wPM	1919
—	21	Kent Constr (1612)	4wDM	1929
—	—	Fowler (4100013)	0-4-0DM	1948
—	—	GEC (USA) (30483)	0-4-4-0DE	1949
—	—	R/Hornsby (305306)	0-4-0DM	1952
Hem Heath	3D	Bagnall (3119)	0-6-0DM	1956
—	—	Hibberd (3906)	4wDM	1959
Toad	37	Fowler (4220015)	0-4-0DH	1962
Fleet	11517	R/Hornsby (458641)	0-4-0DE	1963

Rolling stock
A variety of passenger and freight vehicles are housed on site, including a number of considerable historical importance

grassed areas

Catering facilities: Hot and cold buffet

Length of line: Approx 2 miles

Public opening: Sundays and Bank Holiday Mondays throughout the year. Saturday service July to September inclusive.

Trains run hourly from Brownhills West station, 11.00-15.00. Reduced service hourly 12.00-16.00 during off-peak periods. Check web site for running dates and timetables.

Most services are with steam traction (subject to availability). Industrial diesel locomotives and heritage DMU sets are normally used once a month.

All tickets give unlimited rides on

day of issue

Special events: Vintage Gathering — 11/12 April; Chasewater Park Open Day — 3 May; Spring Gala — 16 May; Bus Rally — 20 June; Vintage Gathering — 29/30 August; Diesel Gala — 12 September; Gricer's Day (with evening running) , 3 October; Collectors' Fair — 21 November; Santa Specials — 5, 12, 19 December

Facilities for disabled: Disabled access to stations, trains and buffet

Membership details: Membership Secretary, Brownhills West Station, Chasewater Country Park, Pool Road, Nr Brownhills, Staffs WS8 7NL

Steam Centre — Chinnor & Princes Risborough Railway — 'The Icknield Line' — Oxfordshire

Member: HRA

The Chinnor & Princes Risborough Railway runs from Chinnor station, close to the beautiful Chiltern Hills and to the Vale of Aylesbury. Originally built in the 1870s to connect the towns of Watlington in Oxfordshire to Princes Risborough in Buckinghamshire, it was closed by British Railways in 1989. Since then a team of volunteers has restored Chinnor station to its

Locomotives

Name	No	Origin	Class	Type	Built
Haversham	13018	BR	08	0-6-0DE	1953
—	D8568	BR	17	Bo-Bo	1963
—	D5801	BR	31	A1A-A1A	1961
—	55023	BR	121	DMBS	1958
—	4247	GWR	4200	2-8-0T	1916

Industrial locomotives

Name	No	Builder	Type	Built
Iris	459515	R/Hornsby (459515)	0-6-0DH	1952

Victorian glory. The railway operates the 3.5-mile ex-Great Western Railway branch line as a tourist attraction for both families and railway enthusiasts. A regular steam-hauled service is provided every Sunday from April to October. Special events are a feature of the programme including Day out with Thomas weekends and Santa Specials. Cream teas are served on selected afternoon trains during the summer months

Location: M40 Junction 6 then B4009 north 4 miles towards Princes Risborough to village of Chinnor. Once in village follow brown tourist signs to station

Operating society/organisation: Chinnor & Princes Risborough Railway Co Ltd, Chinnor Station, Station Road, Chinnor, Oxon OX39 4ER

Contact details: Eric Samual, Press & Publicity Director, 2 Coates Lane, High Wycombe, Bucks HP13 5HE

Telephone: 01844 354117. Talking Timetable 01844 353535. Thomas Booking Line: 01844 354117 (Weekends 10.00-17.00 only)

Internet address: *e-mail:* eric.samual@cprra.co.uk *Web site:* www.cprra.co.uk

OS reference: SP756003

Access by public transport: Nearest main line station — Princes Risborough (4 miles) Chiltern Railways By car: M40 junction 6 then B4009

Stock - coaches
1 ex-LNWR Mess coach, 1 ex-BR Mk 1 NDV, 1 ex-BR Mk 1 RMB, 1 ex-BR Mk 1 CK, 1 ex-BR Mk 1 BSK, 1 ex-BR Mk 2 FK, 12 various wagons, 1 Coles self-propelled crane

---

4 miles direction of Princes Risborough to Chinnor, then follow brown tourist signs

Length of line: 3.5 miles

Journey time: 45min, steam and heritage diesel trains

On site facilities: Souvenir shop, small buffet on Chinnor station. Bar/buffet on most trains (cream teas on selected trains on summer Sunday afternoons). Toilets, free car park, picnic area

Passenger trains: Chinnor-Thame Junction-Chinnor

Public opening: 21, 28 March; 4, 9-12, 18, 25 April; 1-3, 9, 16, 23, 29-31 May; 5/6, 12/13, 19/20, 26/27 June; 3/4, 10/11, 17/18, 24/25, 31 July; 1, 7/8, 14/15, 21/22, 28-30 August; 5, 12, 19, 26 September; 3, 10, 17, 24, 31 October; 4/5, 11/12, 18/19, 28/29 December (Santa Specials)

Special events: Mother's Day — 21 March; Diesel Gala Day — 28 March; Easter Egg Specials — 9-12 April; A Day out with Thomas — 1-3 May; Senior Citizens' Day — 16 May; Branch Line at War Weekend — 30/31 May; Father's Day — 20 June; Grandmother's Day Specials — 11 July; Senior Citizens' Day — 20 July; Day out with Thomas — 7/8 August; Chinnor & Princes Risborough

---

Railway 10th Anniversary Celebration Gala — 21/22 August; Teddy Bear Weekend — 23-25 August; Autumn Gala Weekend — 12 September; Grandfather's Day — 26 September; Children Go Free Day — 10 October; Halloween Specials — 31 October; Santa Specials — 4/5, 11/12, 18/19 December; Mince Pie Specials — 28/29 December.

Cream Teas — 21 March, 4, 18 April; 16, 30/31 May; 6, 13, 20, 27 June; 4, 11, 18, 25 July; 1, 15 August; 5, 26 September; 10 October. Trains leave at 13.30, 15.00, 16.30. Other dates available for party bookings

Special note: Group charter hire and film and photographic facilities. For group bookings contact: 01844 353535.

Advanced booking is strongly recoomended for Day out with Thomas and Santa Specials

Facilities for disabled: Ramp, toilet, accessible parking area. All public areas accessible. Guide dogs welcome

Membership details: Mr Peter Harris, 12 Ann's Close, Aylesbury, Bucks

Membership journal: *The Watlington Flyer* — quarterly

Timetable Service — Cholsey & Wallingford Railway — Oxfordshire

Member: HRA

The Barclay has now returned to steam and has been restored in the guise of GWR 701, a former Swansea Harbour Trust locomotive

Location: Hithercroft Road, Wallingford, Oxfordshire

Sales & Marketing: Jo Clyde

Operating Society: Cholsey & Wallingford Railway Preservation Society, PO Box 16, Wallingford, Oxon OX10 9YN

Telephone: (01491) 835067 (24hr information line)

Locomotives

Name	No	Origin	Class	Type	Built
Unicorn	D3074	BR	08	0-6-0DE	1953
Lion	D3030	BR	08	0-6-0DE	1953
George Mason	D3190	BR	08	0-6-0DE	1955

Industrial locomotives

Name	No	Builder	Type	Built
Spitfire	701	Barclay (1964)	0-4-0ST	1929
Carpenter	3271	Planet (3271)	0-4-0DM	1949
—	803	Alco (77777)	Bo-Bo	1950

Rolling stock — coaches: GWR autocoach, Hawksworth brake coach, GWR full brake, 4 BR Mk 1 coaches, assorted goods stock

England

Internet address: *E-mail:* cwrailyahoo.co.uk *Web site:* www.cholsey-wallingford-railway.com

Access by public transport: Thames Travel X39 from Oxford-London main line trains Cholsey

Public opening: Trains run between 11.00-16.00 (from Wallingford) and 11.30-16.30 (from Cholsey) at hourly intervals on 20/21 March; 10-12, 24/25 April; 2/3, 30/31 May; 20 June; 25 July; 29/30 August; 3-5, 26 September; 30/31 October; 5, 11/12, 18/19 December. Train times may vary in December.

Length of line: 2.5 miles from Wallingford

Journey time: Approximately 20min (one way), 45min (return)

On site facilities: Souvenir and coffee shop, museum, model railway

Special events: Guinness Weekend — 20/21 March; Ivor the Engine — 10-12 April; St George's Celebrations — 24/25 April; May Day Celebrations — 2/3 May; Teddy Bears' Picnic — 30/31May; Beer Festival — 20 June; Wallingford Fun Day — 25 July; Ivor the Engine — 29/30 August; Bunk Festival — 3-5 September; Halloween — 30/31 October; Santa Specials — 5, 11/12, 18/19 December

Special notes: Railway crosses new bypass (A4130) at a level crossing. The Society is running into Cholsey bay platform.

Membership details: John Bennett, at above address

Membership journal: *The Bunk* — 3 issues/year

Churnet Valley Railway

Timetable Service · Staffordshire

Member: HRA

This heritage railway is situated deep in the heart of the Staffordshire moorlands. Cheddleton is an original Victorian country station set in picturesque countryside complete with riverside parking and picnic island. The journey takes you to the idyllic hamlet of Consall Forge and onwards to the newly reinstated station Kingsley & Froghall

Main station/location: Cheddleton Station, Station Road, Cheddleton, Nr Leek, Staffs ST13 7EE

OS reference: SJ 983519

Operating society/organisation: Churnet Valley Railway (1992) plc

Telephone: 01538 360522

Fax: 01538 361848

Internet address: *e-mail:* mgt@cheddcvr.freeserve.co.uk

Web site: www.churnetvalleyrailway.co.uk

Other stations: Consall, Kingsley & Froghall

Car parks: Adjacent to Cheddleton and Froghall stations

Access by public transport: Main line Stoke-on-Trent (10 miles). A regular bus service (No 16) runs from Hanley and Leek to Cheddleton village

On site facilities: Refreshment facilities on all trains and at Cheddleton and Froghall

Souvenir shop: Cheddleton and Froghall

Museum: Small relics museum and locomotive display hall at Cheddleton

Locomotives and multiple-units

Name	No	Origin	Class	Type	Built
—	2	NSR	New L	0-6-2T	1923
—	1	NSR	—	0-4-0BE	1917
—	44422	LMS	4F	0-6-0	1927
—	48305	LMS	8F	2-8-0	1943
—	80136	BR	4MT	2-6-4T	1956
—	5197	USATC	S160	2-8-0	1942
—	411.144	USATC	S160	2-8-0	194?
—	D2334	BR	04	0-6-0DM	1961
—	D3991	BR	08	0-6-0DE	1960
—	20007	BR	20	Bo-Bo	1957
—	20154	BR	20	Bo-Bo	1966
Tamworth Castle	D7672	BR	25	Bo-Bo	1967
—	31442	BR	31	A1A-A1A	1960
—	33102	BR	33	Bo-Bo	1960
Burma Star	33056	BR	33	Bo-Bo	1961
—	37211	BR	37	Co-Co	1961
—	37340	BR	37	Co-Co	1961
—	53455	BRCW	104	DMBS	1957
—	53437	BRCW	104	DMBS	1957
—	53494	BRCW	104	DMCL	1957
—	53517	BRCW	104	DMCL	1957
—	59137	BRCW	104	TSL	1957

Industrial locomotives

Name	No	Builder	Type	Built
—	68030	Hunslet (3777)	0-6-0ST	1952
Cammell	—	YEC	0-4-0DH	1960
Brightside	—	YEC	0-4-0DH	1960

Locomotive notes: Locos expected to be in service: 5197, 68030, 80136, D2334, D3991, 20007, 20154 and 33102.

Stock

Ex-BR Mk 1 coaches: CK (1), BSK (2), SO (3), TSO (2), FK (3), RMB (1) RBR (1), RK (1) and BG (2); ex-BR Mk 2 coaches: BFK (1) and BSO (1); ex-BR suburban coaches: S (1), BS (2), SLO (1); 1 ex-NSR coach body; 1 ex-LMS 6-wheel full brake; 2 ex-LMS goods brake vans; 1

Length of line: 5.25 miles
Public opening: Steam trains Easter-September inclusive; Sundays and Bank Holiday Mondays, Saturdays in July and August. Tuesdays, Wednesdays and Thursdays in August
Special events: Station at War, Day out with Thomas, Wizards Express, Ghost Train and Santa Specials
Facilities for disabled: Access to station areas is possible by wheelchair, train travel by arrangement. Disabled toilet facilities at Consall
Membership details: North Staffordshire Railway Co (1978) Ltd, Membership Secretary, c/o above address
Special notes: Party bookings by arrangement, footplate experience courses, wine & dine dates on application. Licensed for weddings

ex-LMS 6-wheel CCT; 2 ex-LMS box vans; 3 ex-BR box vans; 2 ex-LMS five-plank wagons; 1 ex-LMS hopper wagon; 1 Esso tank wagon; 1 ex-BR standard brake van; 1 ex-BR Oyster; 5 ex-BR General Utility Vans; 2 ex-BR Medfits; 2 ex-BR Catfish; 1 ex-GWR bogie bolster; 2 Flatrols; 1 Lowmac; 7-ton diesel rail-mounted crane; 75-ton rail-mounted diesel crane; 3 ex-BR QQX tool vans; 1 ex-BR QPX staff and dormitory

Owners
44422 the 4F Locomotive Fund
80136 and 68030 the Class 4 Preservation Trust
33056, 33102 and D7672 the NSR Diesel Group
NSR 1 and 2 the National Railway Museum
20007, 20154, 31442, 37211, 37340, D3991 and *Cammell* the Churnet Traction & Rolling Stock Group

---

Cleethorpes Coast Light Railway

Member: HRA

The East Coast's last surviving seaside 15in gauge steam railway. Built in 1948 as a 10.25in line, it was converted in 1972 to 14.25in and then to 15in gauge in 1994.

The railway has a good reputation for galas and events, and continues to improve year on year. In 2000 a new station and viaduct were opened and the line is currently being extended.

The Cleethorpes Coast Light Railway Supporters Association, who help to run services on the line, undertaking a wide range of duties, supports the railway company. This small group provides volunteers from station staff to engine drivers.

2004 will again feature a majority of steam haulage, supported by visiting engines in the summer months

Operating society/organisation: Cleethorpes Coast Light Railway Ltd, Lakeside Station, Kings Road, Cleethorpes, Lincolnshire DN35 0AG
Telephone: (01472) 604657
Fax: (01472) 291903
Internet address: *e-mail:* genoffcclrltd.freeserve.co.uk
Access by public transport: By rail to Cleethorpes station. Local

Locomotives

Name	No	Built/rebuilt	Type	Date
Konigswinter	1	CCLR	2-8-0GH	1992
—	2	Lister	4wDH Tram	—
The Cub/John	3	Minirail/CCLR	4w4DM	1993
—	6	Stanhope/CCLR	0-4-0VBT	1995
—	24	Fairbourne	2-6-2	1989
Seabreeze	—	CCLR	4-6-2	Under construction
Flower of the Forest	—	R&ER	4wVBT	1985
—	—	A. Moss/J. Fowler	4wDH	1995
Battison	—	Battison	1-6-4DH	1958

Rolling stock
10 coaches, 1 x 4-wheel wagon, 1 x 4-wheel van

Sutton Collection

Locomotives

Name	No	Built/rebuilt	Type	Date
Sutton Belle	1	BL/Cannon Ironfoundries	4-4-2	1933
Sutton Flyer	2	Bassett Lowke/Hunt	4-4-2	1950
—	4	G&S Light Engineering	Bo-Bo	1946

Rolling stock
6 closed coaches, 4 open coaches, 4-wheel coal truck

Stagecoach Buses service 9x (all year) and 17 (summer only) pass both Lakeside and Kingsway stations.
By car, Kings Road is the main resort road. Follow brown tourist signs for Lakeside
On site facilities: Large 500 space car park at Lakeside station (pay & display). Station Masters gift shop at Kingsway station. Brief Encounters tea room at Lakeside station. Lakeside picnic area
Period of public opening: Please contact for details

36

Member: HRA, TT

A completely reconstructed country station and railway within sight of a 12th century castle and specialising in entertainment and education. A complementary Farm Park provides interest for all the family (May to September)

Location: Castle Hedingham Station, Yeldham Road, Castle Hedingham, Halstead, Essex CO9 3DZ

OS reference: TL 774362

Operating society/organisation: Colne Valley Railway Preservation Society Ltd

Telephone: Hedingham (01787) 461174

Internet address:
Web site:
www.colnevalleyrailway.co.uk

Car park: At the site (access from A1017 road between Castle Hedingham and Great Yeldham)

Access by public transport: Eastern National bus services 88 Colchester-Halstead, 89 Halstead-Hedingham and Hedingham Omnibuses 4 Braintree-Hedingham, 5 Sudbury-Hedingham. Nearest main line station — Braintree (7 miles)

On site facilities: Depot, museum, souvenir shop, buffet, 4-acre riverside picnic area, toilets, video carriage, exhibition centre, 30 acre farm park

Catering facilities: Buffet carriage when trains operating. Pullman on-train service on selected days for Sunday lunch, private hire and evening wine and dine (pre-booking essential for all Pullman services)

Length of line: 1 mile

Public opening: Steam trains operate every Sunday from 21 March to 31 October, also Wednesdays and Thursdays during school summer holidays, every Bank Holiday (except Christmas & New Year), Wednesdays during other school holidays (except February). Diesel railcar on many other days

Special events: A Day out with Thomas, Santa Specials

Educational events: Diesel trains

Locomotives and multiple-units

Name	No	Origin	Class	Type	Built
Blue Star	35010	SR	MN	4-6-2	1942
—	45163	LMS	5	4-6-0	1935
—	45293	LMS	5	4-6-0	1936
—	D2041	BR	03	0-6-0DM	1959
—	D2184	BR	03	0-6-0DM	1962
—	D3476	BR	10	0-6-0DE	1957
—	31255	BR	31	A1A-A1A	1961
—	47771	BR	47	Co-Co	19??
—	54287	P/Steel	121	DTS	1961
—	55033	P/Steel	121	DTC	1960
—	68009	BR	MLV / 419	DMVL	1961
—	69318	BR	4-BIG / 422	TRBS	1965
—	W79976	AC Cars	—	Railbus	1958
—	E79978	AC Cars	—	Railbus	1958

Industrial locomotives

Name	No	Builder	Type	Built
Victory	8	Barclay (2199)	0-4-0ST	1945
—	WD190	Hunslet (3790)	0-6-0ST	1952
—	68072	Vulcan (5309)	0-6-0ST	1945
Jupiter	60	RSH (7671)	0-6-0ST	1950
—	40	RSH (7765)	0-6-0T	1954
Barrington	—	Avonside (1875)	0-4-0ST	1921
—	1	H/Leslie (3715)	0-4-0ST	1928
—	—	Barclay (349)	0-4-0DM	1941
—	YD43	R/Hornsby (221639)	4wDM	1943
—	—	Hibberd (3147)	4wDM	1947
—	—	Unilok (2109)	4wDM R/R	1982
—	—	Lake & Elliot (1)	4wPM	1924
—	—	R/Hornsby (281266)	4wDM	1950

Locomotive notes: 40, *Barrington* and 190 expected to be operational during 2004. Diesels 31255 and 55033 also operational

Stock

2 ex-Pullman cars, *Aquila* and *Hermione;* 10 ex-BR Mk 1 coaches (2xTSO, SO, 3xCK, SK, 2xBSK); 1 ex-BR Mk 3 SLEP; 9 BR NPCCS, 2 ex-LNER — 1xBTO (16551) 1xTK (42240); 1 LMS BG, 1 GER BTK; 4 goods brake vans (GWR, LNER & 2 BR), 3 oil tank wagons, BR steam crane, LT ballast wagon, BR Sturgeon, BR Conflat, GER van, BR van, BR Medfit, LNER tube wagon, BR diesel crane, BR Flatrol, BR Lowmac

Owners

35010 and 45293 the British Engineman's Steam Preservation Society
54287 and 55033 Pressed Steel Heritage Ltd
31255 and 68009 the Colne Valley Railway Diesel Group
47771 the Class 47 Preservation Project

available every day for school visits (steam on certain days). Special steam school days in June. Victorian Special in October. All educational events must be pre-booked

Family tickets: Available — 2 adults and up to 4 children, giving unlimited train rides except on special events

Facilities for disabled: Access to most areas. Ramps to trains, staff will help. Special carriage available

Special notes: The railway has

England

been completely rebuilt on part of the original Colne Valley & Halstead Railway trackbed. It offers much of educational value specialising in school party visits by appointment at any time of the year

Membership details: Membership Secretary, c/o Castle Hedingham Station

Coventry Railway Centre

Museum — Warwickshire

Member: HRA

The railway is the only standard gauge line in Warwickshire and has been constructed on a greenfield site by members of The 1857 Society, work beginning in 1983. Originally known as the Coventry Steam Railway Centre, the public were first admitted in 1988, after which time the marketing name — Airfield Line — was adopted. Development continues and the site now houses ex-MR Little Bowden Junction signalbox, and the rebuilt 118-year old LNWR North Kilworth station building, to be renamed Thistledown Halt. Work is ongoing to convert the six acre site to an authentic railway setting. The site also contains a collection of vintage road rollers

Location: Within the boundary of Coventry Airport, south of the city. Easily reached via Rowley Road, junction with A45/A46, Coventry eastern bypass — M6/M69/M1 link road. Follow Coventry Airport direction signs — entrance is adjacent to Emergency Exit Gate 2

OS reference: SP 349750

Access by public transport: Main line to Coventry, West Midlands bus route 20/21 from city centre to Toll Bar End

Operating society/organisation: Coventry Railway Centre in conjunction with Carrick Wardale Steam Crane Group, The 1857 Society and Suburban Electric Railway Association

Telephone: Not advised

Intronet address: Web site:http://www.coventryrailwaycentre.org.uk

Length of line: Third of a mile (under construction)

Public opening: Every Sunday from Easter to October, 11.00-17.00, static display. See press for operating days and special events.

Locomotive and multiple-units

Name/Unit Nos	No	Origin	Class	Type	Built
(Leviathan)	50040	BR	50	Co-Co	1968
4732 {	12795	BR	4SUB / 405	DMBSO	1951
	12354	BR	4SUB / 405	TS	1948
	10239	BR	4SUB / 405	TOS	1948
	12796	BR	4SUB / 405	DMBSO	1951
5791/93/ {	65321	BR	2EPB / 416/2	DMBSO	1954
(930053) {	77112	BR	2EPB / 416/2	DTC	1954
4311/ {	61287	BR	2HAP / 414	DMBSO	1959
(6089) {	75407	BR	2HAP / 414	DTCL	1959
6307 {	14573	BR	2EPB / 416/2	DMBSO	1959
{	16117	BR	2EPB / 416/2	DTS	1959
—	68007	BR	MLV / 419	DMVL	1961
—	68008	BR	MLV / 419	DMVL	1961
—	(7)	LOR*	—	TFO	1895
—	28690	LMS	503	DMBSO	1938
—	29289	LMS	503	DTTO	1938
—	29720	LMS	503	TCO	1938
5176	15345	BR	415 / 4EPB	TSO	1954
1523	61383	BR	4CEP / 411	DMSO	1958
1500	70302	BR	4CEP / 411	TSO	1958
2205	69339	BR	4CEP / 411	TSRB	1970
7001	67300	BR	457	DMSO	1981
—	50397	P/Royal	103	DMBSO	1958
210002	67301	BR	210	DTSO	1981

*Liverpool Overhead Railway, built by Brown Marshall & Co

Industrial locomotives

Name	No	Builder	Type	Built
—	(1)	A/Barclay (1772)	0-4-0F	1922
—	(1)	E/Electric (EE905)	4wBE/WE	1935
(C. P. May)	—	Hibberd (2895)	4wPM	1944
—	(L14)	R/Hornsby (235515)	4wDM	1945
Mazda	—	R/Hornsby (268881)	0-4-0DE	1950
(Crabtree)	—	R/Hornsby (338416)	4wDM	1953
—	(L7)	R/Hornsby (349038)	4wDM	1954

Rolling stock

Ex-City & South London Railway trailers Nos 135 and 163
1 BR Mk 1 TSO, 1 steam crane, 1 hand crane, 1 bogie tool van (converted from Maunsell Ironclad coach, 2 fitted vans, 1 LNER brake van, 1 MoD (SR design) brake van, 1 MoD tanker

Owners

Crabtree on loan from North Downs Steam Railway
Unit 4732 the 4SUB Preservation Ltd
Unit 5791/93 and Class 503 vehicles the Electric Train Preservation Ltd
LOR (7), 67300, 67301, C&SLR tailers and Bogie Tool Van the Suburban Electric Railway Association

England

Other times and party visits by prior arrangement. (No access at other times.)
Car park: On site, access off Rowley Road
Facilities for disabled: Site relatively flat. Members willing to assist if prior notice given. No access to buffet coach, no toilets

15396 the 4SUB Preservation Ltd
Steam crane the Carrick & Wardale Crane Group

| Tram Service | Crich Tramway Village | Derbyshire |

Member: HRA, TT
An experience of living transport history with vintage horse-drawn, steam and electric trams running through a re-created townscape of authentic buildings, stone setts, iron railings and historic street furniture. The heart of the Museum is its collection of over 70 vintage trams and you can enjoy the thrill of travelling on the scenic mile-long track. New for 2004 is a woodland walk and sculpture trail
Location: Crich, Nr Matlock, Derbyshire DE4 5DP
OS reference: SK 345549
Manager: John Miller
Operating society/organisation: Tramway Museum Society
Telephone: (01773) 852565
Internet address: Web site: www.tramway.co.uk
Car park: Site; coach parking also available
Access by public transport: By rail, nearest main line stations: Cromford or Alfreton then by bus; or Whatstandwell and steep uphill walk
On site facilities: Souvenir shop, play areas, bookshop and picnic areas. 1-mile electric tramway. Tramway period street, depots, displays, exhibitions and video theatre. Large exhibition hall with new interpretive display depicting the history of the tram and Turn of the Century Trade Exhibition plus other exhibitions/displays
Refreshment facilities: Hot and cold snacks and meals
Public opening: Daily 14-22 February, then weekends until end of March. Daily1 April until 31 October then weekends until 19 December.
Opening times: 10.30-16.00 except April to October (10.00-17.30)

Locomotives

Name	No	Builder	Type	Built
—	—	B/Peacock (2464)	0-4-0VB tram loco	1885
—	—	E/Electric (717)	4wE	1927
Rupert*	—	R/Hornsby (223741)	4wDM	1944
GMJ*	—	R/Hornsby (326058)	4wDM	1952
—*	—	R/Hornsby (373363)	4wDM	1954

*not on display

Trams

No	Operator	Built
1	Derby	1904
1	Douglas Head Marine Drive	1896
1	Leamington & Warwick	1881
1	London Transport	1932
2	Blackpool & Fleetwood	1898
4	Blackpool Corp	1885
5	Blackpool	*1972
5	Gateshead & District	1927
7	Chesterfield	1904
8	Chesterfield	1899
9	Oporto	1873
10	Hill of Howth	1902
14	Grimsby & Immingham	1915
15	Sheffield	1874
21	Dundee & District	1894
22	Glasgow	1922
35	Edinburgh	1948
40	Blackpool & Fleetwood	†1914
40	Blackpool	1926
45	Southampton	1903
46	Sheffield	1899
(47)	New South Wales Govt	1885
49	Blackpool	1926
52	Gateshead & District	*1901
59	Blackpool	*1902
60	Johannesburg	1905
68	Paisley & District	1919
74	Sheffield	1900
76	Leicester	1904
102	Newcastle	1901
106	London County Council	1903
132	Kingston-upon-Hull	§1910
166	Blackpool	1927
167	Blackpool	1928
180	Leeds	1931

[18.30 weekends in June, July and August, plus all Bank Holidays]

Special events: Countdown to D-Day — 11/12 April; Teddy Bears' Outing — 25 April; Models Weekend — 15/16 May; Edwardian Weekend — 22/23 May; Tramathon — 20 June; 1940s Weekend— 14/15 August; Transport Extravaganza — 29/30 August; Beetle Drive — 19 September; Treasure Trail — 20-31 October; Starlight Halloween — 31 October; Santa Special — 11/12, 18/19 December

Family tickets: Available

Facilities for disabled: Access to all public facilities, Braille guide book available. Also 1969 Berlin tram specially adapted to lift and carry people in wheelchairs. Also a 'wheelway', a smooth path routeing around and through cobbled areas

Special notes: Crich houses the largest collection of preserved trams in Europe and has a 1-mile working tramway on which restored electric trams are regularly operated. Special events are arranged at weekends and Bank Holidays throughout the season. Part of tram line occupies route of narrow gauge mineral railway built by George Stephenson

Membership details: From above address

Membership journal: *The Journal* — quarterly

No	Operator	Built
180	Prague	1908
189	Sheffield	1934
264	Sheffield	1937
273	Oporto	—
298	Blackpool	*1937
331	Metropolitan Electric	1930
345	Leeds	*—
399	Leeds	1926
510	Sheffield	1950
600	Leeds	1931/54
602	Leeds	1953
674	New York 3rd Avenue Transit	1939
812	Glasgow	1900
869	Liverpool	1936
1100	Glasgow	1928
1105	Glasgow	1929
1147	Hague	1957
1282	Glasgow	1940
1297	Glasgow	1948
1622	London Transport	1912
3006	Berlin	1969
—	London Tramways	c1895

*stored off-site
†on loan to Blackpool
§on loan to Hull Museum of Transport

Note: In addition to the trams (including examples from Czechoslovakia, Germany, The Netherlands, Portugal, USA and South Africa) — about a third of which have been restored to working order — there are a number of Works Cars not listed

---

Museum	**Darlington Railway Centre & Museum**	County Durham

Located on the original 1825 route of the Stockton & Darlington Railway, the restored North Road station, dating from 1842, is now a museum which forms the centrepiece of an area devoted to railway history and preservation.

The Museum is administered by Darlington Borough Council. The collection includes locomotives, rolling stock and many small exhibits. The site also includes two other historic buildings of the S&DR — the former Goods Shed and the Hopetown Carriage Works.

The Ken Hoole Study Centre houses a collection of reference material on the railways of north-east England including the library

Locomotives

Name	No	Origin	Class	Type	Built
Locomotion	1	S&DR	—	0-4-0	1825
Derwent	25	S&DR	—	0-6-0	1845
—	1463	NER	1463	2-4-0	1885
—	910	NER	901	2-4-0	1875
Blue Peter	60532	LNER	A2	4-6-2	1948

Stock

1 Stockton & Darlington Rly passenger coach (1846)
1 North Eastern Railway Coach body (c1860)
1 NER 20-ton mineral wagon
1 Chaldron wagon

Owners

Locomotion, Derwent, 1463 and 910 are all on loan from the National Railway Museum
60532 on loan via the North Eastern Locomotive Preservation Group

England

of the North Eastern Railway Association (access by appointment).

Arriva train services provide a link to Darlington's main line station and to Shildon, for the Timothy Hackworth Museum

Museum Curator: Mr J. Wilks
Location: North Road Station, Darlington, County Durham DL3 6ST. Approximately three-quarters of a mile north of town centre, off North Road (A167)
OS reference: NZ 289157
Telephone: (01325) 460532
Car park: At museum site
Access by public transport: Rail services to Darlington North Road station. Local bus services along North Road
Catering facilities: Refreshment area open during summer season. Confectionery and drinks at other times
On site facilities: Souvenir and book shop, toilets, meeting room
Public opening: Daily 10.00-17.00 (except Christmas holidays). Days and times may be subject to amendment
Special events: Santa Specials (contact for details)
Facilities for disabled: Access to main museum building for wheelchairs. Disabled person's toilet. Parking spaces for disabled in forecourt
Membership details: Friends of Darlington Railway Museum, Darlington Railway Preservation Society, A1 Steam Locomotive

Darlington Railway Preservation Society
Member: HRA

Locomotives

Name	No	Origin	Class	Type	Built
—	78018	BR	2MT	2-6-0	1954

Industrial locomotives

Name	No	Builder	Type	Built
—	—	Bagnall (2898)	0-4-0F	1948
—	2	RSH (7925)	0-4-0DM	1959
—	1	Peckett (2142)	0-4-0ST	1953
David Payne	185	Fowler (4110006)	0-4-0DM	1950
Smiths Dock Co Ltd	—	Fowler (4200018)	0-4-0DM	1947
—	—	GEC	4wE	1928
—	—	R/Hornsby (279591)	0-4-0DM	1949
—	—	R/Hornsby*	4wDM	—
—	—	R/Hornsby*	4wDM	—
—	—	R/Hornsby*	4wDM	—

*1ft 6in gauge

Stock
Various wagons, steam and diesel cranes

A1 Steam Locomotive Trust
Member: HRA

Locomotives

Name	No	Origin	Class	Type	Built
Tornado	60163	A1SLT	8P6F	4-6-2	Under construction

Trust and North Eastern Railway Association all c/o above address
Note: Some locomotives are located in the former goods shed, where restoration work is being undertaken by the Darlington Railway Preservation Society (limited opening to visitors — times vary; groups by arrangement). Part of the former carriage works has been renovated and is now used by the A1 Steam Locomotive Trust for assembly of the new Peppercorn Pacific *Tornado* (usually open to visitors on Saturdays, please enquire)

Timetable Service	# Dartmoor Railway	Devon

Member: HRA

Dartmoor Railway is a very young railway as far as tourism is concerned although the railway has been in existence for 140 years as the Southern Railway main line from Waterloo to Plymouth. The line only survived because of ballast supplies from Meldon Quarry. The Dartmoor Railway (a partnership between Aggregate Industries, RMS Locotec and Devon County Council) offers a unique experience which encompasses access to Dartmoor National Park for everyone including the disabled, the less energetic and cyclists, views of Meldon Quarry and workings, a small visitor centre and a restored Southern Railway station in the 1950s style at Okehampton.

Headquarters: Dartmoor Railway Ltd, Okehampton Station, Okehampton, Devon EX20 1EJ
Telephone: 01837 55637
Fax: 01837 54588
Internet addresses: e-mail: info@dartmoorrailway.co.uk

Web site: www.dartmoorrailway.co.uk
Managing Director: John Hummel
General Manager: David Payne
Commercial Manager: Robin Townshend
Main station: Okehampton
Other public stations: Meldon Quarry for Meldon Viaduct, access only by rail and National Cyclepath. Sampford Courtenay due to open spring 2004, access by road and rail
Access by public transport: Main line trains on Sundays from end of

May to end of September. Bus on Sundays all year round
Refreshment facilities: Buffet at Okehampton and Meldon
Model & Gift shops: Extensive model and gift shop at Okehampton. Books and souvenirs also available at Meldon
Depot: Meldon Quarry, access only by rail and National Cyclepath
Length of line: 15.5 miles from Coleford Junction-Meldon Quarry
Passenger trains: 'Dartmoor Pony' Okehampton to Meldon Quarry every weekend, four days per week May to end October, every day in school holidays and Bank Holidays. Sunday Rover — Exeter to Okehampton on Sundays from end of May to end of September
Special events: Opening of Sampford Courtenay station. Sunday lunches and evening special trains aboard the new 'Dartmoor Belle' wine and dine train throughout the year
Special notes: 'Dartmoor Pony' has provision for bicycles. Visits for interest groups and education tours. 'Dartmoor Belle' available for private hire. Special function coach can be added in turn for both corporate and special functions. 'Dartmoor Pony' available for private short excursions
Facilities for disabled: Facilities on train and buffets for disabled and accessible by wheelchair
Membership details: Friends of Dartmoor Railway c/o above address. Gives discount to members for train rides, gifts, etc
Membership journal: Three times a year

Locomotives and multiple-units (in use as hauled stock)

Name	No	Origin	Class	Type	Built
Bluebell Mel	08937	BR	08	0-6-0DE	1962
—	25072	BR	25	Bo-Bo	1963
—	31301*	BR	31	A1A-A1A	1962
—	31415*	BR	31	A1A-A1A	1961
—	31423*	BR	31	A1A-A1A	1960
—	31426*	BR	31	A1A-A1A	1960
—	31437*	BR	31	A1A-A1A	1960
—	31439*	BR	31	A1A-A1A	1960
—	47348*	BR	47	Co-Co	1965
—	47716*	BR	47	Co-Co	1966
—	73103*	BR	73	Bo-Bo	1965
—	73117*	BR	73	Bo-Bo	1966
—	73134*	BR	73	Bo-Bo	1966
—	61743	BR	411	DMSO	1956
—	76301	BR	438 / 4TC	DTSO	1967
—	76302	BR	438 / 4TC	DTSO	1967
—	70860	BR	438 / 4TC	DTSO	1967
—	70826	BR	438 / 4TC	DTSO	1967
—	69332	BR			1969
—	69310†	BR	422	TRBS	1965

†static buffet at Meldon
*owned by Fragonset Railways

Locomotive notes:
Fragonset locomotives scheduled to work on services: 47716, 73134
Fragonset locomotives to be restored to work on services: 31437, 73103

Industrial locomotives

Name	No	Builder	Type	Built
—	68006	Hunslet (3192)	0-6-0ST	1944
—	S103	H/Clarke (1864)	0-6-0T	1952
Flying Falcon	MSC 0256	Fowler	0-6-0DE	

Stock
Courier vehicle NXX No 80225; 2 ex-BR Mk 1 RBR 1691, 1697; 3 ex-BR Mk 3 sleeping cars 10518, 10595, 10611; 1 ex-BR sleeping car 10000; ex-GWR Director's saloon; function coach, converted from 99622; Generator coach, DB977335 (Fragonset Railways owned).
Following EMU vehicles for spares reclamation only: 61742, 70812
Selection of maintenance vehicles including horse box S96300 converted to Generator coach for 'Dartmoor Belle'

Owners
Class 31s, 47 and 73s — Fragonset Railways

Timetable Service	**Dean Forest Railway**	Glos

Member: HRA, TT
Passenger services operate between Norchard and Lydney Junction (Severn & Wye Joint), with the extension to Parkend nearing completion during 2004. From Spring 2004 passenger services are extended to Whitecroft (no public platform) by DMU shuttle from Norchard (High Level). Ultimately the line will boast five level crossings, three of which are manually operated
Location: Norchard Railway Centre on the B4234. Signposted off the A48 Lydney bypass to town centre whence B4234 commences
OS reference: SO 629044

Operating society/organisation: Dean Forest Railway Society in conjunction with owning company, Forest of Dean Railway Ltd
Telephone: (01594) 843423 information line; (01594) 845840 (daytime)
Internet address: *Web site:* www.deanforestrailway.co.uk

Car park: At Norchard only, adequate for cars and coaches. No parking at other stations

Access by public transport: Main line station at Lydney. Stagecoach Red & White buses (service 73 Monday-Saturday) Gloucester-Lydney-Newport

On site facilities: Shop at Norchard with museum, riverside walk, picnic site and forest trail

Catering facilities: Hot and cold meals at Coaches Café on Norchard platform on service days. Parties catered for by appointment. Sunday lunchtime service by 'Royal Forester' first class dining car service, runs alternate Sundays in season, advance booking essential

Length of line: Steam operation 2 miles plus DMU 1.5-mile. (Lydney Junction-Parkend will be 4.25 miles)

Public opening: Daily for static display — shop and museum, open every Saturday and Sunday 11.00-17.00 and weekdays late March to Christmas.

Steam train rides: All Sundays 21 March to 31 October; Good Friday, Easter Saturday and all Bank Holiday Sundays and Mondays (Christmas excepted). Wednesdays July to September. Thursdays and Saturdays in August.

Heritage DMU service operates Wednesdays in June, and Saturdays June, July and September

Special events: Day out with Thomas — 15-18 April, 3-6 June, 4/5, 11/12 September; Father's Day — 20 June; Vintage Rally — 8 August; Forties Re-enactment — 24-26 September; Halloween Ghost Trains — 31 October; Carol Service Special (18.30 Norchard to St Mary's Church, Lydney) — 11 December; Santa Specials — 5, 11/12, 18/19, 23/24 December

Facilities for disabled: Access to museum, shop, toilets and trains

Membership details: Mr R. Bramwell, 4 Poole Ground, Highnam, Gloucester GL2 8NA and web site

Membership journal: *Forest Venturer* — half yearly

GWR Prairie tank No 5541 waits at Lydney station on the Dean Forest Railway. *Phil Barnes*

Locomotives and multiple-units

Name	No	Origin	Class	Type	Built
—	28	TVR	O1	0-6-2T	1897
—	5541	GWR	4575	2-6-2T	1928
—	9642	GWR	5700	0-6-0PT	1946
—	9681	GWR	5700	0-6-0PT	1949
—	03128	BR	03	0-6-0DM	1960
—	03141	BR	03	0-6-0DM	1960
Charlie	13308	BR	08	0-6-0DE	1956
—	08734	BR	08	0-6-0DE	1960
Gladys	D3937	BR	08	0-6-0DE	1960
—	D9555	BR	14	0-6-0DH	1965
—†	5386	BR	27	Bo-Bo	1962
—	D7633	BR	25	Bo-Bo	1965
—	D5634	BR	31	A1A-A1A	1960
—	37263	BR	37	Co-Co	1965
—	73901	BR	73	Bo-Bo	1962
—*	73002	BR	73	Bo-Bo	1962
—	E6005	BR	73	Bo-Bo	1962
—§	73906	BR	73	Bo-Bo	1962
—	50619	BR	108	DMBS	1958
—	51914	BR	108	DMS	1960
—	56492	BR	108	DTC	1960
—	56495	BR	108	DTC	1960

†on loan to East Lancashire Railway
§on loan to Severn Valley Railway
*mobile stores vehicle

Industrial locomotives

Name	No	Builder	Type	Built
—	—	Barclay (2221)	0-4-0ST	1946
Uskmouth No 1	—	Peckett (2147)	0-4-0ST	1952
Wilbert	—	Hunslet (3806)	0-6-0ST	1953
Warrior	—	Hunslet (3823)	0-6-0ST	1954
—	—	Hunslet (2145)	0-4-0DM	1940
—	—	Fowler (4210127)	0-4-0DM	1957
—	—	Hibberd (3947)	4wPM	1960

Stock

2 ex-GWR coaches; 12 ex-BR coaches; 1 DFR constructed Cafeteria coach (static at Norchard), 3 Wickham trolleys; 1 steam crane Thos Smith (Rodley) TS 5027 (10ton); Booth 15-24 tonne diesel-hydraulic crane, Schöma p-way tram and trailer

Marketing name: The Friendly Forest Line — re-creating the railway heritage of the Royal Forest of Dean

Owners
28 the National Railway Museum
5541 the Forest Prairie Fund
9642 the South Wales Pannier Group
9681 the Dean Forest Locomotive Group
03128, 03141, 13308, D3937, 08734, 5386, D5634, D7633, 73002, E6005 and 73906 the Dean Forest Diesel Association
Class 108 DMUs the Dean Forest DMU Group

Museum	# Derby Industrial Museum	Derbyshire

Member: TT
As would be expected of a railway town, the museum has an extensive collection of railway material including locomotives and rolling stock (most on display at the Midland Railway Centre). The railway gallery tells the stories of railway industries in Derby, especially as they relate to the Midland Railway and its successors. Replica Midland Railway signalbox and model railway (under construction). The story is brought up to date by the Railway Research Gallery which looks at the role of the Railway Technical Centre and includes a replica of an InterCity 225 driving cab

Location: Silk Mill Lane, Derby
Operating society/organisation: Derby Industrial Museum, Silk Mill Lane, off Full Street, Derby DE1 3AF
Telephone: (01332) 255308
Fax: (01332) 255108
Car park: Local car parks around city
Access by public transport: Bus station quarter mile, railway station three-quarter mile

On site facilities: Shop, baby changing facilities
Opening times: Admission free. Mondays 11.00-17.00, Tuesdays to Saturdays 10.00-17.00, Bank Holidays 14.00-17.00. Sundays 14.00-17.00
Facilities for disabled: Parking by arrangement. Level access to building, lifts and ramps to all gallery areas, toilets, sign language and subtitles in Rolls-Royce gallery

---

Steam Centre	# Derwent Valley Light Railway	North Yorkshire

Member: TT
The Society has completed the rebuilding of Wheldrake station at Murton
Location: Murton Park, Murton Lane, Murton, Nr York YO19 5UF
Operating society/organisation: Derwent Valley Light Railway Society
Telephone: (01904) 489966
Internet address: Web site: www.dvlrs.murton.btinternet.co.uk
OS reference: SE 651537
On site facilities: Refreshments, souvenir shop (Yorkshire Museum of Farming)
Car park: Free, on site
Length of line: Half-mile
Access by public transport: York-Stamford Bridge and York-Hull bus services from York main line station
Facilities for disabled: Toilets, ramped ways, etc
Public opening: Open daily mid-February-end October, for the Yorkshire Museum of Farming, Danelaw (Viking) Village and the Derwent Valley Light Railway. Trains operate Sundays and Bank Holidays Easter-end September and for Santa Specials
Membership details: c/o above address
Society journal: DVLR News (quarterly)

Locomotives

Name	No	Origin	Class	Type	Built
—	03079	BR	03	0-6-0DM	1960

Industrial locomotives

Name	No	Builder	Type	Built
—	8	A/Barclay (2369)	0-4-0ST	1955
—	65	H/Clarke (1631)	0-6-0T	1929
—	ED6	Fowler (4200022)	0-4-0DM	1948
Churchill	—	Fowler (410005)	0-4-0DM	1947
Jim	—	R/Hornsby (417892)	4wDM	1959
Octavius Atkinson	—	R/Hornsby (466630)	4wDM	1962
British Sugar York	—	R/Hornsby (327964)	0-4-0DM	1953

Rolling stock
1 NER coach, 1 NER coach body, 1 Swiss-style coach (newly built in 2003, 12 various freight wagons, and 1 steam rail crane

44

Devon Railway Centre

The Devon Railway Centre features a lovingly restored Victorian Great Western Railway station together with historic locomotives, carriages and wagons as featured on TV. Unlimited passenger rides can be taken on the 2ft gauge railway and miniature railways. There is also a large model railway exhibition featuring 15 working layouts including Polchester and Chiltern Green. All-inclusive admission price

Location: Alongside Bickleigh Bridge over the River Exe on the A396, four miles south of Tiverton and 10 miles north of Exeter

General Manager: Matthew Gicquel

Contact address: Devon Railway Centre, Bickleigh, Nr Tiverton, Devon EX16 8RG

Telephone: 01884 855671

Internet address: *Web site:* www.devonrailwaycentre.co.uk

OS reference: SS 938074

Car park: On site

Access by public transport: Regular bus service from Tiverton and Exeter, routes 55 and 55A

On site facilities: Passenger carrying line, large model railway exhibition, restored GWR station, standard gauge static display, historic narrow gauge collection, miniature railway, refreshments and souvenirs, crazy golf, drive your own miniature railway

Length of line: Half mile, 2ft gauge; quarter mile 7.25in gauge, 200yd standard gauge demonstration line; 100yd 7.25in gauge drive your own train

Opening times: 10.30-17.00. Easter until 31 October. Daily from 30 May until 12 September. Daily during school holidays. Sundays and Bank Holidays at other times. Phone for details of extra openings

Special events: Steam weekend — 7/8 August;Santa Specials — 5, 12, 19 December. Phone for further details

Industrial locomotives (2ft gauge)

Name	No	Builder	Type	Built
Horatio	—	R/Hornsby (217967)	4wDM	1942
Pen-yr-Orsedd	—	R/Hornsby (235711)	4wDM	1945
Ruston	—	R/Hornsby (418770)	4wDM	1957
Claude W. Lane	—†	R/Hornsby (435398)	4wDM	1959
Planet	—	Planet (2201)	4wDM	1939
Lister	—	Lister (6299)	4wPM	1935
—	—	Lister (34025)	4wDM	1949
—	—	Planet (2025)	4wDM	1937
—	—	Kent (1747)	4wPM	1931
Ivor	—	M/Rail (8877)	4wDM	1944
—	—	M/Rail (20073)	4wDM	1950
Sir Tom	—	M/Rail (40s273)	4wDM	1966
—	—*	M/Rail (105H006)	4wDM	1919
—	—	BEV	0-4-0BE	c1970

†2ft 9in gauge
*3ft gauge

Industrial locomotives (standard gauge)

Name	No	Builder	Type	Built
Boris	1	Baguley (3357)	0-4-0DM	1952

Locomotive notes: All locomotives are expected to be be working in 2004, except for *Claude*, Kent and Planet 2025

Rolling stock: All 2ft gauge unless indicated. Two Hudson bogie passenger coaches, Hudson 4-wheel coach, Dinorwic Yellow Coach, 2 slate slab wagons, GWR slate wagon, 7 skip wagons, 4 mine tubs, RAF bomb wagon, Hudson 3-plank wagon, 2 bogie coach chassis. Lochaber incline wagon (3ft gauge), Ravenglass & Eskdale wagon (15in gauge), copper mine tub (20in gauge), Cattybrook brickworks wagon (2ft 10in gauge), assorted works wagons. Standard gauge: 2 ex-BR Mk 1 coaches, 1 ex-BR BG

Miniature railway locomotives (7.25in gauge)

Name	No	Builder	Type	Built
—	D7011*	Cromar White	Bo-BoBE	1969
—	D7029	Cromar White	Bo-BoPM	1972
(Intercity)	—	—	Bo-BoBE	c1995
—	—	Pfeiferbahn	4wPH	c1985
—	—	—	4wPH	c1960
—	7	Parkside	4WBER S/O	2002

*rebuilt from petrol to battery power by DRC during 2002
7 is a drive your own train operated by coin in the slot

Rolling stock: 2 sit-in coaches built by DRC, 1 sit astride coach

Member: HRA, TT

Based around the GWR engine shed and depot, the Centre now has a typical GWR small country station with signalboxes (from Radstock and Frome), re-creation of Brunel's broad gauge railway, two demonstration lines, and a small relics museum

General Manager: Michael Dean

Location: Adjacent to main line station, Didcot, Oxfordshire. Access via station subway

OS reference: SU 525907

Operating society/organisation: Great Western Society Ltd, Didcot Railway Centre, Didcot, Oxon OX11 7NJ

Telephone: Didcot (01235) 817200

Internet address: *Web site:* www.didcotrailwaycentre.org.uk

Car park: Didcot station

Access by public transport: Didcot Parkway main line station

Refreshment facilities: Refreshment room open all days centre is open (lunches, snacks). Picnic area

On site facilities: GWR locomotive depot, replica GWR station, museum and broad gauge demonstration. Souvenir sales. Rides are available on the demonstration lines on Steamdays. Admission price on Steamdays includes train rides

Length of line: 1,000yd

Public opening: Saturdays and Sundays all year. Daily 3-18 April, 29 May-5 September, 16-31 October, 27 December to 1 January. Steamdays first and last Sunday each month from March to October, Bank Holidays, all Sundays July-August, all Wednesdays 14 July to 1 September, all Saturdays in August. Open 10.00-17.00 (November/December 10.00-16.00).

Train rides: On Steamdays there is normally continuous operation of the passenger train, interrupted by Travelling Post Office demonstrations and turning of the locomotives on some days

Special events: Day out with Thomas — 8-10 October; Thomas Santa Special — 10-12, 17-19

Locomotives

Name	No	Origin	Class/builder	Type	Built
—	22	GWR	Diesel Railcar	1A-A1	1940
—	1338	GWR (Cardiff Rly)	Kitson (3799)	0-4-0ST	1898
Trojan	1340	GWR	Avonside (1380)	0-4-0ST	1897
—	1363	GWR	1361	0-6-0ST	1910
—	3650	GWR	5700	0-6-0PT	1939
—	3738	GWR	5700	0-6-0PT	1937
—	3822	GWR	2884	2-8-0	1940
Pendennis Castle	4079	GWR	'Castle'	4-6-0	1924
—	4144	GWR	5101	2-6-2T	1946
—	4866	GWR	4800	0-4-2T	1936
Lady of Legend*	2999	GWR	'Saint'	4-6-0	1929
Earl Bathurst	5051	GWR	'Castle'	4-6-0	1936
—	5322	GWR	4300	2-6-0	1917
—	5572	GWR	4575	2-6-2T	1927
Hinderton Hall	5900	GWR	'Hall'	4-6-0	1931
King Edward II	6023	GWR	'King'	4-6-0	1930
—	6106	GWR	6100	2-6-2T	1931
—	6697	GWR	5600	0-6-2T	1928
Burton Agnes Hall	6998	GWR	'Hall'	4-6-0	1949
—	7202	GWR	7200	2-8-2T	1934
Cookham Manor	7808	GWR	'Manor'	4-6-0	1938
—	D3771	BR	08	0-6-0DE	1959
Pontyberem	2	Burry Port & Gwendraeth Valley Rly		0-6-0ST	1900
Shannon	5	Wantage Tramway		0-4-0WT	1857

*under construction using frames of No 4942 *Maindy Hall*

Industrial locomotives

Name	No	Builder	Type	Built
Bonnie Prince Charlie	1	RSH (7544)	0-4-0ST	1949
—	26	Hunslet (5238)	0-6-0DH	1962

Locomotive notes: Locomotives available in 2004 should be: 22, 1338, 1340, 3822, 3738, 4144, 5051. Locomotives under restoration include: 3650, 4079, 5322, 6023, 7202. Construction of the Firefly Trust's reproduction broad gauge locomotive *Firefly* is being undertaken. 4079 was repatriated from Australia in 2000

Stock
Over 40 ex-GWR coaches are preserved along with numerous ex-GWR freight wagons

Owner
5 on loan from the National Railway Museum

December; New Year Steamings — 1/2 January 2005

Facilities for disabled: Steps at access from station subway may cause problems, but assistance can normally be provided (advance notification is useful)

Membership details: Charles Roberts, at above address

Membership journals: *Great Western Echo* — quarterly; *National Newsletter* — seven times annually

East Anglia Transport Museum

Member: TT

The East Suffolk Light Railway is the title given to the 2ft gauge railway, which winds its way 300yd or so along the northern perimeter of the museum site, between the stations of Chapel Road and Woodside. The railway commenced operation in 1973 and aims to re-create a typical passenger-carrying light railway of years gone by. Many aspects of railway interest can be found along its length. The track came from Leziate sand quarry and Canvey Island, as well as from the Southwold Railway, and signals from various local locations; all of which help to set the overall scene

Location: Carlton Colville, three miles south-west of Lowestoft in Suffolk

OS reference: TM 505903

Operating society/organisation: East Anglia Transport Museum Society Ltd, Chapel Road, Carlton Colville, Lowestoft, Suffolk NR33 8BL

Telephone: (01502) 518459

Internet address: *Web site:* www.eatm.org.uk

Car park: Adjacent

Access by public transport: First Eastern Counties L11, L12, X71 & X74 (Monday-Saturday); First Eastern Counties X71, L18 & L19

Industrial locomotives

Name	No	Builder	Type	Built
Aldeburgh	2	M/Rail (5912)	4wDM	1934
Leiston	4	R/Hornsby (177604)	4wDM	1936
Orfordness	5	M/Rail (22209)	4wDM	1964
Thorpeness	6	M/Rail (22211)	4wDM	1964

Trams

No	Trucks	Body	Date	Operator
11	Maley & Taunton	E/Electric	1939	Blackpool Corp
14	Brill	Milnes	1904	Lowestoft Corp
159	Preston McGuire	Blackpool Corp	1927	Blackpool Corp
474	Beijines	Beijines	1929	Amsterdam
1858	EMB	E/Electric	1930	London Transport

Stock

Locally designed and built covered coach, plus combined coach and brake van, suitable for wheelchairs. Small selection of wagons. Van body ex-Southwold Railway

(Sundays and Bank Holidays) from Lowestoft. Main line rail, Oulton Broad South (1.5 miles)

On site facilities: Refreshments, picnic areas, souvenir and bookshop, toilets (including disabled), working transport museum, including trams, narrow gauge railway, trolleybuses, steamrollers and other commercial and public transport vehicles. Unlimited free rides

Public opening: Easter weekend (please phone), and then Sundays and Bank Holiday Mondays from

2 May to 25 September (11.00-17.30). Wednesdays and Saturdays June to September inclusive (14.00-17.00). Midsummer opening, daily (except Mondays) 27 July to 9 September (14.00-17.00).

Last admission 1 hour before closing

Special events: Please phone for details

Special notes: Limited facilities for the disabled. Pre-booked party rates

Membership details: From the above address

East Anglian Railway Museum

Member: HRA, TT, AIM, EETB, EATL

Adjacent to Chappel Viaduct which is the most spectacular railway structure in East Anglia

Location: Chappel & Wakes Colne Station, near Colchester

OS reference: TL 898289

Chairman: Mike Stanbury

Operating society/organisation: East Anglian Railway Museum, Chappel & Wakes Colne Station, Station Road, Wakes Colne, Essex

CO6 2DS. Registered charity No 1001579

Telephone: Colchester (01206) 242524

Fax: 0870 1258315

Internet address: *e-mail:* info@earm.co.uk
Web site: www.earm.co.uk

Car park: On site

Access by public transport: Great Eastern Chappel & Wakes Colne station. Also Eastern National/Hedingham Omnibus

service No 88 Colchester-Halstead (hourly). Sundays Eastern National No 88C Colchester-Halstead (every 2 hours)

On site facilities: Refreshments, comprehensive bookshop, museum, signalboxes, souvenir shop, picnic area, miniature railway and toilets

Public opening: Daily 10.00-16.30

Special events: Day out with Thomas — 9-12 April; Steam Days — 2/3, 30/31 May; Ride Dennis the Diesel — 2 June; Steam Day &

Teddy Bears' Day — 6 June; 5th Chappel Cider Festival — 10-13 June; DMU Train Rides & Drive a Diesel — 20 June; Steam Day — 4 July; DMU Train Rides & Drive a Diesel — 18 July; MiniRail Day — 28 July; Steam Day — 1 August; MiniRail Day — 4, 11, 14 August; DMU Train Rides & Drive a Diesel — 15 August; Day out with Thomas — 26-30 August; 18th Chappel Beer Festival — 7-11 September; Steam Day and Gauge One Display — 3 October; Young Members' Steam Day — 31 October; Santa Steamings — 11/12, 18/19 December

Family tickets: Available on all days (unlimited rides on steam days)

Special notes: Steam days as in Special Events list. Driver experience courses available on a number of dates throughout 2004; please phone for details or book on line at http://www.earm.co.uk

Three restored signalboxes, large goods shed and restoration shed. Original Victorian country junction station. Schools days and Santa steamings. Disabled visitors welcome — prior advice appreciated. Guided tours by prior arrangement. Light refreshments daily, Signals café on event days

Membership details: Membership Secretary, 50 Ayr Way, Rise Park, Romford, Essex RM1 4UH

Membership journal: *Stour Valley Steam* — 3 times/year

Locomotives and multiple-units

Name	No	Origin	Class	Type	Built
A. J. Hill	69621†	GER	N7	0-6-2T	1924
—	D2279	BR	04	0-6-0DM	1960
—	37003	BR	37	Co-Co	1960
—	50599	BR	108	DMBS	1958
—	51568*	BR	108	DMCL	1959
—	53628*	BR	108	DMBS	1958
—	52053*	BR	108	DMCL	1960
—	54223*	BR	108	DTCL	1959
—	56491	BR	108	DTC	1960
—	51213	BR	101	DMBS	1959
—	51505	BR	101	DMC	1959
—	56358	BR	101	DTC	1959

* on loan to Keith & Dufftown Railway
† on North Norfolk Railway for overhaul

Industrial locomotives

Name	No	Builder	Type	Built
Jubilee	—	Bagnall (2542)	0-4-0ST	1936
—	11	Barclay (1047)	0-4-0ST	1905
Belvoir	—	Barclay (2350)	0-6-0ST	1954
Jeffery	2039	Peckett (2039)	0-4-0ST	1943
Penn Green	54	RSH (7031)	0-6-0ST	1941
Birkenhead	—	RSH (7386)	0-4-0ST	1948
—	AMW144	Barclay (333)	0-4-0DM	1938
—	23	Fowler (4220039)	0-4-0DH	1965
—	2029	Simplex (2029)	0-4-0PM	1920

Stock

1 ex-LNER TSO coach; 1 fully restored GER 6-wheel full brake; 1 GER fully restored 4-wheel coach; 1 ex-GER bogie coach; 1 SR PMV; 1 ex-BR 13-ton open wagon; 2 ex-BR 16-ton mineral wagons; 1 Lomac wagon; 1 ex-LMS 12-ton open wagon; 3 Wickham Trolleys; 1 GWR Toad brake van; 1 ex-BR brake van; Somersham 'pump' trolley, 1 Grafton steam crane, 1 LMS 5 plank wagon, 1 BR cattle van (on loan ex-NRM), 1 BR special cattle van, 1 tube wagon, 1 Pooley van, 1 LNER fish van, 1 BR box van, 2 tank wagons, 1 Molasses tank wagon, 1 Baguley railcar (on loan from GWRPS)

Owner

37003 the Class 37 Locomotive Group
Birkenhead the GWR Preservation Society

East Hayling Light Railway

There are three stations on the line Beachlands, the main station/storage/workshop building located seaward of the funfair. Eastoke Corner 1-mile to the east is the other end of the line. Hornby Halt (sponsored by Hornby the modelmakers) provided with passing loop is between. All stations are provided with ample (Council) pay & display car

Locomotives

Name	No	Builder	Type	Built
Jack	—	A/Keef (23)	0-4-0DH s/o	1988
Alister	—	Ruston (201790)	4wDH	1940
Alan B	—	M/Rail (7199)	4wDM	1937
—	—	EHLR	0-4-0T	*

*under construction

Stock

Glazed and upholstered 4-wheel coaches with a set of bogie coaches under construction

parking and (private) refreshment facilities
Headquarters: 20 Jasmond Road, Cosham, Portsmouth PO6 2SY
Managing Director: Bob Haddock
Telephone:023 9237 2427
Main public station: Beachlands
Other public stations: Eastoke Corner, Hornby Halt
Car parks: Pay & display at all stations

Access by public transport: No information provided
Refreshment facilities: At all stations
Journey time: Not advised
Length of line: 2ft gauge
Period of public operation: Every weekend and Wednesday (market day) all year round, plus school holidays
Facilities for disabled: None

Special events: Please contact for full details,Easter Bunnies, Father's Day, Santa Specials
Special notes: On display are the original BR station signs Hayling Island and Havant for Hayling
Membership details: Terry Mercer 023 9271 7550
Membership journal: *The Hayling Billy* — quarterly

Timetable Service — East Kent Railway — Kent

Member: HRA

The East Kent Light Railway Society was formed in 1985 with the aim of preserving the remaining 3-mile section of the Colonel Stephens light railway which originally ran from Shepherdswell to Wingham. Passenger-carrying operations between Shepherdswell and Eythorne started during 1995, and 1996 saw the first steam on the line for over 30 years. A future halt near Tilmanstone is planned
Location: Shepherdswell (EKR) Station, Shepherdswell, Dover, Kent CT15 7PD
Internet address: *Web site:* www.eastkentrailway.com
OS reference: TR 258483
Operating organisation: East Kent Railway Trust
Car park: Shepherdswell and Eythorne stations
Access by public transport: Main line trains to Shepherdswell station (adjacent) tel: 08457 484950. Bus — Stagecoach East Kent (limited service, not Sundays), tel: 0870 6082608
On site facilities: Light refreshments, book and souvenir shop, museum, plus 3.5/5in gauge steam railway. Picnic area and toilets. Restored signalbox visitor. Eythorne: Signalbox and small shop
Public opening: Weekends throughout the year for static displays and site facilities throughout the year. Passenger trains — Easter to September Sundays and Bank Holidays
Special events: Easter Bunny

Locomotives and multiple-units

Name	No	Origin	Class	Type	Built
Sealion	33065	BR	33/0	Bo-Bo	1962
—	65373*	BR	2EPB/416	DMBS	1953
—	77558*	BR	2EPB/416	DTS	1953
—	68001	BR	MLV/419	MLV	1959
—	53256	M/Cam	101	DMBS	1957
—	54343	M/Cam	101	DTC(L)	1958

*unit No 5759

Industrial locomotives

Name	No	Builder	Type	Built
Richborough Castle	—	E/Electric (D1197)	0-6-0D	1967
The Buffs	—	R/Hornsby (466616)	0-6-0DH	1961
Snowdon	—	Fowler (416002)	0-4-0DM	1952
Coronation	—	NBL (27097)	0-4-0DM	1953
St Dunstan	—	Avonside (2004)	0-6-0ST	1927
Albert	—	Barclay (2248)	0-4-0ST	1948

Rolling stock
Leyland Experimental coach, LMS brake third, 2 x LMS full brake (BG), BR Mk 1s TSO, BSK, FK, BR Mk 2A first brake, BR Mk 2 TSO and a selection of freight vehicles including an SR GUV

Owners
St Dunstan on long-term loan from British Coal
LMS BG the Walmer Model Railway Group
Leyland Experimental Coach the Nene Valley Railway
Multiple-units the EPB Preservation Group
Class 33 the South East Locomotive Group
68001 the EPB Preservation Ltd

Specials — 9-12 April; Teddy Bears' Picnic — 30/31 May; EKR Special Gala — 29/30 August; Heritage Bus Rally — 19 September; Halloween Ghost Trains — 30/31 October; Santa by Train — 4/5, 11/12, 18/19 December. See press for other attractions. Events & site answerphone: 01304 832042

Facilities for disabled: Limited access to buffet, and platforms at both stations
Membership details: Mr B. Hancock, 33 Beaufield, Whitfield, Dover, Kent CT16 3JW
Membership journal: *East Kent Railway News,* 3 times a year

East Lancashire Railway

Member: HRA, TT

A very popular railway run by the East Lancs Railway Society in close co-operation with local authorities, the line won the 1987 ARPS award. Visit the line to find out the cause of the line's popularity and success

Location: Bolton Street Station, Bury, Lancashire BL9 0EY

OS reference: SD 803109

Publicity Director: Graham Vevers

Operating society/organisation: East Lancashire Railway Preservation Society

Telephone: 0161 764 7790

Internet address: *Web site:* www.east-lancs-rly.co.uk

Access by public transport: Main line services to Manchester, Bolton, Rochdale and Burnley. Metrolink from central Manchester to Bury Interchange. Various bus services also operate to Bury, Ramsbottom or Rawtenstall from the main line stations listed

On site facilities: Refreshments normally available when trains are running. Buffet car service on most trains. Souvenir shop, transport museum

Length of line: Approximately 8 miles

Public opening: Steam and diesel-hauled services operate on Saturdays, Sundays and Bank Holidays throughout the year. Santa Specials (advanced booking only) in December

Special events: August — Teddy Bears' Picnic; Santa Specials — weekends in December; Diesel Enthusiasts' Weekend and Friends of Thomas the Tank Engine Days — please apply for details; Irwell Valley Diner, Wine & Dine Trains (advance booking only — please apply for details)

Special Notes: The Society re-opened the Bury-Summerseat-Ramsbottom section in 1987 and the Ramsbottom-Irwell-Rawtenstall section in 1991 with the Bury-Heywood section opening in 2003

Membership details: D. Layland

Membership journal: *The East Lancashire Railway News* — twice yearly

Marketing name: East Lancs

Locomotives and multiple-units

Name	No	Origin	Class	Type	Built
—	7229	GWR	7200	2-8-2T	1935
—	52322	L&Y	27	0-6-0	1896
—	42765	LMS	5P4F	2-6-0	1927
—	44871	LMS	5MT	4-6-0	1945
—	45337	LMS	5MT	4-6-0	1937
—	45407	LMS	5MT	4-6-0	1937
Leander	5690	LMS	'Jubilee'	4-6-0	1936
Princess Elizabeth	6201	LMS	'Princess'	4-6-2	1933
—	46441	LMS	2MT	2-6-0	1950
—	46428	LMS	2MT	2-6-0	1948
—	47324	LMS	3F	0-6-0T	1926
Shaw Savill	35009	SR	MN	4-6-2	1945
Duke of Gloucester	71000	BR	8P	4-6-2	1954
—	76079	BR	4MT	2-6-0	1957
—†	76084	BR	4MT	2-6-0	1957
—	80097	BR	4MT	2-6-4T	1954
Morning Star	92207	BR	9F	2-10-0	1959
—	11506	BR	01	0-4-0DM	1956
—	D2062	BR	03	0-6-0DM	1959
—	D3232	BR	08	0-6-0DE	1956
—	08445	BR	08	0-6-0DE	1958
—	08479	BR	08	0-6-0DE	1958
—	08944	BR	08	0-6-0DE	1962
—	D9531	BR	14	0-6-0DH	1965
—	20087	BR	20	Bo-Bo	1961
—	D5054	BR	24	Bo-Bo	1960
—*	5386	BR	27	Bo-Bo	1962
—	D5705	BR	28	Co-Bo	1958
—	D5600	BR	31	A1A-A1A	1959
—	31467	BR	31	A1A-A1A	1960
—	31556	BR	31	A1A-A1A	1961
—	D7076	BR	35	B-B	1963
—	33117	BR	33	Bo-Bo	1960
—	37197	BR	37	Co-Co	1964
—	37235	BR	37	Co-Co	1964
Caithness	37261	BR	37	Co-Co	1965
—	37423	BR	37	Co-Co	1965
—	D335	BR	40	1Co-Co1	1961
—	D345	BR	40	1Co-Co1	1961
Onslaught	D832	BR	42	B-B	1961
3rd Carabinier	D99	BR	45	1Co-Co1	1961
Gateshead	D1501	BR	47	Co-Co	1962
Valiant	50015	BR	50	Co-Co	1967
Western Prince	D1041	BR	52	C-C	1962
—	51285	Cravens	105	DMBC	1958
—	56121	Cravens	105	DTC	1956
—	65451	BR	504	DMBS	1958
—	77172	BR	504	DTS	1958

*on loan from Dean Forest Railway
†at Riley & Sons Ltd for restoration

Industrial locomotives

Name	No	Builder	Type	Built
Gothenburg	32	H/Clarke (680)	0-6-0T	1903
—	1	Barclay (1927)	0-4-0ST	1927
—	—	Sentinel (10204)	4wDH	1964

Name	No	Builder	Type	Built
MR Mercury	1	Hibberd (3438)	4wDM	1950
Winfield	—	M/Rail (9009)	4wDM	1948
—	4002	H/Clarke (D1076)	6wDM	1959

Stock
44 BR Mk 1 coaches; 11 BR Mk 2 coaches, 1 GWR coach; 1 Bogie guard's coach; Cravens 50-ton steam crane RS1013/50 (1930), NER 5-ton hand crane DB915390 (1880) and Smiths 5-ton diesel crane (1939) plus over 80 goods vehicles

Owners
D335 and D345 the Class 40 Preservation Society
D99 and D5705 the Pioneer Diesel Group
6201 the 6201 Princess Elizabeth Locomotive Trust
Class 37s, Ian Riley Engineering, main line certified
65451 and 77172 The Class 504 Group
Class 37, 35009, 45407 and 76079 Riley & Sons (Railways)
D5054 the Type 2 Group
D1501 Pete Waterman
50015 the Manchester Class 50 Group

East Somerset Railway

Timetable Service

Somerset

The ESR was created by David Shepherd and his friends in the early 1970s. Once home to such locomotives as *Black Prince* and *Green Knight*, Cranmore is still one of the few preserved railways offering only steam-hauled trains. The railway seeks to portray a country branch line, and offers a warm and personal welcome to all visitors who want to experience the sights and sounds of the steam era
Contact: Booking Office
Headquarters: East Somerset Railway, Cranmore, Shepton Mallet, Somerset BA4 4QP
OS reference: ST 664429
Telephone: Cranmore (01749) 880417
Fax: (01749) 880764
Internet address: *e-mail:* info@eastsomersetrailway.org
Web site: www.eastsomersetrailway.org
Main station: Cranmore
Car park: Cranmore — free
Refreshment facilities: The Whistlestop Restaurant at Cranmore offers lunches, snacks, teas, etc. Group catering by arrangement. Picnic areas at Cranmore. Public and private Wine & Dine trains

Locomotives
Name	No	Origin	Class	Type	Built
—	5637	GWR	5600	0-6-2T	1924
—*	B110	LBSCR	E1	0-6-0T	1877
—†	47493	LMS	3F	0-6-0T	1927
—*	30075	JZ	USA	0-6-0T	1950s
—	D3044	BR	08	0-6-0DE	1960

*Undergoing overhaul
†Away on loan

Industrial locomotives
Name	No	Builder	Type	Built
Lord Fisher	1398	Barclay (1398)	0-4-0ST	1915
—	705	Barclay (2047)	0-4-0ST	1937
Lady Nan	1719	Barclay (1719)	0-4-0ST	1920

Stock
Numerous ex-BR Mk 1 coaches; 25 assorted wagons, mostly LMS and SR

Owners
5637 the 5637 loco Group
30075 the Project 62 Group
D3044 on loan from Foster Yeoman

Souvenir shop: Cranmore
On site facilities: Station shop. David Shepherd Gallery with railway and wildlife prints for sale. Children's play area. Engine shed and workshops open for viewing. Small railway museum
Depot: Engine shed and workshop at Cranmore West (.25-mile from Cranmoor)
Length of line: 2.75 miles
Passenger trains: Cranmore to Mendip Vale via Cranmore West and Merryfield Lane. Return trip takes c35min. Ticket allows unlimited travel on normal

operating days. All trains are steam-hauled

Period of public operation: Steaming days: Sundays in January, February, March; weekends in April, May; Wednesdays and weekends in June and July; Wednesdays, Thursdays and weekends in August; weekends in September and October; Sundays in November. Please call for details and train times. Last admission 30min before closing time

Special events: Diesel Weekend 17/18 April; Day out with Thomas — 1-3 May; Jazz Night — 24 July; Day out with Thomas — 31 July, 1, 4/5 August; Cranmore '44 — 28-30 August; Steam Dream — 25/26 September; Santa Specials — Weekends in December
Wine & Dine trains.
Murder Mystery Wine & Dines — 8 May, 10 July, 9 October, Mothers Day — 21 March, Fathers Day — 20 June; Mendip Belle Sunday Lunch — 16 May, 18 July, 15 August, 19 September, 17 October; Halloween — 30 October
Booking required for all Wine & Dine trains and Santa Specials

Facilities for disabled: All public areas and trains are accessible

Special Notes: Footplate experience courses available, both half day and full day. Please call for availability, prices and brochure. School groups, children's parties, private parties and Wine & Dine by arrangement — please call to discuss your requirements

Membership details: Please call for leaflet

Membership journal: *Cuttings* — 4 per year

Steam Centre — Elsecar Heritage Centre — South Yorkshire

Member: HRA

The Elsecar Railway runs between Elsecar Heritage Centre and the canal basin at Hemingfield, through a scenic conservation area alongside the Elsecar branch of the Dearne & Dove Canal

Location/headquarters: Elsecar Heritage Centre, Wath Road, Elsecar, Barnsley, South Yorkshire S74 8HJ

Telephone: (01226) 740203

Fax: (01226) 350239

Internet address: *e-mail:* elsecarheritagecentre@barnsley.gov.uk
Web site: www.barnsley.gov.uk/tourism

Main station: Elsecar

Length of line: 1-mile, 20min journey

Car park location: On site, free

Access by public transport: Main line Elsecar from Sheffield, Huddersfield, Leeds

Refreshment facilities: On site

Souvenir shops: On site

On site facilities: Refreshments, souvenir shop, toilets

Museum: Attractions include Science Track, Educational Workshops, 'Living History Centre', Bottle Collection, Hot Metal Press, Newcomen Beam Engine, working crafts people, various special events. Antiques centres open 7 days a week

Facilities for disabled: There are four disabled persons' toilets at different locations on the site. All buildings are fully wheelchair accessible at ground floor level

Public opening: Site open daily 10.00-17.00. Living History Centre open Tuesday to Sunday 10.30-16.30 (closed Monday except Bank Holidays). Please check for Christmas and New Year openings

The railway operates a public service on Sundays 12.00-14.30 from March to October, also Halloween and Christmas plus special event days and Bank Holidays

Special events: Include Thomas the Tank Engine, Vintage Weekend, Noddy Family Fun Event, Christmas Fair, Halloween Hauntings and Santa Specials on the railway

Special notes: Site and Living History Centre free admission except on special event days. Santa Specials run during December

Industrial locomotives

Name	No	Builder	Type	Built
Countess Fitzwilliam	544996	R/Hornsby (382808)	4wDM	1968
Earl Fitzwilliam	1917	Avonside (1917)	0-6-0ST	1923
Marbi Monster	—	Peckett	0-6-0ST	
Earl of Stafford	2895	YEC (2895)	0-6-0DH	1963
Jenny	7	H/Clarke (1689)	0-4-0	1937
Catherine	—	H/Clarke (1884)	0-6-0T	1955

Stock
4 ex-BR Mk 1 coaches, 1 Wickham trolley

Owners
Catherine and *Jenny* the Brian Harrison Trust

England

Embsay & Bolton Abbey Steam Railway

Member: HRA, TT

Yorkshire's 'Friendly Line' operates from Embsay station built in 1888. The railway is very family-orientated with many events for children. The enthusiast is not forgotten, with one of the finest collections of ex-industrial tank engines in Britain. The railway is currently constructing a new museum and workshop complex, and the line's extension to Bolton Abbey opened in 1997. Bolton Abbey station has been built to the original Midland Railway style. An atmosphere of the rural branch line prevails, which is operated by ex-industrial locomotives

Operating Committee:
Peter Burke

Business & Marketing Manager:
Stephen Walker. Tel: 01756 710614 (ext 3). Fax: 01756 710720

Internet address: *Web site:* www.embsayboltonabbeyrailway. org.uk

Location: Bolton Abbey Station, Bolton Abbey, Skipton, Yorkshire BD23 6AF

OS reference: SE 007533

Operating society/organisation:
Yorkshire Dales Railway Museum Trust

Telephone: 01756 710614, 24hr Talking Timetable 01756 795189

Car parks: Embsay and Bolton Abbey

Access by public transport:
Pennine bus from Skipton, National Park bus from Ilkley

On site facilities: Souvenir shop at Bolton Abbey and Embsay — transport and industrial archaeological bookshop at Embsay

Catering facilities: Buffet and bar on most trains. Buffet at both Bolton Abbey and Embsay stations. Special charters can be arranged, meals for parties can be arranged on normal service trains, subject to advance booking, please write for further details

Length of line: 4.5 miles

Public opening: Steam trains run every Sunday throughout the year, weekends from April to October, Tuesdays in June, early July, September and 28 December. Daily

Locomotives and multiple-units

Name	No	Origin	Class	Type	Built
—	D2203	BR	04	0-6-0DM	1952
—	NCB 38 (D9513)	BR	14	0-6-0DH	1964
—	D8189	BR	20	Bo-Bo	1967
—	LEV2	Derby	—	Railbus	1984
—	52005	BR	107	DMBS	1960
—	52012	BR	107	DMC	1960
—	52031	BR	107	DMCL	1960

Industrial locomotives

Name	No	Builder	Type	Built
Annie	9	Peckett (1159)	0-4-0ST	1908
Gladiator	8	H/Clarke (1450)	0-6-0ST	1922
Slough Estates No 5	—	H/Clarke (1709)	0-6-0ST	1939
Primrose No 2	S121	Hunslet (3715)	0-6-0ST	1952
Ann	—	Sentinel (7232)	4wVB	1927
Beatrice	7	Hunslet (2705)	0-6-0ST	1945
Airedale	3	Hunslet (1440)	0-6-0ST	1923
York No 1	—	Yorkshire (2474)	0-4-0ST	1949
Illingworth	—	H/Clarke (1208)	0-6-0ST	1916
—	140	H/Clarke (1821)	0-6-0T	1948
Spitfire	S112	Hunslet (2414)	0-6-0ST	1942
Wheldale	S134	Hunslet (3168)	0-6-0ST	1944
Sir Robert Peel	8	Hunslet (3776)	0-6-0ST	1952
—	69	Hunslet (3785)	0-6-0ST	1953
Monkton No 1	—	Hunslet (3788)	0-6-0ST	1953
—	22	Barclay (2320)	0-4-0ST	1952
—	68005	RSH (7169)	0-6-0ST	1945
Thomas	4	RSH (7661)	0-4-0ST	1950
H. W. Robinson	—	Fowler (4100003)	0-4-0DM	1946
—	—	Fowler (4200003)	0-4-0DM	1948
—	MDE15	B/Drewry (2136)	4wDM	1938
—	887	R/Hornsby (394009)	4wDM	1955
—	—	Wickham (7610)	2w-2PMR	1957
—	—	Lister (9993)*	4wPM	1938
—	—	Lister (10225)*	4wPM	1938
—	—	R/Hornsby (175418)*	4wDM	1936
—	—	R/Hornsby*	4wDM	—
—	—	M/Rail (8979)*	4wDM	1946
—	—	M/Rail (5213)*	4wDM	1930
—	—	R/Hornsby	4wDM	1957
Meaford	—	Barclay (440)	0-4-0DH	1958
—	36	H/Clarke (D1037)	0-6-0DM	1958

*2ft gauge

Stock

18 ex-BR Mk 1 coaches (SK, CK, 2xBCK, 5xTSO, 2xRMB, 1xBSO(T), 1xRBR and 1xSLS), 4 ex-LNER coaches; 2 SR parcels vans; Freight stock and service vehicles, SR and GW brakes
Stephen Middleton collection of vintage coaches

Owners

Class 107 DMU vehicles the Class 107 Ltd

Note

Items on display may vary

from 19 July (except DMU service on July Monday and Fridays) until the end of August. Steam also operates February and October half term Wednesdays.

DMU service runs February and October half terms, 16-18 July. Additional services operated by DMUs on Sundays in June, July, August and September

Special events: Day out with Thomas — 9-12 April; Children Travel Free Weekend — 1-3 May;

Day out with Thomas — 29-31 May; Teddy Bears Picnic — 24/25 July; Day out with Thomas — 28-30 August; 1940s Weekend — 18/19 September; Harvest of Steam Weekend — 16/17 October; Halloween Specials — 31 October; Santa Trains — Sundays 21, 28 November, 4/5, 11/12, 18/19 December; New Year's Day Specials — 1 January 2005. Certain summer Sundays will be designated Vintage Train days when

in addition to a normal passenger train service a vintage train will operate using historic coaches
Special notes: Steam rides are on the 4.5-mile line to the new station and picnic area at Bolton Abbey. Old Midland Railway buildings, fine collection of industrial locomotives
Membership details: Membership Secretary at above address
Membership journal: *Dale Steam, YDR News* — 4 times/year

Attraction — Evesham Vale Light Railway — Worcestershire

Member: BGLR

The Evesham Vale Light Railway takes you through the apple orchards to a picnic and viewing area overlooking some of the most picturesque scenrey in the Vale of Evesham. Steam locomotives are used on most days and it is possible to break your journey and walk to the river, returning on a later train. The railway is situated within Evesham Country Park, 1 mile to the north of the historic town of Evesham. Enjoy a day out and stroll around the 130 acre estate, including a mile and quarter of the River Avon. Visit the Vale Wildlife Visitor Centre, browse in the relaxe atmosphere of the courtyard shops or try some of the freshly prepared lunches and snacks in the licensed Apple Barn restaurant

Location/headquarters: Evesham Vale Light Railway, Evesham Country Park, Twyford, Nr Evesham, Worcestershire WR1 4TP
Contact: Jim Shackell
Telephone: 01386 422282
Internet address: *e-mail:* enquiries@evlr.co.uk
Web site: www.evlr.co.uk
Main station: Twyford (adjacent to Evesham Country Park car park)
Other station: Evesham Vale (in the country park)
OS reference: SP0446
On site facilities: Large car and coach park, licensed restaurant within park shopping complex. Wildlife Visitor Centre. Small souvenir shop at Twyford station

Locomotives

Name	No	Builder	Type	Built
Prince William	5751	G&S	4-6-2	1949
—	715	Morse	0-4-0	1951
—	—	Lister (41545)	4wDM	1955
—	—	Eddy/Knotwell	4wDM	2002

Length of line: 1.25 miles, 15in gauge
Locomotive and carriage depots: Adjacent to Twyford station
Access by public transport: By train to Evesham main line station then bus — Stagecoach No 28 — from Evesham bus station, hourly service will stop close to park entrance, then 15min walk to Twyford station
Public opening: Weekends and

Bank Holidays throughout the year. Daily 16-20 February, 5-20 April, 1-4 June, 19 July-3 September, 21-29 October, 20 December-5 January 2005 (excluding Christmas and Boxing Days). Please ring information line (01386 422282) for more details. trains run every half-hour from 10.30 to 17.00 (16.00 November to March)
Facilities for disabled: Limited wheelchair facilities on trains

The delightful setting of the Evesham Vale Light Railway in October 2003. *Neville Knight*

England

Member: BGLR
A comparatively new line with purpose-built locomotives and rolling stock around part of Exbury Gardens. Train fare is in addition to entrance fee
Location/headquarters: Exbury Gardens, Exbury, Southampton SO45 1AZ
Contact: Ian Wilson (railway foreman). Tel: 023 8089 2898
Telephone: 023 8089 1203
Internet address: *Web site:* www.exbury.co.uk
Access by public transport: Main line trains to Brockenhurst. Bus from Southampton summer Sundays only
Car park: On site

Industrial locomotives

Name	No	Builder	Type	Built
Rosemary	—	Exmoor (315)	0-6-2T	2001
Naomi	—	Exmoor (316)	0-6-2T	2001
—*	—	Exmoor	2-6-0	2004
—	—	Exmoor	0-4-0DH	2001

*under construction

Stock
6 coaches, with nore under construction

On site facilities: Souvenir shop, refreshments and toilets adjacent to main car park
Length of line: 1.25 miles, 12.25in gauge
Public opening: 28 February to 31 October. Limited winter opening.

Special events: Narrow Gauge in the Gardens — 19/20 June; Steam in the Gardens — 2/3 October
Facilities for disabled: Yes

Member: HRA
The railway was built in 1893 to carry coal from Foxfield Colliery to the North Staffordshire Railway at Blythe Bridge. Following closure of the colliery in 1965 the line was rescued for preservation. The Society is working towards rebuilding the railway a further 0.75 mile down the famous Foxfield Bank to the site of Foxfield Colliery as part of a half million pound lottery grant
Chairman: S. Sutton
Headquarters: Foxfield Steam Railway, Blythe Bridge, Stoke-on-Trent
Postal address: P. O. Box 1967, Stoke-on-Trent, ST4 8YT
Telephone:
01782 396210 (weekends)
01782 643507 (week days)
Fax: 01782 396210
Internet address: *Web site:* www.foxfieldrailway.co.uk
Main station: Blythe Bridge (Caverswall Road)
OS reference: SJ 957421
Car park: Blythe Bridge
Access by public transport: Main

Industrial locomotives

Name	No	Builder	Type	Built
Bellerophon*	—	Haydock Foundry (C)	0-6-0WT	1874
—	1827	B/Peacovk (1827)	0-4-0ST	1879
—	6	R/Heath	0-4-0ST	1886
—	4101	Dubs (4101)	0-4-0CT	1901†
Henry Cort	—	Peckett (933)	0-4-0ST	1903††
Millom	—	Avonside (1563)	0-4-0ST	1908†
Moss Bay	—	K/Stuart (4167)	0-4-0ST	1920††
Cranford	—	Avonside (1919)	0-6-0ST	1924†
Helen	—	Simplex (2262)	4wDM	1924
Marston No 3	—	H/Leslie (3581)	0-6-0ST	1924†
—	—	K/Stuart (4388)	0-4-0ST	1926•
Lewisham	—	Bagnall (2221)	0-6-0ST	1927
Rom River	—	K/Stuart (4421)	6wDM	1929
Boots No 1	—	Barclay (1984)	0-4-0F	1930††
Ironbridge No 1	—	Peckett (1803)	0-4-0ST	1933††
Spondon No 2	—	E/Electric (1130)	4wBE	1939††
Roker	—	RSH (7006)	0-4-0CT	1940††
Hawarden	—	Bagnall (2623)	0-4-0ST	1940
—	WD820	B/Drewry (2157)	0-4-0DM	1942
(Hercules)	242915	R/Hornsby (242915)	4wDM	1946
—	11	Peckett (2081)	0-4-0ST	1947•
Whiston	—	Hunslet (3694)	0-6-0ST	1950
—	9535	Sentinel (9535)	4wVBGT	1952•
Florence No 2	—	Bagnall (3059)	0-6-0ST	1953†
Meaford No 2	—	RSH (7684)	0-6-0T	1951
Wimblebury	—	Hunslet (3839)	0-6-0ST	1956•
(Gas-oil)	88DS	R/Hornsby (408496)	4wDM	1957†
Wolstanton No 3	—	Bagnall (3150)	0-6-0DM	1960

line railway Blythe Bridge (400yd).
PMT bus service to Blythe Bridge
Refreshment facilities: Buffet and
real ale bar at Blythe Bridge
Souvenir shop: Blythe Bridge
Passenger trains: Steam-hauled
trains operate from Blythe Bridge
(Caverswall Road) to Dilhorne Park
and return
Family ticket: Available (2 adults
+ 2 children or 1 adult + 4 children)
Length of line: 3.5 miles. Current
operation over 2.5 miles of line
Period of public operation: Steam
trains operate Sundays and Bank
Holiday Mondays 21 March-end
October inclusive between Blythe
Bridge and Dilhorne Park.
Special events: Steam Gala —
17/18 July; Halloween and Santa
Specials, weekends in December
(both pre-booked events). Please
contact for details
Facilities for disabled: Access to

Name	No	Builder	Type	Built
B. R. C. (Megan)	—	Thomas Hill (103C)	0-4-0DH	1957
Rachel	—	R/Hornsby (423637)	0-4-0DE	1958
(Roman)	165DS	R/Hornsby (424841)	0-4-0DE	1960
Ludstone	—	YEC (3207)	0-4-0DH	1961
Leys	—	Bagnall (2868)	0-6-0DE	1962
Meaford No 4	—	Barclay (486)	0-6-0DH	1964

†under overhaul
††static exhibit
•awaiting overhaul
*on loan for two years

Stock
3 ex-BR Mk 1 CK coaches; 1 ex-BR Mk 2a TSO coach; 4 other coaches;
3 scenery vans (converted for other uses); 79 assorted wagons, 16-ton
mineral wagons; 1 rail-mounted self-propelled diesel-electric crane

Owner
Bellerophon the Vintage Carriages Trust

majority of Caverswall Road station
is on the level; disabled toilets.
Advance notice essential for those
wishing to travel on the train
Membership journal: *Foxfield
News* — quarterly

Timetable Service	# Gartell Light Railway	Somerset

Owned and operated by three
generations of the Gartell family,
the Gartell Light Railway offers
visitors the chance to travel by train
along the route of the old Somerset
& Dorset Joint Railway. A half-
mile section of the line from
Pinesway Junction to Park Lane
runs along the old S&D trackbed,
while work has started on an
extension northwards from
Pinesway Junction along the S&D
formation towards Templecombe.
A flyover has been constructed to
carry the extension over the
existing line to the terminus at
Common Lane and tracklaying has
begun. On most open days a three
train service is operated, with
departures every 15min and trains
crossing at Pinesway Junction. The
GLR is fully signalled using a
variety of upper and lower
quadrant, colour light and shunt
signals controlled by two full size
signalboxes. The GLR's first steam
locomotive, a locally built 0-4-2T,
specially designed to cope with the
steep gradients and sharp curves of
the section from Common Lane up

Industrial locomotives
2ft gauge:

Name	No	Builder	Type	Built
Amanda	1	GLR	Bo-BoDH	2003
Andrew	2	R/Hornsby	4wDH	1964/5
Alison	5	A/Keef (10)	4wDH	1983
Mr G	6	N. Dorset Loco Wks	0-4-2T	1998

Rolling stock — coaches: 9 fully enclosed bogie coaches

Rolling stock — wagons: goods guard's van, bogie PW gang/tool van,
bogie hopper, bogie open, bogie well, bogie flat, bogie crane and open
wagon

to Pinesway Junction, entered
service in 1998.
Location/headquarters: Gartell
Light Railway, Common Lane,
Yenston, Nr Templecombe,
Somerset BA8 0NB
Telephone: 01963 370752
Internet address: *Web site:*
http://www.gartell-light-
railway.co.uk
General Manager: John Gartell
Main station: Common Lane
Other stations: Pinesway Junction,
Park Lane
Car park: Large free car park at

Common Lane
OS reference: ST 718218
Access by public transport: 1.5
miles south-east of Templecombe
railway station
Refreshment facilities:
Refreshment room at Common
Lane serving a range of hot and
cold snacks and drinks. Lakeside
picnic area at Pinesway Junction
Visitor centre: Common Lane
Souvenir shop: Common Lane
Museum: Common Lane —
Templecombe Railway Museum
(collection of artefacts,

photographs, documents, models, etc recording the history of Templecombe station)
Depot: Common Lane (not open to public)
Length of line: 0.75-mile

Facilities for disabled: Two of the three trains in service have accommodation for a disabled visitor in a
Period of public operation: 12 April; 3, 31 May; 27 June; 25 July;

29/30 August; 26 September, 31 October. 10.30-16.30
Special events: Vintage Transport display — 27 June; Santa Specials (must be pre-booked) — 5 and 12 December

---

| Timetable Service | # Gloucestershire Warwickshire Railway | Glos |

Member: HRA
Part of an ambitious project to link Cheltenham with Stratford, much has been done to re-create the railway and buildings that made up this cross-country route. The railway is home to many owners of private locomotives and rolling stock, so from time to time the items on display may vary. The extension from Gotherington to Cheltenham Racecourse opened in April 2003
Location: Toddington station, Toddington
OS reference: SO 050322
Operating society/organisation: Gloucestershire Warwickshire Steam Railway plc, The Station, Toddington, Cheltenham, Glos GL54 5DT
Telephone: Toddington (01242) 621405
Internet address:
e-mail: enquiries@gwsr.plc.uk
Web site: www.gwsr.plc.uk
Main station: Toddington
Other public stations: Winchcombe, Cheltenham Racecourse
Access by public transport: Hourly service from Cheltenham to Greet for Winchcombe station. Local bus service Castleways will answer timetable queries on (01242) 602949. Regular Stagecoach service to Cheltenham station Racecourse Park & Ride (approx half mile to GWR station)
Car park: All stations
On site facilities: Sales, catering, narrow gauge rides, toilets
Length of line: 10 miles
Public opening: On non-operating mid weekdays the station is closed. Public services; weekends, Bank Holiday Mondays, between March and November, some summer weekdays

Locomotives and multiple-units

Name	No	Origin	Class	Type	Built
—	2807	GWR	2800	2-8-0	1905
—	4247	GWR	4200	2-8-0T	1916
—	4270	GWR	4200	2-8-0T	1919
—	4277	GWR	4200	2-8-0T	1920
Raveningham Hall	6960	GWR	6959	4-6-0	1944
Owsden Hall	6984	GWR	6959	4-6-0	1948
—	7069	LMS	—	0-6-0DE	1939
Peninsular & Oriental SNCo	35006	SR	MN	4-6-2	1941
—	8274	LMS	8F	2-8-0	1941
—	76077	BR	4MT	2-6-0	1956
Black Prince	92203	BR	9F	2-10-0	1959
—	03069	BR	03	0-6-0DM	1959
—	D2182	BR	03	0-6-0DM	1952
—	D9539	BR	14	0-6-0DH	1965
—	D9553	BR	14	0-6-0DH	1965
—	D8137	BR	20	Bo-Bo	1966
—	24081	BR	24	Bo-Bo	1960
—	26043	BR	26	Bo-Bo	1959
—	D5541	BR	31	A1A-A1A	1959
—	37215	BR	37	Co-Co	1964
Clydebridge	37324	BR	37	Co-Co	1962
—	45149	BR	45	1Co-Co1	1961
—	47105	BR	47	Co-Co	1963
—	47376	BR	47	Co-Co	1965
—	51950	BR	108	DMBS	1960
—	52062	BR	108	DMC	1960

Industrial locomotives

Name	No	Builder	Type	Built
—	19	Fowler (4240016)	0-6-0DH	1964
—	21	Fowler (4210130)	0-4-0DM	1957
—	—	H/Clarke (D615)	0-6-0DM	1938
John	—	Peckett (1976)	0-4-0ST	1939
King George	—	Hunslet (2409)	0-6-0ST	1942
—	1	Drewry/RSH (2573/7859)	0-6-0DM	1956
—	2	Drewry/RSH (2574/7860)	0-6-0DM	1956

Stock
4 ex-GWR coaches; 55 ex-BR coaches; 4 ex-LMS coaches; Baguley/Drewry inspection vehicle; 2 Wickham trolleys; plus numerous wagons (including 10 brake vans, 45-ton steam crane, 18-ton diesel crane)

Owners
2807 the Cotswold Steam Preservation Ltd (www.gwr2807.co.uk)
4247 the 4247 Preservation Society
4277 Peter Best (undergoing overhaul off-site)

Special events: Day out with Thomas — 24/25 April, 9/10 October; Anniversary Gala — 7-9 May; Transport Nostalgia Days — 27 June, 25 July, 5 September; Autumn Diesel Gala — 16/17 October; Model Railway Exhibition — 13 November; Winter Diesel Gala — 27/28 November; Santa Specials — 4/5, 11/12, 18/19, 22-24 December; Christmas Diesel Day — 27 December

Special notes: The site is being developed as the headquarters of the railway between Cheltenham and Stratford. The GWR owns the railway land between Cheltenham and Broadway and operates over 10 miles from Toddington to Cheltenham Racecourse with an intermediate station at Winchcombe.

Guest locomotives will be operating during the year with very special guest *City of Truro* expected March to May 2004.

Wine & Dine train 'Elegant Excursions' at www.excursions/freeserve.co.uk

Round trip tickets give unlimited travel on day of purchase.

Family tickets available

35006 the P&O Locomotive Society
8274 and 7069 the Churchill (8F) Locomotive Co
92203 David Shepherd (currently undergoing overhaul off-site)
26043 and 45149 the Cotswold Mainline Diesel Group
D9537, D9539 and D9553 Cotswold Diesel Preservation Group
37215 and 37324 the Growler Group
47105 and 47376 the Brush Type 4 Fund
D8137 the English Electric Type 1 group

North Gloucestershire Railway
Industrial narrow gauge locomotives (2ft gauge)

Name	No	Builder	Type	Built
Isibutu	5	Bagnall (2820)	4-4-0T	1946
George B	—	Hunslet (680)	0-4-0ST	1898
Chaka	—	Hunslet (2075)	0-4-2T	1940
Justine	—	Jung (939)	0-4-0WT	1906
Brigadelok	—	Henschel (15968)	0-8-0T	1918
—	2	Lister (34523)	4wDM	1949
—	3	M/Rail (4565)	4wPM	1928
Spitfire	—	M/Rail (7053)	4wPM	1937
—	1	R/Hornsby (166010)	4wDM	1932
—	L5	R/Hornsby (181820)	4wDM	1936
—	—	R/Hornsby (354028)	4wDM	1953

Stock
3 coaches; 11 wagons

Membership details: From above address
Membership journal: *The Cornishman* — quarterly

Great Central Railway

Member: HRA, TT

The original Great Central Railway's extension to London in 1899 was the last main line to be built in this country, most of which was closed in the 1960s. Steam-hauled services operate through attractive rolling Leicestershire countryside, crossing the picturesque Swithland reservoir. The railway's aim is to re-create the experience of British main line operation in the days of steam. The images of a main line are backed up by a double track line with long trains hauled by large locomotives

Headquarters: Great Central Railway plc, Loughborough Central Station, Great Central Road, Loughborough, Leicestershire LE11 1RW
Telephone: Loughborough (01509) 230726

Locomotives and multiple-units

Name	No	Origin	Class	Type	Built
—	4141	GWR	41xx	2-6-2T	1946
Witherslack Hall*	6990	GWR	'Hall'	4-6-0	1948
Ditcheat Manor	7821	GWR	'Manor'	4-6-0	1950
Sir Lamiel	30777	SR	N15	4-6-0	1925
Boscastle	34039	SR	WC	4-6-2	1946
Brocklebank Line	35025	SR	MN	4-6-2	1948
—	45231	LMS	5MT	4-6-0	1936
Alderman A. E. Draper	45305	LMS	5MT	4-6-0	1936
—	46521	LMS	2MT	2-6-0	1953
—	47406	LMS	3F	0-6-0T	1926
—	61264	LNER	B1	4-6-0	1947
—	63601	GCR	8K	2-8-0	1919
—	69523	GNR	N2	0-6-2T	1921
—	90775	MoS	WD	2-10-0	1943
—	73156	BR	5MT	4-6-0	1956
—	78019	BR	2MT	2-6-0	1954
—	D3101	BR	08	0-6-0DE	1955
§—	D4067	BR	10	0-6-0DE	1961
—	D8098	BR	20	Bo-Bo	1961
—	D5185	BR	25	Bo-Bo	1960

England

The Gloucestershire Warwickshire Railway won the Ian Allan Heritage Railway of the Year Award for 2003. Amongst other achievements the railway's restored Cheltenham Race Course station was opened by The Princess Royal. Here Southern Railway 'Schools' class No 30926 *Repton* has been disguised as sister engine No 30925 *Cheltenham. Alan Barnes*

England

Fax: 01509 239791
Internet address: *e-mail:*
booking_office@gcrailway.co.uk
Web site:
www.gcrailway.co.uk
Main stations: Loughborough Central, Leicester North
Other public stations: Quorn & Woodhouse, Rothley
OS reference: SK 543194
Car park: Quorn, Rothley
Access by public transport:
Loughborough Midland station (0.75-mile). Add-on ticket from any National Rail station includes unlimited travel on day of visit. Arriva Fox County, Barton, Kinch, South Notts and Trent Buses serve Loughborough Baxtergate (0.5 mile). Arriva Fox County Nos 126/7 pass end of Great Central Road (A6 Leicester Road, 300yd)
Refreshment facilities: Licensed Griddle Car with hot and cold drinks on majority of trains and at Loughborough Central station. Light refreshment facilities available at all other stations. Luxurious First Class Restaurant Car, for wich advance booking is obligatory, is provided on 13.15 train every Saturday and Sunday. Also provided on 19.30 train every Saturday and every Friday (June-September). Additional service may run at peak times. Private charter trains available, along with more details of all the above, on request
Souvenir shop: Loughborough
Museum: Loughborough
Depot: Loughborough
Length of line: 8 miles
Passenger trains: Loughborough-Leicester North
Period of public operation:
Weekends and Bank Holidays throughout the year. Daily between June and September with additional services at times of peak demand
Special events: 1960s (Steam & Diesel) Gala — 26-28 March; Easter daily running — 5-16 April; Classic Vehicle Rally — 10-12 April; 1950s Experience — 1-3 May; Day out with Thomas — 29 May-1 June; 'Operation Gauntlet' World War 2 experience — 11-13 June; Summer Gala — 24/25 July; Toy & Model Fair — 15 August; Day out with Thomas — 21-30

Name	No	Origin	Class	Type	Built
Harlech Castle	25265	BR	25	Bo-Bo	1963
—	D5830	BR	31	A1A-A1A	1962
—	37255	BR	37	Co-Co	1965
†—	D123	BR	45	1Co-Co1	1961
—	D1705	BR	47	Co-Co	1965
Sir Herbert Walker	E6003	BR	73	Bo-Bo	1966
—	51427	BR	101	DMBS	1959
—	51616	BR	127	DMBS	1959
—	51622	BR	127	DMBS	1959
—	53193	BR	101	DMC	1959
—	53203	BR	101	DMBS	1957
—	53321	BR	101	DMC	1958
—	59276	BR	120	TS	1958

*undergoing overhaul at Tyseley Locomotive Works
§ named *Alfred Thomas & Margaret Ethel Naylor*
† named *Leicestershire & Derbyshire Yeomanry*

Industrial locomotives

Name	No	Builder	Type	Built
(Quag)	(1)	Ruston (37971)	0-4-0DM	1954
(Arthur Wright)	D4279	Fowler (4210079)	0-4-0DE	1952
Duke of Edinburgh	28	A/Barclay (400)	0-4-0DM	1956

Owners
6990 the Witherslack Hall Locomotive Society
7821 the Great Western Steam Locomotives
30777 on loan from the National Railway Museum (under custody of the
34059 the Boscastle Locomotive Syndicate
35025 the Brocklebank Line Association
45321 the Great Central Railway plc
45305 the 5305 Locomotive Association
46521, 73156 and 78019 Loughborough Standard Locomotives Group
47406, D3101, D4067 private
61264 the Thompson B1 Locomotive Society
63601 on loan from the National Railway Museum
69523 the Gresley Society
90775 the Essex Locomotive Society
D5830, D8098 and D1705 the Type 1 Locomotive Co
E6003 the ED Locomotive Group
Class 101s Renaissance Railcars
37255 on loan from Fragonset Railways

August; Quorn Swapmeet — 5 September; Diesel Gala — 24-26 September; Day out with Thomas — 22-24 October; Half term daily running — 25-29 October; Bonfire Night — 5 November; Santa Specials — 27 November-24 December; Christmas Day — 25 December; Boxing Day — 26 December; Christmas Gala — 27-31 December; New Year's Eve Specials 31 December.
Facilities for disabled: Special carriage for wheelchair/disabled persons (advance notice required). Wheelchair access good at Quorn

and Rothley, can be arranged at Loughborough with advance notification. Boarding ramps at all stations
Membership & share details:
Share enquiries: Company Secretary, Great Central Railway plc
Membership: Membership Secretary, Main Line Steam Trust Ltd. Both c/o above address. Friends of Great Central Railway, Friends Co-ordinator c/o above address

Steam Centre | Great Whipsnade Railway | Bedfordshire

Member: HRA
Location: Whipsnade Wild Animal Park, Dunstable, Bedfordshire LU6 2LF
Telephone: (01582) 872171 (extension 2270)
Fax: (01582) 873748
Internet address: *e-mail:* whipsnade-operations@2sl.org
Railway Co-ordinator: Graham Tylor
Main station: Whipsnade Central
Length: 2 miles (2ft 6in gauge)
On site facilities: Car park (100yd), souvenir shop, refreshments (30yd)
Period of public operation: January — no trains; February — half term; March — weekends only; April to July — daily

Locomotives

Name	No	Builder	Type	Built
Chevalier	1	M/Wardle (1877)	0-6-2T	1915
Excelsior	2	K/Stuart (1049)	0-4-2T	1908
Superior	4	K/Stuart (4034)	0-6-2T	1920
Victor	—	Fowler (4160004)	0-6-0DM	1951
Hector	—	Fowler (4160005)	0-6-0DM	1951
Mr Bill	10	R/Hornsby (221625)	0-4-0DM	1944
Hercules	—*	23rd August Works (Bucharest)	0-6-0DH	1981

*Polish State Railways Class LYD2

Rolling stock: 10 carriages, 9 wagons

(Weekdays diesels only/steam at weekends); August daily steam trains; September/October — daily (Weekdays diesels only/steam at weekends); November — school half term; December — no trains
Facilities for disabled: Carriage designed for wheelchairs

Steam Centre | Hollycombe Steam Collection | West Sussex

Member: HRA, TT
An extensive collection of working steam, including railways, traction engines, fairground rides, Bioscope, organs, the oldest Burrell Showman's engine *Emperor*, sawmill and engine from the paddle steamer *Caledonia*, set in woodlands and gardens
Location: Iron Hill, Hollycombe, near Liphook, Hants
OS reference: SU 852295
Operating society/organisation: Hollycombe Steam & Woodland Garden Society, Iron Hill, Midhurst Road, Liphook, Hants GU30 7LP
Telephone: Liphook (01428) 724900 (24hr answerphone)
Fax: 01428 723682

Industrial locomotives

Name	No	Builder	Type	Built
Caledonia	70	Barclay (1995)	0-4-0WT	1931*
Jerry M	38	Hunslet (638)	0-4-0ST	1895*
Commander B	50	H/Leslie (2450)	0-4-0ST	1899
—	16	R/Hornsby	4wDM	1941*

*2ft gauge

Internet address: *Web site:* www.hollycombe.co.uk
Car park: On site
Access by public transport: Liphook main line station (1 mile)
On site facilities: Shop and refreshments, toilets, car park, *dogs allowed in car park only*
Length of lines: Standard gauge – quarter mile
2ft gauge 'Quarry Railway' – 1.5 miles
7.25in gauge – quarter mile
Public opening: All Easter weekend. Sundays and Bank Holidays 4 April-10 October. Daily 1-30 August. 12.00-17.00.
Special events: Please phone for details

Irchester Narrow Gauge Railway Museum

Member: HRA

The aims of the controlling trust are to acquire and preserve narrow gauge railway locomotives, rolling stock and exhibits associated with Northamptonshire and the East Midlands, to display the collection for the benefit of the public and to restore exhibits to working order so they may be demonstrated in a proper manner

Location: Within Irchester Country Park, 2 miles south of Wellingborough

Operating society/organisation: The Irchester Narrow Gauge Railway Trust, 3 St Christopher's Close, Cranwell, Lincs NG34 8XB

On site facilities: Shop, museum, demonstration line, picnic area

Access by public transport: Main line Wellingborough (Midland Road) station, buses to Irchester and Little Irchester

Industrial locomotives

Name	No	Builder	Type	Built
—	85*	Peckett (1870	0-6-0ST	1934
—	86*	Peckett (1871)	0-6-0ST	1934
—	87*	Peckett (2029)	0-6-0ST	1942
Cambrai	—*	Corpet (493)	0-6-0T	1888
—	ND3645*	R/Hornsby (211679)	4wDM	1941
—	—†	R/Hornsby (281290)	0-6-0DM	1949
—	ED10*	R/Hornsby (411322	4wDM	1958
—	—†	M/Rail (1363)	4wPM	1918
The Rock	—*	Hunslet (2419)	0-4-0DM	1941

* metre gauge
† 3ft gauge

Car Parks: Main park car parks

Toilets: Main park complex

Public opening: Every Sunday (summer 10.00-17.00, winter 10.00-16.00), at other times by arrangement. Steam and demonstration weekends are held on last full weekend of the month — March-October

Facilities for disabled: Museum and site on level, staff available if required

Membership details: Membership Secretary, 1 Wilby Street, Northampton NN1 5JX

Ironbridge Gorge Museums

The railway items form only a small part of the displays on two of the museum's main sites: Blists Hill Victorian Town and Coalbrookdale. The Blists Hill site offers an opportunity to see a number of industrial and other activities being operated in meticulously reconstructed period buildings. A working foundry is just one of the exciting exhibits. A full size working replica of Richard Trevithick's 1802 steam locomotive built by the Coalbrookdale Company can also be seen operating at certain times at the Blists Hill site. The Ironbridge Gorge was designated a World Heritage Site in 1987

Location: Ironbridge, Shropshire

OS reference: SJ 694033

Operating society/organisation: Ironbridge Gorge Museum Trust,

Industrial locomotives

Name	No	Builder	Type	Built
—	—	Sentinel/Coalbrookdale (6185)	0-4-0VBT	1925
—	—	Sentinel/M/Wardle (6155)	0-4-0VBT	1925
—	5	Coalbrookdale	0-4-0ST	1865
—	—	A/Barclay	0-6-0ST	1896

All locomotives are at the Museum of Iron site.
Phone 01952 432141 for details

Coach Road, Coalbrookdale, Telford, Shropshire TF8 7DQ

Telephone: Telford (01952) 433522

Fax: (01952) 432204

Internet address: Web site: www.ironbridge.org.uk

Car park: At the sites

Access by public transport: Various operators. Please telephone Telford Travel Link 01952 200005 or 0870 6082608 for further details

Catering facilities: Licensed Victorian pub, sweet shop and tea rooms at the Blists Hill site, serving drinks and mainly cold snacks. Tea, coffee and light refreshments at the Museum of Iron, Coalbrookdale and Coalport China Museum

Public opening: Main sites, including Museum of Iron and Blists Hill, daily (except Christmas Eve and Christmas Day) 10.00-17.00

Special notes: Tickets for all the sites or just for single sites available

Isle of Wight Steam Railway

Member: HRA, TT

Separated from the mainland by the Solent, the line's isolation encouraged the maintenance and retention of Victorian locomotives and coaching stock which still operate on the line today. Its rural charm enhances its attraction for the island's holidaymakers during the summer season

Commercial Director: Jim Loe

Headquarters: Isle of Wight Steam Railway, Haven Street Station, Ryde, Isle of Wight PO33 4DS

Telephone: (01983) 882204

Internet addresses: *e-mail:* ronlee@iwsteamrailway.co.uk *Web site:* www.iwsteamrailway.co.uk

Main station: Haven Street

OS reference: SZ 556898

Other public stations: Wootton, Ashey and Smallbrook Junction

Car park: Haven Street

Access by public transport: 'Island Line' service from Ryde or Shanklin to Smallbrook Jct

Refreshment facilities: Light refreshments available (licensed)

Souvenir shop: Haven Street

Museum: Small exhibits museum at Haven Street

Depot: Haven Street

Length of line: 5 miles

Locomotives

Name	No	Origin	Class	Type	Built
Freshwater	W8 (32646)	LBSCR	A1X	0-6-0T	1876
Newport	W11 (32640)	LBSCR	A1X	0-6-0T	1878
Calbourne	W24	LSWR	O2	0-4-4T	1891
—	D2554	BR	05	0-6-0DM	1956
—	D2059	BR	03	0-6-0DM	1959

Industrial locomotives

Name	No	Builder	Type	Built
Invincible	37	H/Leslie (3135)	0-4-0ST	1915
Ajax	38	Barclay (1605)	0-6-0T	1918
Royal Engineer	198	Hunslet (3798)	0-6-0ST	1953

Owners

Royal Engineer on loan from National Army Museum

Stock

1 IWR coach; 4 LBSCR coaches; 3 SECR coaches; 2 LCDR coaches; 5 IWR coaches (bodies only); 5 LCDR coaches (bodies only); 1 LBSCR coach (body only); 1 crane; 1 Wickham trolley; 30 wagons; 6 parcels vans; 2 ex-LT hoppers; 1 ex-BR Lowmac; 1 LSWR Road van; 1 cattle van (on loan from the National Railway Museum)

Passenger trains: Wootton-Smallbrook Jct

Period of public operation: Daily — June to September. Selected days — March to May and October

Special events: 1940s Weekend — 3/4 July; A Day out with Thomas — 23-26 July; Island Steam Extravaganza — 27-30 August. Santa Specials, in December (please contact for details)

Facilities for disabled: Limited facilities, but can be catered for individually, or in groups (by prior arrangement), toilets available

Membership details: Membership Secretary at above address

Membership journal: *Island Rail News* — quarterly

Keighley & Worth Valley Railway

Member: HRA

1968 saw the reopening of the Worth Valley branch following the first sale of a standard gauge railway to a preservation society. Qualified volunteers have now managed and operated the KWVR every weekend, summer and winter for three decades. The KWVR is justifiably proud of having led the British independent railway movement in establishing the now ubiquitous late 1950s/early 1960s house style. Many have copied, but few succeed so well as the Worth Valley with totems, A5 handbills, period posters, red uniform ties, hanging baskets, gas lights and coal fires. One of the most community-orientated independent railways, being the first to create a 'Resident's Railcard' discount fares scheme

Chairman, Joint Management Committee: Trevor England

Headquarters: Haworth Station, Keighley, West Yorkshire, BD22 8NJ

Telephone: Haworth (01535) 647777 24hr recorded timetable and information service; Haworth (01535) 645214 (other calls)

Internet address: *Web site:* www.kwvr.co.uk

Main stations: Keighley, Ingrow West, Haworth, Oxenhope

Other public stations: Damems, Oakworth

OS reference: SE 034371

63

Car parks: Free at Keighley, Ingrow West, Oakworth and Oxenhope. Parking at Haworth (small charge, part refundable if travelling). Coaches at Ingrow West and Oxenhope only

Access by public transport: Fast and frequent electric Metro trains from Leeds, Bradford and Skipton to Keighley (joint station with KWVR). GNER direct service from King's Cross at 17.50 Monday-Friday. Arriva Trains (Northern) through services from Glasgow, Carlisle, Morecambe, Lancaster to Keighley station. Through bookings to 'Oxenhope KWVR' are available from any travel centre throughout Britain and allow one day's unlimited travel on KWVR. Arriva Trains (North) from Blackpool, Preston, Blackburn, Accrington, Burnley, Manchester to Hebden Bridge for connection via bus service 500 to Oxenhope (tel 01535 603284 for days of operation and timings)

Refreshment facilities: Buffet facilities at Oxenhope and Keighley (open when train service in operation). The only CAMRA-approved 'Real Ale' bar operates on most steam trains (March-October). Wine and Dine services by prior booking only — the 'White Rose Pullman' and 'West Riding Ltd'

Picnic areas: Keighley Station, Haworth Locomotive Depot, Oxenhope Station

Viewing areas: Keighley (Garsdale) Turntable, Haworth Locomotive Depot

Souvenir shops: Keighley, Haworth and Oxenhope stations; Ingrow Vintage Carriages Museum

Museums: Vintage Carriages Trust's carriage and locomotive museum at Ingrow Railway Centre. Open daily 11.00-16.30

Depots: Carriage and wagon — Oxenhope; Motive power/loco works — Haworth, 'Bahamas Locomotive Society' workshops and museum at Ingrow Railway Centre

Length of line: 4.75 miles

Passenger trains: Early morning local shoppers' services worked by diesel railbus/diesel multiple-unit, otherwise all steam-hauled

Frequent bus service between Haworth station and Haworth village top on Sundays (May-

Locomotives and multiple-units

Name	No	Origin	Class	Type	Built
—	43924	MR	4F	0-6-0	1920
—	41241	LMS	2MT	2-6-2T	1949
—	45212*	LMS	5MT	4-6-0	1935
Bahamas	45596	LMS	'Jubilee'	4-6-0	1935
—	48431	LMS	8F	2-8-0	1944
—	47279	LMS	3F	0-6-0T	1925
—	1054	LNWR	—	0-6-2T	1888
—	30072	SR	USA	0-6-0T	1943
City of Wells	34092	SR	WC	4-6-2	1949
—	80002	BR	4MT	2-6-4T	1952
—	75078	BR	4MT	4-6-0	1956
—	78022	BR	2MT	2-6-0	1953
—	5775	GWR	5700	0-6-0PT	1929
—	52044	L&Y	2F	0-6-0	1887
—	19*	L&Y	Pug	0-4-0ST	1910
—	51218	L&Y	Pug	0-4-0ST	1901
—	752	L&Y	—	0-6-0ST	1881
—	85	TVR	02	0-6-2T	1899
—	5820	USATC	S160	2-8-0	1945
—	90733	MoS	WD	2-8-0	1945
—	68077	LNER	J94	0-6-0ST	1947
—	D226	BR	—	0-6-0DE	1956
—	D2511	BR	—	0-6-0DM	1961
—	D3336	BR	08	0-6-0DE	1954
—	D5209	BR	25/1	Bo-Bo	1963
—	D8031	BR	20	Bo-Bo	1960
—	50928	BR	108	DMBS	1959
—	51565	BR	108	DMC	1959
—	79962	W&M	—	Railbus	1958
—	79964	W&M	—	Railbus	1958

Industrial locomotives

Name	No	Builder	Type	Built
Hamburg	31	H/Clarke (679)	0-6-0T	1903
Nunlow	—	H/Clarke (1704)	0-6-0T	1938
Brussels	118	H/Clarke (1782)	0-6-0ST	1945
Tiny	—	Barclay (2258)	0-4-0ST	1949
Merlin	231	H/Clarke (D761)	0-6-0DM	1951
—	MDHB No 32	Hunslet (2699)	0-6-0DM	1944

*away on loan

Stock

30 coaches including examples of pre-Grouping types; BR Mk 1 stock including the oldest vehicle in existence, part of the prototype batch; a Pullman car, NER and L&Y observation cars

Owners

19, 752 and 51218 the L&YRPS Trust
75078 and 78022 the Standard 4 Preservation Society
Bahamas, Nunlow, Tiny the Bahamas Locomotive Society
1054 the National Trust
52044 the Bowers 957 Trust
34092 the City of Wells Syndicate

September) and Bank Holidays, 11.20-17.20

Period of public operation: Steam-hauled passenger services every weekend and Bank Holiday throughout the year (in December diesel-hauled). Daily from mid-June to early September

Special events: Day out with Thomas — 27/28 March, 18/19 September; Diesel Weekend — 19/20 June; Steam Gala Weekend — 8/9 October.
Steam tours of the line — 15-17, 22-23, 29/30 June, 1 July; Santa Specials — weekends 27

November to 19 December; Mince Pie Specials 26 December-1 January 2005
Facilities for disabled: Wheelchairs accommodated in guard's compartments on trains. Please advise before visit, to the Advance Bookings Officer, c/o Haworth station
Special notes: Accompanied children under 5 years of age free. Children 5-15 and senior citizens at 50% discount. Family ticket available (2 adults + 3 children/senior citizen). Free entry to VCT Museum with rover tickets
Membership details: Membership Secretary c/o above address
Membership journal: *Push & Pull* — quarterly
Marketing name: Worth Valley

Timetable Service

Kent & East Sussex Railway

Kent

Member: HRA, TT

The Kent & East Sussex Railway owes much of its charm to its origin as the world's first light railway. The tightly curved line with steep gradients is typical of those country railways that were developed on shoestring budgets to bring the 'iron horse' to sparsely populated areas. Services operate over 10.5 miles of line from the picturesque town of Tenterden to Bodiam.

Pride of the line's coach fleet is the magnificently restored train of Victorian carriages built between 1860 and 1901.

Company Secretary: Nick Pallant
Headquarters: Tenterden Railway Co Ltd, Tenterden Town Station, Tenterden, Kent TN30 6HE
Telephone: Tenterden (01580) 762943 (24 hour talking timetable); Tenterden (01580) 765155 (office)
Internet address: *Web site:* www.seetb.org.uk/kesr
Main station: Tenterden Town
Other public stations: Rolvenden, Wittersham Road, Northiam, Bodiam
Car parks: Tenterden, Northiam
OS reference:
Tenterden TQ 882336,
Northiam TQ 834266
Access by public transport: Stagecoach No 400 from Ashford (Kent) main line station. Arriva No 12 Maidstone-Headcorn station-Tenterden & Rye
Refreshment facilities: Tenterden Town and Northiam. Also on many trains. Lunch and afternoon teas on many trains (advance booking essential). Picnic areas at Tenterden, Wittersham Road and Northiam
Souvenir shop: Tenterden Town Station
Museum: Colonel Stephens

Locomotives and multiple-units

Name	No	Origin	Class	Type	Built
Bodiam	3	LBSCR	A1X	0-6-0T	1872†
Sutton	32650	LBSCR	A1X	0-6-0T	1876
Knowle	2678	LBSCR	A1X	0-6-0T	1880*
—	753	SECR	P	0-6-0T	1909*
Wainwright	DS238	SR	USA	0-6-0T	1943*
Maunsell	65	SR	USA	0-6-0T	1943*
—	1638	GWR	1600	0-6-0PT	1951
—	20	GWR	AEC	diesel railcar	1940
—	68078	LNER	J94	0-6-0ST	1946
Norwegian	376	NSB	21c	2-6-0	1919*
—	D2023	BR	03	0-6-0DM	1958◊
—	D2024	BR	03	0-6-0DM	1958
—	08108	BR	08	0-6-0DE	1955◊
—	48 (D9504)	BR	14	0-6-0DH	1964◊
—	14029 (D9529)	BR	14	0-6-0DH	1965◊
Ashford	D6570	BR	33	Bo-Bo	1961◊
—	51571	BR	108	DMC	1959*
—	53971	BR	108	DMBS	1959*

48 undergoing overhaul at Nene Valley Railway
†in service summer 2004
◊in use for shunting/engineering trains
48 on loan to Network Rail, Whitemoor
14029 on loan to Victa Railfreight Ltd, Chatham

Industrial locomotives

Name	No	Builder	Type	Built
Marcia	12	Peckett (1631)	0-4-0T	1923
Charwelton	14	M/Wardle (1955)	0-6-0ST	1917
Holman F. Stephens	23	Hunslet (3791)	0-6-0ST	1952†
Rolvenden	24	Hunslet (3800)	0-6-0ST	1953*
Northiam	25	Hunslet (3797)	0-6-0ST	1953*
—	40	BTH	Bo-Bo	1932*
—	42	Hunslet (4208)	0-6-0DM	1948
Titan	—	R/Hornsby (423661)	0-4-0DM	1958

*in passenger traffic
†in service summer 2004

Passenger stock in service

SECR family saloon; LNWR 6-wheel director's saloon; SECR 4-wheel full third; SR Maunsell CK; GER 6-wheel composite; District Railway 4-wheel full first; 2 SR Maunsell brake open 1st Class; SR Maunsell non-descript brake-open; BR Mk 1 RU and 5 other BR Mk 1 coaches; 1926 Pullman Parlour Cars *Barbara* and *Theodora* for 2004

Railway Museum at Tenterden Town
Depot: Rolvenden
Length of line: 10.5 miles
Passenger trains: Tenterden-Bodiam. All Bank Holidays and school holidays. Daily 1 June to 29 September. Most days ring for details, full service in August
Special events: Steaming to Victory — 15/16 May; Day out with Thomas — 19-27 June; Hoppers Weekend — 11/12 September; Day out with Thomas — 18-26 September; various special weekends throughout the year, including diesel days, mixed

Stock
2 ex-SECR 'Birdcage' coaches; 2 ex-LSWR coaches; 1 GER observation car; 2 Pullman cars; 3 ex-SR Maunsell coaches; 3 steam cranes; large interesting collection of freight vehicles, totalling 51 vehicles

trains, etc, see leaflet for details
Facilities for disabled: A special coach for disabled people, 'Petros', is conveyed in many trains (telephone for confirmation of availability), reserved parking at Northiam.
Toilets with disabled access at Tenterden and Northiam, and in 'Petros'
Special notes: The Wealden Belle luxury dining car service operates

on most Saturday evenings April to October and selected Wednesdays in the summer. Roast lunch served most Sundays. Advance booking is essential for these trains. Santa Special services operate on each Saturday and Sunday in December. Advance booking recommended
Membership details: Membership Secretary, c/o above address
Membership journal: *The Tenterden Terrier* — 3 times/year

| Steam Centre | **Kew Bridge Steam Museum** | London |

The museum is housed in a magnificent 19th century Pumping Station and centres around the station's five world famous Cornish Beam Engines, two of which can be seen in steam every weekend and Bank Holiday Mondays. Originally used to pump West London's water supply for more than a century, one of them, the 'Grand Junction 90', is the world's largest working beam engine. In surrounding buildings other large engines also work at weekends, demonstrating more modern steam and diesel pumping machinery.

The Water For Life Gallery reveals the fascinating history of London's water supply from Roman toilet spoons to the massive 'high-tec' London ring main.

Many Victorian waterworks had their own railway. At Kew Bridge this is demonstrated by a short line, operated by the Hampshire Narrow Gauge Railway Society. 1998 saw the return to steam of *Cloister* for the first time in 22 years
Location: 100yd from the north side of Kew Bridge, next to the tall Victorian tower
Operating group: Kew Bridge Engines Trust, Green Dragon Lane, Brentford, Middx TW8 0EN
Telephone: 020 8568 4757 (information line)
Internet address: *Web site:* www.kbsm.org

Industrial locomotives
2ft gauge:

Name	No	Builder	Type	Built
Cloister	—	Hunslet (542)	0-4-0ST	1891
Wendy	1	Bagnall (2091)	0-4-0ST	1919
Alister	2	Lister (44052)	4wDM	1958

Car park: Free on site
Access by public transport: *Rail:* SouthWest Trains, Kew Bridge (from Waterloo via Clapham Junction) and North London Line to Gunnersbury; *Bus:* Nos 65, 237, 267, 391; *Tube:* Gunnersbury (District Line, then 237 or 267 bus), Kew Gardens (District Line, then 391 bus)
Length of line/gauge: About 100yd, 2ft gauge
Public opening: Museum: Daily 11.00-17.00 (except Good Friday and 20 December 2004 to 4 January 2005). Railway: see below
Special events: Exhibition :'Liquid History: photographs of the River Thames' from the National Monuments Record — 11 March to 12 April; Stirling Hot Air Engine Rally — 4 April; Magic of Meccano Show 24*/25 April; Historic Fire Engine Rally — 16 May; Kew Bridge Model Boat Show — 12*/13 June; Seminar: 'Murdoch and other forgotten Engineers' (places limited, pre-booking essential) — 15 July; Exhibition: William

Murdoch — right hand man or frustrated genius — 16 July to 26 September; London Open House Weekend — 18*/19 September; Steam Models Show — 2*/3 October; Live Steam Model Railway Show — 20*/21 November; Brentford Charting Change II — paintings and photographs of the canal era — 3 December to 28 February 2005
Tower Open Days: Escorted tours of the tower and other restricted parts of the Museum will take place at 13.30 on the first Sunday of every month from April to September. Pre-booking essential (adults only).
The railway is scheduled to operate every Sunday March to November, plus Saturdays marked *
On site facilities:
Bookshop/toilets/car park. Refreshments available at weekends only
Facilities for disabled: Access to most of museum, including lower floor. Access via ramps and lift. Large print guide available and guide dogs welcome. Partial

England

wheelchair access. Wheelchair loan service and wheelchair accessible toilet
Special note: Groups of 10 or more can be given guided tours and a 10% discount on admission charges. Special steaming can be arranged and touch tours are available for partially sighted groups. All groups

must be pre-booked.
  Children under 13 must be accompanied by an adult.
  Different admission rates apply to selected special events and tower tours. Please contact the museum for details
Museum contact: Kew Bridge Engines Trust, c/o above address

Railway contact: HNGRS, 44 St Thomas' Avenue, Hayling Island, Hants PO11 0EX
Other attractions: Museum displays a selection of stationary steam engines and associated water supply displays

---

Museum	# Kidderminster Railway Museum	Worcestershire

Established in an 1878 GWR warehouse, the museum houses an enormous collection of railway relics, photographs and documents, with a number of 'hands-on' exhibits.
Contact address: Station Approach, Comberton Hill, Kidderminster, Worcestershire DY10 1QX
General Manager: David Postle
Telephone: Kidderminster (01562) 825316

Internet address:
e-mail: krm@krm.org.uk
Web site: www.krm.org.uk
OS reference: SO 837763
Location: Adjacent to SVR station
Car park: SVR car park
Access by public transport: Kidderminster main line station, Midland Red bus service X92 to Kidderminster
Facilities for disabled: Ramp access for wheelchairs to ground level

Special events: Practical signalling courses using Museum and SVR resources. Filmshows, model railway exhibitions, railway art exhibitions, postcard/photograph fairs,
On site facilities: Souvenirs, refreshments
Public opening: Open on SVR operating days

Timetable Service	# Kirklees Light Railway	West Yorkshire

Member: HRA
Location/headquarters: Clayton West, A636 Wakefield-Denby Dale road
Operating society/organisation: Kirklees Light Railway, Park Mill Way, Clayton West, Nr Huddersfield HD8 9XJ
Telephone: (01484) 865727
Main station: Clayton West
Other station: Cuckoos Nest, Skelmanthorpe, Shelley
Length of line: 4 miles, 15in gauge
Car park: Clayton West — free
Access by public transport: Bus No 235 from Huddersfield & Barnsley; 240 from Huddersfield/Scissett; 484 from Wakefield. Rail to Huddersfield, Wakefield or Denby Dale stations
Refreshment facilities: Clayton West, Visitor Centre and Café
Souvenir shop: Clayton West
On site facilities: Toilets, swings,

Locomotives

Name	No	Builder	Type	Built
Fox	—	Taylor	2-6-2T	1987
Badger	—	Taylor	0-6-4T	1991
Tram Engine	7	Taylor	0-4-0	1995
Jay	—	Taylor	4wD	1992
Hawk	—	Taylor	0-4-4-0*	1998
Owl	—	Taylor	4w-4wT*	2000

*articulated

Rolling stock
2 rakes of six carriages (some heated in winter), 4-wheel tool van, 4-wheel ballast/stone wagon, heavy bogie flat car for rail carrying

half-scale roundabouts, lake. HQ of Barnsley Society of Model Engineers
Facilities for disabled: Yes
Period of public operation: Winter— weekends & most school holidays. Summer — daily from Spring Bank Holiday to end August
Special events: Easter Eggspress —

9-13 April; Day out with Thomas — 12/13 June, 24/25 July; Teddy Bears' Picnic — 7/8 August; Halloween Ghost Trains — 30/31 October (evenings); Santa Specials — 28 November, 4/5, 11/12, 18/19, 23/24 December. Please phone or write for details

Lakeside & Haverthwaite Railway

Member: HRA, TT

Originally this Furness Railway branch line carried passengers and freight from Ulverston to Lakeside but now the only part remaining is the 3.5-mile section from Haverthwaite to the terminus at Lakeside where connections are made with the lakeside steamers which ply the 10-mile length of Windermere

General Manager: M. A. Maher

Headquarters: Lakeside & Haverthwaite Railway Co Ltd, Haverthwaite Station, Nr Ulverston, Cumbria LA12 8AL

Telephone: Newby Bridge (015395) 31594

Main station: Haverthwaite

Other public stations: Intermediate station at Newby Bridge. Terminus at Lakeside

OS reference: SD 349843

Car parks: Haverthwaite, Lakeside

Access by public transport: Lakeside steamers on Windermere call at Lakeside. CMS bus to Haverthwaite

Refreshment facilities: Haverthwaite

Souvenir shop: Haverthwaite

On site facilities: Picnic area at Haverthwaite

Depot: All rolling stock at Haverthwaite

Length of line: 3.5 miles

Passenger trains: Steam-hauled Haverthwaite-Lakeside

Period of public operation: 3 April to 31 October 2004.

Locomotives and multiple-units

Name	No	Origin	Class	Type	Built
—	20	FR	A5	0-4-0	1863
—	42073	LMS	4MT	2-6-4T	1950
—	42085	LMS	4MT	2-6-4T	1951
—	17(AD601)	LMS	—	0-6-0DE	1945
—	5643	GWR	5600	0-6-2T	1925
—	8(D2117)	BR	03	0-6-0DM	1959
—	D2072	BR	03	0-6-0DM	1959
—	20214	BR	20	Bo-Bo	1967
—	D5301	BR	26	Bo-Bo	1958
—	52071	BRCW	110	DMBC	1961
—	52077	BRCW	110	DMBC	1961

Industrial locomotives

Name	No	Builder	Type	Built
Caliban*	1	Peckett (1925)	0-4-0ST	1937
Rachel	9	M/Rail (2098)	4wDM	1924
Repulse	11	Hunslet (3698)	0-6-0ST	1950
Princess	14	Bagnall (2682)	0-6-0ST	1942
Alexandra	12	Barclay (929)	0-4-0ST	1902
David	13	Barclay (2333)	0-4-0ST	1953
Cumbria	10	Hunslet (3794)	0-6-0ST	1953
Fluff	16	Hunslet/Fowler	0-4-0DM	1937
—	20	Jones crane	0-4-0DM	1952
Sir James	21	Barclay (1550)	0-6-0F	1917

*under restoration at Steamtown, Carnforth

Stock

10 ex-BR Mk 1 coaches; 1 ex-LNER BG; 1 ex-BR Mk 1 miniature buffet coach, Royal saloon No 5 (built GER, Stratford 1898); selection of freight vehicles

Special events: Santa Specials (advance booking essential) please contact for details

Special notes: Combined railway/lake steamer tickets available, from the station at Haverthwaite and lake steamer piers at Bowness and Ambleside. Lake steamers are operated by Windermere Lake Cruises Ltd

Membership journal: *The Iron Horse* — quarterly

Lappa Valley Railway

Member: TT

Location/headquarters: Benny Halt, St Newlyn East, Nr Newquay, Cornwall TR8 5HZ

Telephone: 01872 510317

Internet address: *web site:* www.lappavalley.co.uk

General Manager: Miss Amanda Booth

Main station: Benny Halt

Other station: East Wheal Rose, Newlyn Downs Halt

Car park: Benny Halt

Access by public transport: Bus service, Newquay to Truro and return. Western National and The Cornishman coaches to St Newlyn East. Signposted, half-mile walk from bus stop to railway. No direct bus service

Refreshment facilities: Café at East Wheal Rose serving hot and cold food, snacks, hot and cold drinks; licensed

Souvenir shop: East Wheal Rose and Benny Halt

On site facilities: 15in, 10.25in and

7.25in gauge railways. Canoes, paddle boats, crazy golf, pedal cars, electric motorbikes, children's play area, brick path maze, listed engine house, walks and a video
Depot: Benny Halt
Facilities for disabled: Yes
Public opening: Easter to end of October, usually daily but ring for early and late season opening days
Special notes: Entry by one all-in price, except for motorbikes.
  Family tickets and reduced afternoon saver fares are available all days. Under 3s free

Locomotives

Name	No	Builder	Type	Built
Muffin	2	Berwyn	0-6-0	1967
		rebuilt Tambling		1991
Zebedee	1	S/Lamb	0-6-4T	1974
		rebuilt Tambling		1990
Gladiator	3	Minirail	4w-4wDH	c1960
Pooh	4	Lister (20698)	4wDM	1942

(all 15in gauge)

Rolling stock
15in gauge — 10 passenger coaches
10.25in gauge — 4 passenger coaches, 2 wagons
7.25in gauge — 1 Mardyke APT set

Timetable Service	# Launceston Steam Railway	Cornwall

Member: HRA, TT
The railway runs through the beautiful Kensey Valley on a track gauge of 1ft 11.5in, following the trackbed of the old North Cornwall line. The locomotives formerly worked on the Dinorwic and Penrhyn railways in North Wales. Launceston station contains a museum of vintage cars and motorcycles and a collection of stationary steam engines which are demonstrated at work. There are catering, gift shop and bookshop facilities. At the far end of the line there are pleasant riverside walks and a shaded picnic area, adjacent to Newmills Farm Park (a popular separate attraction). The covered rolling stock ensures an enjoyable visit whatever the weather
Location: Newport Industrial Estate, Launceston, Cornwall
OS reference: SX 328850
Operating society/organisation: The Spice Settlement Trust Co Ltd, trading as the Launceston Steam Railway, Newport, Launceston PL15 8DA
Telephone: (01566) 775665
Stations: Launceston-Hunts Crossing-New Mills
Car park: Newport Industrial Estate, Launceston
Length of line: 2.5 miles
Gauge: 1ft 11.5in

Industrial locomotives

Name	No	Builder	Type	Built
Lilian	—	Hunslet (317)	0-4-0ST	1883
Velinheli	—	Hunslet (409)	0-4-0ST	1886
Covertcoat	—	Hunslet (679)	0-4-0ST	1898
Sybil	—	Bagnall (1760)	0-4-0ST	1906
Dorothea	—	Hunslet (763)	0-4-0ST	1901
—	—	M/Rail (5646)	4wDM	1933
—	—	M/Rail (9546)	4wDM	1950

Locomotive notes: Only the three Hunslet locomotives (*Lilian, Velinheli, Covertcoat)* are expected to be in use during 2004.

Stock
1 electric inspection trolley; 4 bogie carriages (2 open, 2 closed)

Access by public transport: Main line Gunnislake 13 miles, Plymouth or Bodmin 25 miles
On site facilities: Buffet, transport museum, workshop tours, gift and bookshop, all situated at Launceston
Period of public operation: Good Friday — for 8 days inclusive; Sundays and Tuesdays from Easter to Spring Bank Holiday; Spring Bank Holiday — for 6 days; June — Sundays to Wednesdays inclusive; July-September — daily except Saturdays; October — half term week except Saturday
Public opening: Trains run from 11.00-16.30. Departures about every 40min and more frequently if required. Unlimited riding on date of issue of ticket
Family ticket: Available, 2 adults and up to 4 children
Free travel: Children under three years old
Senior citizens: Discounted tickets
Groups: Discounted tickets
Journey time: Return 30min
Facilities for disabled: Easy access to all areas except bookshop and motorcycle museum. No toilet facilities for disabled. However, public toilets are reasonably accessible
Special events: Double-headed trains on Wednesdays in July and August (whenever possible). Demonstration freight trains (contact for details)

Member: HRA

The Lavender Line is centred around a typical country station, which, somewhat untypically, is in the village it was built to serve. The image portrayed is of the transition steam-diesel era of the 1950s/1960s on the Southern Region of British Railways. The museum is being converted into a OO scale model railway; this will be known as Museum/Model Railway.

Location: Isfield Station, Isfield, Nr Uckfield, East Sussex TN22 5XB. Isfield village is off the A26 between Lewes and Uckfield

OS reference: TQ 452171

Operating society/organisation: The Lavender Line Preservation Society

Telephone/Fax:
Information line: 0891 800645
Business/fax: 01825 750515 (24hr answerphone when not manned)

Internet address: *Web site:* www.lavender-line.co.uk

Car park: On site, free to patrons

Access by public transport: Lewes station and 729 bus (seven days a week). Uckfield station and 729 bus. Tel: South Coast Buses before travelling on 01424 433711 (Mon-Sat 09.00-17.00) for bus details. Tel: National Rail Enquiries on 0345 484950 (24hrs/7 days a week)

On site facilities: 'Cinders' buffet/ restaurant, gift shop, goods shed museum, picnic area, access to signalbox. Children's parties arranged on operating days. Family area. Private functions, weddings and parties etc catered for

Length of line: 1 mile

Public opening: Open Sundays all year, Bank Holidays, weekends in June, July and August.Wednesdays and Thursdays in August. Site open from 10.00-17.00 trains from 11.00
Please note that the Isfield site is not normally open for viewing outside of operating dates.

Facilities for disabled: Access to most facilities on site. No wheel-chair access to toilets at present. Wheelchair access to most of site except Museum/Model Railway, signalbox and trains. A ramp is available for partially disabled access to the trains

Special events: To be arranged, please ring for details. Santa Specials November/December. Ticket price is valid for unlimited rides on day of issue; however, on special event days entry prices, and conditions, may vary. On Vintage Weekend special prices apply (no site entrance only tickets)

Locomotives and multiple-unit

Name	No	Origin	Class	Type	Built
—	D2868	BR	02	0-4-0DH	1961
—	03018	BR	03	0-6-0DM	1958
—	03020	BR	03	0-6-0DM	1958
—	03037	BR	03	0-6-0DM	1959
—	03197	BR	03	0-6-0DM	1961
Alfie	D2272	BR	04	0-6-0DM	1960
Judith	D2324	BR	04	0-6-0DM	1961
—	D2587	BR	05	0-6-0DM	1959
—	07012	BR	07	0-6-0DE	1962
—	69333	BR	422 / 4BIG	TRBS	1965

Industrial locomotives

Name	No	Builder	Type	Built
Annie	945	Barclay (945)	0-4-0ST	1904
Blackie	68012	Hunslet (3193)	0-6-0ST	1944
Austin No 1	—†	Kitson (5459)	0-6-0ST	1932
—	15	Barclay	0-4-0DM	1945
—	16	Barclay	0-4-0DM	1945
—	ND 3827	Hibberd (SC2196/3857)	0-4-0DM	1957
—	ND 10022	Hibberd (SC3986/3968)	0-4-0DM	1960
—	—*	Lister (41803)	4wDM	1955
—	—	Planet (3865)	4wDM	1965

*2ft gauge
†on hire from Llangollen Railway for 2004

Stock

3 ex-BR Mk 1 coaches.

A variety of BR and pre-Nationalisation wagons are in service in a vintage goods train, or are under restoration. A GWR Toad brake van is used on most passenger trains, allowing visitors to ride on the veranda or inside by the stove. The engineering vehicle fleet includes examples from London Transport and pre-Grouping companies

Austin No 1 provides the motive power at Isfield. LL

Location: The Leeds Industrial Museum, Armley Mills, Canal Road, Leeds LS12 2QF
OS reference: SE 275342
Operating society/organisation: Leeds City Council, Department of Learning & Leisure, The Town Hall, Headrow, Leeds LS12 2QF
Curator of Engineering: N. Dowlan
Telephone: (0113) 263 7861
Car park: Cark park adjacent to the Museum
Access by public transport: Nos 5A, 14, 66 and 67 from City Square, Leeds (outside the railway station)
Public opening: April-September: Tuesdays-Saturdays 10.00-17.00, Sundays 13.00-17.00. October-March: Tuesdays-Saturdays 10.00-17.00, Sundays 13.00-17.00. Closed Mondays (except Bank Holidays). NB: last admission 16.00 on all days
Special events: Plant in Steam — Tuesdays 24 July-11 September
On site facilities: Museum shop, refreshments (vending machines), picnic area
Special notes: Facilities for the disabled (toilets etc), lifts. Museum can be viewed by visitors in wheelchairs (most areas are accessible)
Details of locomotive and rolling stock: Locomotive collection includes steam, diesel, mines locomotives and a narrow gauge railway and engines

Industrial locomotives

Name	No	Builder	Type	Built
1ft 6in gauge				
Jack	—	Hunslet 684)	0-4-0WT	1898
Coffin	—*	G/Bat (1326)	0-4-0BE	1933
2ft gauge				
Barber	—	T/Green (441)	0-6-2ST	1908
Cheetal	—	Fowler (15991)	0-6-0WT	1923
Simplex	—	M/Rail (1369	4wPM	1918
Hudson Fordson	—	Hudson (36863)	4wDM	1928
Layer	—*	Fowler (21294)	4wDM	1936
Hudson Hunslet	—	Hunslet (2959)	4wDM	1944
Resin	—	Hunslet (2008)	0-4-0DM	1939
Nacob	—*	Hunslet (5340)	0-4-0DM	1957
Sharlston	—†	H/Clarke (1164)	0-4-0DM	1959
Demtox	—†*	Hunslet (6048)	0-4-0DM	1961
2ft 1in gauge				
Fricl	—*	Hunslet (4019)	0-4-0DM	1948
Pitpo	—*	Hunslet	0-4-0	1955
Calverton	—*	H/Clarke (1368)	0-4-0DM	1965
2ft 6in gauge				
Junin	—	H/Clarke (D557)	2-6-2DM	1930
Fimyn	—†	Hunslet (3411)	0-4-0DM	1947
2ft 8in gauge				
Ficol	—*	Hunslet (3200)	0-4-0DM	1945
2ft 11in gauge				
Lurch	—	H/Clarke (D571)	4wDM	1932
3ft gauge				
Lord Granby	—*	H/Clarke (633)	0-4-0ST	1902
Cement	—*	Fowler (20685)	2-4-0DM	1935
Lofti	—*	Hunslet (4057)	0-6-0DM	1953
3ft 6in gauge				
Pioneer	—	H/Clarke (D634)	0-6-0DM	1946
Festival of Britain	—*	H/Clarke (D733)	0-6-0DM	1951
Standard gauge				
Hodbarrow	—*	Hunslet (299)	0-4-0ST	1882
Aldwyth	—	M/Wardle (865)	0-6-0ST	1882
Capper	—	Fowler (22060)	0-4-0DM	1938
Fort William	—*	Fowler (22893)	0-4-0DM	1940
Trecwn	—	Hunslet (2390)	0-4-0DM	1941
Elizabeth	—	H/Clarke (1888)	0-4-0ST	1958
Southam No 2	—*	H/Clarke (D625)	0-4-0DM	1942
Luton	—	G/Bat (1210)	0-4-0BE	1930
Smithy Wood	—*	G/Bat (2543)	0-4-0WE	1955

Notes
*not currently on public display
†on loan to Red Rose Steam Society/Astley Green Colliery Museum
Simplex is on loan to Moseley Industrial Railway Museum
Barber is on loan to the South Tynedale Railway Trust from February 2004

Leighton Buzzard Railway

Member: HRA, TT

The LBR enables visitors to take a 65min journey into the vanished world of the English light railway. Sharp curves and steep gradients make the locomotives work hard and it is unique with its roadside running. The LBR possesses one of the largest collection of narrow gauge locomotives in Britain together with a varied selection of coaches and wagons — an important part of the national railway heritage. Many items are on permanent display, and some can be seen in action at special events

General Manager: J. Horsley

Headquarters: Leighton Buzzard Railway, Page's Park Station, Billington Road, Leighton Buzzard, Bedfordshire LU7 4TN

OS reference: Page's Park SP 928242

Telephone: (01525) 373888, 24hr answerphone with service and event details

Fax: 01525 377814

Internet address: *e-mail:* info@buzzrail.co.uk
Web site: www.buzzrail.co.uk

Main station: Page's Park. The station is on the A4146 to the south of Leighton Buzzard, near its junction with the A505

Other public stations: Stonehenge Works

Car park: Page's Park, free

Access by public transport: Leighton Buzzard main line station, Silverlink County services from London (Euston), Watford, Hemel Hempstead, Milton Keynes, Northampton, and stations to Birmingham (Tel: 08457 484950). Nearest bus stops at Stanbridge Road (10min walk) and Leighton Buzzard town centre (25min walk). (Tel: 01234 228337 for details)

Refreshment facilities: Dobbers buffet at Page's Park for hot & cold snacks, drinks and ice creams. Refreshments also at Stonehenge Works on busy days

Souvenir shop: Page's Park

Depots: Page's Park and Stonehenge Works

Length of line: 2.85 miles, 2ft gauge

Locomotives

Name	No	Builder	Type	Built
—	740	O&K (2343)	0-6-0T	1907
—	—	O&K (2544)	0-4-0WT	1907
—	778	Baldwin (44656)	4-6-0T	1917
—	—	Freudenstein (73)	0-4-0WT	1901
Sezela No 4	—	Avonside (1738)	0-4-0T	1915
Peter Pan	114	K/Stuart (4256)	0-4-0ST	1922
Chaloner	1	de Winton	0-4-0VBT	1877
Bluebell	1	Hibberd (2631)	4wDM	1938
Pixie	2	K/Stuart (4260)	0-4-0ST	1922
Rishra	3	Baguley (2007)	0-4-0T	1921
Doll	4	Barclay (1641)	0-6-0T	1919
Elf	5	O&K (12740)	0-6-0WT	1936
Falcon	7	O&K (8986)	4wDM	1938
—	8	Ruston (217999)	4wDM	1943
Madge	9	O&K (7600)	4wDM	1934
Haydn Taylor	10	M/Rail (7956)	4wDM	1945
P. C. Allen	11	O&K (5834)	0-4-0WT	1912
—	12	M/Rail (6012)	4wPM	1930
Arkle	13	M/Rail (7108)	4wDM	1937
—	14	Hunslet (3646)	4wDM	1946
—	15	Hibberd (2514)	4wDM	1941
—	16	Lister (11221)	4wDM	1939
Damredub	17	M/Rail (7036)	4wDM	1936
Feanor	18	M/Rail (11003)	4wDM	1956
—	19	M/Rail (11298)	4wDM	1965
—	20	M/Rail (60s317)	4wDM	1966
Festoon	21	M/Rail (4570)	4wPM	1929
—	22	under construction	4wDM	—
—	23	Ruston (164346)	4wDM	1932
—	25	M/Rail (7214)	4wDM	1938
—	24	M/Rail (11297)	4wDM	1965
Yimkin	26	Ruston (203026)	4wDM	1941
—	27	Ruston (408430)	4wDM	1957
RAF Stanbridge	28	Ruston (200516)	4wDM	1940
Creepy	29	Hunslet (6008)	4wDM	1963
—	30	M/Rail (8695)	4wDM	1941
—	31	Lister (4228)	4wPM	1931
—	32	Ruston (172892)	4wDM	1934
—	33	Hibberd (3582)	4wDM	1954
Red Rum	34	M/Rail (7105)	4wDM	1936
Binky	35	Hunslet (6619)	0-4-0DM	1966
Caravan	36	M/Rail (7129)	4wDM	1938
—	37	Ruston (172901)	4wDM	1934
Harry Barnet	38	Lister (37170)	4wDM	1951
T. W. Lewis	39	Ruston (375316)	4wDM	1954
Trent	40	Ruston (283507)	4wDM	1949
—	41	Hunslet (2536)	4wDM	1941
Sarah	42	Ruston (223692)	4wDM	1944
—	43	M/Rail (10409)	4wDM	1954
—	44	M/Rail (7933)	4wDM	1941
—	45	M/Rail (21615)	4wDM	1957
—	46	Ruston (209430)	4wDM	1942
—	47	Hudson (38384)	4wDM	1930
MacNamara	48	Hunslet (4351)	4wDM	1952
—	49	Hibberd (2586)	4wDM	1941
—	50	Hibberd (1568)	4wPM	1927

Journey time: Single 25min, return 70min
Passenger trains: Page's Park-Stonehenge Works
  Group discounts for pre-booked parties of 10 or more people. Packages such as Birthday Breaks, Schools trains and Sunset Specials available, plus train hire
Period of public operation: Sundays 14 March-31 October; Mondays 12 April, 3, 31 May, 30 August; Tuesdays 3-31 August; Wednesdays 14 April, 2 June-1 September, 27 October; Thursdays 3 June, 5 August-2 September; Fridays 18 April; Saturdays 10 April, 1, 29 May, 5 June, 7 August-11 September
Special events: Mothering Sunday — 21 March; Easter Fun — 9-12 April; Teddy Bears' Holiday — 2 May; Father's Day — 20 June; Vintage Vehicles Rally — 27 June; Model Railway Mania — 4 July;

Name	No	Builder	Type	Built
Beaudesert	80	A/Keef (59R)	4wDM	1999
—	3090	M/Rail (1369)	4wPM	1918
—	3098	M/Rail (1377)	4wPM	1918

Pixie on loan to Amerton Railway in 2004

Stock
10 coaches and a wide selection of wagons

Fancy Dress Day - 8 August; Steam Up Weekend — 11/12 September; Steam Glow — 2 October; Halloween Haunting — 26 October
Working Heritage Attractions:
Industry Trains Display — 11 April, 31 May, 20 June, 8 August, 12 September
Sand Quarry — 12 April, 30 May, 27 June, 11 September;
Freight Train — 10 April, 29 May, 28 August
Facilities for disabled: Priority parking at Page's Park. Ramp

access to all facilities including dedicated toilet at Page's Park. Wheelchairs are conveyed in a specially adapted coach. Advance notice appreciated. Leaflets available in large print on request
Membership details: The line is operated by unpaid volunteers. Membership secretary, c/o above address
Membership journal: *Chaloner* — quarterly
Marketing name: The Leighton Buzzard Slow Train

Lincolnshire Wolds Railway

Timetable service | Lincolnshire

Members: HRA
Headquarters: The Railway Station, Ludborough, Grimsby, NE Lincs DN36 5QS
Telephone: 01507 363881
Internet address: *Web site:* www.lincolnshirewoldsrailway.co.uk
Contacts: David Ambler / Frank Street
Main station: Ludborough
OS reference:
Car park: Opposite station site
Access by public transport: No access by rail, very limited Grimsby-Louth bus service
Refreshment facilities: Light refreshments available in buffet car in bay platform on diesel and steam days
Souvenir shop: On site
Museum: On site
Depot: On site
Length of line: 1,200yd at present
Period of public operation: Site open for static viewing all weekends except Christmas. April to September 09.00-16.00, October to March 09.00-15.00. First train leaves at 11.00 on following dates
Special events: Steam dates for

Locomotives and multiple-units

Name	No	Origin	Class	Type	Built
—	D3167	BR	08	0-6-0DE	1955
—	97650	BR	—	0-6-0DE	1953

Industrial locomotives

Name	No	Builder	Type	Built
Lion	—	Peckett (1657)	0-4-0ST	1914
—	—	Peckett (1567)	0-6-0ST	1920
Moorbarrow	47	RSH (7849)	0-6-0ST	1955
M. F. P. No 1	—	Fowler (4210131)	0-4-0DM	1957
M. O. P. No 8	—	Fowler (4210145)	0-4-0DM	1958
Tioxide No 6	6	R/Hornsby (375713)	0-4-0DM	1954
—	4	R/Hornsby (414303)	0-4-0DM	1957
—	7	R/Hornsby (421418)	0-4-0DM	1958

Stock
6 ex-BR Mk 2 coaches, several wagons

Owner
D3167 on loan from Lincoln City Council

2004 are: Mother's Day — 21 March; Easter Specials 11 April; 2, 16, 30 May; Father's Day — 20 June, 4, 18 July; 1, 15, 29 August; 1940s Weekend 11/12 September; 3, 17 October; Halloween — 31 October; Santa Specials — 12, 19

December (pre-booking required)
Diesel trains: 7 November
Facilities for disabled: Full facilities should be available on site for 2004
Membership journal: *On the Line* — 4 times/year

Museum | London's Transport Museum | London

Member: HRA, TT

Spectacular displays of buses, trams and trains reveal a fascinating story of travel, people and the history of London itself. Special exhibitions, family activities, actors, videos and working models all bring the story to life.

Only a small proportion of the museum's collection is on display. The remaining collection is housed at The Depot, a custom-built collections store located at Acton Town. The Depot has regular open days and guided tours. Please call or visit web site for details

Location: Covent Garden, London WC2E 7BB

OS reference: TQ 303809

Operating society/organisation: Transport for London

Telephone: 020 7379 6344. (24hr recorded 020 7567 7299)

Internet address:

Web site: www.ltmuseum.co.uk

Access by public transport: Underground to Covent Garden, Leicester Square or Charing Cross. Buses to Strand/Aldwych

On site facilities: Museum shop, lecture theatre, photo and research libraries (by appointment), resource desk and learning centre

Public opening: Daily 10.00-18.00 (except Fridays 11.00-18.00) (last admissions 17.15). Closed 24-26

Locomotives

Name	No	Origin	Class	Type	Built
—	23	Met Rly	A	4-4-0T	1866
John Hampden	5	Met Rly		Bo-Bo	1922

Industrial locomotives

Origin	Builder	Type	Built
Wotton Tramway	A/Porter (807)	0-4-0TG	1872

Electric stock

4248 District Rly Q23 stock driving motor coach 1923
11182 LPTB 1938 stock driving motor coach
400 Met Rly bogie stock coach 1899
30 City & South London Rly 'Padded Cell' coach 1890
Great Northern Piccadilly & Brompton Railway 'Gate stock' car 1906 (sectioned)

Stock

1 Met Rly milk van; 3 electric trams; 3 horse buses; 7 motorbuses; 1 trolleybus; 1 horse tram; 1 petrol-electric bus chassis

December. Reduced admission prices for students, senior citizens, registered disabled, UB40 holders and pre-booked parties. Children under 16 free.

Facilities for disabled: Disabled toilets available, wheelchair access to all displays. Reduced admission for registered disabled visitors and person accompanying them. Please advise in advance if a party of disabled visitors would like to visit

Special notes: Visitors can put themselves in the driving seat of a bus and a tube simulator; there are also 'hands-on' demonstrations of signals and points. In addition to the vehicles and rolling stock there are models, signs, posters, photographs, audio-visual displays. The museum runs a full programme of events and activities in addition to temporary exhibitions on a variety of topics

Membership details: Details from the Friends of London's Transport Museum who provide volunteer guides and assist with restoration work

Steam Centre | Lynton & Barnstaple Railway | Devon

Member: HRA

Location/headquarters: Lynton & Barnstaple Railway, Woody Bay Station, Martinhoe Cross, Parracombe, Devon EX31 4RA

Telephone: 01598 763487

Internet address: *web site:* www.lynton-barnstaple-railway.org

Chairman L&BR Co: Mike Buse

Chairman L&BR Trust: Roger Ladbury

Main station:
Woody Bay (OS ref: SS684464)

Industrial locomotives

Name	No	Builder	Type	Built
Emmet	—	Haydock	0-4-0T	—
Pilton	—	Drewry	0-6-0DM	—
Snapper	—	R/Hornsby (283871)	4wDM	1950
Titch	—	M/Rail (8729)	4wDM	1941

Other station:
Chelfham (OS ref: SS610357)

Car park: Woody Bay station only

Access by public transport: First Bus service 300 (Taunton-Minehead-Ilfracombe-Barnstaple), 309 and 310 (both Barnstaple-Lynton) all stop at Woody Bay station; the 310 largely follows the original route of the railway and

also stops at Chelfham
Length of line: currently 0.25 mile, 1ft 11.5in gauge
On site facilities: Light refreshments and souvenirs are available at Woody Bay station
Passenger services: Weekends and mid-week April-October
Facilities for disabled: Toilets and access to refreshments/shop
Membership details: Membership Secretary, Barry Marshall, 19 Hazel Coppice, Hook, Hampshire RG27 9RH
(*e-mail:* barry@barrymarshall. freeserve.co.uk
Membership journal: *Lynton & Barnstaple Railway Magazine* — three times a year
Special note: The railway also operates the 1ft 11.5in gauge Lynbarn Railway at the Milky Way adventure park near Clovelly, North Devon

Emmet stands alongside the restored Woody Bay station. *L&BR*

Mangapps Farm Railway Museum

Steam Centre | Essex

Member: HRA

Mangapps re-creates the atmosphere of a rural light railway. Featuring a large museum collection, strong in items of East Anglian interest, railway signalling and goods rolling stock. Other features include original station buildings from Mid-Suffolk Light, Great Eastern and Midland & Great Northern Railways.

Superintendent of the Line: John Jolly
Commercial Manager: June Jolly
Location: Mangapps Farm Railway Museum, Southminster Road, Burnham-on-Crouch, Essex CM0 8QQ. (Entrance on B1021, 1 mile north of Burnham)
Telephone: (01621) 784898
Fax: (01621) 783833
Internet address: *Web site:* www.mangapps.co.uk
Access by public transport: Burnham station approx 1 mile
On site facilities: Station, car park, souvenir shop, toilets, amenity and picnic areas
Refreshment facilities: teas and light refreshments
Length of line: Three-quarter-mile
Public opening: Weekends & Bank Holidays all year (except

Locomotives and multiple-units

Name	No	Origin	Class	Type	Built
—	D2089	BR	03	0-6-0DM	1960
—	03399	BR	03	0-6-0DM	1961
—	D2325	BR	04	0-6-0DM	1961
—	11104	BR	04	0-6-0DM	1953
—	54287	BR	121	DTS	1960
—	59664	BR	115	TCL	1960
—	22624	LT	R38	DMS	1938

Industrial locomotives

Name	No	Builder	Type	Built
Minnie	—	F/Walker (358)	0-6-0ST	1878
Brookfield	—	Bagnall (2613)	0-6-0PT	1940
—	47	Barclay (2157)	0-4-0ST	1943
Empress	—	Bagnall (3061)	0-6-0ST	1954
Hastings	—	Hunslet (469)	0-6-0ST	1888
Elland	No 1	H/Clarke (D1153)	0-4-0DM	1959
—	—	S/Henshaw (7502)	4wDM	1966

Rolling stock

LNER Gresley and BR Mk1 coaching stock, extensive stock of goods wagons. Lynton & Barnstaple Railway (2ft gauge) coach No 7 (being rebuilt)

25/26 December, and daily during Easter and summer school holidays. Closed 2-31 January. Steam trains operate every Sunday in August, Bank Holiday Sunday and Mondays and special event days. Diesel trains run on all other days

Opening times: 13.00-17.30 diesel days; 11.30-17.30 steam days
Special events: Day out with Thomas; Santa Specials — during December; Steam Special — 1 January 2004

75

England

Mid-Hants Railway

Member: HRA

Originally built as the Winchester to Alton link, the Mid-Hants Railway became known as the Watercress Line through regularly carrying this local produce to London markets. Now restored, the line runs from its main line connection at Alton through rolling countryside to its terminus at Alresford. Large and powerful locomotives work impressively over the steeply inclined route, known to railwaymen as 'the Alps'. No 41312 entered service early 1999. No 34016 returned to service in summer 2003. Nos 34016 and 73096 are available for use on the main line

Headquarters: Mid-Hants Railway plc, Alresford Station, Alresford, Hants SO24 9JG

Telephone: 01962 733810

Fax: 01962 735448

Talking timetable: 01962 734866

Internet address: *Web site:* www.watercressline.co.uk

Main station: Alresford

Other public stations: Ropley, Medstead & Four Marks, Alton

OS reference: Alresford SU 588325, Ropley SU 629324

Car park: Alresford, pay & display (free Sundays & Bank Holidays). Alton station pay & display

Access by public transport: *SouthWest Train services* — just over 1hr from London. Through ticketing arrangements available from Waterloo and all main line stations. Alternatively, travel to Winchester station and catch a bus from nearby City Road.

Bus services – operated by Stagecoach 0870 608 2608

Refreshment facilities: Buffet service on most trains; 'West Country' buffet at Alresford; picnic/barbecue area at Ropley; tea/coffee available at Alton when information office open

Catering facilities: The 'Countryman' pre-booked Sunday lunch trains, Christmas specials, and some evening trains. The 'Watercress Belle' operates on certain Saturday evenings April-

Locomotives

Name	No	Origin	Class	Type	Built
—	30499	LSWR	S15	4-6-0	1920
—	30506	LSWR	S15	4-6-0	1920
Harry A. Frith	E828	SR	S15	4-6-0	1923
—*	31625	SR	U	2-6-0	1929
—	31806	SR	U	2-6-0	1926
—	31874	SR	N	2-6-0	1925
Bodmin	34016	SR	WC	4-6-2	1945
249 Squadron	34073	SR	BB	4-6-2	1948
Swanage	34105	SR	WC	4-6-2	1950
Canadian Pacific	35005	SR	MN	4-6-2	1945
—	41312	LMS	2MT	2-6-2T	1952
—	45379	LMS	5MT	4-6-0	1937
Bittern	60019	LNER	A4	4-6-2	1937
—	73096	BR	5MT	4-6-0	1956
—	76017	BR	4MT	2-6-0	1954
—	D3358	BR	08	0-6-0DE	1957
—	12049	BR	11	0-6-0DE	1948
—	D5353	BR	27	Bo-Bo	1961
Captain Bill Smith RNR	D6525	BR	33	Bo-Bo	1960
—	D6593	BR	33	Bo-Bo	1962
—	73104	BR	73	Bo-Bo	1965
—	73139	BR	73	Bo-Bo	1966
—	45132	BR	45	1Co-Co1	1961
—	51363	BR	117	DMBS	1959
—	51405	BR	117	DMS	1959

*currently running as No 5 *James*

Industrial locomotives

Name	No	Builder	Type	Built
—	4	Fowler (22889)	0-4-0DM	1939
Thomas	1	Hunslet (3781)	0-6-0T	1954
Douglas	10	Hunslet (2890)	0-6-0	1943

Stock

26 ex-BR Mk 1 coaches; 24 ex-BR Mk 2 coaches (2 used for accommodation); 4 ex-SR coaches; 1 ex-LSWR coach; 1 ex-LMS coach; 3 steam cranes; Numerous goods vehicles

Owners

30499 and 30506 the Urie Locomotive Society
E828 the Eastleigh Preservation Society
34105 the 34105 Light Pacific Group
35005 Bryherley Ltd
76017 the Standard 4 Locomotive Group
12049 Day Aggregates
73104 and 73139 Fragonset Railways

October. Early booking is essential, please telephone to confirm seat availability for both trains. Real Ale trains run on certain special events and Saturday evenings featuring beers from local breweries and light snacks

Souvenir shops: Alresford, Alton and Ropley

On site facilities: Picnic area, children's play area and viewing facilities at Ropley. Visitor centre at Alresford

Depot: Ropley. Locomotive yard open on operating days 10.30-16.30

Length of line: 10 miles

Passenger trains: Phone Talking Timetable (01962 734866), or visit web site to confirm details. Weekends February to October; various midweek dates May to September (inc), school half terms in February and October. Santa Specials in December (bookings commence October)

Journey time: Round trip 1hr 40min max
Special events: Day out with Thomas — 9-18 April and 7-15 August inclusive; Diesel Weekend — 21-23 May; Steam Gala — 17-19 September; War on the Line — 19/20 June; Bus Rally — 18 July; Santa Specials — December

Facilities for disabled: Toilets at Ropley and the new visitor centre at Alresford station. Passengers in fixed wheelchairs can be carried in the brake compartment on most trains. Ramps are provided to ease entry to trains. No facilities at Alton
Membership details: Membership Secretary, c/o above address

Timetable Service	Mid-Norfolk Railway	Norfolk

Member: HRA

A scheme to preserve part of the former Great Eastern line from Wymondham to Wells-next-the-Sea. The section from Wymondham to Dereham has been purchased and opened for passenger and freight traffic since May 1999. Clearance work is now under way on the Dereham-North Elmham section. The Mid-Norfolk Railway Preservation Trust also operates County School station as a tea room and visitor centre during the summer months

Headquarters: The Railway Station, Station Road, Dereham, Norfolk NR19 1DF
Main station: Dereham
Telephone: (01362) 690633 (answerphone)
Talking timetable: 01362 851723
Fax: 01362 698487
Internet address:
Web site: www.mnr.org.uk
e-mail: info@mnr.org.uk
Car park: At Dereham
Museum: Small relics museum at Dereham
Souvenir shop: Dereham
Refreshment facilities: Railway Buffet at Dereham (all year) and tea room at County School station (summer only)
Access by public transport: Bus from Norwich and King's Lynn. Anglia Railways and Central Trains to Wymondham
Period of public operation:
Regular trains from Dereham to Wymondham operate most of the year. Occasional working freight trains
Special events: Diesel Enthusiasts' Weekend — 20/21 March; Easter Bunnies' Special — 11/12 April;

Locomotives and multiple-units

Name	No	Origin	Class	Type	Built
—	D8069	BR	20	Bo-Bo	1961
—	31235	BR	31	A1A-A1A	1960
—	31530	BR	31	A1A-A1A	1961
—	31538	BR	31	A1A-A1A	1959
Aldeburgh Festival	47596	BR	47	Co-Co	1966
Ramillies	50019	BR	50	Co-Co	1968
—†	51073	Gloucester	119	DMBC	1958
—	51360	BR	117	DMBS	1959
—†	51386	P/Steel	117	DMS	1960
—	51226	M/Cam	101	DMBS	1958
Matthew Smith	51434	M/Cam	101	MBS	1958
—	51499	M/Cam	101	DMBS	1959
—	51503	M/Cam	101	DMC	1959
—	51572	BR	108	DMC(L)	1959
—	56224	BR	108	DTC(L)	1959
—	55006	Gloucester	122	DMBS	1958
—	55009	Gloucester	122	DMBS	1958
—	59117	M/Cam	101	TC	1958
—†	59575	M/Cam	111	TRBSL(L)	1957
—	56301*	Gloucester	100	DTC	1957
—	55508	BR	141	DMS	1983
—	55528	BR	141	DMS(L)	1983
—	68004	BR	MLV / 419	DMVL	1959

*in use as static shop and tea room at County School station
†may not be on site for all of 2004

Industrial locomotives

Name	No	Builder	Type	Built
—§	GET 2	Bagnall (8368)	0-4-0DM	1962
—§	GET 5	Drewry (2566)	0-4-0DM	1955
—§	GET 7	B/Drewry (3733)	4wDE	1977
—§	GET 8	R/Royce (10272)	0-6-0DM	1967
—§	GET 9	R/Hornsby (512842)	0-4-0DE	1965
—§	11103	Drewry (2583)	0-4-0DM	1956

§privately owned, stored at Hardingham and viewable from trains, no public access.

Locomotive notes: D8069, 31235, 31538 and 50019, also various DMUs and Class 141 are in service.

Rolling stock: 1 BR Mk 1 coach. 5 BR Mk 2 coaches. 5 ex-BR Mk 1 NPCCS and breakdown van (ex-Stewarts Lane). BR Mk 2 TSO 5536 used as static bar coach. 10-ton rail-mounted crane. Selection of freight wagons, operational and stored at Hardingham

England

Classic Transport Day — 20 June; Teddy Bears' Specials — 25 July; Late Summer Diesel Enthusiasts' Weekend — 11/12 September; 5th Bygones Extravaganza — 19 October; Carol Service Special (to Thuxton); and Santa Specials in December

Membership details: Membership Secretary c/o Dereham Station
Membership journal: *The Blastpipe* (four times a year)

Owners
50019 and 68004 the Class 50 Locomotive Association
47596 the Stratford 47 Group
31235 the Colne Valley Enterprises Ltd
D8069 the Type One Association
GET the Great Eastern Traction group

Museum — Mid-Suffolk Light Railway — Suffolk

Member: HRA
Location: Wetheringsett, Nr Stowmarket, Suffolk IP14 5PW
OS reference: TM 129659
Operating organisation: Mid-Suffolk Light Railway Company
Telephone: 01449 766899
Internet address: *Web site:* www.mslr.org.uk
Car park: On site
Access by public transport: Some local buses from Ipswich to Diss set down and pick up on the A140 Ipswich-Norwich road near to the museum. Local buses from Stowmarket to Wetheringsett. Services tend to be infrequent and the timetables are subject to change at short notice. Details of services can be obtained from traveline 0870 6082608 or www.traveline.org.uk
On site facilities: Souvenir shop, refreshments, railway walk, railwayana and photographic exhibition, toilets (including disabled) and picnic area
Period of public opening: Usually open on Sundays and Bank

Industrial locomotives

Name	No	Builder	Type	Built
—	1604	H/Clarke (1604)	0-6-0ST	1928
—	304470	R/Hornsby (304470)	0-4-0DM	1951

Rolling stock
GER 5-compartment third, GER 2-compartment brake third, GER 3-compartment first, 1 GER ventilated van, 1 GER non-ventilated van, private owner coal wagon (rebuilt from BR open wagon), BR tube wagon, LNER brake van, NER milk van body, 2 GER 5 compartment third bodies, GER ventilated van body. GER steel outside frame ventilated van, GER horsebox body, conflat (to provide underframe for horsebox), replica contractor open wagon

Holidays from Easter to end September
Special events: Steam days on all Sundays in August and August Bank Holiday Monday. Goods Centenary special event over weekend of 18/19 September 2004
Special notes: Museum dedicated to Mid-Suffolk Light Railway. Original MSLR restored buildings and artefacts. Reproduction MSLR ticket on entry. *Railway World* award winner in 1994 and 2002
Facilities for disabled: Most of the site is accessible for disabled users. A wheelchair is available on request and there is wheelchair access to the demonstration passenger train. Toilets are accessible to wheelchair users
Membership details: Membership Secretary, 4 Felix Road, Stowupland, Stowmarket, Suffolk IP14 4DD
Society journal: *Making Tracks:* quarterly MSLRS Newsletter

Steam Centre — Middleton Railway — Leeds

Member: HRA
This is a preserved section of 'the world's oldest working railway', authorised by the first railway Act of Parliament in 1758, and also the first standard gauge railway to be taken over by volunteers in 1960
Headquarters: Middleton Railway Trust Ltd, Moor Road, Hunslet, Leeds LS10 2JQ

Telephone: 0113 271 0320
Internet addresses: *e-mail:* info@middletonrailway.org.uk
Web site: www.middletonrailway.org.uk

Main station: Moor Road, Hunslet
OS reference: SE 302309
Car park: Moor Road (free)
Access by public transport:
Nearest main line station, Leeds
City. Bus service No 76 from City
Square (opposite Leeds railway
station) to Moor Road station
(every 30min)
Souvenir shop: Moor Road
Museum: In preparation. Depot
open weekends and Bank Holidays
10.00 to 16.30 in season
Length of line: 1.25 miles
(extension pending)
Journey time: Return trip about
25min. Return tickets act as All
Day Rovers
Period of public operation:
Weekends and Bank Holidays 27
March to 26 September, Sundays 3,
10, 17, 24, 31 October, 7
November. Schools' trains 15, 24
June (contact Schools Liaison Offer
on 01904 633906)
Special events: 27/28 March —
Leeds Weekend; Bluebell Walk —
9 May; Mischievous Engines
Weekend — 22/23 May, Happy
Engines Wekend — 10/11 July;
Diesel Weekend — 14/15 August;
Heritage Days — 11/12 September;
Enthusiasts' Weekend — 25/26
Spetember; Halloween — 31
October; Santa's Special Trains —
4/5, 11/12, 18/19, 24 (advance
booking recommended); Santa
trains for schools — 10 December
(contact Schools Liaison Offer on
01904 633906)
Facilities for disabled: Good
access with additional assistance by
prior arrangement
Special notes: Never having closed
since 1758 the railway still operates
under its original Act of Parliament.
The first railway to successfully
commercially use steam
locomotives from 1812. The first
standard gauge railway to be
operated by volunteers from June
1960. Conveyed 10,000 tons of
freight annually from BR to local
works from 1960 to 1983. Part of
South Leeds Heritage Trail,
highlighting former locomotive
works in the area, and other historic
places

Locomotives

Name	No	Origin	Class	Type	Built
—	1310	NER	Y7	0-4-0T	1891
—	68153	LNER	Y1	0-4-0VB	1933
—	385	DSB	HsII	0-4-0WT	1893
John Alcock	7051	LMS	—	0-6-0DM	1932
(Olive)	RDB998901	BR	—	4wDM	1950

Industrial locomotives

Name	No	Builder	Type	Built
John Blenkinsop	—	Peckett (2003)	0-4-0ST	1941
—	—	Peckett (2103)	0-4-0ST	1948
—	—	Bagnall (2702)	0-4-0ST	1943
Henry de Lacy II	—	H/Clarke (1309)	0-4-0ST	1917
Mirvale	—	H/Clarke (1882)	0-4-0ST	1955
Manchester Ship Canal No 67	—	H/Clarke (1329)	0-6-0T	1921
—	11	Hunslet (1453)	0-4-0ST	1925
Picton	—	Hunslet (1540)	2-6-2T	1927
Brookes No 1	—	Hunslet (2387)	0-6-0T	1941
Windle	—	Borrows (53)	0-4-0WT	1909
Matthew Murray	—	M/Wardle (1601)	0-6-0ST	1903
Lucy	—	Cockerill	0-4-0VBT	1890
Sir Berkeley†	—	M/Wardle (1210)	0-6-0ST	1891
—	6	H/Leslie (3860)	0-4-0ST	1935
Carroll	—	H/Clarke (D631)	0-4-0DM	1946
Mary	—	H/Clarke (D577)	0-4-0DM	1932
—	—	Hunslet (1786)	0-4-0DM	1935
—	—	Fowler (3900002)	0-4-0DM	1945
Austin No 1	—	Peckett (5003)	0-4-0DM	1961
—	—	Thomas Hill (138C)	0-4-0DH	1963
Rowntrees No 3	—	R/Hornsby (441934)	4wDM	1960
—*	D2999	Brush (91)/ Beyer Peacock (7856)	0-4-0DE	1958
—	—	G/Batley (420452)	4wDE	1979

*on loan from BSC Orb Works, Newport
†on 10 year loan from Vintage Carriages Trust, but may be away on hire at times

Stock
2 CCTs converted for passenger use Nos 1867 and 2048; CCT as stores van
No 2073; Norwegian brake coach; Various goods vehicles; 5-ton Booth rail
crane; 1 3-ton Smith steam crane; 1 3-ton Isles steam crane; 7.5-ton steam
crane

Owners
1310, 385 the Steam Power Trust
RDB998901 the EM2 Locomotive Society

Midland Railway — Butterley

Member: HRA, TT

The Midland Railway — Butterley is a rapidly developing Preservation Scheme with a difference. The massive 57 acre Museum site and 35 acre Country Park enabled the Centre to become 'More Than Just a Railway' as its publicity says. The seven road Matthew Kirtley Museum allows much of the historic collection to be on display and most of the locomotives to be stored and displayed under cover. A miniature railway (3.5 and 5in gauge) and a 1-mile narrow gauge line (2ft gauge) carries passengers through the Country Park; Brittain Pit Farm Park, with its wide variety of livestock; and of course there is a 3.5-mile standard gauge line complete with Midland signals, three restored signalboxes, Butterley station, the scenic delights of Butterley Reservoir and Golden Valley!

The Victorian Railwaymen's Church, the demonstration signalbox, and all the other many attractions that make up the Midland Railway — Butterley will be open throughout the year

Location: Midland Railway, Butterley Station, Nr Ripley, Derbyshire DE5 3QZ

OS reference: SK 403520

General Manager: John Hett

Operating society/organisation: Midland Railway Trust Ltd

Telephone: Ripley (01773) 747674, Visitor Information Line (01773) 570140.

Fax: (01773) 570271

Internet address:
e-mail: mrc@rapidial.co.uk
Web site: midlandrailwaycentre.co.uk

Car park: Butterley station on B6179 1 mile north of Ripley

On site facilities: Museum, award winning country park, Brittain Pit Farm Park, souvenir shops, miniature railway, narrow gauge railway, garden railway, model railways

Refreshment facilities: Butterley station buffet, Johnson Buffet (Swanwick), on-train bars and extensive 'Wine and Dine' trains,

Locomotives and multiple-units

Name	No	Origin	Class	Type	Built
Princess Margaret Rose	46203	LMS	8P	4-6-2	1935
Duchess of Sutherland	6233	LMS	8P	4-6-2	1938
—	44027	LMS	4F	0-6-0	1924
—	44932	LMS	5MT	4-6-0	1945
—	45491	LMS	5MT	4-6-0	1943
—	47564	LMS	3F	0-6-0T	1928
—	47327	LMS	3F	0-6-0T	1926
—	47357	LMS	3F	0-6-0T	1926
—	47445	LMS	3F	0-6-0T	1927
—	158A	MR	—	2-4-0	1866
—	53809	S&DJR	7F	2-8-0	1925
—	73129	BR	5MT	4-6-0	1956
—	80080	BR	4MT	2-6-4T	1954
—	80098	BR	4MT	2-6-4T	1955
—	92214	BR	9F	2-10-0	1959
—	92219	BR	9F	2-10-0	1959
—	D2858	BR	02	0-4-0DM	1959
—	D2138	BR	03	0-6-0DM	1960
—	08590	BR	08	0-6-0DE	1959
—	12077	BR	11	0-6-0DE	1950
—	D8001	BR	20	Bo-Bo	1957
—	20205	BR	20	Bo-Bo	1967
—	20227	BR	20	Bo-Bo	1968
—	D7671	BR	25	Bo-Bo	1967
—	31271	BR	31	A1A-A1A	1961
Boudicea	31418	BR	31	A1A-A1A	1959
—	31421	BR	31	A1A-A1A	1959
—	33201	BR	33	Bo-Bo	1962
—	37190	BR	37	Co-Co	1964
Aureol	40012	BR	40	1Co-Co1	1959
Great Gable	D4	BR	44	1Co-Co1	1959
Royal Tank Regiment	45041	BR	45/1	1Co-Co1	1962
—	45133	BR	45/1	1Co-Co1	1961
—	46045	BR	46	1Co-Co1	1963
—	47401	BR	47	Co-Co	1963
—	D1516	BR	47	Co-Co	1963
Sir Edward Elgar	50007	BR	50	Co-Co	1967
Tulyar	55015	BR	55	Co-Co	1961
Western Lady	D1048	BR	52	C-C	1962
Electra	27000	BR	EM2	Co+Co	1953
—	50019	BR	114	DMBS	1956
—	55513	BR	141	DMS	1983
—	55533	BR	141	DMS(L)	1983
—	55966	BR	127	DPU	1959
—	55976	BR	127	DPU	1956
—	56006	BR	114	DTC	1956
—	59609	BR	127	TC	1959
—	79018	BR	—	MBS	19??
—	79612	BR	—	DTC	19??
—	29663	M/Cam	—	TC	1931
—	29666	M/Cam	—	TC	1931
—	29670	M/Cam	—	TC	1931
Iris	M79900	BR	—	MBS	1956

Locomotive notes: In service 92214, 6233, 80098, 47357, 46045, 08590, Class 114 and 127 DMU, D4, 33201, 37190, 46045, 47401, 50007, D2138,

'The Midlander' (details from above address)

Length of line: Standard gauge 3.5 miles, narrow gauge 0.8-mile

Public opening: Trains run every Sunday from 25 January to 19 December, every Saturday 14 February to 13 March, 3-17 April, 1 May to 18 September, 2 October to 6 November, 20 November to 18 December. Daily 14-22 February, 7-18 April, 29 May to 6 June, 22 July to 30 August.

On other dates the Midland Railway — Butterley will be open for static display.

Golden Valley Light Railway: Trains will run weekends, Bank Holiday Mondays April to October, daily 29 May to 6 June, 22 July to 30 August. Special steam days — check for details.

Butterley Park Miniature Railway: Trains will run Sundays and Bank Holiday Mondays Easter to September.

Journey time: Approximately 1hr

Special events: Day out with Thomas — 6/7, 13/14 March; Mother's Day Lunch Train — 21 March; Diesel Gala— 3/4 April; Easter Eggstravaganza — 7-18 April; Spring on the Farm — 17/18 April; Railway Experience Day — 24 April; Vintage Train Weekend — 1-3 May; Diesel & Steam Weekend — 15/16 May; Spring Steam Gala — 22/23 May; Day out with Thomas —29 May-6 June; Father's Day Lunch Train — 20 June; Diesel & Steam Weekend — 26/27 June; Free for Disabled — 3/4 July; Diesel & Steam Weekend — 11/12 July; Road Rally — 11 July; Anything Goes Weekend — 24/25 July; Day out with Thomas — 31 July-8 August; Diesel & Steam Weekend — 21/22 August; Narrow Gauge and Garden Railways Event — 21/22 August; Vintage Train Weekend — 28-30 August; Steam Gala — 4/5 September; Diesel & Steam Weekend — 11/12 September; Autumn Diesel Gala — 18/19 September; Railway Experience Day — 25 September; Diesel & Steam Weekend — 2/3 October; Goods Train Gala — 9/10 October; Day out with Thomas — 16/17 October; Wizards Weekend — 23/24 October; Fireworks Nights — 30 October, 6 November; Santa Specials — 20/21, 27/28

40012, 12077, 45133 and D7671. Under restoration: 44027, 45491, 44932, 80080. Awaiting repairs or stored: 46203, D1517, 47445, 92219. Boiler and frames only 47564. Static display: 158A, 27000, 47327 (as 16410). Expected to enter service in 2004: 53809, 73129, *Iris*

Industrial locomotives

Name	No	Builder	Type	Built
Gladys	—	Markham (109)	0-4-0ST	1894
Stanton	24	Barclay (1875)	0-4-0CT	1925
Whitehead	—	Peckett (1163)	0-4-0ST	1908
Victory	—	Peckett (1547)	0-4-0ST	1919
Lytham St Annes	—	Peckett (2111)	0-4-0ST	1949
Brown Bailey	4	N/Wilson (454)	0-4-0ST	1894
Castle Donnington	1	RSH (7817)	0-4-0ST	1954
Neepsend		Sentinel (9370)	4wVBT	1947
Andy	2	Fowler (16038)	0-4-0DM	1923
—	RS9	M/Rail (2024)	0-4-0DM	1921
—	RS12	M/Rail (460)	0-4-0DM	1912
Boots	2	Barclay (2008)	0-4-0F	1935
Castle Donnington	2	Barclay (416)	0-4-0DM	1957
Boots	—	R/Hornsby (384139)	0-4-0DE	1955
—	—	H/Clarke (D1152)	0-6-0DM	1959
Albert Fields	—	H/Clarke (D1114)	0-6-0DM	1958
Princess Elizabeth*	6201	H/Clarke (D611)	4-6-2DM	1938
Princess Margaret Rose*	6203	H/Clarke (D612)	4-6-2DM	1938

*21in gauge

Golden Valley Light Railway
2ft gauge unless otherwise shown

		Builder	Type	Built
—	—	Deutz (10249)	4wDM	1932
Pioneer	—	M/Rail (8739)	4wDM	1942
—	—	M/Rail (8756)	4wDM	1942
Campbell Brick Works	—	M/Rail (60S364)	4wDM	1968
—	—	Lister (3742)	4wDM	1931
—	—	M/Rail (11246)	4wDM	1963
—	2	O&K (7529)	0-4-0WT	1914
—	—	O&K (5215)	4wDM	1936
Wheal Jayne	19	BEV	4wBE	1985
—	—	Ruston (7002/0567/6)	4wDM	1966
Annie	—	Ruston (198297)	4wDM	1939
Berryhill	—	Ruston (222068)	4wDM	1943
Hucknall Colliery	3	Ruston (480678)	4wDM	1961
—	—	Hunslet (7178)	4wDH	1971
Calverton Colliery	22	H/Clarke (1117)	0-6-0DM	1958
High Marnham	—	H/Barclay (441)	0-4-0DM	1949
Natalie	—	H/Barclay (LD 9351)	0-4-0DM	1994
—	—	Lister (53726)	4wDM	1963
—	—	SMH (40SD529)	4wDM	1983
—	NG24	B/Drewry (3703)	4wBE	1974
Calverton No 7	7	Hunslet (8911)	4wDM	1980
Ellison	—	SMH (102T20)	4wDH	1979
Pearl 2	—	T. D. A. Civil (1)	0-4-2T	1997

Locomotive notes: In service: *High Marnham, Boots, Castle Donnington No 2,* NG24, Ruston 222068, SMH (40SD529 & 102T20), *Calverton Colliery No 22,* Lister, Deutz 10249, *Albert Fields,* M/Rail 60S364, *Princess Margaret Rose.* Under restoration: *Andy,* O&K 7529, *Lytham St Annes, Castle Donnington No 1.* Awaiting repairs or stored on display: RS9, Hunslet 7178, M/Rails 5906/11246. Static display: *Gladys,* 4, *Boots No 2,* Sentinel 9370, *Welbeck Colliery, Victory,* RS12, *Stanton* No 24, *Brown Bailey*

November, 4/5, 9, 11/12, 16, 18/19, 22-24 December; Festive Trains — 27 December-2 January 2005
Facilities for disabled: Toilets, special coach, access to shop and cafeteria, special weekend
Membership details: J. Hett, at above address
Membership journal: *The Wyvern* — quarterly
Marketing names: 'More than just a railway'; Golden Valley Light Railway (narrow gauge); Butterley Park Miniature Railway (miniature line)

Stock
Numerous carriages, wagons and cranes. Museum display includes MR Royal saloon, MR 4-wheeled coach, MR brake third, LD&ECR all third, BR horsebox, LMS travelling Post Office, L&YR family saloon, MR motor carvan, MR bogie brake third, restored freight vehicles, LMS 50-ton steam crane, and much more

Owners
158A, 44027 on loan from the National Railway Museum
53809 the 13809 Preservation Group
47357, 47327, 47445, 47564, 73129 Derby City Council
6201, 6203, 6233, 46203, 80080, 80098 the Princess Royal Class Locomotive Trust
55015 the Deltic Preservation Society
D4, 45041 and 46045 the Peak Locomotive Preservation Co Ltd
D7671 Derby Industrial Museum
33201 the Birmingham Railwaymen's Crompton Workgroup
Class 141 and Wickham units the Llangollen Railcar Group

Railway Centre — Midsomer Norton Station — Somerset

Member: HRA

The Midsomer Norton Station Project has secured a foothold on the northern part of the S&D where previous preservation attempts failed. More recently it has been joined by the North Dorset Railway Trust, which has established a prescence on the southern part of the route at Shillingstone. The S&DRHT has the central object of preserving the route and infrastructure wherever the opportunities arise, whether for heritage or conventional railways or, more simply, for public recreation and conservation. In practice, energies are being concentrated at Midsomer Norton, with the longer term aim of extending the running line southwards up the notorious 1 in 53 grade towards Chilcompton, and even northwards down towards Radstock. The station site is on a 25-year lease from Bath & North East Somerset Council and the Trust is in negotiation with three private landowners to secure access further south for nearly a mile. Beyond that lie Chilcompton Tunnels and the first obstacle of the landfilled cutting. Midsomer Norton station is planned to become one of the few significant visitor attractions in this run-down former coal-mining community, with the S&D legend attracting

Industrial locomotives

Name	No	Builder	Type	Built
David James Cook	—	E/Electric (D1120)	0-6-0DE	1966

Rolling stock: 2 Mk 1 dining cars (ex-Pullman), 2 ex-MoD box vans, 2 LMS brake vans, Kilmersdon Colliery coal wagon, ex-WR box van, LMS Wickham platelayers' trolley. Planned acquisitions during 2004 include Mk 1 Restaurant car, Mk 1 brake composite and composite coaches, Sturgeon bogie wagon

national and even international attention. The Trust is working towards an opening event in August 2004, when it is hoped to operate a steam train. An English Electric diesel shunter arrived in September 2003 and will power works and demonstration trains initially in 2004

Main station: Midsomer Norton South
OS Reference: ST 664537
Chairman: John Baxter, Chairman & Acting Treasurer; Peter Russell, Secretary; Jeremy Woodrow, Membership Secretary; Richard Stevens, Vice-President
Headquarters: Somerset & Dorset Railway Heritage Trust, Midsomer Norton Station Project, Silver Street, Midsomer Norton, BA3 2EY
Telephone: 01661 411221
Internet address:
E-mail: info@sdjr.co.uk
Web site: www.sdjr.co.uk
Car park: Limited parking on site

— 200 place free car parking — 300m towards town centre (OS ST 666542)
Access by public transport: Nearest rail stations Bath Spa (13 miles), Frome (13 miles), Trowbridge (15 miles). Bus (First) services 173, 174, 176, 178 drop off at Town Hall weekdays; 173, 778, 969, 984 on Sundays; 184 also connects to Frome station. Updated information on www.firstbadgerline.com
On site facilities: Drinks and sales/information in main station building during opening times; toilets. Static restaurant coach in sidings (for light refreshments) and museum in stable block both planned for opening in 2004
Length of line: Initially 350m of running line being laid through station, plus sidings in goods yard. Medium term scope for extension southwards for approx 1km towards Chilcompton Tunnels. Goods shed

The most recent locomotive to be restored on the Midland Railway is BR-built Class 9F No 92214.
Alan Barnes

The restored station at Midsomer Norton. Tracklaying has begun to enable brake van rides to commence during 2004. *S&DRHT*

England

workshop housing diesel shunter open for viewing

Opening times: Site and buildings open every Sunday 10.00-17.00 throughout the year (staffed), most Mondays (staffed, but please telephone to check). Site only open, but normally unstaffed at other times

Special events: 28/29 August 2004 — official opening of first phase planned (please contact nearer time, see also local and railway press)

Disabled access: Wheelchairs can access station forecourt, down platform and main building (via platform) at present. Museum will include gently ramped access path

Membership details: Jeremy Woodrow, 2 Fir Tree Cottages, Newlands Hill, Portishead, North Somerset BS20 6AT — Rates for 2004 — Life membership £180 (single member) £250 (Family/Corporate). Ordinary Adult £12, Junior or Senior Citizen £8 Family/Household (2 spouses/partners + 2 children under 16) £16; Corporate £20. Membership leaflets available in station

Membership journal: *The Telegraph* — 3 times per annum (April, August and December)

The Museum is one of Britain's finest neo-classical stations and was built in 1848 to commemorate the election of George Hudson as MP for Sunderland. Restored features include the booking office, unchanged since it was installed in 1866, waiting shelter on the west platform and siding area

Location: North Bridge Street, Sunderland SR5 1AP
Telephone: (0191) 567 7075
OS reference: NZ 396576

Rolling stock
NER brake van 1915, LNER CCT van 1939

On site facilities: Car parking on museum forecourt, shop. Self-service refreshment dispenser
Access by public transport: 10min walk from Sunderland Central station. Served by several bus routes from Sunderland city centre, Newcastle and South Shields
Public opening: Daily 1 January-31 December (except New Year's Day, Christmas Day, Boxing Day [please check for Good Friday and Easer Sunday opening times]). Monday to Saturday 10.00-17.00. Sunday 14.00-17.00. Free admission
Access for disabled: Ramped access, suitable for wheelchair users

---

Based in the buildings of the world's oldest passenger railway station (dating from 1830), the Museum has colourful 'hands-on' galleries that amuse, amaze and entertain. Visitors can find out about our industrial past, and walk through a Victorian sewer complete with sounds and smells.

Location: Liverpool Road, Castlefield, Manchester (off Deansgate near Granada TV)
OS reference: SJ 831987
Operating society/organisation: The Museum of Science and Industry in Manchester, Liverpool Road, Castlefield, Manchester M3 4FP

Locomotives

Name	No	Origin	Class	Type	Built
Lion	57	L&MR	—	0-4-2	1838
Pender	3††	IoMR	—	2-4-0T	1873
Novelty	Replica of 1829 locomotive using some original parts				1986
—	3157†	PR	—	4-4-0	1911
—	2352§	SAR	GL	4-8-2+2-8-4	1929
Ariadne	1505 (27001)	BR	EM2 (77)	Co-Co	1954
Hector	26048	BR	EM1 (76)	Bo-Bo cab only	1952
Planet*	—		Replica	—	2-2-0	1992

Industrial locomotives

Name	No	Builder	Type	Built
Lord Ashfield	—	Barclay (1964)	0-4-0ST	1929
—	258	E/Electric (1378)	4wBE	1944

*replica of 1830-built locomotive
††ex-Isle of Man Railways, 3ft gauge, sectioned (B/Peacock 1255)

Telephone: (0161) 832 2244
Internet address: *e-mail:*
marketing@msim.org.uk
Web site: http://www.msim.org.uk
Car parks: On site, plus parking in the area (Museum car park £4 [valid to 31 March 2004])
Access by public transport: Manchester Victoria, Piccadilly, Oxford Road and Deansgate main line stations. GM bus 33. G-Mex Metrolink station
On site facilities: Oldest passenger railway station, listed buildings containing exhibitions about science, industry, aviation, space, water supply and sewage disposal, gas and electricity. Xperiment the 'hands-on' science centre and the 'Out of this world' space gallery. World's largest collection of working steam mill engines in the Power Hall, demonstrated every afternoon. The Collections Centre has research facilities and access to reserve collections. Museum shop,

†ex-Pakistan Railways, 5ft 6in gauge (V/Foundry 3064)
§ex-South African Railways, 3ft 6in gauge (B/Peacock 6693)

Rolling stock
BR Mk 2 SO E5241, 1966
Replica M&BR 1st class carriage c1840 using original fragments
2 replica L&MR 2nd class carriages c1835
c1908 L&YR ambulance carriage rebuilt 1923 as Medical Examination Car, LMS No 10825 (under restoration)
B782903 4-wheeled covered goods van, BR (Wolverton), 1961
B783709 4-wheeled covered goods van, BR (Wolverton), 1962
3-plank loose coupled goods wagon, GCR (Chatham), c1890

Owners
Lion on loan from the National Museums & Galleries on Merseyside
Novelty on loan from the National Railway Museum, York
Industrial locomotives on loan from PowerGen

restaurant, Learning and Conference Centres
Public opening: Daily except 24-26 December, including Saturdays and Sundays, 10.00-17.00. Entrance in Lower Byrom Street. Admission free to permanent galleries,

although prices still apply for special exhibitions. Please ring for details. Groups can book a visit by calling (0161) 833 0027
Special notes: Good wheelchair access, toilets for the disabled, lecture and conference facilities.

Museum	**National Railway Museum**	North Yorkshire

Member: HRA, TT, MLSOG
Location: National Railway Museum, Leeman Road, York YO26 4XJ
OS reference: SE 594519
Operating society/organisation: Part of the National Museum of Science and Industry
Telephone: York (01904) 621261
Car park: Available on site, charge applies. Coach parking is available — pre-booking required
Access by public transport: The Museum is within a few minutes' walking distance of the railway and bus stations in York. The York City & District Bus Service operates to the door
On site facilities: Museum shop, restaurant and toilets. Reference library (free by appointment). Also model railway, miniature railway, baby changing facilities, indoor and outdoor play areas, children's interactive learning centre, conference centre
Public opening: Daily 10.00-18.00. Closed 24-26 December. Admission is free for all

Facilities for disabled: Most areas of the Museum are accessible
Special notes: The Museum has been open since 1975 and has welcomed over 20 million visitors. In 2001 it was awarded the prestigious 'European Museum of the Year' title
It offers the visitor three extensive exhibition halls, the Great Hall, the Station Hall and The Works, which house the world's premier collection of railway related material.
The Great Hall displays are on the theme of railway technology. There is a magnificent display of railway locomotive development round the turntable. Signalling, the modern railway and the Channel Tunnel are also represented. The displays reflect the present and the past and include a full-sized model of the nose cone of a state of the art Transmanche Super Train operating between England and the Continent. A new permanent exhibition now features the only Bullet Train on display outside Japan and tells the story of how this revolutionary high

speed train took the world by storm. Regular temporary exhibitions exploring various aspects of railway history/technology. Displays on the operation of the railways, tape/slide presentations can be found on the Balcony Galleries.
The Station Hall illustrates the concept of travel by train — for passengers and freight. Several trains are drawn up at platforms with a number of footplates and carriages open to visitors. The vehicles displayed range from the superb Royal carriages to humble freight wagons.
The Interactive Learning Centre provides visitors with 'hands-on' experience of various aspects of railway operation.
The Museum's extensive reference library (including the photographic and drawings collections) continues to be free to all booked enquirers every weekday from 10.30-17.00.
The tables which follow indicate the whereabouts (display, on loan, in store) of the National Railway Collection. It must be emphasised

that the appearance of any particular item on public display cannot be guaranteed. If it is vital to discover the exact whereabouts of a specific item, enquirers should contact the Museum in York before the trip.

The National Railway Museum is open for evening hire for private viewings and celebrations; menus and details are available on request.

Details of membership of the Museum's support group, including a quarterly newsletter are available from: The Secretary, Friends of the National Railway Museum, c/o the above address.

Locomotives — Steam

Name	No	Origin	Builder	Class	Type	Built
Agenoria	—	Shutt End Colliery	Foster/Raistrick	—	0-4-0	1829
Sans Pareil	—	—	Hackworth	—	0-4-0	1829
Coppernob	3	FR	Bury, Curtis & Kennedy	—	0-4-0	1846
Pet	—	LNWR	Crewe	—	0-4-0ST	1865
Aerolite	66	NER	Gateshead	X1(LNER)	2-2-4T	1869
—	1	GNR	Doncaster	—	4-2-2	1870
Bauxite	2	Hebburn Works	B/Hawthorn	—	0-4-0ST	1874
—	1275	NER	Gateshead	—	0-6-0	1874
Boxhill	82	LBSCR	Brighton	A1	0-6-0T	1880
Gladstone	—	LBSCR	Brighton	—	0-4-2	1882
Livingston Thompson	—	Ffestiniog Rly	Ffestiniog Rly	—	0-4-4-0	1885
Wren	—	LYR	B/Peacock	—	0-4-0ST	1887
—	1008	LYR	Horwich	—	2-4-2T	1889
Hardwicke	790	LNWR	Crewe	—	2-4-0	1892
—	563	LSWR	Nine Elms	T3	4-4-0	1893
—	1621	NER	Gateshead	M	4-4-0	1893
—	245	LSWR	Nine Elms	M7	0-4-4T	1897
—	673	MR	Derby	—	4-2-2	1899

England

Name	No	Origin	Builder	Class	Type	Built
—	1247	GNR	S/Stewart	J52	0-6-0ST	1899
—	737	SECR	Ashford	D	4-4-0	1901
—	251	GNR	Doncaster	C1	4-4-2	1902
—	1000	MR	Derby	4	4-4-0	1902
City of Truro	3440	GWR	Swindon	'City'	4-4-0	1903
—	87	GER	Stratford	J69	0-6-0T	1904
—	1217	GER	Stratford	J17	0-6-0	1905
—	2818	GWR	Swindon	2800	2-8-0	1905
Lode Star	4003	GWR	Swindon	'Star'	4-6-0	1907
Butler Henderson	506	GCR	Gorton	'Director'	4-4-0	1920
Cheltenham	925	SR	Eastleigh	V/Schools	4-4-0	1934
—	2500	LMS	Derby	4P	2-6-4T	1934
Rocket (replica)	—		R. Stephenson	—	0-2-2	1934
—	5000	LMS	Crewe	5MT	4-6-0	1935
—	607	Chinese Govt Rlys	Vulcan	KF7	4-8-4	1935
Green Arrow	4771	LNER	Doncaster	V2	2-6-2	1936
Mallard	4468	LNER	Doncaster	A4	4-6-2	1938
Duchess of Hamilton	46229	LMS	Crewe	8P	4-6-2	1938
Eustace Forth	15	—	RSH (7063)	—	0-4-0ST	1942
Winston Churchill	34051	SR	Brighton	BB	4-6-2	1946
Ellerman Lines	35029	BR(SR)	Sectioned	MN	4-6-2	1949
—	1	Imperial Paper Mills	Barclay	—	0-4-0F	1956
Frank Galbraith	5	Tees-Side Bridge & Engineering Co	Sentinel	—	4wTG	1957
Evening Star	92220	BR	Swindon	9F	2-10-0	1960
Rocket (replica)	—	—	Loco Enterprises	—	0-2-2	1979
Iron Duke (broad gauge replica)	—	GWR	RESCO	—	4-2-2	1985
Penydarren (replica)	—	Penydarren Iron Works	—	—	0-4-0	—

Locomotives — Electric

Name	No	Origin	Builder	Class	Type	Built
—	75S	W&CR	Siemens (6)	—	Bo electric	1898
—	1	NER	BTH	—	Bo-Bo electric	1904
—	809	GPO	Green Bat	—	2w-2E	1931
—	26020	BR	Gorton/Metrovick	76	Bo-Bo Electric	1951
—	RA.36	TML	Hunslet	—	4wBE/WE	1990

Locomotives — Diesel

Name	No	Origin	Builder	Class	Type	Built
—	—	—	Simplex (4217)	—	4wPM	1925
Hexhamshire	15	CEGB	A/Whitworth (D21)		0-4-0DE	1933
—	—	Yorkshire Water Authority	R/Hornsby (187105)	—	4wDM	1937
—	08064	BR	Darlington	08	0-6-0 DE	1953
BEA Carrington Station*	3	CEGB	RSH (7746)	—	0-6-0 DM	1954
Deltic	—	E/Electric	E/Electric	—	Co-Co	1955
—	D8000	BR	E/Electric	20	Bo-Bo	1957
—	5500	BR	Brush	31	A1A-A1A	1957
—	D200	BR	E/Electric	40	1Co-Co1	1958
—	03090	BR	—	03	0-6-0DM	1960
—	D2860	BR	YEC	02	0-4-0 DH	1960
—	D6700	BR	E/Electric	37	Co-Co	1961
Western Fusilier	D1023	BR	Swindon	52	C-C	1963
—*	41001	BR	Crewe	41	Bo-Bo	1972

*stored at MoD Kineton

England

Locomotives on loan

Livingston Thompson from the Ffestiniog Railway
Penydarren from the Welsh Industrial & Maritime Museum

Rolling Stock Powered Units— Gas Turbine

1972	BR Advanced Passenger Train

Rolling Stock Powered Units — Electric

1916	LNWR Motor Open Third Brake No 28249
1925	SR Motor Third Brake No S8143S
1937	SR Driving Motor Brake Third No S10656S
1937	SR Motor Third Open Brake No S11179S
1937	SR Driving Trailer Composite No S12123S
1940	SR (W&C) Motor Driving Car No 61
1941†	LMS Class 502 BMS No 28361
1941†	LMS Class 502 DTC No 29896
1975	Birmingham Airport Maglev passenger car
1976	Series 'O' Shinkasen No 2214
1983†	BR APT prototype train

Rolling Stock Powered Units — Diesel

1959	BR DMU Class 108 Nos 51562 & 51922
1975	Leyland Motors LEV-1 experimental railbus

Rolling Stock — Departmental

1850	GNR 4-wheel hand crane No 112
1890	GNR Locomotive Tender No 1002
1891	NER Snow Plough No DE900566
1899	GWR Hand Crane No 537
1904	MR Officers' Saloon No 2234
1906	NER Dynamometer Car No 902502
1907	NER Steam Breakdown Crane No CME 13
1907	Match Truck No DE942114
1911	GWR Track Testing Coach
1926	LNER Match Truck No DE320952
1931/2	LNER Petrol-driven platelayers' trolley No 960209
1936	GWR Ballast Wagon No 80659
1938	LMS Mobile test unit No 1, No 45053
1949	BR Matisa tamping machine No 74007
1955	GEC 12.5-ton Coles Crane
1957	BR Track recording trolley No DX 50002 *Neptune*
1969	BR Plasser Tamping & Liner No 73010

Rolling Stock — Passenger

1834	B&WR 1st & 2nd composite
1834	B&WR 2nd class
1834	B&WR 3rd class
1842	L&BR Queen Adelaide's Saloon
1845	S&DR 1st/3rd Composite No 59
1850	NER Brake End (body only)
1851	ECR 1st class No 1
1860	Cornwall Rly broad gauge coach (body only)
1861	NBR Port Carlisle branch 'dandy car'
1869	LNWR Queen Victoria's Saloon
1872	NLR Directors' Saloon No 1032
1885	MR 6-wheel composite brake No 901
1885	WCJS 8-wheel TPO No 186
1887	GNR Brake Van No 848
1887	GWR 6-wheel tricomposite No 820
1897	Lynton & Barnstaple Rly brake composite No 6992

1898	ECJS 3rd class No 12
1899	Privately owned Duke of Sutherland's Saloon No 57A
1900	LNWR (ex-WCJS) Dining Car LMS 76
1902	LNWR King Edward's Saloon No 800
1902	LNWR Queen Alexandra's Saloon No 801
1903	LSWR Tricomposite brake No 3598
1905†	LNWR Corridor 1st Brake 5154 (Royal Train)
1905†	LNWR Corridor 1st Brake 5154 (support vehicle)
1908†	ECJS Royal Saloon No 395
1908†	ECJS Passenger Brake Van No 109
1913	Pullman Car Co 1st class parlour car *Topaz*
1914	MR Dining car No 3463
1925	LMS 3rd class vestibule No 7828 *(on loan from LMS Carriage Association)*
1928	LMS 3rd Sleeping Car No 14241
1930	L&MR 1st *Huskinson* (replica)
1930	L&MR 1st *Traveller* (replica)
1930	L&MR 2nd (replica)
1930	L&MR 2nd (replica)
1936	CIWL Night Ferry sleeping car No 3792
1937	LNER Buffet Car No 9135
1937	LMS corridor 3rd class brake No 5987,
1938	GJR TPO (replica)
1941	LMS Royal Saloon 799 (armoured car)
1945†	GWR Royal Saloon No 9006
1945	GWR Royal Saloon No 9007
1955	BR Lavatory composite No E43046
1960†	BR Griddle car No Sc1100
1960	Pullman Car Co 1st class Parlour car No 326 *Emerald*
1962†	BR Prototype Mk II 1st class corridor No 13252
1962	BR Mk II 2nd brake corridor No 35468
1962†	BR Mk II 1st corridor No 21274
1969	BR Mk IIb 2nd open No 5455
1985	GWR 3rd (broad gauge replica)

Rolling Stock — Freight & Non Passenger Carrying

1815	Little Eaton (Derby Canal) Gangroad Wagon
1815	Peak Forest Canal Tramway Wagon No 174
1816	Grantham Canal Tramway Truck
1828	Dandy Cart
1840	Stratford & Moreton Tramway Wagon
1850	South Hetton Colliery Chaldron Wagon No 1155
1870	Seaham Harbour Colliery Chaldron Wagon
1889	Shell-Mex oil tank wagon No 512
1894	LSWR Brake van No 99
1901	Shell/BP Tank Wagon No 3171
1907	NER 16-ton bogie stores van No 041273
1908	LNWR Open carriage truck No 11275
1912	NER Sand wagon No DE14974
1912	GNR 8-ton van No E432764
1917	MR 8-ton open wagon
1917	GCR Box Van
1917	LNWR Box Van
1920	GCR single bolster wagon

England

1920	GNR double bolster wagon
1924	LMSR Van
1926	GWR Fitted open wagon No 108246
1927	LNER 40-ton flat wagon No DE633433
1931	GWR Fruit Van No 112884
1931	Stanton Iron Works 12-ton wagon
1933	LMSR 20-ton Goods Brake Van No 295987
1935	SR Bogie goods brake van No 56297
1935	GWR Motor car van No 126438
1935	PLM Train Ferry Van No 475014
1936	LMSR 3 plank open wagon No 472867
1936	LMS Tube wagon No 499254
1936	ICI hopper wagon No19154
1937	GWR Siphon bogie milk van No 2775
1937	LMSR Milk Tank Wagon No 44057
1937	2 x Yorkshire Water Authority side-tipper wagons
1938	LMS Single bolster wagon No 722702
1940	WD Warflat No 161042
1944	LMS Lowmac No M700728
1944	GWR 13-ton open wagon No DW143698
1946	SNCF 16-ton mineral wagon No ADB192437
1946	LNER 20-ton hopper wagon No E270919
1949	BR Bogie bolster D No B941000
1950	BR 24-ton iron ore hopper wagon No B436275

1950	BR 20-ton Weltrol No B900805
1951	ICI Liquid chlorine tank wagon No 47484
1951	BR(SR) Show cattle wagon No S3733S
1951	BR 8-ton cattle wagon No B893343
1952	BR 30-ton bogie bolster wagon No B943139
1953	Buxton Lime Quarries 23-ton bogie hopper wagon No 19154
1954	BR 27-ton Iron Ore Tippler No B383560
1954	National Benzole oil tank wagon No 2022
1955	BR china clay tip wagon No B743141
1957	BR Horse box No S96369
1959	BR Conflat No B737725
1960	BR Banana Van No B882593
1961	BR Presflo cement wagon No B873368
1961	BR 30-ton bogie bolster No B923123
1962	BR Speedfreight container No BA 4324B
1965	BR Boiler Wagon Nos DB902805, DB902806, DB902807, DB902808
1966	Milk Marketing Board 6-wheel tank No 42801
1970	Phillips Petroleum 100-ton GLW tank wagon No PP85209
1970	BR 2,000gal Road/Rail Milk Tank No ADM707111
1989	TML side-tipping muck cart No R T239
	†stored at MoD Kineton

Items on Loan from the NRM
Locomotives

Original type/No/Name	Location	Builder	Built
Wylam Colliery	Science Mus	—	1813
Hetton Colliery 0-4-0	Beamish	G. Stephenson	1822
SDR 0-4-0 *Locomotion*	Darlington	R. Stephenson & Co	1825
L&MR 0-2-2 *Rocket*	Science Mus	R. Stephenson & Co	1829
L&MR 0-2-2 *Novelty*	Museum of Science & Technology (Manchester)	Braithwaite & Ericsson	1829
SDR 'Collier' class *Etherley* (tender only)	Shildon	—	1840
SDR 0-6-0 No 24 *Derwent*	Darlington Nth Rd Mus	A. Kitching	1845
LNWR 2-2-2 No 3020 *Cornwall*	Crewe	Crewe	1847
GJR 2-2-2 *Columbine*	Science Mus	Crewe	1845
Wantage Tramway 0-4-0WT No 5 *Shannon*	Didcot Rly Ctr	G. England	1857
LNWR 0-4-0ST 1439	East Lancs	Crewe	1865
MR 2-4-0 No 158A	Midland Rly Ctr	Derby	1866
South Devon Rly 0-4-0WT *Tiny*	South Devon Rly	Sara	1868
LSWR 2-4-0WT No 0298	Bodmin	B/Peacock	1874
NER 0-6-0 No 1275	Darlington	Duds & Co	1874
NER 2-4-0 No 910	Darlington Nth Rd Mus	Gateshead	1875
NER 2-4-0 No 1463	Darlington Nth Rd Mus	Gateshead	1885
C&SL No 1	LT Museum	B/Peacock	1890
S&MR 0-4-2WT *Gazelle*	Col Stephens Rly Mus	Dodman	1893
GER 2-4-0 No 490	Bressingham	Stratford	1894
GWR 0-6-0 No 2516	Steam	Swindon	1897
TVR 0-6-2T No 28	Dean Forest	TVR	1897
GNR No 990 *Henry Oakley*	Bressingham	Doncaster	1899
LSWR 4-4-0 No 120	Bluebell Rly	Nine Elms	1899
LT&SR 4-4-2T No 80 *Thundersley*	Bressingham	R. Stephenson	1909
GCR 2-8-0 No 102	Great Central	Gorton	1911
NSR 0-4-0wE No 1	Churnet Valley	Bolton	1917
WD No 1377 (2ft Gauge)	LBR	Simplex	1918
NER 0-8-0 No 901	North York Moors Rly	Darlington	1919
NSR No 2	Churnet Valley	Stoke	1922
GWR 4-6-0 No 4073 *Caerphilly Castle*	Steam	Swindon	1923
LMS 0-6-0 No 4027	Midland Rly Ctr	Derby	1924

Original type/No/Name	Location	Builder	Built
GWR 2-2-2 *North Star* (replica)	Steam	R. Stephenson	1925
SR 4-6-0 No 777 *Sir Lamiel*	GCR	N/British	1925
SR 4-6-0 No 850 *Lord Nelson*	Eastleigh Works†	Eastleigh	1926
GWR No 6000 *King George V*	Steam	Swindon	1927
LMS 2-6-0 No 2700	Barrow Hill	Derby	1934
SR 0-6-0 No 33001	Bluebell Rly	Eastleigh	1942
GWR 0-6-0PT No 9400	Steam	Swindon	1947
BR 4-6-2 No 70013 *Oliver Cromwell*	Bressingham	Crewe	1951
BR Bo-Bo No E5001	Crewe	Eastleigh	1958
BR Bo-Bo No E3036	Barrow Hill	N/British	1960
BR Co-Co D9000 *King's Own Yorkshire Light Infantry*	Deltic9000	E/Electric	1961

†private site

Powered Units

NER	electric parcels van No 3267, G. Stephenson Mus	
GWR	diesel railcar No 4, Steam	

Departmental Stock

1932	LMS Ballast plough brake van No 197266, Embsay
1949	BR(LMS) Dynamometer car No 3, No 45049, Barrow Hill

Passenger Stock

1846	SDR 1st & 2nd composite No 31, Darlington Nth Rd Mus
1850	SDR 3rd No 179, Timothy Hackworth Mus, Shildon
1850	NER 4-wheel coach body, Darlington
1908	ECJS Passenger Brake van LNER No 396, Bressingham
1910	GCR Open 3rd class No 666, Nottingham
1925	GWR 3rd class dining car No 9653, Severn Valley Rly
1925	GWR 3rd class dining car No 9654, Severn Valley Rly
1934	GWR Buffet Car No 9631, Steam,
1936	LNER 3rd Open, No 13254, NYMR
1939	SR TPO No 4920, Nene Valley
1941	LMS Royal saloon No 798, Glasgow Museum of Transport
1950	BR (LMS) 3rd brake, No 27093, Midland Rly Ctr
1960	Pullman Car Co 1st class Kitchen car No 311 *Eagle,* Bluebell

Freight & Non Passenger Carrying Stock

1826	Cramlington Colliery Chaldron Wagon, Science Museum, Wroughton
1870	S&DR Chaldron Wagon (replica), Timothy Hackworth Museum
1898	CR well trolley bogie crocodile, Bo'ness
1902	NER 20-ton wooden hopper wagon No 4551, Tyne & Wear
1909	GWR Girder Wagon Set (Pollen E) Nos DW84997, 84998, 84999, 85000, Didcot
1912	LBSCR Open wagon No 27884, Yeovil
1912	LSWR Gunpowder van No KDS61209, Yeovil
1914	GWR Shunters' truck No W94988, Steam
1920	LSWR Lowmac, No DE563024, NYMR
1922	LBSCR cattle truck No 7116, Isle of Wight Steam Rly
1928	ICI Nitric acid tank wagon No 14, Yeovil
1939	SR postal sorting van No 4920, Nene Valley Rly
1941	LNER 20-ton brake van, No 246710, NYMR
1948	BR(SR) 12-ton shock absorbing wagon No 14036, NYMR
1950	BR 12-wheel well wagon, No KDB901601, East Lancs
1955	BR 16-ton mineral wagon No B227009, Middleton
1959	BR Fish van No B87905, Hull
1970	S&D Chaldron Wagon (replica), Shildon

Museum — National Waterways Museum — Glos

Member: HRA

The museum completed a Lottery update of the galleries and site in 2001

Location: Gloucester Docks — signposted 'Historic Docks'

OS Reference: SO 826183

Operating society/organisation: National Waterways Museum, The Waterways Trust, Llanthony Warehouse, Gloucester Docks, Gloucester GL1 2EH.

Tel: (01452) 318200

Fax: (01452) 318202

Internet address: *e-mail:* bookingsnwm@thewaterwaystrust.org

Web site: www.nwm.org.uk

Car parks: Pay & display outside museum. Free coach parking

Access by public transport: Main line Gloucester station, 1 mile

On site facilities: Tea room, souvenir and specialist bookshop (canal-related with some railway literature). School room/children's holiday activities. Working

Industrial locomotives

Name	No	Builder	Type	Built
—	1	A/Barclay (2126)	0-4-0F	1942

Ex-Gloucester Corporation, Castle Meads Power Station, Gloucester Docks. Now on static display

Rolling stock

William Balmforth of Rodley crane, c1880. Small collection of GW, Midland, LMS and BR vans with local connections. Sharpness Docks open wagons and Gloucester-built flat wagon, Manchester Ship Canal (ex-GWR) Toad brake van

demonstrations vary. Tug driving and blacksmith courses. Trip boats and other museums in docks

Facilities for disabled: Full facilities, lifts, ramps, toilets. All indoor displays, quaysides and tea room accessible. Floating exhibits not accessible

Public opening: Daily, 10.00-17.00, except 25 December. Admission charged. Last admissions 16.00

Special events: Preservation, modellers' & craft events; leisure learning courses (send for further information)

Membership details: 'Friends' support organisation. Membership Secretary, c/o Museum address, Volunteers active in restoration/fundraising. Winter Meetings programme.

Membership journal: *Llanthony Log* — quarterly

Timetable Service — Nene Valley Railway — Cambs

Member: HRA, TT

This unique railway's collection includes locomotives and coaches from 10 countries and two continents. It is a regular location for TV and film makers — from films like *Goldeneye* with Pierce Brosnan as 007 to ITV's *London's Burning*. The railway and the pleasant Cambridgeshire countryside have doubled for locations as diverse as Russia and Spain

General Manager: Mr M. A. Warrington

Headquarters: Nene Valley Railway, Wansford Station, Stibbington, Peterborough, Cambs PE8 6LR

Telephone: Stamford (01780) 784444; Talking Timetable (01780) 784404

Locomotives

Name	No	Origin	Class	Type	Built
Mayflower	1306	LNER	B1	4-6-0	1948
92 Squadron	34081	SR	BB	4-6-2	1948
City of Peterborough	73050	BR	5MT	4-6-0	1954
—	D9516	BR	14	0-6-0DH	1964
—	D9523	BR	14	0-6-0DH	1964
Atlantic Conveyor	D306	BR	40	1Co-Co1	1960
—	64.305-6	DB	64	2-6-2T	1936
—	7173	DB	52	2-10-0	1943
—	656	DSB	F	0-6-0T	1949
—	101	SJ	B	4-6-0	1944
—	1178	SJ	S	2-6-2T	1914
—	3.628	Nord	3500	4-6-0	1911
—	5485	PKP	Typ	0-8-0T	19xx
—	51401	BR	117	DMS	1959
—	51347	BR	117	DMBS	1959
—	59508	BR	117	TCL	1959

Main station: Wansford
Other public stations: Orton Mere, Ferry Meadows, Peterborough NVR (15min walk from city centre)
OS reference: TL 903979
Car park: Wansford, Orton Mere, Ferry Meadows, Peterborough NVR
Access by public transport: Buses from Peterborough to Orton Mere and Ferry Meadows
Refreshment facilities: Wansford, bar coach on most trains
Souvenir shops: Wansford
Exhibition: Wansford
Depot: Wansford
Length of line: 7.5 miles
Passenger trains: Yarwell Junction-Wansford-Ferry Meadows-Orton Mere-Peterborough NV
Period of public operation: Sundays from mid-February; weekends from Easter to end of October; Wednesdays from May, plus other midweek services in summer. Santa Specials at end of November and throughout December (telephone for details)
Special events: Take place throughout the year including Thomas' Weekend, Gala Weekend, Steamin' Blues and Vintage

Industrial locomotives

Name	No	Builder	Type	Built
—	—	Avonside (1945)	0-6-0ST	1926
Toby	—	Cockerill (1626)	0-4-0VBT	1890
Muriel	—	E/Electric (1123)	0-4-0DH	1966
Rhos	—	H/Clarke (1308)	0-6-0ST	1918
Derek Crouch	—	H/Clarke (1539)	0-6-0ST	1924
Thomas	—	H/Clarke (1800)	0-6-0T	1947
Jacks Green	—	Hunslet (1953)	0-6-0ST	1939
—	75006	Hunslet (2855)	0-6-0ST	1943
—	—	R/Hornsby (294268)	4wDM	1951
Doncaster	—	YEC (2654)	0-4-0DE	1957
—	11	Rebuilt Hill	4wD	1963
Stanton No 50	—	YEC (2670)	0-6-0DE	1958
—	DL83	R/Royce (10271)	0-6-0DH	1967

Stock
15 BR Mk 1 coaches; Wagons Lits sleeping car, Italian-built; Wagons Lits dining car, Belgian-built; 6 coaches from Denmark; 1 coach from France; 4 coaches from Belgium; 2 steam rail cranes; SR Travelling Post Office; TPO coach M30272M; 20 12-ton Vanfits plus items of freight stock

Rail/Mail Weekend (telephone for details). The shop, café, bookshop, model railway and exhibition are open on operating days and the locomotive yard is open all year for viewing. NVR is also the home of *Thomas* the children's favourite engine
Facilities for disabled: Ramp access to all stations and shops. Full toilets in Wansford station, souvenir shop. Disabled persons and helpers are eligible for concessionary fares. Passengers can be assisted on and off trains
Membership details: Bill Foreman, c/o above address
Membership journal: *Nene Steam* — 3 times/year
Marketing name: Britain's International Steam Railway

Timetable Service	North Norfolk Railway	Norfolk

Member: HRA, TT
Part of the former Midland & Great Northern Joint Railway, other elements of the LNER have crept in in the guise of the 'B12' and a Gresley buffet car. The GER 'J15' has been restored. Guest locomotives can be viewed at various times throughout the year. The line runs through beautiful coast, wood and heathland scenery with a nature trail running along its side between Weybourne and Kelling Heath
General Manager: Geoff Gowing
Headquarters: North Norfolk Railway, Sheringham Station, Sheringham, Norfolk NR26 8RA
Telephone: Sheringham (01263) 820800
Fax: (01263) 820801

Locomotives and multiple-units

Name	No	Origin	Class	Type	Built
—	564	GER	J15	0-6-0	1912
A. J. Hill	69621	GER	N7	0-6-2T	1924
—	8572	LNER	B12	4-6-0	1928
—	D2280	BR	04	0-6-0DM	1960
Camulodunum	D3940	BR	08	0-6-0DE	1960
—	D3935	BR	08	0-6-0DE	1961
—	12131	BR	11	0-6-0DE	1952
—	D5207	BR	25	Bo-Bo	1962
—	5580	BR	31	A1A-A1A	1960
—	31207	BR	31	A1A-A1A	1960
Mirage	D6732	BR	37	Co-Co	1962
—	47367	BR	47	Co-Co	1965
—	51228	M/Cam	101	DTSL	1958
—	54062	M/Cam	101	DMBS	1957
—	79960	W&M	—	Railbus	1958
—	79963	W&M	—	Railbus	1958

England

Internet address: *Web site:*
www.nnrail.co.uk
Main station: Sheringham
Other public stations:
Weybourne, Kelling Heath Park,
Holt
OS reference: Sheringham TG
156430, Weybourne TG 118419
Car parks: Sheringham,
Weybourne, Holt
Access by public transport: By
train to Sheringham station
(200yd)
Refreshment facilities:
Sheringham, Weybourne, Holt
Souvenir shops: Sheringham,
Weybourne, Holt
Museum: Sheringham
Depot: Weybourne
Length of line: 5.25 miles
Passenger trains: Steeply graded,
Sheringham-Weybourne-Holt
Period of public operation:
Weekends in March, daily from
mid-April to end September,
certain dates through October and
November. Santa Specials through
December
Special events: Mother's Day —
21 March; Easter Event — 9-12
April; 'Beside the Seaside' — 1-3

Industrial locomotives

Name	No	Builder	Type	Built
Ring Haw	—	Hunslet (1982)	0-6-0ST	1940
—	3809	Hunslet (3809)	0-6-0ST	1954
—	68009	Hunslet (3825)	0-6-0ST	1953
Wissington	—	H/Clarke (1700)	0-6-0ST	1938
—	—	Bagnall (2370)	0-6-0F	1929

Stock
3 ex-LNER coaches, GNR quad set, 7 ex-BR coaches, 3 coach King's Cross
suburban set; small number of wagons and Southern Railway PMV

Owners
564 and 8572 the Midland & Great Northern Railway Society
69621 East Anglian Railway Museum, on site for overhaul
5580 A1A Locomotives
47367 The Stratford Class 47 Group

May; Father's Day — 20 June;
Vintage Transport — 3/4 July; Beer
Festival — 16-18 July; Steam Gala
— 3-5 September; 1940s Weekend
— 18/19 September; Diesel Gala
— 2/3 October; Day out with
Thomas — 22-25 October; Santa
Specials — 4/5, 11/12, 17-19, 21-24
December; Mince Pie Specials —
26 December to 2 January 2004
Facilities for disabled: Wheelchair
facilities provided on certain trains.

Recommended telephone before
travelling. No disabled toilet
facilities as yet
Membership details: Midland &
Great Northern Joint Railway
Society, Mr S. Kennedy, Walnut
House, Walnut Gardens, Claydon,
Oxon OX17 1NA
Membership journal: *Joint Line* —
quarterly
Marketing name: The Poppy Line

Museum — North Woolwich Old Station Museum — London

This attractive Victorian terminus
building overlooks the Thames.
Railway artefacts, documents,
drawings, etc, are well displayed in
glass cases or on the walls, the
stock being stabled in the platform
area. Convenient for City Airport
and connections for the Docklands
Light Railway
Location: North Woolwich Old
Station Museum, Pier Road, North
Woolwich, London E16 2JJ
OS reference: TQ 433798
Organisation: Newham Museum
Service
Telephone: 020 7474 7244
Car park: Only in adjoining streets
Public transport: Train: Silverlink
services. Buses: 101, 473 and 474

Locomotives

Name	No	Origin	Class	Type	Built
—	229	GER	209	0-4-0ST	1876

Industrial locomotives

Name	No	Builder	Type	Built
—	—	Hibberd (3294)	4wDM	1948

Stock
1 ex-LNER coach; 2 compartment sections of LTSR coach; NLR Luggage
Van; 1 ex-Royal Arsenal Ammunition Van (18in gauge)

Facilities: Museum shop
Public opening: Open Weekends
January-November 13.00-17.00.
Daily during Newham children's
school holidays only 13.00-17.00
Admission: Free

England

North Yorkshire Moors Railway

Member: HRA, TT

This 18-mile line runs through the picturesque North York Moors National Park and is host to an extensive collection of main line locomotives

General Manager: Peter Pay

Headquarters: Pickering Station, Pickering, North Yorkshire YO18 7AJ

Telephone: Pickering (01751) 472508 for passenger enquiries, charter and diner bookings

Internet address: *e-mail:* admin@nymrpickering.fsnet.co.uk *Web site:* www.northyorkshiremoorsrailway.com

Main station: Pickering

Other public stations: Grosmont, Goathland, Levisham

OS reference: Pickering NZ 797842, Levisham NZ 818909, Goathland NZ 836013, Grosmont NZ 828053

Car parks: Grosmont, Goathland, Levisham, Pickering

Access by public transport: Arriva Northern rail service to Grosmont from Whitby and Middlesbrough. Bus services Leeds-York-Malton-Pickering-Goathland-Whitby; Helmsley-Pickering-Scarborough

Refreshment facilities: Available on most trains and at Grosmont, Goathland and Pickering

Souvenir shops: Pickering, Goathland, Grosmont and Grosmont MPD

Locomotive Depot: Grosmont

Length of line: 18 miles

Passenger trains: Steam-hauled services Grosmont-Pickering. Pullman evening dining service and 'Moorlander' Sunday lunch service run regularly. Saloons are also available for special occasions (eg wedding parties, conferences, etc)

Special events: Throughout the season, ring for details

Period of public operation: Daily 27 March-31 October, Santa Specials and other Xmas services in December/January

Facilities for disabled: The NYMR welcomes disabled visitors and special attention will gladly be

Locomotives and multiple-units

Name	No	Origin	Class	Type	Built
George Stephenson	44767	LMS	5MT	4-6-0	1947
Eric Treacy	45428	LMS	5MT	4-6-0	1937
—	2392	NER	P3	0-6-0	1923
—	2238	NER	T2	0-8-0	1918
—	901	NER	T3	0-8-0	1919
Sir Nigel Gresley	60007*	LNER	A4	4-6-2	1937
—	62005	LNER	K1	2-6-0	1949
—	69023	LNER	J72	0-6-0T	1951
—	3814	GWR	2884	2-8-0	1940
—	6619	GWR	5600	0-6-2T	1928
—	825**	SR	S15	4-6-0	1927
—	30830	SR	S15	4-6-0	1927
Repton	30926	SR	V	4-4-0	1934
Hartland	34101	SR	WC	4-6-2	1950
The Green Knight	75029	BR	4MT	4-6-0	1951
—	80135	BR	4MT	2-6-4T	1956
Dame Vera Lynn	3672	MoS	WD	2-10-0	1943
—	2253	USATC	S160	2-8-0	1943
—	D2207	BR	04	0-6-0DM	1953
—	08556	BR	08	0-6-0DE	1959
—	4018	BR	08	0-6-0DE	1961
Helen Turner	D5032	BR	24	Bo-Bo	1959
—	D5061	BR	24	Bo-Bo	1960
The Diana	D7541	BR	25	Bo-Bo	1965
The Sybilla	D7628	BR	25	Bo-Bo	1965
Lion	50027	BR	50	Co-Co	1968

*undergoing major overhaul at Grosmont
**restored incorporating parts from 30841

Industrial locomotives

Name	No	Builder	Type	Built
—	29	Kitson (4263)	0-6-2T	1904
—	5	R/Stephenson (3377)	0-6-2T	1909
Antwerp	—	Hunslet (3180)	0-6-0ST	1944
Neil D. Barker	12139	E/Electric (1553)	0-6-0DE	1948
—	16	Drewry	0-4-0DM	1941
—	2	R/Hornsby (421419)	4wDM	1958
—	3*	R/Hornsby (441934)	4wDM	1960
—	1	Vanguard (129V)	0-4-0DM	1963
—	2	Vanguard (131V)	0-4-0DM	1963

*on loan to Middleton Railway

Stock

5 pre-Grouping, 12 pre-Nationalisation, 32 x BR Mk 1, 4 x Pullman, 5 other BR coaches, 2 x Camping Coach, 1 x BR Mk 3 sleeper, 11 x brake vans, 4 x diesel cranes, 2 x 45-ton steam cranes, 88 other vehicles

Owners

825 and 30830 the Essex Locomotive Society
2238, 2392, 62005, 69023 the North Eastern Locomotive Preservation Group
60007 Sir Nigel Gresley Locomotive Preservation Trust
75014 the 75014 Steam Locomotive Operators group
901 on loan from the National Railway Museum
Antwerp the National Mining Museum
29 Lambton Locomotive Trust

provided if advance notice is given
Special notes: Operates through North York Moors National Park

D5032 T. J. Thomson & Co
D5061 the Class 24 Society
50027 the Class 50 Support Group
5, 2253, 3814, 6619, 34101, 34767, 75029 and 80135 private

Northampton & Lamport Railway

Steam Centre

Northants

Member: HRA
Headquarters: Pitsford & Brampton Station, Pitsford Road, Chapel Brampton, Northampton NN6 8BA
Location: About 5 miles north of Northampton, Pitsford Road off A5199 (formerly A50) or A508
Chairman: Dr Colin Wilson
Operating company: Northampton Steam Railway Ltd
Telephone: 01604 820327. Sundays and weekday afternoons, recorded announcements other times
Internet address: *Web site:* www.nlr.org.uk
Access by public transport: None
On site facilities: NLR souvenir shop, buffet coach, toilets, second hand bookshop
Length of line: 1.3 miles, extension to bridge 14 now open
Public opening: Every Sunday and Bank Holiday Monday from 7 March to 31 October. Santa Specials every Saturday and Sunday from 28 November to 19 December. Plus some Saturdays during special events
Special events: Mother's Day — 21 March; Easter Egg Specials — 10-12 April; Day out with Thomas — 1-3 May; Teddy Bears' Holiday — 29-31 May; Classic Car Show — 6 June; Vintage Transport Weekend — 7/8 August; Day out with Thomas — 28-30 August and 16/17 October; Santa Specials — 28 November, 4/5, 11/12, 18/19 December (pre-booking essential); Mince Pie Specials — 1 January 2005
Membership details: Mr G. Gibbons, Pitsford & Brampton Station, Pitsford Road, Chapel Brampton, Northampton NN6 8BA
Membership journal: *Premier Line* — 4 times a year

Locomotives and multiple-units

Name	No	Origin	Class	Type	Built
—	3862	GWR	2884	2-8-0	1942
Castell Dinas Bran	25035*	BR	25	Bo-Bo	1963
—	26010†	BR	26	Bo-Bo	1959
—	27056	BR	27	Bo-Bo	1962
—	31289	BR	31	A1A-A1A	1961
The Royal Artilleryman	45118	BR	45	1Co-Co1	1962
—	PMW651	BR	97	0-6-0DM	1959
—	51359	BR	117	DMBS	1959
—	51367	BR	117	DMBS	1959
—	51402	BR	117	DMS	1959
—	55001	BR	122	DMBS	1958

*undergoing restoration on the Great Central Railway
†may be transferred to the Great Central Railway for restoration

Industrial locomotives

Name	No	Builder	Type	Built
Colwyn	45	Kitson (5470)	0-6-0ST	1933
Westminster	1378	Peckett 1378)	0-4-0ST	1914
—	2104	Peckett (2104)	0-4-0ST	1948
Vanguard	5374	Chrzanow (5374)	0-6-0T	1959
Bunty	146C	Fowler (4210018)/ rebuilt T/Hill	0-4-0DH	1950 1964
—	21	Fowler (4210094)	0-4-0DH	1955
—	1	R/Hornsby (275886)	4wDM	1949
Sir Gyles Isham	7646	R/Hornsby (319286)	0-4-0DM	1953

Stock

Coaches: 2 x BR Mk 1 TSO; 1 x BR Mk 1 BSO; 1 x BR Mk 1 SK; 1 x BR Mk 1 CK; 1 x BR Mk 1 RBR; 1 x Mk 2 BSO (trolley buffet); 1 x BR Mk 1 NAV; 2 x BR NJV; 2 x SR PMV; 1 x GWR full brake; 1 x LMS CCT
Wagons: A number of various types

Owners

Colwyn the Colwyn Preservation Society
7646 the Northampton Locomotive Co
31289 on loan from Fragonset Railways

Northamptonshire Ironstone Railway Trust

Member: HRA
Location: Hunsbury Hill Industrial Museum, Hunsbury Hill Country Park, Hunsbury Hill Road, Camp Hill, Northampton
OS reference: SP 735584
Operating organisation: Northamptonshire Ironstone Railway Trust Ltd
Telephone: 01604 702031
Contact: W. Nile, 14 Lyncrest Avenue, Dunston, Northampton. (Tel: 01604 757481)
Access by public transport: Northampton Transport bus routes, 24, 25 to Camp Hill from Greyfriars bus station
On site facilities: Light refreshments, shop, toilets. Children's play areas and picnic areas
Length of line: 2.25 miles with yard, engine shed and workshops, 2 stations and level crossing
Public opening: Museum and shed/yard for viewing most weekdays and weekends. Train service from Easter Sunday to end of September on Sundays and Bank Holiday Mondays plus December for Santa Specials. Parties can be catered for on weekdays by appointment
Times of opening: 10.00 to 16.00 for viewing with train service from 13.00 to 17.00 on Sundays and Bank Holidays
Facilities for the disabled: Passenger coach can accommodate wheelchairs
Special notes: Museum to the Ironstone Industry of Northamptonshire, the museum houses photographs, documents and other items connected with the ironstone industry. The railway is laid on the old trackbed of the quarry system and partly on a new formation with remains of the quarry face and cuttings available for exploration
Membership details: Mr R. Coleman, c/o above address

Multiple-units

Name	No	Origin	Class	Type	Built
—	13004	SR	4DD	DMBS	1949
—	56285	BR	121	DTS	1960
—	70284	BR	4CEP / 411	TS	1956
—	70296	BR	4CEP / 411	TS	1956
—	69304	BR	4BIG / 422	TSRB	1965
—	14352†	BR	415 / 4EPB	DMS	1954
—	15396†	BR	415 / 4EPB	TS	1954
—	14351†	BR	415 / 4EPB	DMS	1954

†unit No 415176

Industrial locomotives

Name	No	Builder	Type	Built
Vigilant†	—	Hunslet (287)	0-4-0ST	1882
Belvedere◊	—	Sentinel (9365)	0-4-0TG	1946
Musketeer◊	—	Sentinel (9369)	0-4-0TG	1946
Hylton	—	Planet (3967)	0-4-0DH	1961
—	—	Fowler (422001)	0-4-0DH	1965
Lois	—	Fowler (422033)	0-4-0DH	1965
Muffin	46	R/Hornsby (242868)	4wDM	1946
—	16	Hunslet (2087)	0-4-0DM	1940
AMOCO	56	R/Hornsby	0-4-0DM	1956
Shire Lodge	53	R/Hornsby	0-4-0DM	1954
Sir Alfred	53	R/Hornsby (319214)	0-6-0DM	1953
—	5	R/Hornsby (338489)	0-4-0DM	1956
—*	87	Peckett (1871)	0-6-0ST	1934
Northampton†	1	Bagnall (2565)	0-4-0ST	1934
Cherwell**	—	Bagnall (2654)	0-6-0ST	1942
—	—	Grafton	Steam crane	1934

* metre gauge on loan to Irchester Country Park
◊ static display
† being rebuilt
**3ft gauge

Owners

13004, unit No 415176 the Bulleid Preservation Enterprises
70284/70296 Northampton Social Services

Member: HRA

Location: On the A60 just south of Ruddington, 3 miles south of Nottingham city centre, off A52, 7 miles north of Loughborough. Signposted

Operating society/organisation: Great Central (Nottingham) Ltd, Nottingham Heritage Centre, Mere Way, Ruddington, Nottingham NG11 6NX

Telephone: (0115) 940 5705

Fax: (0115) 940 5905

Internet address:
Web site: www.nthc.co.uk

Access by public transport: Buses from city centre and Broad Marsh (tel: [0115] 924 0000), via Nottingham Midland station

On site facilities: Car park, shop and cafe, picnic area and country park walks. 700m long passenger-carrying miniature railway. Extensive bus museum

Length of line: 7 mile steam train ride

Facilities for disabled: Accessible, and access to toilets

Public opening: Sundays & Bank Holidays 11 April to end of October, plus Santa Specials. 10.45-17.30

Special events: Great Easter Egg Hunt — 12 April; East Nidlands Bus Gala — 2 May; Model Railway Exhibition — 16 May; Day out with Thomas — 19/20, 26/27 June; Diesel Gala — 17/18 July; Bus Gala — 1 August; 60s Day — 15 August; Great Central Society Gala — 5 September; Autumn Steam Gala — 18/19 September; End of Season Vehicle Rally — 3 October; Hallowe'en Special Ghost Train — 30 October; Firework Display — 6 November; Santa Specials — 27/28 November, 4/5, 11/12, 18/19 December

Membership details: Great Central Northern Development Association, c/o above address

Society journal: Quarterly

Visiting Class B1 4-6-0 No 61264 running as No 61039 near Ruddington on 5 April 2003.
Alan Barnes

Locomotives and multiple-units

Name	No	Origin	Class	Type	Built
—	D4115	BR	08	0-6-0DE	1962
—	13180	BR	08	0-6-0DE	1955
—	D7629	BR	25	Bo-Bo	1965
—	D8048	BR	20	Bo-Bo	1959
—	D9520	BR	14	0-6-0DH	1964
—	37075	BR	37	Co-Co	1962
—	51138	BR	116	DMBS	1958
—	51151	BR	116	DMS	1958
—	52060	BR	108	DMSL	1959
—	53645	BR	108	DMBS	1958
—	53926	BR	108	DMBS	1959
—	59389	BR	108	TS	1958
—	68088	LNER	Y7	0-4-0T	1923
—	—	USATC	S160	2-8-0	

Industrial locomotives

Name	No	Builder	Type	Built
Victor	2996	Bagnall (2996)	0-6-0ST	1951
—	54	H/Clarke (1682)	0-6-0ST	1937
—	1684	Hunslet (1684)	0-4-0T	1931
—	56	RSH (7667)	0-6-0ST	1950
—	63	RSH (7761)	0-6-0ST	1954
Rhiwnant	—	M/Wardle (1317)	0-6-0ST	1895
Dolobran	—	M/Wardle (1762)	0-6-0ST	1910
Abernant	—	M/Wardle (2009)	0-6-0ST	1921
Northampton	7646	Chrzanow (5387)	0-6-0T	1959
Staythorpe	D2959	R/Hornsby	0-4-0DE	—
Toby	—	R/Hornsby (235513)	4wDM	1945

Rolling stock: 1 BR Mk 1 FO, 1 BR Mk 2 BSO, 1 BR Mk 2 BFK, 1 BR (ex-WR) cinema coach, GCR coach (body) CBL No 1663 (oldest surviving GCR coach, built 1903), 4 Barnum coaches, suburban coach, 2 MS&LR 6-wheel coaches, 1 'Internation' concert coach (used as display area and will not run), 1 LNER 45-ton steam breakdown crane, 1 SR GUV, various goods wagons

Owners
37075 the 5C Locomotive Group
Class 108 and 116 DMUs the Nottingham (GC) DMU Group

Paignton & Dartmouth Steam Railway

The line from Paignton is the holiday line with steam trains running for seven miles in Great Western tradition along the spectacular Torbay coast to Churston and through the wooded slopes bordering the Dart estuary to Kingswear. The scenery is superb, with seascapes right across Lyme Bay to Portland Bill on clear days. Approaching Kingswear is the beautiful River Dart, with its fascinating craft, and on the far side, the 'olde worlde' town of Dartmouth and Britannia Royal Naval College, Butterwalk, Bayard's Cove and Dartmouth Castle

Director & General Manager: J. B. S. Cogar

Headquarters: Paignton Queen's Park station, Paignton, Devon

Telephone: Paignton (01803) 555872

Main station: Paignton Queen's Park

Other public stations: Goodrington, Churston, Kingswear (for Dartmouth)

OS reference: SX 889606

Car parks: Paignton municipal car park, Goodrington, Dartmouth (ferry to Kingswear)

Access by public transport: Adjacent to both Paignton main line station and Devon General bus station

Refreshment facilities: Paignton and Kingswear

Locomotives and multiple-units

Name	No	Origin	Class	Type	Built
Warrior	4555	GWR	4500	2-6-2T	1924
Trojan	4588	GWR	4575	2-6-2T	1927
Goliath	5239	GWR	5205	2-8-0T	1924
Ajax	6435	GWR	6400	0-6-0PT	1937
Lydham Manor	7827	GWR	7800	4-6-0	1951
Braveheart	75014	BR	4MT	4-6-0	1951
Ardent	D2192	BR	03	0-6-0DM	1962
Volunteer	D3014	BR	08	0-6-0DE	1954
Mercury	D7535	BR	25	Bo-Bo	1965
—	59003*	BR	116	TS	1957
—	59004*	BR	116	TS	1957
—	59488*	P/Steel	117	TCL	1959
—	59494*	P/Steel	117	TCL	1959
—	59503*	P/Steel	117	TCL	1959
—	59507*	P/Steel	117	TCL	1959
—	59513*	P/Steel	117	TCL	1959
—	59517*	P/Steel	117	TCL	1959

*converted to locomotive-hauled vehicles

Stock

15 ex-BR Mk 1 coaches; 1 Pullman observation coach; 2 auto-coaches; 1 ex-GWR coach

Depot: Churston

Length of line: 7 miles

Passenger trains: Paignton-Kingswear, views of Torbay and Dart estuary, 495yd tunnel

Period of public operation: Easter to October

Facilities for disabled: Limited, special ramp to take wheelchairs onto trains. Disabled toilets at Paignton

Special events: Santa Specials — please see timetable and press for details. Combined river excursions available

Membership details: Devon Diesel Society

Membership journal: Devon Diesel Society

Special note: The railway also operates excursion vessels on the River Dart. Combined river excursions available, boat trains and Round Robin tickets. Boat train — single journey to Kingswear, 1hr 30min boat cruise to Totnes and bus back to Paignton

---

Peak Rail plc

Member: HRA

Location: *Registered Office:* Matlock Station, Matlock, Derbyshire DE4 3NA

OS reference: Matlock SK 060738

Operating society/organisation: Peak Rail plc, Matlock Station, Matlock, Derbyshire DE4 3NA

Telephone: (01629) 580381

Internet address: *Web site:*

Locomotives and multiple-units

Name	No	Origin	Class	Type	Built
—	48624	LMS	8F	2-8-0	1943
—	D2953	BR	01	0-4-0DM	1956
—	D2854	BR	02	0-4-0DH	1960
—	D2866	BR	02	0-4-0DH	1961
—	03027	BR	03	0-6-0DM	1958
—	03084	BR	03	0-6-0DM	1959
—	03099	BR	03	0-6-0DM	1960
—	D2139	BR	03	0-6-0DM	1960

www.peakrail.co.uk
Car parks: Matlock station, Darley
Dale, Rowsley South station
Length of line: 4 miles — Matlock
Riverside-Rowsley South.
A 2ft gauge railway is under
construction at Rowsley
On site facilities: Shop at Matlock.
Shops and buffets at Darley Dale
and Rowsley South. Picnic area and
riverside walk
Public opening: Sundays
throughout the year, Saturdays
April to October. Midweek during
summer. Timetable varies
Facilities for disabled: Darley
Dale and Rowsley. Matlock
Riverside unsuitable for disabled
passengers
Period of public operation: Not
advised, see timetable supplement
Special events: Please contact for
details

Name	No	Origin	Class	Type	Built
—	03158	BR	03	0-6-0DM	1960
—	D2229	BR	04	0-6-0DM	1955
—	D2284	BR	04	0-6-0DM	1960
Dorothy	D2337	BR	04	0-6-0DM	1961
—	07013	BR	07	0-6-0DE	1961
Geoff L. Wright	D3023	BR	08	0-6-0DE	1953
—	D9502	BR	14	0-6-0DH	1964
—	31270	BR	31	A1A-A1A	1961
Penyghent	D8	BR	44	1Co-Co1	1959
Renown	50029	BR	50	Co-Co	1968
Repulse	50030	BR	50	Co-Co	1968
—	50627	BR	108	DMBS	1958
—	51566	BR	108	DMSL	1959
—	51567	BR	108	DMSL	1959
—	51933	BR	108	DMBS	1960
—	53933	BR	108	DMBS	1959
—	54484	BR	108	DTC	1960
—	54504	BR	108	DTC	1960
—	59387	BR	108	TS	1958
—	51973 (977806)	BR	108	DMBS	1958

Industrial locomotives

Name	No	Builder	Type	Built
The Duke	2746	Bagnall (2746)	0-6-0ST	1944
Quarryman	68006	Hunslet (3183)	0-6-0ST	1944
Warrington	150	RSH (7136)	0-6-0ST	1944
Zebedee	—	RSH (7597)	0-6-0ST	1949
Vulcan	—	V/Foundry (3272)	0-4-0ST	1918
—	—	T/Hill	0-6-0DH	
Lucky	48	T/Hill	0-6-0DH	
Castlefield	—	H/Clarke	0-6-0DH	
—	20	R/Hornsby (432479)	0-4-0DM	1959
Rotherham	—	YEC (2480)	0-4-0DM	
Bigga	—	Fowler (4200019)	0-4-0DM	1947
Ken	—	Sentinel (10180)	0-6-0DH	1964

Rolling stock — coaches: 2 BR Mk 1 RMB, 1 BR Mk 1 SLF, 3 BR Mk 1
TSO, 2 BR Mk 1 SO, 3 BR Mk 1 SK, 1 BR Mk 1 BSK, 2 BR Mk 1 BG, 1
BR Mk 1 GUV, 1 BR Mk 2 SO, 1 BR Mk 2 BSO, 1 BR Mk 2 BFK, 1 LMS
TK, 2 LMS BCK, 1BTK, 1 Bullion coach, 3 parcels vans

Rolling stock — wagons: 1 5 plank, 1 LMS 5 plank, 3 match wagons,
1 LNER flat wagon, 1 LMS 5 plank tube, 1 LMS 2 plank tube, 1 BR
Grampus 20-ton ballast, 1 LNER flat, 1 LMR water bowser, 1 Plasser &
Theurer tamper, 2 LMS fish vans, 2 Austrian ferry wagons, 1 SR parcels
van, 1 Shell tank wagon, 1 Esso tank wagon, 2 tank wagons, 2 LNER
2 plank dropsides, 3 BR 12-ton box vans, 1 12-ton van (wooden
underframe), 2 BR Pallet vans, 1 Charles Roberts covered van, 1 LNER
crane, 2 LMS brake vans, 1 BR brake van, 1 MR brake van, 1 BR Sturgeon
rail wagon, 1 BR Lowmac, 1 BR Welltrol, 1 BR Salmon, 2 BR Dogfish
ballast hoppers

Owners
03158 the Amber Valley Locomotive Group
50029 and 50030 The Renown Repulse Restoration Group
D8 the North Notts Loco Group
Vulcan the Vulcan Loco Trust
7597 Peak Rail and Peak Rail Heritage Trust
D3023 the Heritage Shunters Trust

Derbyshire Dales Narrow Gauge Railway
Industrial narrow gauge locomotives (2ft gauge)

Name	No	Builder	Type	Built
—	—	M/Rail (22070)	4wDM	1960
—	—	R/Hornsby (264252)	4wDM	1952
—	—	R/Hornsby (393325)	4wDM	1956
—	—	R/Hornsby (487963)	4wDM	1963

Steam Centre — Plym Valley Railway — Devon

Member: HRA
A scheme dedicated to the restoration of services over the former GWR Marsh Mills-Plym Bridge line, a distance of 1.5 miles
Location: 5 miles from centre of Plymouth, Devon, north of A38. From Marsh Mills roundabout, take B3416 to Plympton, follow signs
Internet address: *Web site:* www.plymrail.co.uk
OS reference: SX 517564
Operating society/organisation: Plym Valley Railway Co Ltd, Marsh Mills Station, Coypool Road, Marsh Mills, Plymouth, Devon PL7 4NW
Access by public transport: Buses from Plymouth, Nos 20, 20A, 21, 22A, 51 stop close to site
On site facilities: Shop and refreshments at Marsh Mills, Coypool (Sundays only)
Public opening: Sundays from 10.00, and other selected days
Length of line: Half-mile currently in use for passenger rides
Special events: Please see press for details

Locomotives and multiple-units

Name	No	Origin	Class	Type	Built
—	75079	BR	4MT	4-6-0	1956
—	13002	BR	08	0-6-0DE	1953
William Cookworthy	37207	BR	37	Co-Co	1963
—	51365	BR	117	MBS	1960
—	51407	BR	117	DMS	1960

Industrial locomotives

Name	No	Builder	Type	Built
Byfield No 2	—	Bagnall (2655)	0-6-0ST	1941
—	3	H/Leslie (3597)	0-4-0ST	1926
—	—	T/Hill (125V)	4wDH	1963
—	—	Hibberd (3281)	4wDM	1948

Rolling stock: 3 x BR Mk 1 coaches, 1 LBSCR compartment coach (body only), 2 x BR GUVs, 3 x brake vans, various wagons. Self-propelled Smith & Rodley diesel crane of 1956

Special notes: Visitors are advised that, at the moment, the railway and two locomotives are still under restoration. 2 working locomotives and DMU. The line was extended beyond the first bridge in 2003. Train rides behind the 13002 on some Sundays (normally 2nd in the month)

Membership details: Den Fairchild, Plym Valley Railway, Marsh Mills Station, Coypool Road, Marsh Mills, Plymouth, Devon PL7 4NW
Membership journal: *Plym Valley Railway News* — 3/year
Marketing name: The Woodland Line

Steam Centre — The Railway Age, Crewe — Cheshire

Location: Crewe Heritage Centre, Vernon Way, Crewe
OS reference: SJ 709552
Operating society/organisation: Crewe Heritage Trust Ltd
Telephone: (01270) 212130
Internet address: *Web site:* www.therailwayage.co.uk
Car park: On site, town centre, Forge Street, Oak Street

Locomotives and multiple-units

Name	No	Origin	Class	Type	Built
Cornwall	3020	LNWR	—	2-2-2	1888
—	485	LNWR	G2	0-8-0	1921
—	5224§	GWR	4200	2-8-0T	1924
—	6638	GWR	5600	0-6-2T	1928
Britannia	70000	BR	7MT	4-6-2	1951
—	D2073	BR	03	0-6-0DM	1959
—	D8233	BR	15	Bo-Bo	1959
—	31442	BR	31	A1A-A1A	1960

Access by public transport: Main line Crewe

Refreshment facilities: Adjacent Safeway superstore

On site facilities: Gift shop, picnic area, children's corner, weekend train rides, standard gauge and miniature railway, exhibition hall, main line viewing area, 3 working signalboxes with 'hands-on' visitor operation

Public opening: Daily 10.00-16.00 (last admission 15.00). Family tickets available. Please contact for details of events

Facilities for disabled: Toilets

Membership details: Heritage Centre Supporters Association, c/o above address

Notes: Steam locomotives passed for use over main line tracks are stabled between duties from time to time

Name	No	Origin	Class	Type	Built
—	D120†	BR	45	1Co-Co1	1961
Cornwall	3020	LNWR	—	2-2-2	1888
Ixion	D172†	BR	46	1Co-Co1	1962
—	D1842	BR	47	Co-Co	1965
Royal Oak	50017*	BR	50	Co-Co	1968
—	18000	BR	—	A1A-A1A	1949
—	55032*	P/Steel	121	DMBS	1960

†on site occasionally, but usually kept at private locations
*may not be on site for all of 2003
§on loan to West Somerset Railway

Industrial locomotives

Name	No	Builder	Type	Built
Robert	—	H/Clarke (1752)	0-6-0T	1943

Rolling stock
APT vehicle Nos 48103, 48106, 48404, 48602, 48603, 48606, 49002; 1 BR Mk 1 BSK; various ex-BR coaches and passenger brake vans from time to time for repairs

Owners
485 and *Cornwall* — the National Railway Museum

Museum	**Railworld**	Cams

Member: HRA

Railworld is primarily an exhibition centre. In addition it has a museum which is mainly about Peterborough's railway history, its model railway is impressive. There are also 'Age of Steam' exhibits and a database of over 7,000 names of local railworkers since the 1840s (50p extra access charge)

Location: Situated alongside the Town station of the Nene Valley Railway. Walk — 15min walk from train and bus stations. By car — turn off A605 Oundle Road (town end) into Council's long stay car park, drive through to Railworld. The Railworld car park is free to visitors. By bike — situated on the 'Green Wheel' cycle route. By boat — alongside river quay (tel: 01933 680743 for details of boat trips)

OS reference: TL 189981

Operating society/organisation: Railworld, Oundle Road, Peterborough, Cambridgeshire PE2 9NR

Contact: Rev Richard Paten

Telephone/fax: 01733 344240

Internet address: *Web site:* www.railworld.net

Locomotives

Name	No	Origin	Class	Type	Built
—	996	DSB	4MT	4-6-2	1950

Industrial locomotives

Name	No	Builder	Type	Built
—	804	Alco (77778)	Bo-Bo	1949
Nutty*	5	Sentinel (7701)	4wVBT	1929
—†	740	O&K (2343)	0-6-0T	1907

*2ft 6in gauge
† 2ft gauge and on loan to Leighton Buzzard Railway
remainder standard

Other stock: Britain's RTV 31 Hovertrain vehicle, Presflo 2-axle flyash wagon (No B874076 of 12965) and a 2-axle 8,650gal tank wagon (No 55223 of 1966). Birmingham International Airport Maglev car No 01 of 1984 supplied by Metro-Cammell, operational 1984-1995 — the world's first train without wheels in commercial service

On site facilities: Buffet and small shop, open weekends March to October. Picnic area and floating restaurant nearby. Model railway

Public opening: Daily March-October 11.00-16.00. Also Monday to Fridays November-March 11.00-16.00

Special events: National Science Week — 12-21 March; 'Environment Week' (Integrated Transport) — 26 June-11 July

Access for disabled: Reasonable wheelchair access

Admission charge: Adult £4, Child £2, Concessions £3, Family £10 (2A+4C)

Membership details: John Crane, 21 St Margarets Road, Peterborough PE2 9EA

Membership journal: *Friends of Railworld* — quarterly

Ravenglass & Eskdale Railway

Cumbria

Member: HRA

From the coast through two of Lakeland's loveliest valleys to the foot of England's highest mountain, small steam engines haul trains in the heart of the national park

General Manager:
Trevor Stockton

Headquarters: Ravenglass & Eskdale Railway, Ravenglass, Cumbria CA18 1SW

Telephone: (01229) 717171

Fax: (01229) 717011

Internet address: *E-mail:* rer@netcomuk.co.uk

Web site: www.ravenglass-railway.co.uk

Main station: Ravenglass

Other public stations: Muncaster Mill, Irton Road, The Green, Beckfoot, Eskdale (Dalegarth)

OS reference: SD 086964

Car parks: All stations

Access by public transport: Main line services to Ravenglass; bus service from Whitehaven

Refreshment facilities: Ravenglass, Dalegarth. Bar meals at 'Ratty Arms'

Picnic areas: At both termini

Souvenir shops: Ravenglass, Dalegarth

Museum: Ravenglass

Length of line: 7 miles, 15in gauge

Passenger trains: Steam or diesel-hauled narrow gauge trains

Locomotives

Name	No	Builder	Type	Built
River Irt	—	Heywood	0-8-2	1894
River Esk	—	Davey Paxman (21104)	2-8-2	1923
River Mite	—	Clarkson (4669)	2-8-2	1966
Northern Rock	—	R&ER	2-6-2	1976
Bonnie Dundee	—	K/Stuart (720)*	0-4-2	1901
Shelagh of Eskdale	—	R&ER/Severn-Lamb	4-6-4D	1969
			rebuilt	1998
Quarryman	—	Muir-Hill (2)	0-4-0P/Paraffin	1928
Perkins	—	Muir Hill (NG39A)	0-4-4DM	1929
Silver Jubilee	—	R&ER	DMU	1977
Lady Wakefield	—	R&ER	B-B	1980
Synolda	—	Bassett-Lowke	4-4-2	1912
—	—	Greenbat (2782)	0-4-0BE	1957
Cyril	—	Lister	0-4-0DM	1987

*rebuilt to 15in gauge 1981

Ravenglass-Dalegarth

Period of public operation: Daily late March-early November. Limited winter service November-March

Family ticket: All day travel at reduced price

Facilities for disabled: Special coaches for wheelchair passengers. Advance notice preferred. Wheelchair access to toilets, café and museum at Ravenglass; toilets, shop and cafe at Eskdale (Dalegarth)

Special notes: At Ravenglass the R&ER has two camping coaches

and the company also operates the 'Ratty Arms' public house formed by conversion of the former BR station buildings. During the high summer, mid-July through August, five steam locomotives are normally in use Monday-Thursday

Membership details: Mr N. Dickinson, 3 Clifton Terrace, Ravenglass, Cumbria CA18 1SE

Membership journal: *The R&ER Magazine* — quarterly

Marketing names: 'la'al Ratty' — Cumbrian dialect for little narrow track, now a watervole stationmaster!

Romney, Hythe & Dymchurch Railway

Kent

Member: HRA

This line was built in 1926/27 as a one-third size miniature main line, and is by far the longest and most fully equipped 15in gauge railway in the world. It carries not only daytrippers and holidaymakers but also children to and from the local school at New Romney.

Headquarters: Romney, Hythe & Dymchurch Railway, New Romney Station, Kent TN28 8PL

Telephone: (01797) 362353/

363256

Fax: 01797 363591

Internet addresses: *e-mail:* rhdr@romneyrail.fsnet.co.uk

Web site: http://www.rhdr.org.uk

OS reference: TR 074249

Main station: New Romney

Other public stations: Hythe, Dymchurch, St Marys Bay, Romney Sands, Dungeness

Car parks: Hythe, Dymchurch, New Romney, Dungeness

Access by public transport:

Folkestone Central station (South Eastern Trains) and then bus to Hythe (4 miles) or Rye station (SouthCentral) and then bus to New Romney (8 miles)

Refreshment facilities: Cafeterias at New Romney and Dungeness, picnic areas at Dymchurch, New Romney and Dungeness. Also licensed observation coach on certain trains

Souvenir shops: Hythe and New Romney (plus Dymchurch and

Dungeness in main season)
Toy and Model Museum: New Romney, with displays of old, and not so old, toys; plus two large operating model railways
Depot: New Romney
Length of line: 13.5 miles, 15in gauge
Passenger trains: Train frequency depends on the time of year: maximum frequency is 45 minutes
Period of public operation: Trains run daily from 1 April to 30 September. Also weekends from 14 February until 5 November. Out of season the school train departs New Romney at 15.00 with limited public accommodation (Monday-Friday, term times only)
Special events: Steam & Diesel Gala — 15/16 May; Autumn Steam Extravaganza — 2/3 October. Santa Specials in December (pre-booking essential)
Special notes: Senior citizen concessions any day except Bank Holiday and advertised special events. Family tickets available. Special trains can be run at most times by prior arrangement. Parties can be catered for at New Romney and Dungeness cafés. Evening dining train service on selected Saturdays in the summer

Locomotives

Name	No	Builder	Type	Built
Green Goddess	1	Davey Paxman	4-6-2	1925
Northern Chief	2	Davey Paxman	4-6-2	1925
Southern Maid	3	Davey Paxman	4-6-2	1926
The Bug	4	Krauss (8378)	0-4-0TT	1926
Hercules	5	Davey Paxman	4-8-2	1926
Samson	6	Davey Paxman	4-8-2	1926
Typhoon	7	Davey Paxman	4-6-2	1926
Hurricane	8	Davey Paxman	4-6-2	1926
Winston Churchill	9	YEC (2294)	4-6-2	1931
Doctor Syn	10	YEC (2295)	4-6-2	1931
Black Prince	11	Krupp (1664)	4-6-2	1937
John Southland	12	TMA Birmingham	Bo-Bo	1983
Captain Howey	14	TMA Birmingham	Bo-Bo	1989
—	PW1	M/Rail (7059)	4wDM	1938
—	PW2	RH&DR	4wPM	1965
Redgauntlet	PW3	Jacot/RH&DR	4wPM	1963
Trembly*	—	Lister (37658)	4wDM	1952

*on loan fitted with a *Toby* body for Thomas the Tank events

Stock
40 saloon bogie coaches; 12 open bogie coaches; 5 luggage/brake saloons; 1 parlour car; 1 mess coach; 40 assorted wagons

Facilities for disabled: Ramps and level crossings at all stations for easy access. Special wheelchair coach available on any train by prior arrangement. Stair lift between café and 'Toy & Model Museum'. Disabled toilets at Hythe, Dymchurch, New Romney and

Dungeness
Membership details: RH&DR Association, 26 Norman Close, Battle, East Sussex TN33 0BD
Membership journal: *The Marshlander* — quarterly

Diesel Centre — Rother Valley Railway — East Sussex

The original section of what was to become known as the Kent & East Sussex Railway was thought to be lost to preservation for ever following decisions of Transport Minister, Barbara Castle, in the late 1960s. However, more enlightened attitudes in recent years mean that work is now in hand to reinstate the missing link between Robertsbridge and the K&ESR at Bodiam
Location/headquarters: Robertsbridge Station, Robertsbridge, East Sussex TN32 4DG
Telephone: 01580 881833
Operating society/organisation: Rother Valley Railway (East Sussex) Ltd, Bedford House, 62 London Road, Maidstone, Kent

Industrial locomotives

Name	No	Builder	Type	Built
Titan	43	Vulcan/Drewry	0-4-0DM	1955
—	7	Sentinel	0-4-0DH	1959

Rolling stock (under restoration)
Ex-SR brake van, ex-SR Maunsell brake third, ex-SR corridor Comp (converted to General Manager's saloon), ex-BR Mk 1 2nd open, ex-SR GBL, 4 parcels vans, 5 box wagons, 2 open wagons, 1 flat wagon, 1 hopper wagon, 2 tank wagons and 2 lowmacs
NB: This list is subject to change during the course of the year

ME16 8QL, and the Rother Valley Railway Supporters Association, 375 New Hythe Lane, Larkfield, Aylesford, Kent ME20 6RY
OS reference: TQ 734235
Access by public transport: Connex SouthEastern trains on Charing Cross and Tunbridge Wells

to Hastings service call at Robertsbridge station. Arriva bus service 4 and 5 on Maidstone-Hastings service call at High Street, Robertsbridge
Car parks: Robertsbridge station and Station Road, Robertsbridge
On site facilities: Visitor centre

housed in former VSOE lounge with souvenir shop and buffet. Rolling stock under restoration, picnic area
Facilities for disabled: Access to the visitor centre, buffet, shop and all public areas
Length of line: Standard gauge — c400yd at present. When restored, length to Bodiam will be 3.5 miles, with end-on connection to K&ESR
Public opening: Every Sunday and Bank Holiday Monday (except Christmas and Boxing Day). 10.30-17.00 (dusk if earlier)
Special events: Annual model railway exhibition. Subject to Ministry approval brake van rides will commence this year
Membership secretary: Peter Coombs, 375 New Hythe Lane, Larkfield, Aylesford, Kent ME20 6RY. (Tel: 01622 717491)
Society journal: *The Phoenix* — quarterly

Steam Centre — Ruislip Lido Railway — London

Member: HRA

The 12in gauge line is operated by enthusiast volunteers as an attraction within Ruislip Lido, a country park which is maintained by the London Borough of Hillingdon

Location: Ruislip Lido, Reservoir Road, Ruislip, Middlesex

Operating society/organisation: Ruislip Lido Railway Society Ltd, Membership Secretary, Mrs S. E. Simmons, 9 Wiltshire Lane, Eastcote, Pinner, Middx HA5 2LH

Telephone: 020 8866 9654

Car park: Available at Lido

Access by public transport: Ruislip Underground station (Metropolitan and Piccadilly lines) then by bus H13 or 331 nearby (daily). Lido is off the A4180 road

Refreshment facilities: New family pub/restaurant (Brewers Fayre) on site. Picnic areas also available

Length of line: 1.25-mile single journey, 2.5 miles return including new extension now open which

Locomotives

Name	No	Builder	Type	Built
Robert	3	Severn-Lamb	B-2 DH	1973
Lady of the Lakes	5	Ravenglass & Eskdale Railway	B-B DM	1985
Mad Bess	6	RLRS	2-4-0ST+T	1998
Graham Alexander	7	Severn-Lamb	B-B DM	1990
Bayhurst	8	Severn-Lamb	B-B DM	2003

Locomotive notes: All locomotives are normally available for service. Limited steam-hauled service

Stock

6 open coaches; 9 closed coaches; miscellaneous service stock

terminates near the main entrance to car park

Public opening: The line is open at weekends throughout the year; Daily from 26 June to 5 September; 15-17, 22-24 September and daily during Hillingdon school holidays.

24-hour recorded train information service (01895) 622595. Full service leaflet on request to 020 8866 9654. Party bookings (01895) 637400

Journey time: Single 20min, return 40min

Facilities for disabled: Wheelchair passengers can travel on all trains

Membership details: c/o above address

Membership journal: *Woody Bay News* — 3 issues per year

Steam Centre — Rutland Railway Museum — Rutland

Member: HRA

This museum is dedicated to portraying the railway in industry, particularly iron ore mining, and has a wide range of industrial locomotives and rolling stock. Indeed, its collection of quarry freight rolling stock is probably the most comprehensive in the country and regular demonstrations are a feature of the 'steam days'.

Location: Cottesmore Iron Ore Mines Siding, Ashwell Road, Cottesmore, near Oakham, Rutland — museum situated midway between villages of Cottesmore and Ashwell, approximately 4 miles north of Oakham (locally signposted)

OS reference: SK 886137

Operating society/organisation: Rutland Railway Museum, Cottesmore Iron Ore Mines Siding, Ashwell Road, Cottesmore, Nr Oakham, Rutland LE15 7BX

Telephone: Oakham (01572) 813203

Car park: Free car park on site
Access by public transport:
Nearest main line station, Oakham.
Bus service, Paul James,
Nottingham-Melton Mowbray-
Ashwell-Oakham,
Corby/Peterborough-Oakham-
Ashwell (service 19).
On site facilities: Free train rides,
demonstration freight trains,
refreshments, toilets, museum,
shop, picnic sites, demonstration
line with lineside walk and viewing
areas, static displays of over 30
steam and diesel locomotives; over
50 wagons, vans and coaches
(believed to be the largest
collection of preserved quarry
freight stock in the UK)
Length of line: Three-quarter-mile
Passenger trains: Regular shuttle
service operates on open days
(approximately every 15min)
Public opening: Open weekends or
by arrangement, some weekdays
(please telephone prior to visit).
Open 11.00-17.00. (Leaflets
available, SAE please)
Special events: Easter Steam Days,
Easter Bunny Children's
Competition — 11/12 April; May
Steam Days, Teddy Bear Weekend
— 2/3 May; Whitsun Steam Days
— 30/31 May; Steam Open Day —
13 June; Summer Steam Weekend
& Model Railway Exhibition —
29/30 August; Steam Open Day —
26 September; Santa Steam
Specials — December (dates to be
confirmed
Facilities for disabled: Site
relatively flat. Members willing to
assist.
Special notes: The open air
museum houses an extensive
collection of industrial locomotives
and rolling stock typifying past
activity in local ironstone quarries,
nationwide mines and factories. A
demonstration line approximately
three quarters of a mile long has
been relaid on the former MR
Cottesmore mineral branch
(originally built to tap local
ironstone quarries), on which
restored locomotives and stock are
run
Membership details: Membership
Secretary, c/o above address

Locomotives and multiple-units

Name	No	Origin	Class	Type	Built
—	D2118	BR	03	0-6-0DM	1959
—	D2302	BR	04	0-6-0DM	1960
—	06003	BR	06	0-4-0DH	1959
NCB No 7	(D9518)	BR	14	0-6-0DH	1964

Industrial locomotives

Name	No	Builder	Type	Built
Dora	—	Avonside (1973)	0-4-0ST	1927
Firefly	—	Barclay (776)	0-4-0ST	1896
BSC No 2	—	Barclay (1931)	0-4-0ST	1927
Drake	—	Barclay (2086)	0-4-0ST	1940
Sir Thomas Royden	—	Barclay (2088)	0-4-0ST	1940
Uppingham	—	Peckett (1257)	0-4-0ST	1912
Elizabeth	—	Peckett (1759)	0-4-0ST	1928
Singapore	—	H/Leslie (3865)	0-4-0ST	1936
—	24	Hunslet (2411)	0-6-0ST	1941
Coal Products No 6	—	Hunslet (2868)/	0-6-0ST	1943
		(Rebuilt Hunslet 3883)		1963
—	65	Hunslet (3889)	0-6-0ST	1964
—	8	Peckett (2110)	0-4-0ST	1950
—	7	Sentinel (9376)	4wVBT	1947
—	—	Sentinel (9596)	4wVBT	1955
—	—	Barclay (352)	0-4-0DM	1941
—	1	Barclay (415)	0-4-0DH	1957
—	20-90-01	Barclay (499)	0-4-0DH	1965
—	8	Bagnall (3209)/	0-4-0DH	1962
		RSH (8364)		
—	—	Brush (804)	0-6-0DE	1978
—	BSC 1	E/Electric (D1049)	0-6-0DH	1965
—	—	E/Electric (D1231)	0-6-0DH	1967
—	4	Fowler (4240012)	0-6-0DH	1961
—	—	Fowler (4240015)	0-6-0DH	1962
Phoenix	—	Hibberd (3887)	4wDM	1958
—	21	H/Clarke (D707)	0-6-0DM	1950
—	No 1	Hunslet (6688)	0-4-0DH	1968
—	3	N/British (27656)	0-4-0DH	1957
Betty	8411/04	R/Royce (10201)	0-4-0DH	1964
—	D21	R/Royce (10270)	0-6-0DH	1967
—	—	R/Hornsby (305302)	4wDM	1951
—	—	R/Hornsby (306092)	4wDM	1950
—	—	R/Hornsby (347747)	0-6-0DM	1957
—	20-90-02	R/Hornsby (504565)	0-4-0DH	1965
Hays	—	R/Hornsby (544997)	0-4-0DE	1969
—	—	T/Hill (120c)	4wDH	1962
		(Rebuild of Sentinel 9619/1957)		
—	RoF No 1	T/Hill (132c)	0-4-0DH	1963
		(Rebuild of Fowler 22982/1942)		
—	CEGB 24	T/Hill (188c)	4wDH	1967
		(Rebuild of Sentinel 9597/1955)		
—	10	T/Hill (234v)	4wDH	1971
—	—	YEC (2641)	0-6-0DE	1957
—	20	YEC (2688)	0-6-0DE	1959
—	No 28	YEC (2791)	0-6-0DE	1962
—	1382	YEC (2872)	0-6-0DE	1962

Locomotive notes: In service Dora, Singapore, 7, D9555, Betty, 1, 20-90-01,
8 (Bagnal 3209), No 1 (HE6688), 21, Phoenix, CEGB 24, RoF No1, D2118
and BSC 1
Stock
1 coaches; 4 brake vans; 14 covered goods vans; 57 wagons (includes rakes of
wagons as used in local ironstone and industrial railways); 3 rail cranes

Museum — Science Museum — London

Built on land acquired with the profits from the Great Exhibition of 1851, the Science Museum was one of the first to include industrial archaeology. The railway exhibits are drawn from the collection based at the National Railway Museum. They form part of a major gallery, 'Making the Modern World', which opened in June 2000 on the site of the former Land Transport gallery

Location: South Kensington
OS reference: TQ 268793
Operating society/organisation: Science Museum, Exhibition Road, South Kensington, London SW7 2DD
Telephone: 020 7942 4000
Internet address: *Web site:* www.sciencemuseum.org.uk
Access by public transport: South

Locomotive

Name	No	Origin	Class	Type	Built
Rocket	—	Liverpool & Manchester Railway	—	0-2-2	1829
Columbine	—	Grand Junction Railway	—	2-2-2	1845
Puffing Billy	—	Wylam Colliery	—	0-4-0	1813

Locomotive note: Restored to static display condition

Kensington Underground station
Catering facilities: Cafés on ground floor, hot meals, tea, coffee, sandwiches, etc. Picnic area in basement
On site facilities: Bookshop, toilets on most floors
Public opening: Daily 10.00-18.00. Closed 24-26 December
Special events: All organised by

the National Railway Museum, York, which is part of the Science Museum. Telephone (01904) 621261 for details
Facilities for disabled: Toilets on most floors, ramp and lifts to all floors. Parties should contact before arrival if extra assistance is required
Special notes: Static exhibits only in 'Making the Modern World'

Timetable Service — Seaton & District Electric Tramway — Devon

Member: HRA, South West Tourism
A unique 2ft 9in gauge electric tramway, operating on the trackbed of the former Southern Railway branch line between Seaton, Colyford and Colyton in east Devon. Panoramic views of the beautiful Axe Valley and estuary together with a host of wading birds and other wildlife

Location: Harbour Road Car Park, Seaton; Swan Hill Road, Colyford (next to White Hart Inn); Station Road, Kingsdon, Colyton
OS reference: SY 252904
Operating society/organisation: Modern Electric Tramways Ltd t/a Seaton Tramway, Car Depot, Harbour Road, Seaton, Devon EX12 2NQ
Telephone: 01297 20375
Fax: 01297 625626
Internet address: *e-mail:* info@tram.co.uk
Web site: www.tram.co.uk
Access by public transport: Nearest railway station: Axminster.

Trams

No	Prototype based on	Type	Built
2	London Metropolitan Tramways	A	1964
4	Blackpool	'Boat'	1961
6	Bournemouth (later Llandudno & Colwyn Bay)	'open top'	1954
7	Bournemouth (later Llandudno & Colwyn Bay)	'open top'	1954
8	†—	—	1968
12	London Metropolitan Tramways	'Feltham'	1966
14*	London Metropolitan Tramways	A	1904
16*	Bournemouth		1921
17	Manx Electric Tramway	'toastrack'	1988
19*	Exeter Corporation	—	1906
9	new build	double-deck	2001
10	new build	double-deck	2001
11	new build	double-deck	2001

†a larger version of the ex-Bournemoth design of cars 6 and 7
*rebuilds of actual prototypes
9, 10, 11 are based on elements of designs from Plymouth and Blackburn

Buses: Axe Valley Mini Travel service 885 from Axminster, service 899 from Lyme Regis and Sidmouth. First Southern National service X53 from Weymouth and

Exeter, service 20 from Taunton and Honiton. Bus enquiries 0870 608 2608 or www.devon.gov.uk/devonbus
On site facilities: Gift shops at

Seaton and Colyton. Restaurant and picnic area at Colyton
Length of line: 3 miles, 2ft 9in gauge
Period of public operation and departure times (2004):
Daily 14-22 February, 10.00-16.00. Saturdays & Sundays 28 February-28 March, 10.00-16.00. Daily 3 April-24 July, 10.00-17.00. Daily 25 July-4 September, 10.00-20.40. Daily 5 September-23 October, 10.00-16.00. Daily 24-31 October, 10.00-16.00. Saturday & Sunday 6 November-19 December, 10.00-16.00. Santa Specials — 5, 12, 19, 24 December, enquire for details.

Private hire all year round for groups of 25+
Special events: Vintage Vehicle Rally — 12 June; Gala Day — 13 June; Seaton Carnival Late Night Service — 4 September; Colyton Carnival Late Night Service — 11 September; End of Season Gala — 30/31 October
Fares: Seaton to Colyton return fares — Adult £5.40, OAP £4.85, Child £3.80. Single fares and rover tickets also available. Discounts for local residents, families and parties of 12 or more
Facilities for disabled: Tramcar No 17 carries up to 12 wheelchairs.

Please note that it has open sides and is therefore exposed to the weather. It is sometimes possible to accommodate individuals at short notice, but groups should book in advance. Disabled toilets at Seaton and Colyton
Special notes: Tram driving lessons available through the season except 25 July-4 September. Bird watching trips available January to May and September to December. Enquire for details. Service operated by open-top double-deck bogie cars (enclosed saloon cars during inclement weather)

Severn Valley Railway

Member: HRA, TT
The railway hosts more main line engines than any other preserved line in the country, enjoying the back-up of a large volunteer and professional workforce and extensive engineering workshops and equipment. Railway travel like it used to be
General Manager: Alun Rees
Headquarters: Severn Valley Railway Co Ltd, Railway Station, Bewdley, Worcs DY12 1BG
Telephone: Bewdley (01299) 403816; 24hr timetable — 0800 600900
Internet address: Web site: http://www.svr.co.uk
Main stations: Bridgnorth, Bewdley, Kidderminster Town
Other public stations: Arley, Highley, Hampton Loade, Northwood Halt, Country Park Halt
OS reference: Bridgnorth SO 715926, Bewdley SO 793753
Car parks: At all main stations
Access by public transport: First Bus service 192 to Kidderminster and Bewdley and 125 & 297 to Bridgnorth. Rail service to Kidderminster (main line) with immediate connections to SVR station. Through tickets available from all manned main line stations
Refreshment facilities: At most stations, but not on all operating days and on most trains. Fully licensed bars at Bridgnorth and

Locomotives and multiple-units

Name	No	Origin	Class	Type	Built
The Great Marquess	61994	LNER	K4	2-6-0	1938
Union of South Africa	60009	LNER	A4	4-6-2	1937
Gordon	AD600	LMR	WD	2-10-0	1943
—	43106	LMS	4MT	2-6-0	1951
—	46443	LMS	2MT	2-6-0	1950
RAF Biggin Hill	45110	LMS	5MT	4-6-0	1935
—	47383	LMS	3F	0-6-0T	1926
—	48773	LMS	8F	2-8-0	1940
—	42968	LMS	5P4F	2-6-0	1933
—	813	GWR	—	0-6-0ST	1901
—	2857	GWR	2800	2-8-0	1918
—	5164	GWR	5101	2-6-2T	1930
—	4150	GWR	5101	2-6-2T	1947
—	5764	GWR	5700	0-6-0PT	1929
—	7714	GWR	5700	0-6-0PT	1930
—	4566	GWR	4500	2-6-2T	1924
Bradley Manor	7802	GWR	'Manor'	4-6-0	1939
Erlestoke Manor	7812	GWR	'Manor'	4-6-0	1939
Hinton Manor	7819	GWR	'Manor'	4-6-0	1939
Hagley Hall*	4930	GWR	'Hall'	4-6-0	1929
Taw Valley	34027	SR	WC	4-6-2	1946
—	1501	GWR	1500	0-6-0PT	1949
—**	7325	GWR	4300	2-6-0	1932
—	75069	BR	4MT	4-6-0	1955
—	80079	BR	4MT	2-6-4T	1954
Greyhound	D821	BR	42	B-B	1960
Western Ranger	D1013	BR	52	C-C	1962
Western Courier	D1062	BR	52	C-C	1963
—	D3022	BR	08	0-6-0DE	1952
—	08133	BR	08	0-6-0DE	1955
—	D3586	BR	08	0-6-0DE	1953
—	12099	LMS	11	0-6-0DE	1952
—†	D7029	BR	35	B-B	1962
—	D5410	BR	27	Bo-Bo	1962
Hood	D431	BR	50	Co-Co	1968

Kidderminster Town
Souvenir shops: Bridgnorth, Kidderminster Town
Depots: Bridgnorth (locomotives), Bewdley and Kidderminster (stock)
Model railways: At Bewdley, Kidderminster and Hampton Loade
Length of line: 16.5 miles
Passenger trains: Steam-hauled trains running frequently from Kidderminster Town to Bewdley and Bridgnorth. Diesel-hauled service on limited occasions as advertised
Period of public operation: Every weekend, Santa Steam Specials weekends in December. Daily service 8 May to 26 September, plus February, April and October local school holidays. Open for limited viewing at other times
Special events: Day out with Thomas — 8/9, 15/16 May; Heavy Horse Power Weekend — 5/6 June; 1940s Weekends — 26/27 June, 3/4 July; Severn Valley in Bloom — 31 July/1 August; Day out with Thomas — 4/5, 11/12 September; Autumn Steam Gala — 24-26 September; Diesel Gala — 1-3 October; Classic Vehicle Day — 10 October; Railcar 50 — 15-17 October; Santa Steam Specials — 4/5, 11/12, 18/19, 24 December. Festive Season service — 26 December-3 January 2005
Facilities for disabled: Facilities available, special vehicle available to carry wheelchairs by prior arrangement. Disabled people's toilets and ramp access to refreshment facilities at Kidderminster and Bridgnorth. Enlarged versions of all leaflets are available for the visually impaired from staffed booking offices
Special notes: A number of special enthusiasts' weekends and special events are held when extra trains are operated. In addition, supplementary trains with diesel haulage are run as advertised. 'Severn Valley Limited' and 'Severn Valley Venturer' Restaurant Car service operates on Sundays, some Wednesdays and as required on other occasions. Advance booking required. Charter trains with or without dining facilities can be arranged
Membership details: Mrs Kate

Name	No	Origin	Class	Type	Built
Ark Royal	50035	BR	50	Co-Co	1968
Exeter	D444	BR	50	Co-Co	1968
Defiance	D449	BR	50	Co-Co	1967
—	51935	BR	108	DMBS	1960
—	51941	BR	108	DMBS	1960
—	52064	BR	108	DMC	1960
—	56208	BR	108	DTCL	1958
—	59250	BR	108	TBS	1958

*on display at the McArthur Glen complex, Swindon
**on display at Steam: Museum of the Great Western Railway, Swindon
†at private site for overhaul

Industrial locomotives

Name	No	Builder	Type	Built
Warwickshire	—	M/Wardle (2047)	0-6-0ST	1926
The Lady Armaghdale	—	Hunslet (686)	0-6-0T	1898
—	—	Ruston (319290)	0-4-0DM	1953
—	—	R/Hornsby (414304)	0-4-0DM	1957
—	—	R/Hornsby (408297)	0-4-0DM	1957

Stock
27 ex-GWR coaches; 13 ex-LMS coaches; 24 ex-BR Mk 1 coaches; 8 ex-LNER coaches; numerous examples of ex-GWR, LMS and other freight vehicles and two 30-ton steam cranes

Owners
813 the GWR 813 Fund
1501 the 15xx Fund
2857 the 2857 Fund
42968 the Stanier Mogul Fund
4150 the 4150 Locomotive Fund
4566 the 4566 Fund
5164 the 51xx Fund
5764, 7714 the Pannier Tank Fund
34027, 60009, 61994 and D1013 are privately owned
7325 the Great Western (SVR) Association
7802 and 7812 the Erlestoke Manor Fund
7819 the Hinton Manor Fund
43106 the Ivatt 4 Fund
46443 the SVR 46443 Fund
47383 the Manchester Rail Travel Society
48773 the Stanier 8F Locomotive Society
D431, 50035 and D444 the 50 Fund
D449 Operation Defiance
75069 the 75069 Fund
80079 the Passenger Tank Fund
AD600 the Royal Corps of Transport Museum Trustees
D821 and D7029 the Diesel Traction Group
D1062 the Western Locomotive Association
D3022 the Class 08 Society
D5410 Sandwell Metropolitan Council
4930 and 45110 the SVR(H) plc

Kirk, c/o above address
Membership journal: *Severn Valley Railway News* — quarterly
Share details: Mrs W. Broadhurst, c/o above address

Shildon Railway Village

Museum — **County Durham**

The Timothy Hackworth Museum closed in its current form in October 2003 and will reopen in September 2004 as part of the Shildon Railway Village, the newest addition to the National Museums of Science & Industry

Museum Manager: Dr George Muirhead

Location/address: Shildon Railway Village, 4 Soho Cottages, Shildon DL4 1PQ

Telephone/Fax: 01388 777999

Internet address: e-mail: dill.hamer@lycos.co.uk or a.warren.srv@lycos.co.uk

Car parking: Available on site including accessible parking

Access by public transport: Shildon main line station

Locomotive and multiple units

Name	No	Origin	Class	Type	Built
Sans Pareil	—*	L&MR	—	0-4-0	1980
—	10656	SR	2BIL	DMBSK	1937
—	12123	SR	2BIL	DTCK	1937

(Middlesbrough to Bishop Auckland line), connecting to East Coast main line at Darlington. Local bus services to Shildon through Arriva buses (0191 384 3323)

On site facilities: From September 2004 — café, refreshments and gift shop

Length of line: Currently 200m will extend to approx 1km in September 2004

Public opening: The new museum will be open Easter to end of October daily 10.00-17.00 and November to Easter Wednesdays to Sundays 10.00-16.00

Access for disabled: The site will be accessible to wheelchair users including accessible toilets

Special note: The current locomotive is a replica of Sans Pareil which runs on event days only, and will run approximately 30 times per annum at the new attraction

Sittingbourne & Kemsley Light Railway

Steam Centre — **Kent**

Member: HRA, TT

The Sittingbourne & Kemsley Light Railway is part of the 2ft 6in gauge railway built to convey paper and other materials between mills at Sittingbourne and Kemsley and the Dock at Ridham on the banks of the Swale. The first section of the line opened in 1906 and two of the engines then in use remain on the line today.

The railway is now leased from Metsa Serla and is operated as a tourist attraction. Passenger trains are normally steam-hauled and are formed of a varied selection of open and covered coaches. For the first half mile of the journey the train twists and turns through Milton Regis on a concrete viaduct which was one of the first reinforced concrete structures to be built

Headquarters: Sittingbourne & Kemsley Light Railway Ltd, PO Box 300, Sittingbourne, Kent ME10 2DZ

Telephone: 0871 871 4606 (talking timetable). Other enquiries: 01622 755313 or 07944 135033

Locomotives

Name	No	Builder	Type	Built
Alpha	—	Bagnall (2472)	0-6-2T	1932
Triumph	—	Bagnall (2511)	0-6-2T	1934
Superb	—	Bagnall (2624)	0-6-2T	1940
Unique	—	Bagnall (2216)	2-4-0F	1924
Premier	—	K/Stuart (886)	0-4-2ST	1905
Leader	—	K/Stuart (926)	0-4-2ST	1905
Melior	—	K/Stuart (4219)	0-4-2ST	1924
Edward Lloyd	—	R/Hornsby (435403)	4wDM	1961
Victor	—	Hunslet (4182)	4wDM	1953

Industrial standard gauge locomotives

Name	No	Builder	Type	Built
—	4	H/Leslie (3718)	0-4-0ST	1928
Bear	—	Peckett (614)	0-4-0ST	1896
—	1	Barclay (1876)	0-4-0F	1925

Locomotive notes: In service: Superb, Melior, Triumph. Under repair: Leader, Premier. On static display: Alpha, Unique and standard gauge exhibits

Stock

10 bogie coaches (4 ex-Chattenden & Upnor Railway); 2 open coaches; various wagons

England

Internet address: *Web site:* http://www.sklr.demon.co.uk
Main station: Sittingbourne
Car park: Sittingbourne
Party bookings and enquiries: Sittingbourne & Kemsley Light Railway Ltd, PO Box 300, Sittingbourne, Kent ME10 2DZ. Tel: 01227 369606 or 01622 755313
Access by public transport: Sittingbourne main line station, A2 and M2 roads
OS reference: Sittingbourne TQ 905643, Kemsley Down TQ 920662
Refreshment facilities: Kemsley Down

Souvenir shop: Kemsley Down
Depot: Kemsley Down (access by rail only)
Length of line: 2 miles, 2ft 6in gauge
Passenger trains: Southeast England's only former industrial narrow gauge railway
Journey time: 15min in each direction
Period of public operation: Every Sunday from beginning of April to end of September. Also on Good Friday, Easter Saturday and the Saturday and Monday of all Bank Holiday weekends. Every Wednesday during local school summer holidays
Special events: Not advised, please contact for details
Special notes: There is no public access to Kemsley Down other than by the railway on operating dates. When the line is closed all stock is stored in security compounds, on the mill premises. Family ticket available, special rates for parties and senior citizens. Picnic area at Kemsley Down
Membership details: Alan James, S&KLR, PO Box 300, Sittingbourne, Kent ME10 2DZ.
Marketing name: Sittingbourne Steam Railway

Museum	Snibston Discovery Park	Leicestershire

Members: TT
Location: Snibston Discovery Park, Ashby Road, Coalville, Leicestershire LE67 3LN
Telephone: (01530) 278444
Fax: (01530) 813301
Operating group: Leicestershire County Council, Heritage Services, Community Services Dept. Tel: 01530 278452
Internet address: *e-mail:* npell@leics.gov.uk
Museum contact: Mr N. Pell, Snibston Discovery Park, Ashby Road, Coalville, Leicestershire LE67 3LN
Public opening: Daily 10.00-17.00. Closed Christmas Day, Boxing Day and two weeks in January
Car & coach parking: On site, free
Access by public transport: Arriva Fox from Loughborough and Nottingham (route 99); from Leicester (route 117); from Swadlincote (route 118), Mon-Sat; route 217/8 Sun & Bank Holiday Mondays; Hinckley (route 159); routes 118 and 254 also run from Leicester. Connections at Ashby with Burton upon Trent. Further information, tel: 0870 608 2608
On site facilities: Shop, toilets, car park, café. Conference facilities,

Multiple-unit

Name	No	Origin	Class	Type	Built
—	70576	BR	4CEP/411	TBC	1956

Industrial locomotives (standard gauge)

Name	No	Builder	Type	Built
Mars II†	—	RSH (7493)	0-4-0ST	1948
—	2	Barclay (1815)	0-4-0F	1924
—*	—	Brush (314)	0-4-0ST	1906
Cadley Hill No 1†	—	Hunslet (3851)	0-6-0ST	1962
—	16	Hunslet (6289)	0-6-0DM	1966
—	—	R/Hornsby (393304)	4wDM	1955
—	—	Brush	4wDE	1955

Industrial locomotives (2ft 6in gauge)

Name	No	Builder	Type	Built
—	—	E/Electric (2416)	4wBE	1957
—	—	H/Clarke (DM1812)	0-6-0DM	1960
—	—	Hunslet (7385)	4wDMF	1976
—	63/000/449	Hunslet (8973)	4wDH	1979

Locomotive notes: 2004 operational locomotives for passenger trains will be *Yvonne*, R/Hornsby (393304) and Hunslet 6289
†locomotive is stored, but may be brought out for display on special events
*originally Powlesland & Mason No 6 taken over by GWR in 1924 and numbered 921
Plus 2ft 6in gauge English Electric battery-operated electric man-riding locomotives — ex-NCB

Rolling stock: 1 ex-BR Mk 1 TBCK, 1920 Midland Railway brake van, 15 other goods vehicles

tourist information centre (tel: [01530] 813608). Family tickets, picnic areas, science play area,

Sheepy Magna wheelwrights workshop. Special event days, nature reserve, golf driving range,

England

colliery building tours
Railways on site: Approx one third of a mile of standard gauge track with passenger trains on selected days. Please telephone for further information. Track to be extended in 2004.

Narrow gauge railway about 350yd in length (non operational).

Volunteers to help run the railway are welcome to join our 'Friends of Coaltracks' support group; please contact Mr N. Pell at above address if interested

---

| Museum | **Somerset & Dorset Railway Trust** | Somerset |

Member: HRA
Situated at Washford on the West Somerset Railway, the Trust Museum houses Somerset & Dorset memorabilia and artefacts to stir memories of cross-country travel in the era of steam. The sidings and restoration shed give the visitor a chance to see locomotives, wagons and carriages close up
Headquarters: Washford Station, Minehead Road, Washford, Somerset TA21 0PP
Telephone: 01984 640869
Internet address: *Web site:* http://www.sdrt.org
Car park: Small car park by main road
Access by public transport: West Somerset Railway trains on operating days, March to end October. Nearest main line station: Taunton. First Bus service 28 (Taunton-Minehead) passes the station

Locomotive

Name	No	Origin	Class	Type	Built
—*	53808	S&DJR	7F	2-8-0	1925

*undergoing heavy overhaul at Minehead

Industrial locomotives

Name	No	Builder	Type	Built
Isabel*	—	H/Leslie (3437)	0-6-0ST	1919
Kilmersdon	—	Peckett (1788)	0-4-0ST	1929

*undergoing restoration at Washford

Stock
3 Somerset & Dorset 6-wheeled coaches undergoing restoration. Large wagon collection. Display of narrow gauge equipment from Sedgemoor peat railways

On site facilities: Souvenir counter at the station. No refreshments on station but adjacent inn offers food and children are welcome
Public opening: 10.30-16.30 throughout June, July, August and September, plus Bank Holiday weekends and Gala Days
Membership details: Ian Briggs, S&DJR Trust, 24 Preston Close, Stanton-under-Bardon, Markfield, Leics LE67 9TX
Membership journal: *Pines Express* (4 issues/year, plus newsletter)

| Timetable Service | **South Devon Railway -** | Devon |

Member: HRA, TT
A typical West Country branch line meandering up the Dart Valley to Buckfastleigh which is home to the railway's workshops, a butterfly and otter farm and several other attractions. The line is accessible from Totnes (main line) via a footbridge (4min walk)
General Manager: R. Elliott
Headquarters: South Devon Railway, Buckfastleigh Station, Buckfastleigh, Devon TQ11 0DZ
Telephone: 0845 345 1470
Internet addresses: *e-mail:* southdevonrailway.org

Locomotives and multiple-units

Name	No	Origin	Class	Type	Built
—	1420	GWR	1400	0-4-2T	1933
—	1369	GWR	1366	0-6-0PT	1934
—	3205	GWR	2251	0-6-0	1946
—	3803	GWR	2884	2-8-0	1939
Dumbleton Hall	4920	GWR	'Hall'	4-6-0	1929
—	5526	GWR	4500	2-6-2T	1929
—	5786	GWR	5700	0-6-0PT	1930
—	D2246	BR	04	0-6-0DM	1956
—	D3666	BR	09	0-6-0DE	1959
—	D8110	BR	20	Bo-Bo	1962
—	20118	BR	20	Bo-Bo	1962
—	25901	BR	25	Bo-Bo	1966
—	37037	BR	37	Co-Co	1962
Superb	50002	BR	50	Co-Co	1967

England

111

Main station: Buckfastleigh
Other public stations: Staverton,
Totnes (Littlehempston)
OS reference:
Buckfastleigh SX 747663,
Staverton SX 785638
Car park: Buckfastleigh (free),
Staverton (free). Totnes — use
main line pay & display or council
car parks
Access by public transport: Bus,
X38/9 Exeter-Plymouth; 88
Newton Abbot-Buckfastleigh; X80
Plymouth-Torquay. Main line trains
to Totnes
Refreshment facilities:
Buckfastleigh, Totnes (café at
Totnes Rare Breeds Centre adjacent
to and only accessible via SDR
station
Souvenir shop: On the train and
Buckfastleigh station
Museum: Buckfastleigh
Depot: Buckfastleigh
Vintage bus: Operates to Buckfast
Abbey and Buckfastleigh town
most days (free service)
Miniature railway: Operates most
Sundays and gala days at
Buckfastleigh (7.25in gauge, half
mile
Model railway: Extensive 00
gauge model railway at
Buckfastleigh. Admission included
in train fare
Length of line: 7 miles
Passenger trains: Buckfastleigh-
Totnes alongside the River Dart
Period of public operation: Daily
April to October
Facilities for disabled: Good
Membership details: South Devon

Name	No	Origin	Class	Type	Built
—	51592	BR	127	DMBS	1959
—	51604	BR	127	DMBS	1959
—	55000	BR	121	DMBS	1959
—	59659	BR	115	TS	1960
—	59719	BR	115	TCL	1960
—	59740	BR	115	TS	1960

Broad gauge — 7ft 0.25in

Name	No	Origin	Class	Type	Built
Tiny	—	SDR	—	0-4-0VBT	1868

Industrial locomotives

Name	No	Builder	Type	Built
Ashley	1	Peckett (2031)	0-4-0ST	1942
Lady Angela	1690	Peckett (1690)	0-4-0ST	1926
Sapper	WD132	Hunslet (3163)	0-6-0ST	1943
Glendower	—	Hunslet (3810)	0-6-0ST	1954
Carnarvon	47	Kitson (5474)	0-6-0ST	1935
—	—	Fowler (421014)	0-4-0DM	1958
Errol Lonsdale	68011	Hunslet (3796)	0-6-0ST	1953

4ft 6in gauge

Name	No	Builder	Type	Built
Lee Moor No 2	—	Peckett (784)	0-4-0ST	1899

Stock
13 ex-BR Mk 1 coaches; 7 ex-GWR coaches; 3 ex-GWR auto trailers;
25 wagons. Lee Moor Tramway china clay wagon (4ft gauge)

Owners
Tiny, 7ft 0.25in gauge, part of the National Collection
3803 the South Devon Railway Trust
Glendower is privately owned
Errol Lonsdale the South Devon Railway Trust
1420 the South Devon Railway Association
5526 the 5526 Ltd
D2246 and 50002 the Devon Diesel Society
D8110, 20118 and 25901 the South Devon Diesel Traction Group
5786 the Worcester Locomotive Society
Sapper & 4920 the South Devon Railway Trust
1369 the South Devon Railway Association

Railway Association, c/o above
address
Membership journal: Bulliver —
quarterly

Timetable Service

South Tynedale Railway

Cumbria

Member: HRA
A narrow gauge line passing
through the attractive scenery of the
South Tyne valley, in the North
Pennine area of outstanding natural
beauty
Location: Approximately 0.75-mile
north of Alston town centre, on
A686 Hexham road
OS reference: NY 717467
Operating society: South Tynedale

Railway Preservation Society, The
Railway Station, Alston, Cumbria
CA9 3JB
Telephone: Alston (01434) 382828
(timetable information); (01434)
381696 (other enquiries)
Internet address: Web site:
www.strps.org.uk
Car park: Alston station
Access by public transport: Bus
services are infrequent and vary

seasonally. Routes include
Haltwhistle-Alston, Carlisle-Alston
and Newcastle-Hexham-Alston-
Penrith. Please check with local
Tourist Information Centres or, for
public transport information in
Cumbria, phone 0870 608 2608
On site facilities: Book and
souvenir shop, picnic area, toilets
(including disabled persons),
parking, lineside footpath

Catering facilities: Most weekend trains serve coffee, tea, soft drinks and snacks at Kirkhaugh from a converted brake van on the train. (Tea room at Alston is not operated by Society.) Confectionery, ice cream and soft drinks on sale in the railway shop at Alston

Length of line: 2.25 miles, 2ft gauge from Alston to Kirkhaugh

Public opening: Trains will run: 9-18, 24/25 April;1-3, 8/9, 15/16, 22/23, 29-31 May; 1-6, 12/13, 19/20, 26/27, 29/30 June; daily in July EXCEPT 2, 5, 9, 12, 16; daily in August; 4/5, 11/12, 18/19, 25/26 September; 3, 10, 17, 24, 26-28 October; 4/5, 11/12, 18/19 December

Steam haulage scheduled for: 11/12 April; 1-3, 30/31 May; 6, 13, 20, 26/27 June; 4, 11, 18-31 July; daily in August; 30/31 October; 4/5, 11/12, 18/19 December

Special events: Family Fun Days — 1-3 May: Teddy Bears' Picnic — 5/6 June; Steamathon Weekend — 26/27 June; Halloween Specials — 30/31 October; Santa Specials — 4/5, 11/12, 18/19 December.

Facilities for disabled: A carriage with access for wheelchairs users is available. Advance booking is recommended: tel: 01434 381696. Wheelchair accessible toilet at Alston

Special notes: The line has been constructed on the trackbed of the former BR Haltwhistle-Alston branch

Membership details: Membership

Locomotives

Name	No	Builder	Type	Built
Barber	—	T/Green (441)	0-6-2ST	1908
Naworth	4	H/Clarke (DM819)	0-6-0DM	1952
Thomas Edmondson	6	Henschel (16047)	0-4-0T	1918
—	9	Hunslet (4109)	0-4-0DM	1952
Naklo	10	Chrzanow (3459)	0-6-0WTT	1957
Cumbria	11	Hunslet (6646)	0-4-0DM	1967
—	13	Hunslet (5222)	0-4-0DM	1958
Helen Kathryn	14	Henschel (28035)	0-4-0T	1948
—	—	Hunslet (4110)	0-4-0DM	1952
—	—	H/Clarke (DM1167)	0-6-0DM	1960
—	15	H/Clarke (DM1366)	0-6-0DM	1965
—	—	EE/Baguley (2519/3500)	4wBE	1958
—	—	B/Drewry (3704)	4wBE	1973
		rebuilt A/Barclay (6526)		1987
Carlisle	16	Hunslet (1859)	0-4-2T	1937
Permanent Way	DB965062			
Trolley		Wickham (7597)	4wDM	1957

Owners

4, 6, 9, 10 & 16 the South Tynedale Railway Preservation Society 11, 13, 14, 15, DM4110, DM1167, 2519/3500, DB965082 and Baguley/Drewry are privately owned

Stock

5 bogie coaches; 1 brake vans; 3 bogie open wagons; 8 4-wheel open wagons; 1 4-wheel box van; 3 4-wheel flat wagons; 1 4-wheel fuel tank wagon; 2 bogie well wagons, 4 4-wheel skip wagons; 5 bogie flat wagons; 6 bogie hopper wagons; 1 4-wheel hopper wagon; 1 4-wheel weed-killer wagon; 1 bogie compressor wagon; 2 4-wheel chassis

Owner

Barber is on loan from Leeds Industrial Museum

Secretary, c/o above address
Membership journal:
Tynedalesman — quarterly
Marketing name: England's Highest Narrow Gauge Railway

Timetable Service	Spa Valley Railway	Kent

Member: HRA

This railway originally formed part of a system of cross-country lines in East Sussex running through the Wealden countryside

Location: The main station at Tunbridge Wells West is located in the western end of the town close to the A26 road and the popular 'Pantiles' area

OS reference: Tunbridge Wells West station TQ 577384

Operating society/organisation: Tunbridge Wells & Eridge RPS,

Locomotives and multiple-units

Name	No	Origin	Class	Type	Built
—	47493	LMS	3F	0-6-0T	1927
—	1928	SJ	S1	2-6-4T	1953
—	09004	BR	09	0-6-0DE	1959
Colonel Tomline	D3489	BR	10	0-6-0DE	1958
—	15224	BR	12	0-6-0DE	1949
—	6583	BR	33	Bo-Bo	1962
—	73140	BR	73	Bo-Bo	1966
—	51669	BR	115	DMBS	1960
—	51849	BR	115	DMBS	1960

Tunbridge Wells West Station, Nevill Terrace, Tunbridge Wells, Kent TN2 5QY
Telephone: 01892 537715
Internet address: *Web site:* www.spavalleyrailway.co.uk
Car parking: Tunbridge Wells West – several car parks nearby in town centre. Note: Sainsbury's car park, adjacent to station, is limited to 2 hours for their customers only. High Rocks — large free car park. There is *no* parking at Groombridge
Access by public transport: National Rail services to Tunbridge Wells, then 15min walk, or short bus ride. Nearest bus stop served by many local bus services is at Sainsbury's, Tunbridge Wells, then approx 100yd walk
Refreshment facilities: Static buffet car at Tunbridge Wells West. Also bar car *Kate* on some trains
Souvenir shop: Tunbridge Wells West (within engine shed)
Depot: Tunbridge Wells West shed is an original LBSCR design dating from 1891 and consists of four roads which house various items of rolling stock and motive power
Length of line: 3 miles Tunbridge Wells-Groombridge. Plus future extension planned to Eridge, 2 miles

Industrial locomotives

Name	No	Builder	Type	Built
Scottie*	—	R/Hornsby (412427)	4wDM	1957
Samson*	57	RSH (7668)	0-6-0T	1950
North Downs*	13	RSH (7846)	0-6-0T	1955
Princess Margaret	—	Barclay (376)	0-4-0DM	1947
Lady Ingrid	—	Barclay (2315)	0-4-0ST	1951
Southerham	—	Drewry/Vulcan (D2591)	0-4-0DM	1959
Topham*	—	Bagnall (2193)	0-6-0ST	1922
Fonmon	—	Peckett (1636)	0-6-0ST	1924
Spartan	—	Chrzanow (3135)	0-6-0T	1954
Hotspur*	—	Chrzanow (2944)	0-6-0T	1952

*undergoing overhaul

Stock
6 BR Mk 1 coaches; 1 BR Mk 2 coaches; buffet car from Classs 420 EMU; 2 ex-London Transport T stock coaches; 1 LCDR coach body; 2 brake vans, 4 cranes; various freight wagons

Passenger trains: Weekends and Bank Holidays from 14 March to 29 October plus some weekdays in in July and August. Santa Specials in December. Normal service 27 December-2 January 2005
Special events: Mother's Day — 21 March; Day out with Thomas — 27/28 March, 3/4 April; Easter Bunny Specials — 9-12 April; Father's Day — 13 June; Steam Gala — 21/22 June; Steam Gala — 3/4 July; Diesel Gala — 7/8 August; Mixed Traction Gala — 18/19 September; Day out with Thomas — 2/3, 9/10 October; Santa Specials — 4-24 December
Facilities for disabled: Separate disabled persons' toilet at Tunbridge Wells West station. Level or ramp access to all station platforms. Ramps available for wheelchair access to trains
Membership details: c/o Tunbridge Wells West Station
Membership journal: *Spa Valley Starter* and *Eridge Express*

STEAM — Museum of the Great Western Railway

Museum   Wiltshire

Member: HRA
STEAM — Museum of the Great Western Railway tells the remarkable story of the men and women who built, operated and travelled on the Great Western Railway. Situated on the old Swindon Railway Works site, the museum is housed in a 72,000sq ft Victorian machine shop. As well as locomotives, carriages and wagons the story is told through reconstructions, videos and interactive exhibits
Keeper: T. Bryan AMA
Location: Kemble Drive, Swindon, Wiltshire SN2 2TA
OS reference: tba

Locomotives

Name	No	Origin	Class	Type	Built
—	2516	GWR	2301	0-6-0	1897
—	4248	GWR	4200	2-8-0T	1916
Caerphilly Castle	4073	GWR	'Castle'	4-6-0	1923
King George V	6000	GWR	'King'	4-6-0	1927
—	9400	GWR	9400	0-6-0PT	1947
North Star*	—	GWR	—	2-2-2	1837
—	4	GWR	Diesel railcar	Bo-Bo	1934
Hagley Hall†	4930	GWR	'Hall'	4-6-0	1929
—	7325	GWR	4300	2-6-0	1932
Glorious	50033	BR	50	Co-Co	1968

*broad gauge (7ft 0.25in) replica
†on display in McArthur Glen's 'Designer Outlet' shopping centre located in the old works

Operating society/organisation:
Swindon Borough Council
Telephone: Swindon (01793)
466646
Internet address: *Web site:*
www.steam-museum.org.uk
Car park: Shared with the Great
Western Designer Outlet Village
complex
Access by public transport:
Swindon main line station 1 mile
(20 minutes' walk)
On site facilities: Café, shop
Facilities for disabled: Fully
accessible

Owners
4930 and 7325 on loan from Severn Valley Railway
All other locomotives are part of the National Railway Museum Collection

Period of public opening:
Winter (November-March) Monday
to Saturday 10.00-17.00, Sunday
11.00-17.00. Closed Christmas Day,
Boxing Day and New Year's Day.
Summer (April-October)
Monday to Saturday 10.00-17.30,
Sunday 11.00-17.30
Membership details: The Friends

of Swindon Railway Museum, c/o
Steam
Membership journal: *North Star*
— quarterly

Stephenson Railway Museum & North Tyneside Railway

Steam Centre

Tyne & Wear

Member: HRA
A display in buildings which began
life as the Tyne & Wear Metro Test
Centre now features locomotives
and exhibitions which illustrate
railway development from
waggonways to the present day
Location: Middle Engine Lane,
West Chirton
OS reference: NZ 396576
Internet address: *NTSRA web site:*
ntsra.freeserve.co.uk
Operating society/organisation:
The Stephenson Railway Museum
and the North Tyneside Railway
are managed as a partnership
between North Tyneside Council,
Tyne & Wear Museums and the
North Tyneside Railway
Association (NTSRA). Each can be
contacted c/o Stephenson Railway
Museum, Middle Engine Lane,
West Chirton, North Shields, Tyne
& Wear NE29 8DX
Car park: On site, free
Length of line: North Tyneside
Railway, 2 miles, Stephenson
Railway Museum to Percy Main
Village
Access by public transport: Bus
services 300 from Newcastle
(Haymarket bus station); 337/339
from Wallsend (Metro station
interchange). Ring 0870 608 2608
for times and fares. Tyne & Wear
Metro to Percy Main (then short
walk to NTR station) when North
Tyneside Railway is in operation

Locomotive and multiple-unit

Name	No	Origin	Class	Type	Built
—	D2078	BR	03	0-6-0DM	1959
—	3267	NER	—	DMLV	1904

Industrial locomotives

Name	No	Builder	Type	Built
Billy	—	Killingworth or RS & Co (1)	0-4-0	c1826
—	A No 5	Kitson (2509)	0-6-0PT	1883
Ashington No 5 / Jackie Milburn	5	Peckett (1970)	0-6-0ST	1939
Ted Garrett, JP, DL, MP	1	RSH (7683)	0-6-0T	1951
—	E4	Siemens-Schuckert (457)	Bo-BoWE	1909
Thomas Burt MP 1837-1902	401	Bagnall (2994)	0-6-0ST	1950
—	10	Consett Iron Co	0-6-0DM	1958

Stock
1 LNER Gresley BFK; 3 BR Mk 1 non-gangwayed coaches, 2 BR Mk 2
coaches, 1 LNER Gresley BGP

Owner
NER van National Railway Museum

Public opening: May to September:
Museum — daily (except Fridays),
admission free; railway — Sundays
and Bank Holiday Mondays, also
Saturdays during local school
holidays. Closed October to April.
Write, phone (0191 200 7146) or
visit the NTSRA web site for
details, including early/late season
variations and special events
Special notes: Stephenson Railway
Museum and North Tyneside

Railway share facilities in
buildings. North Tyneside Steam
Railway Association operates and
maintains exhibits from the
Museum Collection
Facilities for disabled: Access for
wheelchairs to Museum building at
Middle Engine Lane. Access to
stations; also wheelchair ramp onto
train

Swanage Railway — 'The Purbeck Line'

Member: HRA

Overlooked by the historic ruins of Corfe Castle, this railway is slowly extending towards Wareham and a connection to the main line network

Location: Swanage station

Operations Manager: Paul McDonald

Passenger Services Manager: David Green

Operating society/organisation: Swanage Railway Co Ltd, Station House, Swanage, Dorset BH19 1HB

Telephone: Swanage (01929) 425800. Talking Timetable — (01929) 425800

Fax: (01929) 426680

Internet addresses: *e-mail:* general@swanrail.freeserve.co.uk *Web site:* www.swanagerailway.co.uk

Other public stations: Herston Halt, Harman's Cross, Corfe Castle and Norden

OS reference: SZ 026789

Car park: Norden park & ride signposted off A351 Wareham-Swanage road on the approach to Corfe Castle. Limited parking available at Swanage station

Access by public transport: Regular bus services operated by Wilts & Dorset from Bournemouth, Poole and Wareham to Swanage and Norden park & ride

On site facilities: Souvenir shop at Swanage. Buffet car on most trains. Picnic areas at Swanage, Harman's Cross and Norden. Exhibition and cinema coach at Corfe. 5in gauge railway at Swanage on some weekends. Travel Agency at Swanage station

Length of line: 6 miles, Swanage-Herston Halt-Harman's Cross-Corfe Castle-Norden

Public opening: Swanage station open every day except Christmas Day. Trains operate weekends all year round. Daily from 1 April until 31 October. Also 26 December 2004 to 2 January 2005

Special events: Not advised, please contact for details

Facilities for disabled: Access to shop and toilets; disabled facilities

Locomotives and multiple-units

Name	No	Origin	Class	Type	Built
—	6695	GWR	5600	0-6-2T	1928
—	30053	LSWR	M7	0-4-4T	1905
Eddystone	34028	SR	WC	4-6-2	1946
257 Squadron	34072	SR	BB	4-6-2	1948
Port Line	35027	SR	MN	4-6-2	1948
—	80078	BR	4MT	2-6-4T	1954
—	80104	BR	4MT	2-6-4T	1955
—	D3591	BR	08	0-6-0DE	1958
—	D9521	BR	14	0-6-0DH	1964
—	20188	BR	20	Bo-Bo	1967
Stan Symes	D6515	BR	33	Bo-Bo	1960
—	33034	BR	33	Bo-Bo	1960
—	52048	BR	108	DMCL	1960
—	51919	BR	108	DMBS	1956
—	51341*	P/Steel	117	DMBS	1959
—	51346	P/Steel	117	DMBS	1959
—	51353*	P/Steel	117	DMBS	1959
—	51356*	P/Steel	117	DMBS	1959
—	51388	P/Steel	117	DMS	1959
—	51392*	P/Steel	117	DMS	1959
—	51395*	P/Steel	117	DMS	1959
—	51398*	P/Steel	117	DMS	1959
—	59486*	P/Steel	117	TCL	1960
—	59492*	P/Steel	117	TCL	1960
—	59516	P/Steel	117	TCL	1960
—	59521*	P/Steel	117	TCL	1960

*undergoing overhaul of-site

Industrial locomotives

Name	No	Builder	Type	Built
May	2	Fowler (4210132)	0-4-0DM	1957
Beryl	—	Planet (2054)	4wPM	1937
Progress	—	Peckett (1611)	0-4-0ST	1923

Locomotive notes: 30053, 80078 and 80104 will be away periodically on short-term loan

Stock

3 ex-LSWR coach bodies; 4 ex-SR vans; 9 ex-SR coaches; 18 ex-BR Mk 1 coaches; 15 various types of wagons; 1 ex-BR Mk 3 Sleeping coach; 1 ex-SR 15-ton diesel-electric crane; 1 ex-BR Corridor 2nd converted to disabled persons' coach. Brake vans from SR, LMS, LSWR including 3 'Queen Marys', GWR

Owners

6695 the Great Western Railway Preservation Group
34028, 34072, 80078 and 80104 the Southern Locomotives Ltd
30053 the Drummond Locomotive Society
D6515 and 33034 the 71A Locomotive Group

on most trains

Membership details: Sue Payne, c/o Southern Steam Trust at above address

Membership journal: *Swanage Railway News* — quarterly

Marketing name: The Purbeck Line

Member: HRA, TT
This is the only preserved section of the former Midland & South Western Junction Railway, the society having had to re-lay track and associated works. There is a new station and the engine shed complex at Hayes Knoll
Location: Tadpole Lane, Blunsdon (approximately midway between Blunsdon St Andrew and Purton)
Chairman: J. Larkin
Operating society/organisation: Swindon & Cricklade Railway, Blunsdon Station, Blunsdon, Swindon, Wiltshire SN25 2DA
Telephone: 01793 771615
Internet address: *Web site:* www.swindon-cricklade-railway.org
Station: Blunsdon
OS reference: SU 110897
Length of line: 1 mile
Car park: Tadpole Lane, Blunsdon
Refreshment facilities: Blunsdon station in former Norwegian State Railways coach. Buffet car at Hayes Knoll on open days. Picnic area
Toilet: Blunsdon station amenities building
Souvenir shop: Blunsdon station. Various sales stands on Open Days around station area. Museum currently being enlarged to reopen in 2004
Depot: Hayes Knoll
Public opening: Site open: 10.00-16.00 Saturdays, Sundays and Bank Holidays throughout the year.
Passenger trains: Trains run on Sundays and Bank Holidays (11.00-16.00) when special events are not scheduled
Special events: Planned for steam haulage unless noted otherwise. Trains will run 11.00-16.00 unless otherwise noted.
Hot Cross Bun Specials (diesel) —

Locomotives and multiple-units

Name	No	Origin	Class	Type	Built
Foremarke Hall	7903	GWR	'Hall'	4-6-0	1949
—*	5637	GWR	5600	0-6-2T	1924
—	3845	GWR	2800	2-8-0	1942
—	2022	BR	03	0-6-0DM	1958
—	03152	BR	03	0-6-0DM	1960
—	13261	BR	08	0-6-0DE	1956
—	51074	GRCW	119	DMBC	1959
—	51104	GRCW	119	DMS	1958

*on loan to East Somerset Railway

Industrial locomotives

Name	No	Builder	Type	Built
Swordfish	—	Barclay (2138)	0-6-0ST	1941
Salmon	—	Barclay (2139)	0-6-0ST	1942
—	—	Barclay (2352)	0-4-0ST	1954
Richard Trevithick	—	Barclay (2354)	0-4-0ST	1954
Woodbine	—	Fowler (21442)	0-4-0DM	1936
—	—	Fowler (4210137)	0-4-0DM	1958
—	—	Fowler (4220031)	0-4-0DH	1964
—*	70	H/Clarke (1464)	0-6-0T	1921
Slough Estates No 3	—	H/Clarke (1544)	0-6-0ST	1924
—	—	H/Clarke (1857)	0-6-0T	1952
Gunby	—	Hunslet (2413)	0-6-0ST	1941

*on loan to Avon Valley Railway

Stock
6 BR Mk 1 coaches; 2 GWR coaches; Selection of goods rolling stock; Wickham railcar

Owners
7903 the Foremarke Hall Locomotive Group
5637 the 5637 Locomotive Group
Slough Estates the Slough & Windsor Railway Society
51074 and 51104 the Gloucester Railcar Trust

9/10 April; Easter Bunny — 11/12 April; Treasure Hunt — 3 May; Ivor the Engine meets Jack the Station Cat— 30/31 May; Steam + Radio Fun Days (in conjunction with Swindon & District Amateur Radio Club) — 10/11 July; Vintage Transport Weekend — 7/8 August; Bicentennial of Steam Weekend — 28/29 August; Military Weekend — 11/12 August; Halloween Ghost Train — 30 October (evening); Santa Specials — 28 November, 4/5, 11/12, 18/19 December
Facilities for disabled: Access to trains, locomotive shed, toilets and refreshments
Membership details: Membership Secretary, c/o above address
Membership journal: S&CR magazine, quarterly

Tanfield Railway

Member: HRA

The oldest railway in the world, featuring 1725 route, 1725 Causey embankment, 1727 Causey arch, 1766 Gibraltar bridge and 1854 Marley Hill engine shed. Also collection of local engines, Victorian carriages and vintage workshop

Location: Off the A6076 Sunniside to Stanley road

OS reference: NZ 207573

Operating society/organisation: The Tanfield Railway, Marley Hill Engine Shed, Sunniside, Gateshead NE16 5ET

Telephone: (0191) 388 7545

Internet address: *Web site:* www.tanfield-railway.co.uk

Main stations: Andrews House, Sunniside, Causey, East Tanfield

Car park: Marley Hill, Causey picnic area, East Tanfield

Access by public transport: X30 (weekdays) stops outside main entrance; 705, 706, 770 Sundays to Sunniside only, near to Sunniside station

Catering facilities: Light refreshments available on operating days

On site facilities: Shop and toilets

Length of line: 3 miles

Public opening: Trains run every Sunday and Bank Holiday Monday from January to November. Also Wednesdays and Thursdays in summer. Santa trains in December before Christmas. Marley Hill engine shed open daily for viewing

Special events: Easter Eggstravaganza — 9-12 April; Over 60s Day — 9 May; Military Weekend — 22/23 May; Spring Bank Holiday Weekend — 30/31 May; Teddy Bear Day — 13 June; Father's Day — 20 June; Children's Day — 18 July; Goods Train Day — 1 August; Victorian Bank Holiday Weekend — 29/30 August; Vintage Workshop Day — 12 September; Teddy Bear Day — 26 September; Coal Train Day — 10 October; Santa Specials — 28 November, 4/5, 11/12, 18/19, 22-24 December (pre-booking essential); Mince Pie Specials — 26/27 December

Locomotive

Name	No	Origin	Class	Type	Built
—	M2*	TGR	M	4-6-2	1951

*3ft 6in gauge, Tasmanian Government Railways (RSH 7630)

Industrial locomotives

Name	No	Builder	Type	Built
—	9	AEG (1565)	4w-4wE	1913
Gamma	—	Bagnall (2779)	0-6-0ST	1945
Horden	—	Barclay (1015)	0-6-0ST	1904
—	6	Barclay (1193)	0-4-2ST	1910
—	17	Barclay (1338)	0-6-0T	1913
—	32	Barclay (1659)	0-4-0ST	1920
Beryl	—	S/Crossley (7697)	0-6-0DM	1953
—	3	E. Borrows (37)	0-4-0WT	1898
—	6	Fowler (4240010)	0-6-0DH	1960
Enterprise	—	R&W Hawthorn (2009)	0-4-0ST	1884
Cyclops	112	H/Leslie (2711)	0-4-0ST	1907
—	2	H/Leslie (2859)	0-4-0ST	1911
Stagshaw	—	H/Leslie (3513)	0-6-0ST	1923
—	3	H/Leslie (3575)	0-6-0ST	1923
—	13	H/Leslie (3732)	0-4-0ST	1928
—	3	H/Leslie (3746)	0-6-0F	1929
Irwell	—	H/Clarke (1672)	0-4-0ST	1937
—	38	H/Clarke (1823)	0-6-0T	1949
—	501	Hunslet (6612)	0-6-0DH	1965
—	4	Sentinel (9559)	0-4-0T	1953
Twizell†	3	Stephenson (2730)	0-6-0T	1891
—	L2	R/Hornsby (312989)	0-4-0DE	1952
—	35	R/Hornsby (418600)	0-4-0DE	1958
—	158	RSH (6980)	0-4-0DM	1940
Hendon	—	RSH (7007)	0-4-0CT	1940
—	62	RSH (7035)	0-6-0ST	1940
—	3	RSH (7078)	4w-4wE	1940
—	49	RSH (7098)	0-6-0ST	1943
Progress	—	RSH (7298)	0-6-0ST	1946
Cochrane	—	RSH (7409)	0-4-0ST	1948
—	44	RSH (7760)	0-6-0ST	1953
—	38	RSH (7763)	0-6-0ST	1954
—	21	RSH (7796)	0-4-0ST	1954
—	47	RSH (7800)	0-6-0ST	1954
—	1	RSH (7901)	0-4-0DM	1958
—	16	RSH (7944)	0-6-0ST	1957
FGF	—	Barclay (D592)	0-4-0DH	1969
—	2	A/Whitworth (D22)	0-4-0DE	1933

†on long-term loan from Beamish

2ft gauge

Name	No	Builder	Type	Built
Escucha	11	B/Hawthorn (748)	0-4-0ST	1883
—	—	Clayton (133141)	4wBE	1984
—	—	Hunslet (7332)	4wDM	1973
—	—	L/Blackstone (53162)	4wDM	1962
—	—	L/Blackstone (54781)	4wDM	1962
—	—	R/Hornsby (323587)	4wDM	1952
—	—	R/Hornsby (244487)	4wDM	1946
—	25	RSH (8201)	4wBE	1960
—	—	W/Rogers	4wBE	—

Family tickets: Available
Facilities for disabled: Access to East Tanfield and Andrews House stations and Marley Hill engine shed. Toilets at Causey car park and Andrews House station
Membership details:
Miss E. Martin, 33 Stocksfield Avenue, Fenham, Newcastle upon Tyne NE5 2DX
Membership journal: *Tanfield Railway News* — 4 times/year

Stock
19 4-wheel carriages; 3 6-wheel carriages; 1 6-wheel van; 14 hopper wagons; 9 contractors bogies; 3 brake vans; 3 steam cranes; 8 covered wagons; 4 open wagons; 4 black wagons; 3 flat wagons

Special notes: Families can alight at Causey station for 2 miles of walks through the picturesque Causey Woods; picnic facilities and toilet available in car park

---

Telford Horsehay Steam Trust

Steam Centre — Shropshire

Member: HRA
Telford Steam Railway is based at Horsehay & Dawley station and goods yard in Telford on the Great Western branch from Wellington to Craven Arms via Ironbridge. The site at Horsehay has a longer history, being at the site of one of the Coalbrookdale companies first blast furnaces. The line saw its last passenger train in 1962 but the route from Lightmoor to Horsehay was kept open for freight traffic until 1979. The TSR acquired the former goods yard at Horsehay & Dawley in 1983. The railway is now extending northwards to Lawley Common, and southwards to Doseley. Excavation of Lawley Common cutting is continuing
Location: Horsehay, Telford, Shropshire
OS reference: SJ 675073
Operating society/organisation:
Telford Horsehay Steam Trust, The Old Loco Shed, Horsehay, Telford, Shropshire TF4 2LT
Sales line: 07765 858348
Internet address: *Web site:* www.telfordsteamrailway.co.uk
On site facilities: Extensive model railway display, tea room, picnic area, children's play equipment, narrow gauge steam tramway, miniature railway operated by Phoenix Model Engineers (separate charge); ticket gives unlimited

Locomotives and diesel multiple-units

Name	No	Origin	Class	Type	Built
—	5619	GWR	5600	0-6-2T	1925
—	50531	BRCW	104	DMC	1957
—	50479	BRCW	104	DMBS	1957
—	50556	BRCW	104	DMC	1957
—	59228	BRCW	104	TBSL	1958

Industrial locomotives

Name	No	Builder	Type	Built
—	MP1	Barclay (1944)	0-4-0F	1944
Wemyss Private Rly	15	Barclay (1944)	0-6-0ST	1945
Tom	27414	N/British (27414)	0-4-0DH	1954
—	D2959	R/Hornsby (382824)	4wDM	1955
Folly	—	R/Hornsby (183062)	4wDM	1937
Idris	—	R/Hornsby (207102)	4wDM	1941
Ironbridge No 3	—	Peckett (1990)	0-4-0ST	1940
—	—	R/Hornsby	0-4-0DH	1968
—	—	R/Hornsby (544998)	0-4-0DE	1969
—	—	YEC	0-4-0DE	?
Thomas	—*	Kierstead	4wVBT	1979

*2ft gauge

Stock
4 ex-BR Mk 1 coach; 1 ex-BR Mk 3 sleeper; 1 ex-GWR auto-trailer; 1 ex-GWR Toad brake van; 1 ex-GWR 3-ton hand crane; 1 Wickham trolley; Permaquip PW transporter vehicle No 68800; Various wagons

travel (except miniature railway)
Public opening: Every Sunday and Bank Holiday from Easter until last Sunday in September including Bank Holidays 11.00-16.00 (-17.00 on steam weekends). Last Sunday in

month steam-hauled and also steam on Bank Holidays, but steam tram every Sunday. Also pre-Christmas weekends in December when Thomas the Tank pays a visit

Museum — Tiverton Museum of Mid Devon Life — Devon

The Museum, dominated by No 1442, affectionately known as the 'Tivvy Bumper', houses a large collection of railway relics
Location: Tiverton, Devon
OS reference: SS 955124
Operating society/organisation: Tiverton & Mid Devon Museum Trust, Becks Square, Tiverton, Devon EX16 6PH
Telephone: (01884) 256295
Car park: Adjoining access by

Locomotives

Name	No	Origin	Class	Type	Built
(Tivvy Bumper)	1442	GWR	1400	0-4-2T	1935

public transport: Rail to Tiverton Parkway, then by bus, or bus from Exeter
On site facilities: Museum, shop and toilets
Public opening: February to

Christmas: Monday to Friday — 10.30-16.30; Saturdays — 10.00-13.00; closed Sundays
Special notes: Disabled access to view locomotive

Steam Centre — Tyseley Locomotive Works — Birmingham

Member: HRA
Location: 670 Warwick Road (A41), Tyseley, Birmingham B11 2HL
OS reference: SP 105841
Operating organisation: Vintage Trains
Supporting society: Vintage Trains Society
Telephone: (0121) 707 4696
Fax: (0121) 764 4645
Internet address: *Web site:* www.vintagetrains.co.uk/brm.htm
Car park: Site
Access by public transport: Travel West Midlands route No 37 from city centre. Main line rail service to Tyseley station (Central Trains and Chiltern Railways)
On site facilities: The Museum is on the site of a former GWR/BR steam shed and has been equipped with specialised railway engineering machinery. It carries out many contract repairs to steam locomotives and rolling stock. Souvenir shop, restaurant, passenger demonstration line and station, viewing gallery, schools' education service
Refreshment facilities: Available in visitor centre
Length of line: Third of a mile
Public opening: Weekends and Bank Holidays only 10.00-16.00.
Special events: 'Shakespeare Express' runs from July to

Locomotives

Name	No	Origin	Class	Type	Built
Kinlet Hall	4936	GWR	'Hall'	4-6-0	1929
Pitchford Hall	4953	GWR	'Hall'	4-6-0	1929
Rood Ashton Hall	4965	GWR	'Hall'	4-6-0	1929
Earl of Mount Edgcumbe	5043	GWR	'Castle'	4-6-0	1936
Defiant†	5080	GWR	'Castle'	4-6-0	1939
Clun Castle	7029	GWR	'Castle'	4-6-0	1950
—	4110	GWR	5101	2-6-2T	1937
—	4121	GWR	5101	2-6-2T	1937
—	7752	GWR	5700	0-6-0PT	1930
—	7760	GWR	5700	0-6-0PT	1930
—	9600	GWR	5700	0-6-0PT	1945
Kolhapur§	5593	LMS	'Jubilee'	4-6-0	1934
—	670	LNWR*	Bloomer	2-2-2	1986
—	13029	BR	08	0-6-0DE	1953
—	D3429	BR	08	0-6-0DE	1958
—	31301	BR	31	A1A-A1A	1962
—	31461	BR	31	A1A-A1A	1959
—	31558	BR	31	A1A-A1A	1962
—	37264	BR	37	Co-Co	1965
—	40118	BR	40	1Co-Co1	1961
—	47524	BR	47	Co-Co	1967
Royal Oak	50017	BR	50	Co-Co	1968
Rodney	50021	BR	50	Co-Co	1968
Fearless	50050	BR	50	Co-Co	1967
—	51375	BR	117	DMS	1960
—	55034	BR	121	DMBS	1958

*replica built at Tyseley Locomotive Works
†on loan to Buckinghamshire Railway Centre
§on loan to Barrow Hill Roundhouse

Industrial locomotives

Name	No	Builder	Type	Built
Cadbury No 1	—	Avonside (1977)	0-4-0T	1925
—	1	Peckett (2004)	0-4-0ST	1942
—	—	Baguley (800)	0-4-0PE	1920

September 2004. Running from Birmingham Snow Hill to Stratford-upon-Avon

Special notes: Tyseley is a centre for 'Steam on the Main Line' railtours over a large area of the national rail network. Full education service providing guided tours, worksheets and live presentation. The Museum is noted for its driving experience courses where members of the public can actually drive and fire a steam locomotive.

Membership details: Membership is available to the public, providing free entry to site events and four copies of *Steam in Trust* magazine

Facilities for disabled: Disabled

Note: Not all locomotives are on site, and some are undergoing restoration. Contract restoration work includes Nos (GWR) 3850, 6024, 6990 and industrials RSH 7289/1945, Sentinel 7109/1927 and DHR 778; locomotives away on loan include 5593 and *Henry* (Barrow Hill)

Stock
19 BR Mk 2 coaches, 4 BR Mk 1 coaches, 9 Pullman Cars, goods and departmental vehicles, saloon, steam and diesel cranes

Owner/Operator
Class 31s — Fragonset Railways (stored)

access to Shakespeare Express available, but must be notified in advance
Note: All attractions and facilities are advertised subject to availability

---

Museum	Vintage Carriages Trust Museum	West Yorkshire

Member: HRA, TT, AIM, ABTEM

A fascinating collection of elderly railway carriages and small locomotives, interestingly presented. Sit in a fully restored, prize winning 1876-built Manchester, Sheffield & Lincolnshire Railway carriage or relive the dark days of wartime travel in one of the three Metropolitan Railway carriages. Listen to the 'Travellers' Tales' and view the collection of railway posters and other items. Video presentation. The carriages and locomotives have appeared in over 50 cinema and television productions including *Inside Out* (2003), *He Knew He Was Right* (2003), *The Forsyte Saga* (2002), *Calendar* (2003), *Hound of the Baskervilles* (2002), *No Man's Land* (2002), *Turner — The Man Who Painted Britain* (2002), *A for Acid* (2001), *The Hours* (2001), *The Way We Live Now* (2001), *The Cazalets* (2000), *Possession* (2000), *The Railway Children* (1970 and 1968 versions)

Location: Vintage Carriages Trust Museum, Ingrow Station Yard, Halifax Road, Keighley, West Yorkshire BD22 8NJ. On the A629 road

Stock

Railway	BR or previous owner Number	Type	Date built	Seats	Weight	Length
MS&LR	176	4-wheel 1st/2nd/3rd/ luggage	1876	34	12T	28ft 0in
GNR	589	6-wheel 3rd brake	1888	40	14T	34ft 11in
MR	358	6-wheel 1st/3rd/ luggage	1886	32	15T	34ft 0in
Met	427	BS	1910	84	30T	54ft 0in
Met	465	S	1919	108	30T	54ft 0in
Met	509	F	1923	84	30T	54ft 0in
SR (SECR)	S3554S	BSK	1924	42	33T	65ft 3in
BR (SR)	S1469S	TSO	1951	64	32T	67ft 1in
GN	2856	Non vestibule composite, lav brake	1898	34	?	45ft 0in

Industrial locomotives

Name	No	Builder	Type	Built
Bellerophon*	—	Haydock Foundry (C)	0-6-0WT	1874
Sir Berkeley†	—	M/Wardle (1210)	0-6-0ST	1891
Lord Mayor	—	H/Clarke (402)	0-4-0ST	1893

*on loan to the Foxfield Railway for two years
†on 10 year loan to Middleton Railway

Operations Manager: Michael Cope, Hon Secretary, VCT
Operating society/organisation: Vintage Carriages Trust (a

Registered Charity No 510776)
Telephone: Keighley (01535) 680425
Fax: (01535) 610796

Internet address: *e-mail:* admin@vintagecarriagestrust.org *Web site:* www.vintagecarriagestrust.org

The web site includes database on over 4,000 preserved carriages, with over 3,000 photos. Also on CD-Rom

Car Park: Yes. Also coach parking at Ingrow station

Access by public transport: Arriva through trains from Carlisle, Settle, Morecambe, Lancaster to Keighley (one mile). Fast and frequent Metro Train services from Bradford Forster Square, Leeds, Shipley, and Skipton to Keighley. Then either KWVR train to Ingrow West (adjacent) or buses 500, 502, 663, 664, 665, 696, 697 from Keighley bus station. Calderline bus 500 (limited winter service) from Hebden Bridge. Calderline bus 502 from Huddersfield and Halifax. Keighley & District buses 696 and 697 from Bradford via Thornton

and Denholme. Numerous buses from Keighley bus station. Tel: (0113) 245 7676 for bus and Metro Train information

On site facilities: Transport relics shop specialising in out of print magazines, lamps and hardware. Hot and cold drinks, ice cream and chocolate available. Toilets with full disabled access. A determined effort has been made to provide a museum which will interest the casual visitor who is not knowledgeable about railways

Public opening: Daily 11.00-16.30, openings outside these times can be arranged for groups. Closed 25 December

Facilities for disabled: The museum building is level with easy access for wheelchair users. A stairlift has been provided to allow wheelchair users to view carriage interiors, and enter guards' brake areas, though naturally wheelchairs

are too wide to enter individual passenger compartments. Toilets with full access for wheelchair users**.** Braille leaflet, guidebook and audio tape for loan during visit. Special facilities for visitors with hearing difficulties. Wheelchair available for loan.

Winner of the 1998 Adapt Museum Award for best practice in access for disabled and older people. Runners up for the 1998 Yorkshire Electricity/Yorkshire & Humberside Museums Council Access Awards. Highly commended in the 1999 White Rose Tourist For All Awards

Special notes: Visitors are welcome to either browse in the shop or visit the museum

Membership details: Membership Secretary, c/o above address

Marketing names: Vintage Carriages Trust or VCT

Wells & Walsingham Light Railway

Timetable Service · Norfolk

Member: HRA, TT

One man's railway, the life and love of retired naval commander, Roy Francis, this delightful line which is totally uncommercialised runs along the old Wells branch to Walsingham where the old station has been transformed into a Russian Orthodox Church by the addition of an onion-shaped dome to its roof. A must if you find yourself nearby

Location: On A149, Stiffkey Road, Wells next the Sea, Norfolk

General Manager: Lt-Cdr R. W. Francis

Operating organisation: Wells & Walsingham Light Railway, Wells

next the Sea, Norfolk NR23 1RB

Talking timetable: 01328 710631

Car park: Yes

Access by public transport: Eastern Counties buses

On site facilities: Souvenir shop, toilets and tea shop

Length of line: 4 miles, 10.25in gauge

Public opening: Daily Good Friday to the end of October

Special notes: Journey may be commenced at either end. Believed to be the world's longest 10.25in gauge line. Built on the old Wells & Fakenham Railway trackbed. Old Swainsthorpe signalbox on site at

Wells. Motive power is provided by a Garratt and a tram locomotive.

Life passes in the form of a gilt edged enamel medallion now available, please enquire for details

Facilities for disabled: Disabled can be seated in normal carriages and wheelchairs carried in luggage van. Occupied wheelchairs cannot be carried due to limitations of track gauge

Membership details: Membership Secretary, Wells & Walsingham Light Railway Support Group, c/o above address

Membership journal: Newsletter — quarterly

Wensleydale Railway

Timetable Service · North Yorkshire

The Wensleydale Railway Association was formed in 1990 with a view to restoring the route from Northallerton to Garsdale. in 2000 agreement was reached to

transfer the remaining 22 miles of line from Northallerton to Redmire to Wensleydale Railway plc. In 2003 services started between Leeming Bar and Leyburn. Medium

term plans are to extend eastwards to Northallerton and in the west from Redmire and then on towards Aysgarth. The ultimate aim is to restore the entire route from

Northallerton to Garsdale
Membership: HRA
Name of contact:
Scott Handley
Headquarters: Wensleydale
Railway plc, 35 High Street,
Northallerton, North Yorkshire
DL7 8EE
Ticketline: 08454 505474
Fax: 01609 776240
Internet addresses: *e-mail:*
admin@wensleydalerailway.com
Web site:
www.wensleydalerailway.com
Main stations: Leeming Bar and
Leyburn
Car Parking: On site
Access by public transport: Yes
Refreshment facilities: Leeming
Bar and Leyburn stations
Souvenir shops: Leeming Bar and
Leyburn
Depots: Leeming Bar
Length of line: 22 miles (12
operated in 2003, more in 2004; 18

Locomotives and multiple-units

Name	No	Origin	Class	Type	Built
—	52006	BR	107	DMBS	1960
—	52025	BR	107	DMCL	1960
—	59791	BR	107	TSL	1960
—	51813	BRCW	110	DMBC	1961
—	51842	BRCW	110	DMCL	1961

Owners
Class 107 dmus by Class 107 Ltd

miles to rebuild)
Passenger trains: See above
Period of public operation:
Easter to Autumn and Santa
Special Events (titles and dates)
Phone ticketline for current
brochure 08454 505474 or see web
site
Facilities for disabled:
Under improvement, but ramp to
facilitate access to trains and access
to both platforms are wheelchair
friendly

Membership details:
Wensleydale Railway Association:
Secretary, Ruth Annison, Dyke
House, Askrigg, Leyburn, N Yorks.
DL8 3HG
Membership journal:
Relay – 3 per year.
Special notes: Very helpful tourist
information centre at Leyburn – tel
01969 623069 – will deal with a
wide range of enquires including
Wensleydale Railway matters

Steam Centre	# West Lancashire Light Railway	Lancashire

Member: HRA
The WLLR is located in the village
of Hesketh Bank, midway between
Preston and Southport. Built by
enthusiasts in 1967 in an endeavour
to conserve some of the mainly
industrial equipment that was fast
disappearing. The railway serves as
a working museum for a variety of
historic locomotives and other
railway equipment from industrial
sites from Britain and overseas
Location: Alty's Brickworks,
Station Road, Hesketh Bank, Nr
Preston, Lancashire PR4 6SP
OS reference: SD 448229
Operating society/organisation:
The West Lancashire Light
Railway Association, Secretary, 8
Croft Avenue, Orrell, Wigan, Lancs
WN5 8TW
Telephone: (01772) 815881
Railway (24hr) or (01695) 622654
Secretary (evenings)
Internet address:
e-mail: sec@westlancs.org
Web site: www.westlancs.org
Car parks: On site
Access by public transport: Main
line rail to Preston or Southport.

Industrial locomotives

Name	No	Builder	Type	Built
Clwyd	1	R/Hornsby (264251)	4wDM	1951
Tawd	2	R/Hornsby (222074)	4wDM	1943
Irish Mail	3	Hunslet (823)	0-4-0ST	1903
Bradfield	4	Hibberd (1777)	4wPM	1931
—	5	R/Hornsby (200478)	4wDM	1940
—	7	M/Rail (8992)	4wDM	1946
Pathfinder	8	H/Hunslet (4480)	4wDM	1953
Joffre	9	K/Stuart (2405)	0-6-0T	1915
—	10	Hibberd (2555)	4wDM	1946
—	16	R/Hornsby (202036)	4wDM	1941
—	19	Lister (10805)	4wPM	1939
—	20	Baguley (3002)	4wPM	1937
—	21	H/Hunslet (1963)	4wDM	1939
—	25	R/Hornsby (297054)	4wDM	1950
—	26	M/Rail (11223)	4wDM	1963
Mill Reef	27	M/Rail (7371)	4wDM	1939
—	30	M/Rail (11258)	4wDM	1964
Montalban	34	O&K (6641)	0-4-0WT	1913
Utrillas	35	O&K (2378)	0-4-0WT	1907
—	36	R/Hornsby (339105)	4wDM	1953
Jonathan	37	Hunslet (678)	0-4-0ST	1898
—	38	Hudswell (D750)	0-4-0DM	1949
—	39	Hibberd (3916)	4wDM	1959
—	40	R/Hornsby (381705)	4wDM	1959
—	41	Lister (29890)	4wPM	1946
—	43	Greenbat (1840)	4wBE	1942
Welsh Pony	44	Wingrove (640)	4wWE	1926
—	45	Chrzanow (3506)	0-6-0T+WT	1957

Bus routes 100 and 102, between Preston and Southport
On site facilities: Gift shop, light refreshments, picnic tables, 2ft gauge line
Public opening: Every Sunday 4 April to 31 October, plus Good Friday and Bank Holiday Mondays. Opening times 12.30-17.30
Special events: Friendly Engines Day — 4 April; Easter — Good Friday (9 April) Easter Monday (12 April); Teddy Bears' Day — 16 May; Gala Weekend — 14/15 August, Fun Trains (Industrial) Day — 10 October; Santa Specials — 12, 18/19 December
Membership details: The Hon Secretary, WLLR, Station Road, Hesketh Bank, Nr Preston, Lancashire PR4 6SP

Name	No	Builder	Type	Built
Stanhope	46	K/Stuart (2395)	0-4-2ST	1917
—	47	Henschel (14676)	0-8-0T	1917
—	48	Fowler (15513)	0-4-2T	1920

Stock
Toastrack coach built 1986 by WLLR
Semi-open coach built 1993 by WLLR
Brake van built 1987 by WLLR
Large collection of goods rolling stock

Irish Mail and *Stanhope* wait for their next duties during the August 2003 Gala. *WLR*

<table>
<tr><td>Timetable Service</td><td colspan="2">West Somerset Railway</td><td>Somerset</td></tr>
</table>

Member: HRA, TT

Running for 20 miles, this is Britain's longest preserved railway and evokes all the atmosphere of a country railway from a more leisured age. The line is host to several societies and groups, and several stations have their own museum, such as the Somerset & Dorset Trust at Washford. There are some idyllic country stations in the Quantock Hills, and Dunster station serves as the model for Hornby Dublo's branch line station

Managing Director: Mark L. Smith

Headquarters: West Somerset Railway, The Railway Station, Minehead, Somerset TA24 5BG

Telephone: Minehead (01643) 704996

Internet address: *e-mail:* info@west-somerset-railway.co.uk
Web site: www.west-somerset-railway.co.uk
WAP-phone: www.wapdrive.com/wsrwap/

Locomotives and multiple-units

Name	No	Origin	Class	Type	Built
—	53808	S&DJR	7F	2-8-0	1925
—	3850	GWR	2884	2-8-0	1942
—	4160	GWR	5101	2-6-2T	1948
—	4561	GWR	4500	2-6-2T	1924
—	5193	GWR	5101	2-6-2T	1934
—	5542	GWR	4575	2-6-2T	1928
—	6412	GWR	6400	0-6-0PT	1934
Dinmore Manor	7820	GWR	'Manor'	4-6-0	1950
Odney Manor	7828	GWR	'Manor'	4-6-0	1950
Braunton	34046	SR	WC	4-6-2	1946
—	80136	BR	4MT	2-6-4PT	1956
—	D2119	BR	03	0-6-0DM	1959
—	D2133	BR	03	0-6-0DM	1959
—	D2271	BR	04	0-6-0DM	1952
—	D3462	BR	08	0-6-0DE	1957
—	D9526	BR	14	0-6-0DH	1964
—	25173	BR	25	Bo-Bo	1963
—	33018	BR	33	Bo-Bo	1960
—	D6566	BR	33	Bo-Bo	1961
—	D7017	BR	35	B-B	1962
—	D7018	BR	35	B-B	1964
Western Campaigner	D1010	BR	52	C-C	1962
—	50413	P/Royal	103	DMBS	1957
—	51352	P/Steel	117	DMBS	1959

England

Main station: Minehead

Other public stations: Dunster, Blue Anchor, Washford, Watchet, Williton, Doniford Beach Halt, Stogumber, Crowcombe, Bishops Lydeard

OS reference: Minehead SS 975463, Williton ST 085416, Bishops Lydeard ST 164290

Car parks: Free parking at Bishops Lydeard, Dunster and Williton. Pay and display at Minehead and Watchet. No parking at Doniford Beach

Access by public transport: Nearest main line station, Taunton. First Bus (01823) 272033

Refreshment facilities: Minehead, Bishops Lydeard (limited opening). Dining Trains from Minehead (tel: 01643 704996) and Bishops Lydeard (01823 433856). Please contact for dates, reservations essential.
Buffet car on most steam trains

Souvenir shops: Minehead, Bishops Lydeard

Museum: Somerset & Dorset Railway Museum Trust, Washford (contact 01984 640869 for opening times). GWR Museum at Blue Anchor (open Sundays & Bank Holidays WSR operating season). Gauge Museum at Bishops Lydeard (open daily). Diesel Heritage Visitor Centre open Saturdays May-September

Depots: Bishops Lydeard, Williton, Washford, Minehead

Length of line: 20 miles

Passenger trains: Steam and diesel trains to Bishops Lydeard

Period of public operation: 7, 13/14, 25-28 March; daily April (EXCEPT 2, 5, 19, 23, 26, 30); daily May (EXCEPT 10, 14, 17, 21, 24); daily 25 May to 30 September (EXCEPT 24, 27 September); daily October (EXCEPT 4, 8, 11, 15, 18, 22, 25, 29); 27/28 November; 3-6, 11-13, 18/19, 23/24, 27-31 December, 1/2 January 2005

Main special events: Spring Steam Gala — 25-28 March, Diesel Gala — 7-9 May; Days out with Thomas — 3/4 July; Steam Fayre & Vintage Rally at Bishops Lydeard — 7/8 August; Diesel Gala — 14/15 August, Real Ale Festival at Minehead station — 11/12

Name	No	Origin	Class	Type	Built
—	51376	P/Steel	117	DMS	1959
—	51663	BR	115	DMBS	1960
—	51852	BR	115	DMBS	1960
—	51887	BR	115	DMBS	1960
—	56169	P/Royal	103	DTCL	1957
—	59505	P/Steel	117	TC	1959
—	59678	BR	115	TC	1960

Note: 5193 is being rebuilt as a 2-6-0 tender locomotive and will enter service in 2004
7828 may not be on site for all of 2004 season

Industrial locomotives

Name	No	Builder	Type	Built
Isabel	—	H/Leslie (3437)	0-6-0ST	1919
Kilmersdon	—	Peckett (1788)	0-4-0ST	1929
—	24	Ruston (210479)	4wDM	1941
—	—	Ruston (183062)	4wDM	1937
—	16	Sentinel (10175)	0-6-0DM	1964
—	501	Brush/Bagnall (3066)	0-4-0DE	1954
—	512	Brush/Bagnall (3102)	0-4-0DE	1954

Stock
21 ex-BR Mk 1 coaches; 2 ex-BR Restaurant cars; 1 ex-BR Sleeping car; 3 ex-S&DJR 6-wheel coaches, 7 ex-GWR camping coaches; 1 ex-GWR Sleeping coach; 1 ex-GWR 5-ton hand crane; more than 40 freight vehicles

Owners
53808, *Isabel, Kilmersdon* the Somerset & Dorset Museum Trust
D1010, D7017, D7018 & D9526 the Diesel and Electric Preservation Group
D2119, D3462 and D7523 Dr John F. Kennedy
5542 the 5542 Ltd
3850 and 7820 the Dinmore Manor Locomotive Ltd
4160 the 4160 Ltd
5193 and D2271 the WSR plc
33018 the Birmingham Railwaymen's Crompton Workgroup
Class 117 vehicles the Ministry of Defence (Army)

September; Autumn Steam Gala— 1-3 October, Grand Trains Extravaganza — 23/24 October, Dunster by Candlelight — 3/4 December; Carol Trains — 6, 13 December; Santa Specials — 27/28 November, 4/5, 11/12, 18/19, 23/24 December; Winter Festival — 29 December

Other special events: Mother's Day Specials — 21 March; DMU Jazz Evenings — 19 June, 17 July, 11 September; Father's Day Specials — 20 June; Halloween Special — 30 October (booking essential).
Fish & Chip Specials (advance booking essential) — 17 April, 15 May, 5 June, 10 & 24 July, 14 & 25 August, 25 September, 2 January 2005.
Murder Mystery Night Specials

(advance booking essential) — 18 June, 9 July, 3 September.
Sunset Specials — Wednesday evenings June to September

Facilities for disabled: Trains have limited accommodation for passengers in wheelchairs. There is level or ramped access to all stations except Doniford, and RADAR key access toilets at Bishops Lydeard and Minehead. Advance booking essential for groups

Membership details: West Somerset Railway Association, The Railway Station, Bishops Lydeard, Taunton TA4 3BX.
Tel: 01823 433856

Membership journal: *WSR Journal* — quarterly

Museum — Winchcombe Railway Museum — Glos

One mile from Winchcombe station on the Gloucestershire Warwickshire railway, the diverse collection includes signalling equipment, lineside fixtures, horse-drawn road vehicles, tickets, lamps, etc. Indoor and outdoor displays set in half an acre of traditional Victorian Cotswold garden. Visitors are encouraged to touch and operate exhibits
Location: 23 Gloucester Street, Winchcombe, Gloucestershire

OS reference: SP 023283
Operating society/organisation: Winchcombe Railway Museum Association, 23 Gloucester Street, Winchcombe, Gloucestershire
Telephone: Winchcombe (01242) 609305
Car park: On street at entrance
Access by public transport: Bus service from Cheltenham operated by Castleways Ltd
On site facilities: Relics and souvenir shop

Public opening: Easter to end October 2004.
Wednesdays, Thursdays, Fridays, weekends and Bank Holiday Mondays — 13.30-17.00; daily throughout August. 13.30-17.00.
Facilities for disabled: Access to all parts except toilets
Special notes: Many visitor-operated exhibits, picnic area, pet animals

Attraction — Windmill Farm Railway — Lancashire

Location: Situated with in the grounds of Windmill Animal Farm
Headquarters: Windmill Animal Farm, Red Cat Lane, Burscough, L40 1UQ
Name of contact: Austin Moss
Telephone: Farm 01704 892282; Austin Moss 07971 221343;

Internet address: *Web site:* www.windmillfarmrailway.co.uk
Main station: At Farm
Other station: Lakeview, 1/2 mile away
Car parking: On site
Access by public transport: None
On site facilities: Farm café, shop

Depots: At farm site
Length of line: 1/2 mile each way (1 mile return) 15in gauge
Period of public operation: March-November 10.00-17.00; Weekends March-December, Daily June to September plus school holidays Trains every 1/2 hour from

A selection of locomotives on display in the main station area. *WFR*

England

11.00 until 16.00
Special events: None planned but see web site
Facilities for disabled: Accessibility for wheelchairs around farm facilities etc, prior warning on railway
Membership details: No membership as such, just volunteer. Contact Austin Moss for details
Fare: 75p adults, 50p children plus farm entry fee.

Industrial locomotives

Name	No	Builder	Type	Built
'Cagney'	44	McGarigle	4-4-0	c1902
Blue Pacific	4	Guinness	4-6-0VB	1935
Whippet Quick	–	Lister	4w-4DM	1935
Gwril	–	Lister	4wPM	1943
Prince William	5751	G&SLE	4-6-2	1946
Princess Anne	—	Barlow	4-6w-2DE	1948
Duke of Edinburgh	—	Barlow	4-6-2	1950
Katie	—	Guest	2-4-2	1953
Siân	—	Guest	2-4-2	1963
Neptune / (St Nicholas)	–	Severn-Lamb	2-8-0GH	1978
–	14	Walker	2w-2PM	1985
City Of London Jubilee	2870	Volante	4-6-0DH	1987
'The Bar Stool'	—	Moss	2w-2PM	1989
St Christopher	—	Exmoor	2-6-2T	2001

Railway Centre — Yeovil Railway Centre — Somerset

Member: HRA

The Yeovil Railway Centre is operated by the South West Main Line Steam Co and is adjacent to the former London & South Western Railway main line at Yeovil Junction. It features the original British Railways turntable
Location: Adjacent to the main line at Yeovil Junction on the London (Waterloo)-Salisbury-Exeter line
Chaiman: Richard Abbott
Contact address: South Western Main Line Steam Co (Yeovil Railway Centre), Yeovil Junction Station, Stoford, Nr Yeovil, Somerset BA22 9UU
Telephone: 01935 410420
Fax: 01935 478373
Internet address: *Web site:* www.yeovilrailway.free servers.com
Car park: On site. Follow signs to Yeovil Junction from Yeovil town centre or from A35 Dorchester-Yeovil road
Access by public transport: SouthWest Trains to Yeovil Junction or First Bus from Yeovil town centre
On site facilities: Exhibition of relics and photographs in the newly acquired transfer shed (dating from 1864) and shop. Light refreshments when brake van rides are operating
Length of line: 500 metres

Locomotive

Name	No	Origin	Class	Type	Built
—	20059	BR	20	Bo-Bo	1961
—	20177	BR	20	Bo-Bo	1966

Industrial locomotive

Name	No	Builder	Type	Built
Pectin	—	Peckett (1579)	0-4-0ST	1921
—	—	Fowler (22900)	0-4-0DM	1941
—	—	Fowler (22900)	0-4-0DM	1947
Yeo	—	R/Hornsby (4000007)	4wDM	1961

Locomotive notes: Main line locomotives occasionally present for servicing during railtours. *Pectin* is likely to be out of use for part/all of season for overhaul

Rolling stock: Selection of freight wagons

Owner
20059 and 20177 the Somerset & Dorset Locomotive Co (located nearby on privately owned sidings)

Opening times: Shop open Sundays mornings throughout the year (except Christmas/New Year). Train Days are planned for Easter Sunday and 1st and 3rd Sundays May to September inclusive. 11.00-16.00 when brake van rides, shunting and turntable demonstrations feature. Also open on days when main line steam is being serviced (telephone or see web site for details) and for Santa Specials in December

Disabled access: To site, but no wheelchair access (at present) to brake van rides
Membership details: Richard Abbott, The Nut Tree, 108 Westfield Grove, Yeovil, Somerset BA21 3DN
Membership journal: *The Turntable*, quarterly

Scotland

Steam Centre — Alford Valley Railway — Aberdeenshire

The Alford Valley Railway operates from the restored station yard which once marked the terminus of the branch line linking the villages of upper Donside with Kintore Junction, thence to Aberdeen

Location: On A944, 25 miles west of Aberdeen, adjacent to Grampian Transport Museum

Headquarters: Alford Valley Railway Co Ltd, Alford Station, Alford, Aberdeenshire

Internet adress: *Web site:* www.alford.org.uk/avr.htm

Main station: Alford

Car park: On site

Length of line: 3km, 2ft gauge

Museum: Grampian Transport Museum adjacent

Depot: Alford station

Period of public operation: Railway operates: April, May September — weekends only (13.00-17.00); June, July and August — daily 13.00-17.00. Trains depart at 30min intervals.

Industrial locomotives

Name	No	Builder	Type	Built
Saccharine	—	Fowler (13355)	0-4-2T	1914
Hamewith	—	Lister (3198)	4wDM	c1930
—	—	A/Keef (63)	4wDM	2001
—	—	M/Rail (22129)	4wDM	1962
—	—	M/Rail (2221)	4wDM	1964
James Gordon	—	Keef (63)	0-4-0T (SO)	2001
Aberdeen Corporation Gas Works	3*	A/Barclay (1889)	0-4-0ST	1926

*standard gauge

Rolling stock

Two 24-seat coaches, 50-seat coach, 24-seat ex-Aberdeen tramcar, various wagons

Seasonal tickets available. Alford Heritage Centre is open daily (10.00-17.00)

Special notes: Steam-operated on first Sunday of each month from April to September. Special bookings available, tel: (01975) 562811

Special events: Easter Fayre, Santa

Specials — please contact for details

Membership details: Membership Secretary, AVR Association, Creagmwor, Main Street, Alford, Aberdeenshire AB33 8AD

Museum — Almond Valley Heritage Trust — West Lothian

Member: HRA

Part of a wide-ranging heritage centre containing a museum of Scotland's shale oil industry with award winning children's exhibits, working watermill, farmsteading with traditional livestock. indoor play areas, countryside walks and farmhouse kitchen tea room.

Operating society/organisation: Almond Valley Heritage Centre, Millfield, Livingston Village, West Lothian EH54 7AR

OS reference: NT 034667

Telephone: 01506 414957

Fax: 01506 497771

Internet address: *e-mail:* info@almondvalley.co.uk

*Web site: www.*almondvalley.co.uk

Access by public transport: Main line trains to Livingston North (1 mile)

On site facilities: Children's exhibits, indoor play areas, tea room

Public opening: Daily (except 25/26 December, 1/2 January)

10.00-17.00.

Trains operate weekends from March-September, daily July and August and certain public holidays

Length of line: 500m 2ft 6in gauge line from Livingston Mill to Almondhaugh stations, with plans to extend

Facilities for disabled: Full disabled access to site, but not to coaches

Industrial locomotives

Name	No	Builder	Type	Built
05/576	—	Barclay (557)	4wDH	1970
Oil Company No 2	—	Baldwin (20587)	4wWE	1902
—	20	Brook Victor (612)	4wBE	1972
—	38	Brook Victor (698)	4wBE	1972
—	42	Brook Victor (700)	4wBE	1972
—	—	Brook Victor (1143)	4wBE	1972
3585	13	Greenwood (1698)	4wDE	1940
ND3059	Yard No B10	Hunslet (2270)	0-4-0DM	1940
—	7330	Hunslet (7330)	4wDM	1973
—	—	Simplex (40SPF522)	4wDM	1981

Note

Barclay 557 and Hunslet 2270 operate passenger services

Bo'ness & Kinneil Railway

West Lothian

Member: HRA, TT, Registered Museum

Historic railway buildings, including the station and train shed, have been relocated from sites all over Scotland. In two purpose-built exhibition halls, the Scottish Railway Exhibition tells the story of the development of the railways in Scotland, and their impact on the people. The rich geology of the area, with its 300 million year old fossils, is explained during a conducted tour of the caverns of the former Birkhill Fireclay Mine

Operating society/location:
Scottish Railway Preservation Society, Bo'ness Station, Union Street, Bo'ness, West Lothian, EH51 9AQ

Access by public transport:
Nearest ScotRail station — Linlithgow. Bus services from Linlithgow, Falkirk, Stirling, Edinburgh and Glasgow

OS reference: NT 003817

Telephone: Train services & Events 01506 825855

Talking timetable: 01506 822298.

Fax: 01506 828766

Internet address: *E-mail:* administration@srps.org.uk
Web site: www.srps.org.uk

Main station: Bo'ness

Other station: Birkhill

Car parks: At Bo'ness and Birkhill (free)

Refreshment facilities: Extensive (unlicensed) buffet at Bo'ness.

Locomotives

Name	No	Origin	Class	Type	Built
—	419	CR	439	0-4-4T	1908
Morayshire	246	LNER	D49	4-4-0	1928
Glen Douglas	256	NBR	D34	4-4-0	1913
—	42	NBR	Y9	0-4-0ST	1887
Maude	673	NBR	J36	0-6-0	1891
—	80105	BR	4MT	2-6-4T	1955
—	D2774	BR	—	0-4-0DH	1960
—	08443 (D3558)	BR	08	0-6-0DE	1958
—	14901 (D9524)	BR	14	0-6-0DH	1964
—	D8020	BR	20	Bo-Bo	1959
—	25235 (D7585)	BR	25	Bo-Bo	1965
—	26004 (D5303)	BR	26	B0-Bo	1958
—	26024 (D5323)	BR	26	Bo-Bo	1959
—	27001 (D5347)	BR	27	Bo-Bo	1961
—	D5351	BR	27	Bo-Bo	1961
—	37025	BR	37	Co-Co	1961
—	47643	BR	47	Co-Co	1968

Industrial locomotives

Name	No	Builder	Type	Built
Clydesmill	3	Barclay (1937)	0-4-0ST	1928
—	3	Barclay (2046)	0-4-0ST	1937
—	24	Barclay (2335)	0-6-0T	1953
Texaco	—†	Fowler (4210140)	0-4-0DM	1958
(Lord King)	—	H/Leslie (3640)	0-4-0ST	1926
—	19	Hunslet (3818)	0-6-0ST	1954
DS3	—	R/Hornsby (275883)	4wDM	1949
DS4	P6687	R/Hornsby (312984)	0-4-0DE	1951
(Ranald)	—	Sentinel (9627)	4wVBT	1957
—	970214	Wickham (6050)	2w-2PMR	c1951
—	—	Matisa (48626)	—	—
—	5	Hunslet (3837)	0-6-0ST	1955
—	(7)	Bagnall (2777)	0-6-0ST	1945
Borrowstounness	—*	Barclay (840)	0-4-0T	1899
—	—*	M/Rail (110U082)	4wDH	1970
—	—	Wickham (10482)	2w-2PMR	1970
—	(17)	Hunslet (2880)	0-6-0ST	1943

Picnic tables at both stations
Souvenir shop: Bo'ness
Depot: Bo'ness
Length of line: 3.5 miles
Period of public operation:
Weekends 3 April-31 October,
daily 5 July-30 August (Mondays
diesel-hauled)
Special events: Easter Egg — 9-12
April; May Diesel Gala — 1-3
May; Day out with Thomas —
15-17 May; Father's Day Vintage
Vehicle Rally — 20 June; Day out
with Thomas — 6-8 August; Diesel
Gala — 4/5 September; Wizards &
Witches event — 30/31 October;
Santa Specials — 27/28 November,
4/5, 11/12, 18/19 December
Facilities for disabled: Disabled
access to platform and a specially
adapted carriage for wheelchair
users. Toilets at Bo'ness station. No
facilities for wheelchairs at Birkhill
Fireclay Mine
Special notes: The S&T
Department were winners of the
1998 Westinghouse Signalling
Award in the Ian Allan Railway
Heritage Awards. Achieved full
museum registration in 1999.
Birkhill Fireclay Mine and Scottish
Railway Exhibition open same days
as trains operate (except December)

Name	No	Builder	Type	Built
—	970213	Wickham (6049)	2w-2PMR	c1951
—	17†	Barclay (2296)	0-4-0ST	1952
Lady Victoria	3	Barclay (1458)	0-6-0ST	1916
The Wemyss Coal				
Co Ltd	20	Barclay (2068)	0-6-0T	1939
—	(6)	Barclay (2127)	0-4-0CT	1942
No 1	—	Barclay (343)	0-6-0DM	1941
City of Aberdeen	—	B/Hawthorn (912)	0-4-0ST	1887
F82 (Fairfield)	—	E/Electric (1131)	4wBE	1940
Kelton Fell	13	Neilson (2203)	0-4-0ST	1876
Lord Roberts	1§	N/Reid (5710)	0-6-0T	1902
(Tiger)	—	N/British (27415)	0-4-0DH	1954
Kilbagie	DS2	R/Hornsby (262998)	4wDM	1949
—	—	R/Hornsby (321733)	4wDM	1952
DS6	(1)	R/Hornsby (421439)	0-4-0DE	1958
St Mirren	(3)	R/Hornsby (423658)	0-4-0DE	1958
—	D88/003	R/Hornsby (506500)	4wDM	1965
(Denis)	—	Sentinel (9631)	4wVBT	1958
—	—	Arrols (Glasgow)	2w-2DM	c1966

*3ft 0in gauge
†at present off site at the Scottish Vintage Bus Museum, Lathalmond, Fife
§official licensed 'Thomas' replica locomotive

Stock
A large selection of coaching stock, many built by Scottish pre-Grouping
companies, ex-BR Class 126 DMU, and an appropriate collection of early
freight vehicles

Owners
80105 and (Denis) owned by Locomotive Owners Group (Scotland)
246 and 24 owned by Royal Museum of Scotland
256 the Glasgow Museum of Transport
27001 the Class 27 Preservation Group
26004 and 26024 the 6LDA Group37025 the Scottish Class 37 Group

---

Timetable Service	Caledonian Railway (Brechin)	Angus

Member: HRA
This Scottish country steam railway
is a classic branch line starting at
the Strathmore line junction station
of Bridge of Dun, last stomping
ground of the Gresley 'A4' Pacific
locomotives, and climbs some steep
gradients through scenic farmland
with assorted wildlife and flora.
The summit is reached at the Edzell
& Forfar junction just short of
Brechin station, itself one of the
most impressive of Britain's
preserved railways.
  The National Trust for Scotland
property House of Dun, built by
William Adam in 1730, is
approximately 1 mile from Bridge

Locomotives

Name	No	Origin	Class	Type	Built
Brechin City	D3059	BR	08	0-6-0DE	1954
*—	MP228 (12052)	BR	11	0-6-0DE	1949
*—	MP229 (12093)	BR	11	0-6-0DE	1951
—	25083	BR	25	Bo-Bo	1963
—	D5314	BR	26	Bo-Bo	1959
—	D5314	BR	26	Bo-Bo	1959
—	27024	BR	27	Bo-Bo	1962
—	37097	BR	37	Co-Co	1962

*on loan from Scottish Industrial Railway centre
All expected to be operational during 2004

Industrial locomotives

Name	No	Builder	Type	Built
Harlaxton†	—	Barclay (1863)	0-4-0ST	1926
—†	—	Barclay (2107)	0-6-0T	1941
BAC No 1	—	Peckett (1376)	0-4-0ST	1915

of Dun station, which is also close to the Montrose Basin, a tidal wildlife centre. Brechin itself has many attractions including the cathedral and round tower and the new Pictavia centre.

The railway is run entirely by volunteer members of the Brechin Railway Preservation Society

Headquarters: Caledonian Railway (Brechin) Ltd, The Station, 2 Park Road, Brechin, Angus DD9 7AF

Telephone: 01356 622992 (or 07740 363958)

Internet address: *E-mail:* calrail@engineer.com *Web site:* www.caledonianrailway.co.,uk

Main stations: Brechin and Bridge of Dun

OS reference: NO 603603

Car park: Brechin, Bridge of Dun

Access by car: Via A90 Dundee/Aberdeen to Brechin bypass. Brown tourist signs to stations. Free parking

Access by public transport: By ScotRail, GNER and Virgin services to Montrose (5 miles). By bus from Montrose, Strathtay Scottish — Dundee (01382) 228054/227201

Refreshment facilities: Light refreshments at Brechin on operating days

Picnic area: Bridge of Dun

Souvenir shop: Brechin

Museum: Brechin

Length of line: 4 miles 22 chains

Depot: Brechin

Passenger trains: Industrial steam and heritage diesel-hauled trains between Brechin and Bridge of Dun

Period of public operation: Steam trains rum every Sunday 30 May to 5 September plus other dates as shown below. Brechin station is open daily for static viewing Tuesday-Friday 11.00-16.00, Bridge of Dun site open daily all week

Special events: Easter Specials _ 10/11 April; Diesel Gala — 2/3 May; Front Line Branch line (1940s Weekend — 5/6 June; Day

Name	No	Builder	Type	Built
Menelaus	—	Peckett (1883)	0-6-0ST	1935
FC Tingey†	—	Peckett (2084)	0-6-0ST	1948
	—	Peckett (2153)	0-6-0ST	1954
Diana No 1	—	Hunslet (2879)	0-6-0ST	1943
	6	Bagnall (2749)	0-6-0ST	1944
	16	Bagnall (2759)	0-6-0ST	1944
	DY 326	Hibberd (3743)	4wDM	1955
	—	Hibberd (3743)	4wDM	1955
	—	R/Hornsby (421700)	4wDM	1959
Dewar Highlander†	48	R/Hornsby (458957)	4wDM	1961

† expected to be operational during 2004, others in store/under restoration

Coaching Stock
In service 7 x BR Mk 1, 3 x BR Mk 2s
Stored 4 x BR Mk 1s

Engineer's Stock
c50 wagons including: 1 ex-BR diesel-electric crane, 2 Dogfish, 1 Mermaid, 4 warflats, 3 rectanks, 1 Ferry van, 2 Lowmacs, 2 minfit, 1 21-ton minfit, 2 LNER vans, 2 LMS vans, 2 demountable tank wagons, 1 ex-BR bolster

Departmental Stock
1 CR origin electrification coach, 1 ex-BR BCK, various vans

Owners
No 1 and *Menelaus*the the Angus Railway Steam Engineers
68189 private
D5314 the Class Twenty Six Preservation Group
D3059, 26035 and 27024 the Caledonian Diesel Group
51993 and 52012 the DMU Group

In addition to above the following is under restoration adjacent to Bridge of Dun station

Locomotives

Name	No	Origin	Class	Type	Built
—	46464	LMS	2MT	2-6-0	1950

out with Thomas — 3/4, 10/11 July; Steam Gala — 28/29 August. Santa Specials — 5, 11/12, 18/19 December. Murder Mystery Evenings — 29 May, 19 June, 24 July, 16 August

Facilities for disabled: Ramp access to both stations. Vehicular access to Brechin platforms by prior arrangement. Coach converted to take wheelchairs and attendants, prior notice required for access and car parking

Family tickets: Available

Disclaimer: The Caledonian Railway (Brechin) Ltd reserves the

right to amend, cancel or add to these events. And whilst every effort will be made to maintain the above services, the company does not guarantee that trains will depart or arrive at the time stated and reserves the right to suspend or alter any train without notice and will not accept any liability for loss, inconvenience or delay thereby caused

Membership details: M. Jackson, c/o above address

Membership journal: Quarterly

Marketing name: The Friendly Line

Museum — Glasgow Museum of Transport — Glasgow

Member: HRA, TT

Glasgow's magnificent railway collection represents one of the best efforts by a municipal authority to preserve a representative collection of items appropriate to the 'locomotive builders of the Empire'. In 1989 the collection opened to view once again in its new setting at the former Kelvin Hall

Access by public transport: Strathclyde PTE Underground. Kelvinhall: Strathclyde Buses 6, 6A, 8, 8A, 9, 9A, 16, 42, 42A, 57, 57A, 62, 62A, 62B, 64; Kelvin Scottish Buses 5, 5A; Clydeside Scottish Buses 17

Operating society/organisation: Glasgow City Council, Dept of Cultural & Leisure Services

Location: Museum of Transport, Kelvin Hall, 1 Bunhouse Road, Glasgow G3 8DP

Telephone: (0141) 287 2623 or (0141) 287 2721

Fax: (0141) 287 2692

Locomotives

Name	No	Origin	Class	Type	Built
—	123	CR	123	4-2-2	1886
—	9	G&SWR	5	0-6-0T	1917
—	103	HR	—	4-6-0	1894
Gordon Highlander	49	GNSR	F	4-4-0	1920

Industrial locomotives

Name	No	Builder	Type	Built
—	1	Barclay (1571)	0-6-0F	1917
—	—	Chaplin (2368)	0-4-0TG	1888
—	—	BEV (583)	B	1927

Stock

Glasgow District Subway car 39T; Glasgow Corporation Underground cars 1 and 4; LMS King George VI's saloon 498 of 1941

Car park: Opposite Museum entrance

On site facilities: Toilets, cafeteria, shop and public telephone, cloaking facility

Public opening: Monday-Thursday 10.00-17.00; Friday and Sunday 11.00-17.00. Closed 1/2 January and 25/26 December only. Please check before travelling

Facilities for disabled: Both single-sex and uni-sex disabled facilities now available. A passenger lift to allow disabled access at the front entrance is now in operation

---

Timetable Service — Keith & Dufftown Railway — Banffshire

Member: HRA

Opened to Keith in 2001. The line links the two towns famous round the world for names such as Chivas Regal and Glenfiddich

Operating society/organisation: Keith & Dufftown Railway Association, Dufftown Station, Dufftown, Banffshire AB55 4BA

Contact: Maureen H. Webster (Chairman)

Telephone: (01340) 821181

Internet address: *e-mail:* kdra@dial.pipex.com

Web site: www.keith-dufftown.org.uk

Main station: Dufftown

Other public stations: Drummuir (access by rail only), Keith Town (not the ScotRail station)

Length of line: 11 miles With 42 bridges and the twin span

Locomotives and multiple-units

Name	No	Origin	Class	Type	Built
—	51568	BR	108	DMC(L)	1959
—	54223	BR	108	DTC(L)	1959
—	53628	BR	108	DMBS	1958
—	52053	BR	108	DMC(L)	1960
—	55500*	BR	140	DMS	1981
—	55501*	BR	140	DMS	1981
—	Car 87§	M/Cam	5BEL	TPS	1932
—	Car 91§	M/Cam	5BEL	DMPBS	1932

§ex-'Brighton Belle' Pullman cars, converted to locomotive-hauled
Class 108s on hire from East Anglian Railway Museum
*unit No 140001

Industrial locomotives

Name	No	Builder	Type	Built
Spirit o' Fife	—	E/Electric (D1193)	0-6-0DH	1967
Wee Mac	—	Clayton	4wDH	1979

60ft high Fiddich Viaduct
Car park: Dufftown, Keith
Access by public transport:
ScotRail station at Keith (short
walk to Keith Town)
Refreshments: Dufftown
Souvenirs: Dufftown
On site facilities: Visitor
Information centre, with artefacts
about Keith & Dufftown Railway
in the Class 140.
Woodland walks from Drummuir
station and access to the Walled
Garden at Drummuir Castle
Period of public operation:
Weekends, Easter to end September
Special events: Spring and autumn
Whisky Festivals, please contact
for dates. Santa Specials — 1/5,
11/12, 18/19 December
Membership details: Membership
Secretary, c/o above address
Membership journal: *The Keith &
Dufftown Express* — quarterly

Rolling stock
3 Canadian 'Speeder' vehicles
A selection of freight vehicles for maintenance purposes

Diesel multiple-units supply the motive power on the
Keith & Dufftown line. *K&DR*

Leadhills & Wanlockhead Railway

Member: HRA
Situated in the Lowther Hills
between Abington and Sanquhar,
the society was formed in 1983 to
construct and operate a 2ft gauge
tourist railway between the villages
of Leadhills and Wanlockhead. The
track now extends to the old county
boundary between Lanarkshire and
Dumfriesshire. The highest
adhesion worked railway in Great
Britain at 1,498ft above sea level.
Signalbox built using terracotta
bricks from the demolished viaduct
at Risping Cleuch, with a variety of
pre-Grouping signalling &
telegraph equipment (eg North
British Railway lever frame and
Caledonian Railway lattice post
signal.
Operating society/organisation:
Leadhills & Wanlockhead Railway
c/o A. Ireland, 23 Pinnacle Hill
Park, Kelso, Borders TD5 8HA
Telephone: 01573 223691
Internet address: *Web site:*
www.leadhillsrailway.co.uk
Main station: Leadhills
Access by public transport:
ScotRail trains stop at Sanquhar on
Nith Valley Line (approx 10 miles)
every 1hr 30min-2 hours. Bus

Industrial locomotives

Name	No	Builder	Type	Built
Charlotte	—	O&K	0-4-0T	1913
Elvan	2	M/Rail (9792)	4wDM	1955
Luce	4	R/Hornsby (7002/0467/2)	4wDM	1966
Little Clyde	5	R/Hornsby (7002/0467/6)	4wDM	1966
Clyde	6	Hunslet (6347)	4wDH	1975
Nith	8	H/Clarke (DM1002)	0-4-0DMF	1956
Mennock	10	H/Barclay (LD 9348)	0-4-0DM	1994

Rolling stock
2 air-braked passenger coaches and guard's van built at Leadhills. 1 air-
braked coach chassis built by Talyllyn Railway, with the L&WR
completing the bodywork. Assorted permanent way wagons

service (Western Scottish
Stagecoach) to Leadhills (please
check for times). Nearest motorway
— M74 — J14 from south/J15 from
north. From A76 take B797 to
Leadhills
Length of line: 1 mile
Journey time: Approx 30min
round trip
On site facilities: Shop, ticket
office, small museum and picnic
tables. Extensive country walks.
Also on 'Southern Upland Way'.
Scottish Lead Mining Museum at

Wanlockhead (1 mile)
Period of public operation: Easter
weekend; weekends April-October.
Saturdays 11.00-17.00, Sundays
11.00-17.00. Schools and private
charters by prior arrangement —
50% discount available
Special events: Steam Fair
weekend (usually late July)
Membership details: c/o above
address
Society journal: Quarterly

133

Member: HRA, TT
Commercial Manager:
Graham E. Ellis
Operations Manager: D. Moseley
Operating society/organisation:
Mull & West Highland (NG)
Railway Co Ltd, Old Pier Station,
Craignure, Isle of Mull PA65 6AY
Telephone: (01680) 812494
Fax: (01680) 300595
Internet address: *e-mail:*
mullrail@deeemm.co.uk
Web site: www.mullrail.co.uk
OS reference: NM 725369
Car park: At Craignure, free
Access by public transport:
Caledonian MacBrayne ferry from
Oban (40min sail)
On site facilities: Gift shop, car
park (free)
Family ticket: Available (2 adults
& 2 children under 14)
Length of line: 1.25 miles/10.25in
gauge
Public opening: Easter week to
mid-October
Facilities for disabled: No steps
on railway, two compartments for
wheelchairs

Locomotives

Name	No	Builder	Type	Built
Lady of the Isles	—	Marsh	2-6-4T	1981
Waverley†	—	Curwen	4-4-2	1952
—	—	Alcock	4w-4PM	1973
Glen Auldyn	—	Davies	B0-B0 DH	1986
Victoria*	—	Vere	2-6-2T	1993
Frances	—	Vere	B0-B0 DH	1999

†visiting Rudyard Lake for 2004
*largest tank engine built for 10.25in gauge

Rolling stock
12 coaches (two with wheelchair accommodation); 3 bogie wagons;
1 4-wheel wagon

Owner
Waverley — The Waverley Group

Membership details: Friends of
Mull Rail, David Crombie,
1 Mulberry Drive, Dunfermline,
Fife KY11 8BZ. Tel: (01383)
728652
Membership journal: *Crankpin
Journal* — annual
Special notes: First island passenger
railway in Scotland, runs to Torosay
Castle and 12 acres of gardens,
superb panoramic views of
mountains and sea. Group discount
available for 20+ pre-booked
passengers. Special trains can be
chartered within and outside
timetable hours. Joint Torosay
Castle/Mull Rail tickets available

Member: TT, Heritage Afloat
Paddle steamers: *Waverley* &
Kingswear Castle. Pleasure cruise
ship: *Balmoral*
The Paddle Steamer *Waverley* was
built for the London & North
Eastern Railway in 1946, and
replaced a vessel of the same name
which was sunk off Dunkirk during
May 1940. Sold to the PSPS — a
Registered Charity — in 1974,
Waverley sails on day trips and
afternoon cruises from ports and
piers in most coastal areas and river
estuaries of the United Kingdom,
from Easter until October each year.

Also in the 'fleet' is the traditional
motor cruiser *Balmoral* and the
river paddle steamer *Kingswear
Castle* which sails from Chatham
Historic Dockyard on the River
Medway
Commercial Director:
Kathleen O'Neil
Operations Director:
Ian McMillan
Headquarters: Waverley
Excursions Ltd, Waverley Terminal,
Anderston Quay, Glasgow G3 8HA
On ship facilities: Self service
restaurants, bars, toilets (disabled
toilets on *Waverley*), souvenirs

Membership details: Paddle
Steamer Preservation Society,
PO Box 365, Worcester WR3 7WH
Membership journal:
Paddlewheels — quarterly
Details of the full programme of
cruises operated by the three ships
can be obtained from the National
Booking Office, Waverley
Excursions Ltd, Waverley Terminal,
Anderston Quay, Glasgow G3 8HA.
Tel: 0845 130 4647.
Book on-line at:
www.waverleyexcursions.co.uk

Steam Centre — Prestongrange Industrial Heritage Museum — East Lothian

Location: On the B1348 between Musselburgh and Prestonpans.
OS reference: NT 734737
Operating society/organisation: East Lothian Museum Service, Library & Museum Headquarters, Dunbar Road, Haddington, East Lothian EH41 3PJ
Telephone: (0131) 653 2904 (Prestongrange Visitor Centre), (01620) 828203 (Museum Service)
Internet address: e-mail: elms@eastlothian.gov.uk
Car park: On site
On site facilities: Once part of the Scottish Mining Museum, Prestongrange is being developed as a museum which tells the story of people and industries in East Lothian — local coal deposits encouraged the growth of numerous other industries; such as pottery, pipe making, soap, glycerine, brewing and weaving
Visitor centre: Changing exhibitions of local industries. Displays of local art and crafts — one-off events, demonstrations, workshops. Cornish beam engine, installed 1874 to pump water from the mine. Colliery locomotives restored by Prestongrange Railway Society are housed here
Toilets: Visitor centre
Refreshment facilities: Available at visitor centre
Public opening: April to October, 11.00-16.00, last tour at 15.00
Length of line: 400m (standard gauge), extension in progress
Facilities for disabled: Access and toilet at visitor centre. Access to powerhouse exhibition, and footpaths along the site
Special events: Events held throughout the season
Membership details: Friends of Prestongrange. Contact Peter Gray, Museums Officer — c/o operating organisation
Contact: For Prestongrange Railway Society — Colin Boyd, 3 Stuart Wynd, Craigmount View, Edinburgh EH2 8XU

Industrial locomotives

Name	No	Builder	Type	Built
—	6	A/Barclay (2043)	0-4-0ST	1937
—	17	A/Barclay (2219)	0-4-0ST	1946
Prestongrange	7	G/Ritchie (536)	0-4-2ST	1914
Tomatin	1	M/Rail (9925)	4wDM	1963
—	—*	Hunslet (4440)	4wDM	1952
—	32	R/Hornsby (458960)	4wDM	1962
George Edwards	33	R/Hornsby (221647)	4wDM	1943
—	—	E/Electric (D908)	4wDM	1964

*2ft gauge

Rolling stock
Steam crane, Whittaker No 30, c1890, occasionally in steam

Diesel Centre — Royal Deeside Railway — Banffshire

Operating society/organisation: The Royal Deeside Railway
Contact: (Chairman) Peter Mearns c/o 6A St Swithern Street, Aberdeen
Telephone: 01224 582654
Internet address: e-mail: petemearns@hotmail.com
Web site: www.deeside-railway.co.uk
OS reference: NO 914962
Main Station: Milton of Craithes
Car Parking: On site
Access by public transport: ScotRail to Aberdeen (11 miles) By road to Craithes via A93 (11 miles)
On site facilities: Light refreshments on board restored

Locomotives and multiple-units

Name	No	Origin	Class	Type	Built
—	03134†	BR	03	0-6-0DH	1960
—	D9551	BR	14	0-6-0DM	1965
—	79988*	BR	—	BDMBS	1958
—	79999*	BR	—	BDMBS	1958

†rebuilt with hyraulic drive
*battery-powered multiple-unit

Industrial locomotives

Name	No	Builder	Type	Built
—	—	Barclay (807)	0-4-0ST	1897

Rolling stock
2 BR Mk 2 coaches, GNSR full brake, GNSR 5-comp lav third (body only), GNSR 5-comp third (body only), GNSR 4 comp First (body only),

coach (seasonal weekend opening)
Length of line: Passenger service planned, 4km to Banchory when initial phase complete
Public opening: Weekends April-September 12.00-17.00

Special events: Santa Specials — December weekends
Membership details: Cindy Blackmore, Membership Secretary, 57 Leslie Road, Aberdeen AB24 4HU

Membership journal: *The Queen's Messanger* (quarterly)
Note: Most locomotives and rolling stock undergoing restoration off-site

---

| Steam Centre | ## Scottish Industrial Railway Centre | Ayrshire |

Member: HRA, TT, AIM
The Scottish Industrial Railway Centre is based on part of the former Dalmellington Iron Co railway system which was one of the best known industrial railway networks in Britain. Steam worked up until 1978 when the collieries it served in the scenic Doon Valley closed. It is the aim of the centre to preserve part of the railway. The Ayrshire Railway Preservation Group also owns the former G&SWR station at Waterside, half a mile from the Centre.
During the winter of 2002/3 the ARPG moved its operations from the former colliery at Minnivey to the Dunaskin Ironworks site at Waterside, and is now based in the former NCB locomotive shed and wagon works there. Working in conjunction with the Dalmellington & District Conservation Trust as part of Doon Valley Heritage, an industrial heritage centre has now been established at the old Dunaskin Ironworks, based on the iron, coal and brickmaking industries
Location: 10 miles south east of Ayr on the A713 to Castle Douglas
Contact address: Scottish Industrial Railway Centre, Dunaskin Ironworks, Waterside, Panta, Ayrshire KA6 7JF
OS reference: NS 438085
Operating society/organisation: Ayrshire Railway Preservation Group
Telephone: Doon Valley Heritage Office (01292) 531144. ARPG Secretary (01292) 313579 (evening & weekends)
Internet address: *e-mail:* agcthoms@aol.com
Web site: www.arpg.org.uk
Length of line: Approx 0.3 mile

Locomotives

Name	No	Origin	Class	Type	Built
*—	MP228 (12052)	BR	11	0-6-0DE	1949
*—	MP229 (12093)	BR	11	0-6-0DE	1951

*on loan to Caledonian Railway

Industrial locomotives

Name	No	Builder	Type	Built
—	16	A/Barclay (1116)	0-4-0ST	1910
—	8	A/Barclay (1296)	0-6-0T	1912
—	19	A/Barclay (1614)	0-4-0ST	1918
—	8	A/Barclay (1952)	0-4-0F	1928
Harlaxton	—	A/Barclay (2107)	0-6-0ST	1941
—	10	A/Barclay (2244)	0-4-0ST	1947
NCB No 23	—	A/Barclay (2260)	0-4-0ST	1949
—	25	A/Barclay (2358)	0-6-0ST	1954
—	1	A/Barclay (2368)	0-4-0ST	1955
—	118	A/Barclay (366)	0-4-0DM	1940
—	7	A/Barclay (399)	0-4-0DM	1956
Lily of the Valley	—	Fowler (22888)	0-4-0DM	1943
Tees Storage	—	N/British (27644)	0-4-0DH	1959
—	—	R/Hornsby (224352)	4wDM	1943
Blinkin Bess	—	R/Hornsby (284839)	4wDM	1950
Johnnie Walker	—	R/Hornsby (417890)	4wDM	1959
—	—	R/Hornsby (421697)	0-4-0DM	1959
—	107	Hunslet (3132)	0-4-0DM	1944
—	—	Sentinel (10012)	4wDM	1959
—	—	Donnelli (163)	4wDMR	1979
3ft gauge				
—	—	R/Hornsby (256273)	4wDM	1949
—	—	Hunslet (8816)	4wDH	1981
2ft 6in gauge				
—	2	R/Hornsby (183749)	4wDM	1937
—	3	R/Hornsby (210959)	4wDM	1941
—	1	R/Hornsby (211681)	4wDM	1942

Note: Not all vehicles on public display
*on loan to Caledonian Railway

Stock

1 BR Mk 1 TSO, 1 BR Mk 1 BSK, 2 Wickham trolleys; 1 steam crane; various other items

Access by public transport:
Nearest rail station, Ayr (10 miles). Half hourly Stagecoach bus service from Ayr. Tel: (01292) 263382

On site facilities: Steam-hauled brake van rides (over 0.3 mile) subject to HMRI inspection. Small museum of railway relics and

photographs, café and souvenir shop
Public opening: The Dunaskin Experience is open April to October, 10.00-17.00
Special events: Steam days (with at least one engine in steam) will be held on: Sundays 4, 11, 18, 25 July; 1, 8, 15, 22, 29 August; 5 September. Opening times 11.00-16.30. Rides subject to HMRI approval
Membership details: Mr Frank Beattie, 1 McKnight Avenue, Waterside, Fenwick, Kilmarnock, Ayrshire KA3 6JE
Special notes: For further information and details of special events, telephone the Doon Valley Heritage Office (01292) 531144, or the secretary Gordon Thomson (01292) 313579, or write to 8 Burnside Place, Troon, Ayrshire KA10 6LZ

Timetable Service — Strathspey Railway — Inverness-shire

Member: HRA, TT

Scotland's steam railway in the Highlands connects the busy tourist resort at Aviemore to the more traditional highland village of Boat of Garten, famed as one of the few nesting places of the osprey (viewing site 3 miles from station). The golf course here was designed by James Braid, who also designed Gleneagles. Beyond Boat of Garten the scenery changes as the 'strath' opens out giving fine views of the Spey en-route to Broomhill. This station appears as 'Glenbogle' in the TV series 'Monarch of the Glen'. Broomhill is approximately 3.5 miles from Grantown on Spey, the railway's ultimate goal

Superintendent of the Line: Laurence Grant

Enquiries: Aviemore Station, Dalfaber Road, Aviemore, Inverness-shire PH22 1PY (SAE for copy of timetable brochure)
Telephone: 01479 810725.
Internet address: *e-mail:* information@strathspeyrailway.co.uk
Web site: www.strathspeyrailway.co.uk
Main station: Aviemore. The railway occupies one platform at the main line Aviemore station
Other public stations: Boat of Garten and Broomhill
OS reference: Aviemore NH 898131, Boat of Garten NH 943789
Car parks: Aviemore (Strathspey Railway side of station (off Dalfaber Road) for railway customers only, Boat of Garten and Broomhill
Access by public transport: ScotRail services and express bus to Aviemore. Local service to Boat of Garten

Locomotives and multiple-units

Name	No	Origin	Class	Type	Built
—	5025	LMS	5MT	4-6-0	1934
E. V. Cooper, Engineer	46512	LMS	2MT	2-6-0	1952
—	828	CR	812	0-6-0	1899
—	D2774	BR	—	0-4-0DH	1960
—	08490	BR	08	0-6-0DE	1958
—	D5302	BR	26	Bo-Bo	1958
—	26025	BR	26	Bo-Bo	1959
—	D5394	BR	27	Bo-Bo	1962
—	31327	BR	31	A1A-A1A	1962
—	51990	BR	107	DMBS	1960
—	52008	BR	107	DMBS	1960
—	52030	BR	107	DMC	1960
—	54047	BR	114	DTC	1960

Industrial locomotives

Name	No	Builder	Type	Built
—	48	Hunslet (2864)	0-6-0ST	1943
Cairngorm	9	RSH (7097)	0-6-0ST	1943
—	60	Hunslet (3686)	0-6-0ST	1948
Niddrie	6	Barclay (1833)	0-6-0ST	1924
Forth*	10	Barclay (1890)	0-4-0ST	1926
Balmenach	2	Barclay (2020)	0-4-0ST	1936
—	17	Barclay (2017)	0-6-0T	1935
Inveresk	16	R/Hornsby (260756)	0-4-0DM	1950
Inverdon	15	Simplex (5763)	4wDM	1957
—	14	North British (27549)	0-4-0DM	1951
Queen Anne	20	R/Hornsby (265618)	4wDM	1948

*not on site

Locomotive notes: In service: 17, 46512, 08490, 26025, 54047 & 52008. Under restoration: 60, 828, D5394

Stock
20 ex-BR coaches; 4 ex-LMS coaches; 2 ex-LMS sleeping cars; 1 ex-LNER sleeping car; 1 ex-HR coach; 1 ex-NBR coach; numerous examples of rolling stock

Owners
6, 17 and 46512 the Highland Locomotive Co Ltd
828 the Scottish Locomotive Preservation Trust Fund
5025 the Watkinson Trust
D5302 and 26025 the Highland Diesel Locomotive Co Ltd

Refreshment facilities: On-train buffet car or facilities on many trains. Picnic tables at Boat of Garten (for use of ticket purchasers). No refreshment facilities on 'Branch Line Days' services

Souvenir shop: Boat of Garten and Aviemore

Museum: Static model of Boat of Garten station, c1963 at Boat of Garten

Depot: Aviemore (not open to public), sidings at both stations are not open to the public

Length of line: 10 miles

Journey time: Aviemore-Boat of Garten 15min; Aviemore-Broomhill 45min (outward) 35min, (inward). Round trip takes approximately 90min

Passenger trains: Steam-hauled services. Aviemore-Boat of Garten/Broomhill. Most Saturdays, unless a special event is taking place, services are run with a 'branch line' set

Period of public operation: 28, 31 March; 4, 7, 14, 18, 21, 25, 28 April; 1-3, 5/6, 8/9, 12/13, 15/16, 19/20, 22/23, 26/27, 29-31 May; daily June to September; 2/3, 6/7, 9/10, 13/14, 16/17, 20/21, 23/24, 27/28, 31/31 October; 5, 12, 18/19, 23/24, 26/27, 31 December; 1/2 January 2005

Special events: Day out with Thomas — 29-31 May, 14-22 August; Santa Specials — 5, 12, 18/19, 23/24 December

Facilities for disabled: Access possible at Aviemore, Boat of Garten and Broomhill. Please contact in advance for directions and if a party involved

Special notes: First and third class travel available on most trains. Family fares available for third class travel. Special rates/arrangements for parties. Luncheon on the train — Sundays 28 March until 31 October, also on Fridays 4 June until 24 September. Evening diner, the 'Strathspey Highlander', every Wednesday 2 June until 8 September. Bicycles carried at a 'flat fee' of £1 — groups must give prior notice (bicycles must not be ridden on platforms or pedestrian pathways)

Membership details: Strathspey Railway Association at above address

Membership journal: *Strathspey Express* — quarterly

Summerlee Heritage Park

Museum — Lanarkshire

Social and industrial history museum, interprets the communities in the west of Scotland in the 19th and 20th centuries. Working machinery in reconstructed workshops; miners' rows, reconstructed coal mine, art gallery, working tramway

Manager: Neil Ballantyne

Operating society/organisation: Summerlee Heritage Park, Heritage Way, Coatbridge, ML5 1QD (operated by North Lanarkshire Council)

Telephone: (01236) 431261

Fax: (01236) 440429

Public opening: Daily 10.00-16.00, except 25/26 December and 1/2 January

Access by public transport: STP electric service from Glasgow Queen Street Low Level to Coatbridge Sunnyside (Airdrie/Drumgelloch line). Or from Glasgow Central via Motherwell to Coatbridge Central. Trains also run from Cumbernauld to Coatbridge Central, but not on Sundays

Car park: Opposite site

Locomotives

Name	No	Origin	Class	Type	Built
Springbok	4112	SAR	GMAM	4-8-2+2-8-4	1956
(3ft 6in gauge/built by North British Loco Co)					
Unit 936103	977844	BR	303	DTS	1960
(303103)	977845	BR	303	DTS	1960
	977846	BR	303	MBS	1960

Industrial locomotives

Name	No	Builder	Type	Built
—	—	Barclay (472)	0-4-0DH	1966
—	—	H/Clarke (895)	0-6-0T	1909
—	—	G/Hogg	0-4-0T	1898
Robin	—	Sentinel (9628)	4wTG	1957

Stock

2 rail-mounted steam cranes.

Also on site are two former Glasgow trams, one , the Coplawhill Motor School training car, has just entered service at Summerlee; the second, a 'Coronation' class car, will shortly commence a full restoration to operational standards

On site facilities: Tea room, gift shop. Working electric tramway with cars from Motherwell, Düsseldorf, Brussels and Graz; underground mine tour and miners' cottages

Special events: Organised events from April-October, details on request

Facilities for disabled: Toilets, wheelchair available

Wales

Bala Lake Railway (Rheilffordd Llyn Tegid)

Gwynedd

Member: HRA, TT

This delightful narrow gauge railway follows the route of the former Bala-Dolgellau Railway, along the shore of Wales' largest natural lake. The railway's headquarters are to be found in the fine old station building at Llanuwchllyn at the south-western end of the line. Do not be deterred by the fact that the railway runs down the opposite shore of the lake to the main road — it is well worth the detour

General Manager: Roger Hine

Headquarters: Rheilffordd Llyn Tegid (Bala Lake Railway) Llanuwchllyn, Bala, Gwynedd LL23 7DD

Telephone: Llanuwchllyn (01678) 540666

Internet address: *Web site:* www.bala-lake-railway.co.uk

Main station: Llanuwchllyn

Other public stations: Llangower, Bala. Request halts at Pentrepiod and Bryn Hynod

OS reference: Llanuwchllyn SH 880300, Bala SH 929350

Car parks: Llanuwchllyn, Llangower and Bala town centre

Access by public transport: Arriva service No 94 to both Bala

Industrial locomotives

Name	No	Builder	Type	Built
Holy War	3	Hunslet (779)	0-4-0ST	1902
Alice	3	Hunslet (802)	0-4-0ST	1902
Maid Marian	5	Hunslet (822)	0-4-0ST	1903
Triassic	1270	Peckett (1270)	0-6-0ST	1911
Meirionnydd	11	Severn-Lamb (7322)	Bo-Bo	1973
Chilmark	12	R/Hornsby (194771)	4wDM	1939
Bob Davies	—	YEC (L125)	4wDM	1983
Indian Runner	—	R/Hornsby (200744)	4wDM	1940
Cernyw	—	R/Hornsby (200748)	4wDM	1940
Lady Madcap	—	R/Hornsby (283512)	4wDM	1949

Locomotive notes: *Holy War* and *Maid Marian* are in regular use, remainder are on static display
Triassic is awaiting overhaul

and Llanuwchllyn (from Wrexham or Barmouth)

Road access: Off the A494 Bala-Dolgellau road

Refreshment facilities: Llanuwchllyn. Large picnic site with toilet facilities by lake at Llangower

Souvenir shop: Llanuwchllyn

Depot: Llanuwchllyn

Length of line: 4.5 miles, 1ft 11.625in gauge

Passenger trains: Llanuwchllyn-Bala. Journey takes 25min in each direction

Period of public operation: 3 April to 3 October (except some Mondays and Fridays)

Facilities for disabled: Facilities available on most trains

Special notes: Small parties (10/12) may just turn up, but a day's notice required for larger groups

Family tickets: Available for all round trip journeys

Membership details: Membership Secretary, c/o Llanuwchllyn station

Membership journal: *Llanuwchllyn Express* — approx 4 times a year

Brecon Mountain Railway

Merthyr Tydfil

A narrow gauge passenger-carrying railway close to Merthyr Tydfil built on part of the trackbed of the former Brecon & Merthyr Railway. Gradually being extended northwards, the railway has some interesting narrow gauge steam

locomotives imported from East and West Germany and South Africa

General Manager: A. J. Hills

Headquarters: Brecon Mountain Railway, Pant Station, Dowlais, Merthyr Tydfil CF48 2UP

Telephone: Merthyr Tydfil (01685)

722988

Fax: (01685) 384854

Main station: Pant

Car park: Pant station

OS reference: SO 063120

Access by public transport: Bus to Pant Cemetery — half hour

frequency from Merthyr bus station. Main line rail service to Merthyr from Cardiff Central
Depot: Pant
Length of line: 3.5 miles, 1ft 11.75in gauge
Period of public operation: Daily 27 March-28 October.
EXCEPT for: 29 March; 2, 5, 19, 23, 26 April; 10, 14, 17, 21, 24, 28 May; 20, 24, 27 September; 1, 4, 8, 11, 15, 18, 22, 25 October
Refreshment facilities: Cafés at Pant and Pontsticill
Special events: Halloween weekend in October; Santa Specials — December
Facilities for disabled: Facilities for disabled include ramps, toilets and carriage designed to carry wheelchairs
Special notes: There is no road access to Pontsticill

Locomotives

Name	No	Builder	Type	Built
—	2	Baldwin (61269)	4-6-2	1930
—	—	Baldwin (15511)	2-6-0	1898
Sybil	—	Hunslet (827)	0-4-0ST	1903
Graf Schwerin-Löwitz	—	Arn Jung (1261)	0-6-2WT	1908
Pendyffryn	—	de Winton	0-4-0VBT	1894
Redstone	—	Redstone	0-4-0VBT	1905
—	77*	Hanomag (10629)	2-6-2+2-6-2	1928
—	146*	Henschel	2-8-2	1959
—	—	Brecon MR (001)	0-6-0DH	1987

*former South African Railways locomotives

Stock
Two balcony end 39-seat coaches; 2 balcony end 40-seat coaches; 1 19-seat Caboose; 4 flat cars, crane and tamper, miscellaneous rail-carrying and ballast wagons; Wickham petrol trolley

---

Museum	# Conwy Valley Railway Museum	Betws-y-coed (Conwy CB)

Conveniently situated alongside Betws-y-coed railway station, the Museum presents some well-displayed distractions to pass the time including model train layouts to delight both adult and child
Location: Adjacent to Betws-y-coed station
OS reference: SH 796565
General Manager: Mr C. M. Cartwright
Operating society/organisation: Conwy Valley Railway Museum, The Old Goods Yard, Betws-y-coed, Conwy LL24 0AL
Telephone: 01690 710568
Fax: 01690 710132
Car park: On site
Access by public transport: Betws-y-coed main line station
On site facilities: Refreshments in buffet car. Bookshop and model/gift shop in museum foyer, operating train layouts, miniature railway (1.25-miles, 7.25in gauge) steam-hauled. Picnic area.
  15in Tramway (operates daily) with 1989-built single-deck bogie tram

Locomotives

Name	No	Builder	Type	Built
Britannia	70000	TMA Engineering (1ft 3in gauge)	4-6-2	1988
Old Rube*	—	Milner Eng	2-8-0	1983
Siân*	—	Humphries	0-4-2T	1989
Shoshone*	—	Simkins/Milner	2-8-0	1975
Union Pacific*	—	R. Greatrex	Bo-Bo	1991
Crocodile*	—	Donfifer/B. Howarth	0-6-0+0-6-0	1985
Princess Elizabeth*	—	Barton (Lewis Shaw)	4-6-2	1960

*7.25in gauge

Stock
Standard gauge: 1 GWR fitter's van; 1 LMS 6-wheel van; 1 LNER CCT van; 1 BR Mk 1 coach; 2 SR luggage vans; 1 Pullman coach; 15in bogie tramcar
7.25in gauge: 5 articulated sit-in coaches; 2 sets 3 articulated sit-in open coaches; 4 wagons plus 'self-drive' 0-4-0 'Toby Tram'
15in gauge: 1 wagon

Public opening: Daily Easter-end of October, 10.00-17.30, then daily 10.00-16.00 (winter opening)
Facilities for disabled: Access to café, museum and toilets from car park. Toilets are adapted for disabled

Corris Railway and Museum

Member: HRA

In the heart of Wales' 'narrow gauge country', the Corris Railway provides a 50min round trip on the restored section of Mid Wales' first public narrow gauge railway. The Museum, situated in the remaining buildings of Corris station, displays relics, photographs and models of the railway

Location: In Corris village off A487 trunk road. Turn opposite Braichgoch Hotel, five miles north of Machynlleth and 11 miles south of Dolgellau

OS reference: SH 755078

Operating society: The Corris Railway Society, Corris Station Yard, Gwynedd (postal address: Corris, Machynlleth, Powys SY20 9SH)

Telephone: 01654 761303

Internet address:
e-mail: alfo@corris.co.uk
Web site: www.corris.co.uk

Car park: Adjacent

Access by public transport: Central Trains services to Machynlleth. Bus Gwynedd services 2 (Aberystwyth-Dolgellau-Machynlleth), 30 (Machynlleth-Tywyn) and 34 (Machynlleth-Aberllefenni); Dyfi Valley service 530 (Tywyn-Machynlleth-Abergynolwyn)

Catering facilities: Snacks, teas

Locomotives

Name	No	Builder	Type	Built
Alan Meaden	5	M/Rail (22258)	4wDM	1965
—	6	R/Hornsby (51849)	4wDM	1966
—	7	—	0-4-2ST	—
—	8	Hunslet (7274)	4wDM	1973

Locomotive notes: 5 and 6 operational. 7 under construction (based on Corris No 4 now Talyllyn No 4 *Edward Thomas*) and due for completion in 2004. 8 undergoing restoration off site, due for service in 2004

Stock
Three carriages, brake van, 17 works wagons and 7 historic wagons

Owner
8 on loan from the National Mining Museum

and light refreshments

On site facilities: Souvenir shop, toilets and children's playground; close to Corris Craft Centre and King Arthur's Labyrinth; two miles from Centre for Alternative Technology

Passenger trains: Corris to Maespoeth

Length of line: Three-quarter-mile, 2ft 3in gauge track. Planning permission for a further two miles of track has been granted

Public opening: Railway — passenger trains operate at weekends and Bank Holidays from Easter to October, plus Santa Specials in December.

Museum — Bank Holidays from Easter, daily, June to September. Half term week in October. Times as advertised locally. Special trains and Museum openings can be booked by prior arrangement. Please check web site or write for further details

Special events: Model Railway Exhibition, Machynlleth — 28-30 August

Facilities for disabled: Disabled access carriage on all trains. Access to display area of Museum and shop

Membership details: Membership Secretary, c/o above address

Fairbourne Railway

Member: Britain's Great Little Railways

Since 1986 this railway has been regauged from 15in to 12.25in and has been transformed by the introduction of new locomotives and rolling stock, a tunnel through the sand dunes, signalboxes, new workshops, a café overlooking the Mawddach estuary. During the main season a two-train service is in operation. A free indoor nature attraction and small museum are open at Fairbourne terminus

Headquarters: North Wales Coast Light Railway Co Ltd, Fairbourne & Barmouth Steam Railway, Beach Road, Fairbourne, Gwynedd LL38 2PZ

Telephone: (01341) 250362

Fax: (01341) 250240

Internet address: *e-mail:* fairbourne.railway@btinternet.com
Web site: http://www.fairbournerailway.com

Main station: Gorsaf Newydd (Fairbourne)

Other public stations: Gorsafawddachaidraigodanhed-dogleddollonpenrhynareurdraeth-ceredigion, Penrhyn Point (Barmouth Ferry Station)

OS reference: SH 616128

Car parks: Gorsaf Newydd

Access by public transport: Fairbourne railway station. Bus Gwynedd service (No 28)

Refreshment facilities: Penrhyn Point café, tea shop on platform at

Wales

Gorsaf Newydd (Fairbourne)
Souvenir shop: Gorsaf Newydd (Fairbourne)
Depot: Fairbourne
Length of line: 2.5 miles, 12.25in gauge
Passenger trains: A 2.5-mile journey connecting with ferry at Penrhyn Point to Barmouth. 20min single journey. Through tickets to Barmouth (including ferry) available
Period of public operation: Daily service Easter week 8-18 April. Daily service 1 May to 21 September and 23-31 October. Santa Specials operate 11/12 December
Special events: Open Day (including free footplate rides) — 11 April; Friendly Fairbourne Engines — 2/3 May, 1/2 June, 25/26 July, 17/18 August; Bob Morris Classic Car Rally & Craft Fair — 14/15 June; 'Ride a

Locomotives

Name	No	Builder	Type	Built
Beddgelert	—	Curwen	0-6-4ST	1979
Yeo	—	Curwen	2-6-2T	1978
Sherpa	—	Milner	0-4-0STT	1978
Russell*	—	Milner	2-6-4T	1985
Lilian Walter†	—	FLW	A1-1AD	1985
Gwril	—	FLW	4wBE	1987

FLW — Fairbourne Locomotive Works
*built as replica Leek & Manifold *Elaine*, rebuilt to present form 1985 at FLW
†originally built by G&S Engineering in 1961 as 15in gauge *Sylvia*. Rebuilt at Fairbourne in 1985

Stock
18 coaches; 15 freight

Lifeboat' along the line at Penrhyn Point — 28 July; Official Half Term 23-31 October; Santa Specials — 11/12 December
Membership details: Fairbourne Railway Supporters' Association, c/o 26 Gwydyr Road, Dolgarrog,

Conwy LL32 8JS
Special notes: During inclement weather the service may be restricted or cancelled. Extra trains and special parties by arrangement with the manager

---

Timetable Service · Ffestiniog Railway · Gwynedd

Member: HRA
In many ways, evocative of the early Swiss mountain railways as it climbs high above Porthmadog with some breathtaking views, the railway still operates an interesting variety of locomotives including some unusual Victorian survivors. Passengers have replaced slate as the principal traffic over this former quarry line
General Manager: Paul Lewin
Headquarters: Ffestiniog Railway Co, Harbour Station, Porthmadog, Gwynedd, LL49 9NF
Telephone: Porthmadog (01766) 516073
Internet address: Web site: http://www.festrail.co.uk
Main stations: Porthmadog Harbour, Blaenau Ffestiniog
Other public stations: Boston Lodge, Minffordd, Penrhyn, Plas Halt, Tan-y-Bwlch, Dduallt, Tanygrisiau
OS reference: SH 571384
Car parks: Porthmadog, Tan-y-Bwlch, Tanygrisiau, Blaenau Ffestiniog

Locomotives

Name	No	Builder	Type	Built
Princess	1	G/England (199/200)	0-4-0STT	1863
Prince	2	G/England	0-4-0STT	1863
Palmerston	4	G/England	0-4-0STT	1863
Welsh Pony	5	G/England (234)	0-4-0STT	1867
Earl of Merioneth	—	FR	0-4-4-0T	1979
Merddin Emrys	10	FR	0-4-4-0T	1879
David Lloyd George	12	FR	0-4-4-0T	1992
Taliesin	—	FR	0-4-4T	1999
Moelwyn	—	Baldwin (49604)	2-4-0DM	1918
Lilla*	—	Hunslet (554)	0-4-0ST	1891
Blanche	—	Hunslet (589)	2-4-0STT	1893
Linda	—	Hunslet (590)	2-4-0STT	1893
Britomart*	—	Hunslet (707)	0-4-0ST	1899
Mountaineer	—	Alco (57156)	2-6-2T	1917
Livingston Thompson†	3	FR	0-4-4-0T	1886
Harlech Castle	—	B/Drewry (3767)	0-6-0-DH	1983
Ashover	—	Hibberd (3307)	4wDM	1948
Conway Castle	—	Hibberd (3831)	4wDM	1958
Moel Hebog	—	Hunslet (4113)	0-4-0DM	1955
Mary Ann	—	M/Rail (596)	4wDM	1917
Criccieth Castle	—	FR	0-6-0DH	1995
The Colonel	—	M/Rail (8788)	4wDM	1943
Diana	—	M/Rail (21579)	4wDM	1957
Stefcomatic	—	Matisa (48589)	2-2-0DH	1956
Vale of Ffestiniog	—	Funkey	Bo-Bo	1968

*privately owned
†on loan to National Railway Museum

Wales

Access by public transport: Minffordd and Blaenau Ffestiniog main line stations. Porthmadog, Minffordd and Blaenau Ffestiniog served by local buses
Refreshment facilities: Licensed restaurant at Porthmadog, café at Tan-y-Bwlch, refreshments also on most trains
Souvenir shops: Porthmadog, Tan-y-Bwlch, Blaenau Ffestiniog
Museum: Interesting artyfacts in Spooner's Bar, Porthmadog
Depot: Boston Lodge
Length of line: 13.5 miles, 1ft 11.5in gauge
Passenger trains: Porthmadog-

Stock
34 bogie coaches; 6 4-wheel coaches; 3 brake vans, plus numerous service vehicles

Blaenau Ffestiniog
Period of public operation: Daily late March-early November, limited winter service
Special events: The Ffestiniog Railway Society is celebrating its 50th anniversary in 2004/5 so there will be several events to support this. Please visit our web site for details
Facilities for disabled:

Porthmadog and Blaenau Ffestiniog easily accessible for wheelchairs. Limited facilities on trains for disabled in wheelchairs by prior arrangement
Membership details: Ffestiniog Railway Society (see above address)
Membership journal: *Ffestiniog Railway Magazine* — quarterly

---

Great Orme Tramway

Timetable Service | Conwy

Member: HRA
A cable-hauled street tramway to the summit of the Great Orme is operated as two sections involving a change half-way. Opened in July 1902, it includes gradients as steep as 1 in 3.9
Location: Great Orme Tramway, Victoria Station, Church Walks, Llandudno
OS reference: SH 7781
Operating society/organisation: Conwy County Borough Council, Tourism Services, 1-2 Chapel

Street, Llandudno LL30 2SY
Telephone: Llandudno (01492) 575275
Internet address: *e-mail*: enq@greatormetramway.com
Web site: www.greatormetramway.com
Car park: Approximately 100yd from Lower Terminal or adjacent to Summit Terminal
Access by public transport: Good
On site facilities: Shop
Period of public operation: March to end of October (daily) 10.00-

18.00 (17.00 October). Can be subject to change
Special notes: The only remaining cable-hauled street tramway in Britain. 1 mile long rising to 650ft (3ft 6in gauge)
Stock: 4 tramcars each seating 48, built 1902/3
Family tickets: Available, along with joint tickets for Great Orme Mine — Bronze Age Heritage Centre

---

Gwili Railway (Rheilffordd Gwili)

Timetable Service | Carmarthenshire

Member: HRA, TT
Runs alongside the River Gwili on part of the former Carmarthen-Aberystwyth line. Attractions include a fully restored signalbox and historic station building. Extension to Danycoed opened in April 2001. A 7.25in gauge miniature railway and a riverside picnic site at Llwyfan Cerrig.
Headquarters: Gwili Railway Co Ltd, Bronwydd Arms Station, Bronwydd Arms, Carmarthen, SA33 6HT
Telephone: Carmarthen (01267)

230666
Internet address: *e-mail:* gwili@talk21.com
Web site: www.gwili-railway.co.uk
OS reference: Bronwydd Arms SN 417239
Llwyfan Cerrig SN 405258,
Main station: Bronwydd Arms
Other public station: Llwyfan Cerrig, Danycoed
Car park: Bronwydd Arms (free) (not 9-13 April when Park & Ride from Carmarthen must be used)
Access by public transport: Carmarthen railway station, then

First Cymru services (Info Line: 0870 608 2306)
Refreshment facilities: Bronwydd Arms, Llwyfan Cerrig (picnic site)
Souvenir shop: Bronwydd Arms
Depot: Llwyfan Cerrig, stock also kept at Bronwydd Arms, Cynwyl Elfed
Length of line: 2.5 miles
Passenger trains: Bronwydd Arms-Llwyfan Cerrig-Danycoed, approximately 1¼ hour service
Period of public operation: 9-13 April; 2/3, 9, 16, 23, 30/31 May; 1-3, 6, 9, 13, 16, 20, 23, 27, 30

June; 4, 7, 11, 14, 18, 21, 15, 28
July; daily – 31 July to 31 August;
5, 12, 19, 26 September; 28-30
October; 11/12, 18/19, 22-24
December

Public opening: Trains leave
Bronwydd Arms at 11.15, 12.30,
14.00, 15.15 and 16.30 on most
operating days. A more frequent
service operates in December

Facilities for disabled: Access to
stations and trains

Special events: Day out with
Thomas — 9-13 April; Summer
Nights events — 31 July, 7 August;
Santa Specials — 11/12, 18/19, 22-
24 December, details: Booking
Hotline 01656 663925

Special notes: Family tickets
available except for Day out with
Thomas and Santa Special events.
Trains may be hired for special
events, tour parties, birthdays, etc

Locomotives

Name	No	Origin	Class	Type	Built
—†	12061	BR	11	0-6-0DE	1949
—**	D2178	BR	03	0-6-0DM	1962

Industrial locomotives

Name	No	Builder	Type	Built
Trecatty	—	R/Hornsby (421702)	0-6-0DM	1959
Olwen	—	RSH (7058)	0-4-0ST	1942
Welsh Guardsman	71516	RSH (7170)	0-6-0ST	1944
Nellie	02101	YEC(2779)	0-4-0DE	1960
Victory	—	A/Barclay (2201)	0-4-0ST	1945
Sir John†	—	Avonside (1680)	0-6-0ST	1914
—†	3	H/Clarke (D1246)	0-4-0DM	1961
Swansea Vale No 1*	—	Sentinel (9622)	4wVBTG	1958
Swansea Jack*	—	R/Hornsby (393302)	4wDM	1955
Dylan Thomas*	—	N/British (27654)	0-4-0DH	1956
—	114	N/British (27878)	0-4-0DH	1962
—	21	H/Leslie (3931)	0-6-0ST	1938
Haulwen†*	—	V/Foundry (5272)	0-6-0ST	1945

Stock

8 ex-BR Mk 1 coaches; 1 ex-BR griddle car; 1 ex-BR Mk 3 sleeper;
1 ex-TVR coach (built 1891); Coles diesel rail crane; 1 Booth diesel-
hydraulic crane; 2 ex-GWR Mink vans; 2 ex-GWR Fruit D; 1 ex-GWR
Crocodile; 1 GWR Bloater; 2 ex-GWR Loriot D; 3 GWR Toad brake vans;
2 GWR bogie bolster wagons; 1 SECR parcels van; 2 SR parcels vans; 1 SR
bogie parcel van; 1 LMS 20-ton brake van; 1 LNER open wagon; 5 LNER
vans; 2 Army vans; 6 BR open wagons; 2 BP tank wagons; 2 tar tankers; 3
open wagons

Owners

*The Railway Club of Wales
** Caerphilly Railway Society
†Vale of Neath Railway Society
†*National Museum of Wales Industrial & Maritime Museum in care of
Caerphilly Railway Society

Timetable Service	**Llanberis Lake Railway (Rheilffordd Llyn Padarn)**	Gwynedd

Member: HRA

A narrow gauge passenger-carrying
railway starting at the historic
Dinorwic Quarry workshops (now
part of the National Museum of
Wales) and running along the
shores of the Llanberis lake using
the trackbed of the former slate
railway line to Port Dinorwic.
Excellent views of Snowdonia and
good picnic spots along the line

General Manager:
Mr B. Yarborough

Headquarters: Llanberis Lake
Railway, Gilfach Ddu, Llanberis,
Gwynedd LL55 4TY

Telephone: Llanberis (01286)
870549

Industrial locomotives

Name	No	Builder	Type	Built
Elidir	1	Hunslet (493)	0-4-0ST	1889
Thomas Bach/Wild Aster	2	Hunslet (849)	0-4-0ST	1904
Dolbadarn	3	Hunslet (1430)	0-4-0ST	1922
Topsy	7	R/Hornsby (441427)	4wDM	1961
Twll Coed	8	R/Hornsby (268878)	4wDM	1956
—	—	R/Hornsby (425796)	4wDM	1958
Garrett	11	R/Hornsby (198286)	4wDM	1939
—	18	M/Rail (7927)	4wDM	1941
Llanelli	19	R/Hornsby (451901)	4wDM	1961
Una*	—	Hunslet (873)	0-4-0ST	1905

*not part of the railway's motive power stock. Housed at the adjacent slate
museum and can sometimes be seen working demonstration freight trains

Stock

13 bogie coaches; 20 wagons

Internet address: *e-mail:* info@lake-railway.co.uk *Web site:* www.lake-railway.co.uk **Main station:** Llanberis (Padarn station/Gilfach Ddu) **Other public stations:** Cei Llydan **OS reference:** SH 586603 **Car park:** Llanberis (Padarn station) **Refreshment facilities:** Padarn station

Souvenir shop: Padarn station **Length of line:** 2.5 miles, 1ft 11.5in gauge **Passenger trains:** Gilfach Ddu-Llanberis-Penllyn-Gilfach Ddu The half mile extension from Gilfach Ddu to Llanberis village is now open **Journey time:** 60min return trip **Period of public operation:** Mondays to Thursdays in March and October. Sundays to Fridays,

April to September. Saturdays July and August. Family tickets available, under 5s free **Facilities for disabled:** Level approaches throughout shop, café and to train. Special toilet facilities provided. Specially adapted carriage for wheelchair users **Marketing names:** Rheilffordd Llyn Padarn Cyfyngedig (Padarn Lake Railway Ltd); Llanberis Lake Railway

---

Timetable Service — Llangollen Railway — Denbighshire

Member: HRA, TT

The line, which is presently 7.5 miles long, is the only operational preserved standard gauge heritage line in North Wales. Situated in the Dee Valley, it follows the course of the River Dee for much of its route, and affords good views of the dramatic Welsh countryside between Llangollen and Carrog, the latter station having been reached

Locomotives and multiple-units

Name	No	Origin	Class	Type	Built
—	2859	GWR	2800	2-8-0	1918
—	3802	GWR	2800	2-8-0	1938
—	5199	GWR	5101	2-6-2T	1934
—	5532	GWR	4575	2-6-2T	1928
—	6430	GWR	6400'	0-6-0PT	1937
—	7754	GWR	5700	0-6-0PT	1930
Foxcote Manor	7822	GWR	'Manor'	4-6-0	1950
—	47298	LMS	3F	0-6-0T	1924
Magpie	44806	LMS	5MT	4-6-0	1944

in 1996. In that year the railway was the winner of the Ian Allan 'Independent Railway of the Year' award. The section from Glyndyfrdwy to Carrog was the venue for BBC 2's reinactment of the Railhill Trials using the replica locomotives *Rocket*, *Sans Pareil* and *Novelty* in 2002, whilst 2003 saw the renovation of the Berwyn Viaduct and reinstatement of the cantilevered platform extension receive a 'Historic Bridge and Infrastructure Award' at the Institute of Civil Engineers. An extension of 2.5 miles westward from Carrog to the small town of Corwen is planned and will require construction of a new terminus. There are many pleasant walks through the scenic splendour of the Dee Valley beginning and ending at the railway's stations

Location: Llangollen station, Abbey Road, A542 from Ruthin, A539 from Ruabon, A5 from Shrewsbury/Betws-y-coed

Chairman: Gordon Heddon

Operating company: Llangollen Railway plc

Supporting organisation/ leaseholder: Llangollen Railway Trust Ltd, The Station, Abbey Road, Llangollen, Denbighshire LL20 8SN (both organisations)

Telephone: General enquiries: 01978 860979 (office hours). Talking Timetable: 01978 860951 (24hr). Santa booking: 01978 861241 (1 October to 24 December).

Fax: 01978 869247

Internet address: *Web site:* http://www.llangollen-railway. co.uk/

Main station: Llangollen

Other stations: Berwyn, Deeside Halt (by request), Glyndyfrdwy, Carrog

OS reference: SJ 214422

Car park: Llangollen (Market St) and Mill St (Lower Dee Mill), Carrog — station car park on B5437 off A5 west of Llangollen

Access by public transport: Nearest station: Ruabon (5 miles) on Shrewsbury-Chester line, then by bus
Bus services: Bryn Melyn bus services Wrexham-Llangollen via Ruabon station half-hourly Monday-Saturday, also Arriva service 94 Wrexham to Barmouth

Name	No	Origin	Class	Type	Built
—	80072	BR	4MT	2-6-4T	1954
—	03162	BR	03	0-6-0DM	1960
—	13265	BR	08	0-6-0DE	1956
—	D8142	BR	20	Bo-Bo	1966
Chirk Castle	25313	BR	25	Bo-Bo	1966
—	37240	BR	37	Co-Co	1964
Mirlees Pioneer	37901	BR	37	Co-Co	1963
—	46010	BR	46	1Co-Co1	1961
Oribi	D1566	BR	47	Co-Co	1962
—	50416	Wickham	109	MBS	1958
—	50447	BRCW	104	DMBS	1957
—	50454	BRCW	104	DMBS	1957
—	50528	BRCW	104	DMC	1957
—	51118†	Gloucester	100	MBS	
—	51618	BR	127	DMBS	1959
—	51907	BR	108	DMBS	1960
—	54490	BR	108	DTC	1960
—	55513†	BR	141	DMS	1984
—	55533†	BR	141	DMSL	1984
—	56097†	Gloucester	100	DTCL	
—	56171	Wickham	109	DTC	1958
—	56456	Cravens	105	DMBS	1958

†at Midland Railway Centre for restoration

Industrial locomotives

Name	No	Builder	Type	Built
Eliseg	—	Fowler (22753)	0-4-0DM	1939
Jennifer	—	H/Clarke (1731)	0-6-0T	1942
Jessie	—	Hunslet (1873)	0-6-0ST	1937
Darfield No 1	—	Hunslet (3783)	0-6-0ST	1953
Austin No 1†	—	Kitson (5459)	0-6-0ST	1932
—	391•	YEC (2630)	0-6-0DE	1959
—	398•	YEC (2769)	0-6-0DE	1959
—	D2892	YEC/BTH (2782)	0-4-0DE	1960
—	D2899	YEC (2854)	0-6-0DE	1961
John Brunner	—	E/Electric (1901)	0-6-0DE	1951

†on hire to Lavender Line for 2004
•on five year loan from Wilmott Bros, Ilkeston

Stock: *coaches, 45 in total including* — Service sets of Mk 1 stock, 4 BR suburban coaches; 1 LNER Thompson lounge car; 2 GWR autocoaches; 1 GN brake, etc, some under restoration

Stock: *wagons, approx 50 including* — 2 Bolster wagons; 3 GWR Toad brake vans; 1 BR(E) brake van; 4 BR ballast wagons; 1 BR Presflow wagon; 1 GWR 'Fruit D'; 2 GWR Tube wagons; 1 Esso tank wagon; 1 Shell tank wagon. plus various other items of freight stock

Stock: *maintenance* — Cowans 50-ton breakdown crane, ARD96718 ex-Laira; 1 Matisa track recording machine; 1 Trackmaster light shunting vehicle; O&K road-railer;

Llangollen Railway is also home to the 6880 *Bretton Grange* project, which is poised to make substantial progress towards the creation of the 81st 'Grange' class locomotive.

Owners
2859 and 5532 the Llangollen Railway GW Locomotive Group
3802 the GW 3802 Ltd
5199 the 5199 Project
7754, 13265, *Jennifer* and *Austin No 1* the Llangollen Railway Trust Ltd
7822 the Foxcote Manor Society

Wales

service (6 a day).
For up-to-date bus information please call Wrexham Bus Enquiries: 01978 266166
Refreshment facilities: Llangollen, Berwyn (weekends only), Glyndyfrdwy (weekends only) and Carrog (closed Christmas to end of January, not Mondays except for special events)
Souvenir shop: Llangollen
Length of line: 7.5 miles
Passenger trains: Llangollen-Carrog
Period of public operation: Daily services from 9 April to 10 October, most weekends at other times plus school holidays including half-term (see timetable for details). Party rates are available for more than 10 passengers

80072 the 80072 Steam Locomotive Co Ltd
03162 the Wirral Borough Council
All DMUs the Llangollen Railcar group
All main line diesel fleet (except 37901) plus *John Brunner* the Llangollen Diesel Group

Special events: Spring Steam Gala — 27/28 March; May Steam Gala — 29-31 May; Railways in Transition, Mixed Traction Gala — 24 July to 1 August; Autumn Steam Gala — 18/19 September; Diesel Gala weekend — 8-10 October; Day out with Thomas — 23-31 October; Santa Specials (on selected dates 4-24 December; Mince Pie Specials — 26-31 December, 2 January 2005
Driver experiences: The railway offers a varied programme of

footplate and railway experience courses from early spring through to late autumn, ranging from the basic Summer Evening Ramble to the more advanced all-day railway experience. A brochure is available from Llangollen station
Facilities for disabled: Special passenger coach for wheelchairs.
Membership details: Mr Graham Hoyland, Llangollen Railway Trust Ltd, c/o above address
Membership journal: *Steam at Llangollen* — quarterly

Museum Penrhyn Castle Industrial Railway Museum Conwy

Member: HRA
A collection of historic industrial steam locomotives, both standard and narrow gauge, displayed in Penrhyn Castle, a well-known National Trust property in the area regularly open to visitors
Location: Llandegai, near Bangor. One mile east of Bangor on the A5
OS reference: SH 603720
Operating society/organisation: National Trust, Penrhyn Castle, Industrial Railway Museum, Llandegai, Nr Bangor LL57 4HN
Telephone: Bangor (01248) 353084
Internet address: *Web site:* www.nationaltrust.org
Car park: Within castle grounds
Access by public transport: By rail: Bangor (3 miles). Bus: Arriva Cymru 5, 6, 7 and 675X
On site facilities: The castle is open to the public, and contains a gift shop. Light refreshments are available
Public opening: Daily 27 March-31 October. July/August — 10.00-17.00. Other months —

Industrial locomotives

Name	No	Builder	Type	Built
Kettering Furnaces No 3	—	B/Hawthorn (859)	0-4-0ST	1885*
Watkin	—	de Winton	0-4-0VBT	1893*
Fire Queen	—	Horlock	0-4-0	1848†
Hawarden	—	H/Clarke (526)	0-4-0ST	1899
Vesta	—	H/Clarke (1223)	0-6-0T	1916
Charles	—	Hunslet (283)	0-4-0ST	1882§
Hugh Napier	—	Hunslet (855)	0-4-0ST	1904§
—	1	Neilson (1561)	0-4-0WT	1870
Haydock	—	Stephenson (2309)	0-6-0T	1879
Acorn	—	R/Hornsby (327904)	0-4-0DM	1948

*3ft gauge
†4ft gauge
§1ft 10.75in gauge

Stock
10 narrow gauge rolling stock exhibits from the Padarn/Penrhyn system. The small relics section includes a comprehensive display of railway signs and model locomotives in the upper stable block

11.00-17.00. Last admission 30min before closing
Facilities for disabled: Access to castle and museum
Special notes: For those interested in stately homes the castle is well worth a visit. The entrance fee

covers both the castle and the railway exhibits housed in the castle courtyard. Ruston Hornsby locomotive *Acorn* can be seen operating on some occasions during opening times

Pontypool & Blaenavon Railway

Member: HRA

The historic Blaenavon site, complete with its railway installations and locomotives, can easily be included in a visit to Big Pit Mining Museum

Location: Just off the B4248 between Blaenavon and Brynmawr. Signposted as you approach Blaenavon

OS reference: SO 237093

Operating society/organisation: Pontypool & Blaenavon Railway Co (1983) Ltd, Council Offices, 101 High Street, Blaenavon NP4 9PT

Telephone/Fax: (01495) 792263

Internet address: *E-mail:* railwayoffice@aol.com
Web site: www.pontypool-and-blaenavon.co.uk

Car park: Adjacent to railway terminus

On site facilities: Light refreshments and souvenir shop on train

Public opening: 10-12, 18, 25 April; 1-3, 9, 16, 23, 30/31 May; weekends in June, July, August (also daily 23-27, 30); 4/5, 12, 19, 26 September. All services will be either DMU or diesel-locomotive hauled

Special events: Easter Bunny Specials — 11/12 April; Teddy Bears' Picnics — 2/3 May; Lucky Dip Specials — 30/31 May; Father's Day Specials — 20 June; Railwayana Exhibition — 31 July/1 August, Transport Gala — 29/30 August; Santa Specials — 4/5,

Locomotives

Name	No	Origin	Class	Type	Built
—	2874	GWR	2800	2-8-0	1918
—	3855	GWR	2884	2-8-0	1942
—	4253	GWR	4200	2-8-0T	1917
—	5668	GWR	5600	0-6-2T	1926
Bickmarsh Hall	5967	GWR	'Hall'	4-6-0	1937
—	9629	GWR	5700	0-6-0PT	1946
—	51351	P/Steel	117	DMBS	1959
—	51397	P/Steel	117	DMS	1959
—	51942	BR	108	DMCL	1960
—	52044	BR	108	DMCL	1960
—	54270	BR	108	DTCL	1960
—	53632	BR	108	DMCL	1960
—	59520	P/Steel	117	TC	1959

Industrial locomotives

Name	No	Builder	Type	Built
Nora	5	Barclay (1680)	0-4-0ST	1920
Harry	—	Barclay (1823)	0-4-0ST	1926
—	8	RSH (7139)	0-6-0ST	1944
Llanwern	104	E/Electric (D1249)	0-6-0DH	1968
—	106	E/Electric (D1226)	0-6-0DH	1971
—	1	Fowler (22497)	0-6-0DM	1938
Ebbw Vale	170	Hunslet (7063)	0-8-0DH	1971
—	10083	R/Royce (10083)	0-4-0DH	1961

Stock

8 ex-BR Mk 1 coaches, 5 ex-GWR coaches, 2 ex-LSWR coaches, 36 other vans, china clay, coke and tank wagons

11/12, 18/19 December. Please visit web site for up-to-date information.

Special notes: The railway incorporates the former mineral/LNWR passenger lines running through Big Pit. Both north and southward extensions are being considered. Service currently operates between Furnace Sidings platform and Whistle Inn platform. The railway runs near to the Garn Lakes — ideal for picnics after a train ride

Membership details: c/o above address, or phone (01873) 857539

Rheilffordd Eryri — Welsh Highland Railway (Caernarfon)

Member: HRA

The Welsh Highland Light Railway Ltd has been incorporated to reconstruct much of the original WHR line. The new northern terminus is at Caernarfon, with re-opening to Porthmadog in stages over the next 7 years.

General Manager: Paul Lewin

Headquarters: Ffestiniog Railway Co, Harbour Station, Porthmadog LL49 9NF

Telephone: Porthmadog (01766) 516073

Internet address: *Web site:* http://www.festrail.co.uk

Main station: Caernarfon

Other public station: Dinas,

Waunfawr, Rhyd Ddu
OS reference: SH 481625
Car parks: Caernarfon
Access by public transport:
Caernarfon is served by local buses.
The station at Bangor is served by
Virgin and Arriva Trains (Wales).
There is a regular bus service
between Bangor and Caernarfon
Depot: Dinas
Length of line: 12 miles, 1ft 11.5in
gauge
Passenger trains: Caernarfon-
Rhyd Ddu
Future extensions: Rhyd Ddu-
Porthmadog
Period of public operation: Daily
late March-early November, limited
winter service
Facilities for disabled: Limited
facilities on trains for disabled in
wheelchairs by prior arrangement
Refreshments: A refreshment
trolley is available on most trains.
Snowdonia Parc Hotel is situated at
Waunfawr station serving a large
selection of snacks, meals and real
ale

Locomotives

Name	No	Builder	Type	Built
—†	K1	B/Peacock (5292)	0-4-0+0-4-0	1909
—**	133	S. F. Belge	2-8-2	1953
—**	134	S. F. Belge	2-8-2	1953
Millennium/ Mileniwm*	138	B/Peacock	2-6-2+2-6-2	1958
—*†	140	B/Peacock	2-6-2+2-6-2	1958
—*	143	B/Peacock	2-6-2+2-6-2	1958
Castell Caernarfon	—	Funkey	Bo-Bo	1968
Upnor Castle	—	Hibberd (3687)	4wDM	1954

*former South African Railways NGG16 class locomotives
**former South African Railways NG15 class locomotives
†not on site
The above locomotives may not be on site. Ffestiniog Railway Co
locomotives may operate some services

Stock
10 bogie coaches, numerous service vehicles

Souvenir shop: There is a small
gift shop at Caernarfon
Special event: Super Power —
September
Membership details: Welsh
Highland Railway Society (see
above address)
Membership journal: *Snowdon
Ranger* — quarterly

Steam Centre | Rhyl Miniature Railway | Denbighshire

Member: Britain's Great Little
Railways
Operating society/organisation:
Rhyl Steam Preservation Trust
Location: Marine Lake,
Wellington Road, Rhyl,
Denbighshire
Internet address: *Web site:*
www.rhylminiaturerailway.co.uk
Trust secretary: Simon Townsend
Postal address: 10 Cilnant, Mold,
Flintshire CH7 1GG.
Telephone: 01352 759109
OS reference: SN 072124
Length: Approx 1 mile (1ft 3in
gauge)
On site facilities: Car park
Access by public transport:
Approx 1 mile from Rhyl main line

Locomotives

Name	No	Builder	Type	Built
Joan	101	Barnes	4-4-2	1920
—	44	Cagney	4-4-0	c1910
Clara	—	Guest & Saunders LE	0-4-2DM (SO)	1961
—	—	Lister	4wDM	1938

Rolling stock: 5 bogie 'cars de luxe' built in the 1910s and a similar vehicle
built in 2001, 2 Cagney bogie coaches built c1904. Ballast wagon

station, buses to Towyn and
Abergele pass by
Period of public operation:
Operation (steam) Bank Holiday
Sundays and Mondays, every
Sunday from mid-June to early
September, every Thursday and
Saturday during school holidays;
all weather permitting from 13.00 or
earlier
Membership details: Friends of
Rhyl Miniature Railway, details
from 01745 339477, newsletters
twice a year

Snowdon Mountain Railway

Member: HRA

The only public rack and pinion railway in the British Isles, opened in 1896, this bustling line climbs the slopes of Snowdon, often through the clouds, to the café at the top

General Manager: Alan Kendall
Engineering Manager: Sam Reeves
Commercial Manager: Vince Hughes
Marketing Co-ordinator: Melanie Mynard
Headquarters: Snowdon Mountain Railway, Llanberis LL55 4TY
Telephone: 0870 458 0033 (advance bookings available via telephone)
Fax: (01286) 872518
Internet address: *e-mail:* info@snowdonrailway.co.uk
Web site: www.snowdonrailway.co.uk
Main station: Llanberis
Other public stations: Summit, also Clogwyn/Rocky Valley when Summit is inaccessible
OS reference: SH 582597
Car park: Llanberis
Access by public transport: Bangor railway station then by bus, either direct, or alternatively via Caernarfon. Snowdon Sherpa Services to/from Beddgelert and Betws-y-coed stop outside the station
Refreshment facilities: Llanberis, Summit
Souvenir shops: Llanberis, Summit

Locomotives

Name	No	Builder	Type	Built
Enid	2	SLM (924)	0-4-2T	1895
Wyddfa	3	SLM (925)	0-4-2T	1895
Snowdon	4	SLM (988)	0-4-2T	1896
Moel Siabod	5	SLM (989)	0-4-2T	1896
Padarn	6	SLM (2838)	0-4-2T	1922
Ralph*	7	SLM (2869)	0-4-2T	1923
Eryri*	8	SLM (2870)	0-4-2T	1923
Ninian	9	Hunslet (9249)	0-4-0DH	1986
Yeti	10	Hunslet (9250)	0-4-0DH	1986
Peris	11	Hunslet (9305)	0-4-0DH	1991
George	12	Hunslet (9312)	0-4-0DH	1992

All steam locomotives were built by Swiss Locomotive Works, Winterthur
All diesel locomotives were built by Hunslet Engine Co, Leeds
*currently stored out of service (boilerless)

Stock

8 closed bogie coaches; 1 bogie works car; 1 4-wheel open wagon; a 3-car diesel-electric railcar set built 1995 by HPE Tredegar (fleet Nos 21, 22, 23 [Works Nos 1074/5/6])

Depot: Llanberis
Length of line: 7.5km, 800mm gauge
Passenger trains: Llanberis-Summit. Journey time approx 60min. Departures from Llanberis at 30min intervals during peak periods. Round trip approx 2hr 30min
Period of public operation: Daily 15 March-1 November
Facilities for disabled: Those requiring wheelchair access should please telephone in advance to discuss their particular requirements. Disabled parking is available and there are suitable toilet facilities in both Llanberis station and the Summit. Only officially registered support dogs can travel on the trains
Special notes: All trains subject to weather. Prior to mid-May and in severe weather conditions trains cannot proceed all the way to the summit and terminate at Clogwyn or Rocky Valley. Advantageous group booking rates are available. Please contact the Marketing Co-ordinator.
'Early Bird' half price fare available on 09.00 departure (08.30 departure in August). Any train may be steam- or diesel-hauled

Swansea Vale Railway

Member: HRA
Location/headquarters: Swansea Vale Railway Upper Bank, Pentrechwyth, Swansea SA1 7DB
Telephone: (01554) 770041
Internet address: *Web site:* www.swanseavalerailway.co.uk
Main stations: Six Pit Junction, Nant-Y-Ffin Road, Llansamlet (Swansea)
Llansamlet is situated 2 miles north of the City of Swansea, opposite Comet store

Other stations: Cwm Halt and Upper Bank Junction (awaiting development)
OS reference: Six Pit Junction — SN 683969, Upper Bank Junction — SN 668953
Car parks: Free car parks at Six Pit

150

Wales

Facilities for disabled: All facilities including portable steps and wide door for wheelchairs in two coaches

Period of public operation: Daily from 3-18 April, closed Thursdays and Fridays 22 April to 28 May, closed Fridays 11 June to 16 July. Daily from 17 July to 5 September. Closed Thursdays and Fridays September and October.

Special events: Steam Gala 17/18 July; Halloween (evening trains), Santa Specials in December. Please contact for further details

Special notes: Pay once only and ride all day

Membership details: Teifi Valley Railway Society, c/o Henllan station

Membership journal: *Right Away* — quarterly

Industrial locomotives

Name	No	Builder	Type	Built
Alan George	—	Hunslet (606)	0-4-0ST	1894
Sgt Murphy	—	K/Stuart (3117)	0-6-2T	1918
Sholto	—	Hunslet (2433)	4wDM	1941
Simon	—	M/Rail (7126)	4wDM	1936
Sammy	—	M/Rail (605)	4wDM	1959

Steam Centre — Vale of Glamorgan Railway — Vale of Glamorgan

Member: HRA

Steam hauled rides over 1.5 miles of track including new extension

Location: Barry Island Station, Barry Island, South Wales

Operating society: Vale of Glamorgan Railway Co

Car park: Large public car park near site

OS reference: ST 115667

Access by public transport: Frequent train services from Cardiff to Barry Island for cross platform interchange (Cardiff Railway Co)

On site facilities: Museum, shop, light refreshments

Public opening: Open for viewing Monday to Friday most of the year. Services operate: Bank Holidays, weekends July and August and special events

Special events: Easter Bunny — 9-12 April; Day Out With Thomas — 16-18 April; visiting locomotive — 3, 31 May; Day Out With Thomas — 10-19 July; Vintage Transport — mid July; Teddy Weekend — 31 July/1 August; Day Out With Thomas — 3-8 September.

Santa Specials — see local press for details or ring 01446 748816

Length of line: 1.5 miles

Further information: The Chairman, Vale of Glamorgan Railway Co, Barry Island Station, South Wales CF36 5TH

Membership details: Membership Secretary c/o above address

Locomotives and multiple-units

Name	No	Origin	Class	Type	Built
—	2861	GWR	2800	2-8-0	1918
—	4115	GWR	4101	2-6-2T	1936
—	5227	GWR	5205	2-8-0T	1924
—	5538	GWR	4575	2-6-2T	1928
—	5539	GWR	4575	2-6-2T	1928
—	6686	GWR	5600	0-6-2T	1928
Willington Hall	7927	BR	'Hall'	4-6-0	1950
—	44901	LMS	5MT	4-6-0	1945
—	48518	LMS	8F	2-8-0	1944
—	80150	BR	4MT	2-6-4T	1956
—	92245	BR	9F	2-10-0	1958
—	51339	P/Steel	117	DMBS	1959
—	51382	P/Steel	117	DMS	1959
—	54279	BR	108	DTC	1959

Locomotive notes: In store, not on public view, except 5538 on site. Several of the locomotives listed above are expected to be used as a source of parts for 're-creation' projects

Industrial locomotives

Name	No	Builder	Type	Built
Pamela	—	Hunslet (3840)	0-6-0ST	1956
Ugly	62	RSH (7673)	0-6-0ST	1950
—	7705	RSH (7705)	0-4-0ST	1952
—	52/001	Barclay (1966)	0-4-0F	1929
Bill Caddick	—	H/Clarke (1168)	0-6-0DM	1959
—	—	Unilok (2183)		1964

Stock

BR Mk 1 coaches, TVR coach No 153, operational steam crane, various freight vehicles

Vale of Rheidol Railway

Member: GLTW

This narrow gauge railway offers a 23-mile round trip from Aberystwyth to Devil's Bridge providing spectacular views which cannot be enjoyed by road. At Devil's Bridge there are walks to the Mynach Falls and Devil's Punch Bowl. Many artists have been inspired by the magnificence of Devil's Bridge and the Rheidol Valley

General Manager: N. Thompson

Headquarters: Vale of Rheidol Railway, The Locomotive Shed, Park Avenue, Aberystwyth SY23 1PG

Telephone: (01970) 625819

Fax: (01970) 623769

Internet address: *Web site:* www.rheidolrailway.co.uk

Main station: Aberystwyth (adjacent to main line station)

Other public stations: Devil's Bridge, Rhiwfron, Rheidol Falls, Aberffrwd, Nantyronen, Capel Bangor, Glanrafon, Llanbadarn

OS reference: SN 587812

Car parks: Aberystwyth, Devil's Bridge

Access by public transport: Aberystwyth main line station: and bus services to Aberystwyth

Refreshment facilities: Aberystwyth (not railway owned), Devil's Bridge (not railway operated)

Souvenir shop: Aberystwyth

Depot: Aberystwyth (not open to the public)

Length of line: 11.75 miles, 1ft 11.75in gauge

Journey time: Single 1hr, return 3hr

Passenger trains: Aberystwyth-Devil's Bridge

Period of public operation: Daily 3 April-30 October, with some exceptions in April, May, September and October

Locomotives

Name	No	Origin	Ex-BR Class	Type	Built
Owain Glyndŵr	7	GWR	98	2-6-2T	1923
Llywelyn	8	GWR	98	2-6-2T	1923
Prince of Wales	9	GWR	98	2-6-2T	1924
—	10	Brecon MR (002)	98/1	0-6-0DH	1987

Stock

16 bogie coaches; 1 4-wheel guard's van; 14 wagons for maintenance use; 1 inspection trolley

The following locomotives are stored on the railway pending restoration and future display

Name	No	Builder	Type	Built
—	4	Decauville (1027)	0-4-0T	1926
Kathleen	—	de Winton	0-4-0VBT	1877
—	6	Fowler (10249)	0-6-0T+T	1905
—	21	Fowler (11938)	0-4-2T	1909
—	23	Fowler (15515)	0-6-2T	1920
Margaret	—	Hunslet (605)	0-4-0ST	1894
—	31	Mafei (4766)	0-8-0T	1916
—	—	H/Clarke (D564)	4wDM	1930
—	—*	R/Proctor (50823)	4wPM	1918
—	—	K/Stuart (3114)	0-4-0ST	1918

*metre gauge

Also Henschel bogie tender (11854/25 of 1917)

Welsh Highland Railway — Porthmadog

Member: HRA, GLToW

The Welsh Highland Railway Ltd operates services at the south-western end of the old Welsh Highland line and has its base in the bustling holiday town of Porthmadog. The company is developing an exciting project to enhance visitor facilities at the Gelert's Farm site. Extension to Pont Croesor is now underway.

Locomotives

Name	No	Builder	Type	Built
Moel Tryfan	—	Bagnall (3023)	0-4-2T	1953
Gelert	—	Bagnall (3050)	0-4-2T	1953
—	—	Baldwin (44699)	4-6-0T	1917
Russell	—	Hunslet (901)	2-6-2T	1906
Pedemoura	—	O&K (10808)	0-6-0WT	1924
Karen	—	Peckett (2024)	0-4-2T	1942
Glaslyn	1	R/Hornsby (297030)	4wDM	1952
Kinnerley	2	R/Hornsby (354068)	4wDM	1953
Cnicht	36	M/Rail (8703)	4wDM	1941

The WHR is very much a family orientated attraction and adults have the opportunity to purchase a footplate pass

Location: Tremadog Road, Porthmadog, immediately adjacent to main line railway station and opposite the Queen's Hotel

OS reference: SH 571393

Operating society/organisation: Welsh Highland Railway Ltd, Gelert's Farm Works, Madoc Street West, Porthmadog, LL49 9DY

Telephone:
Porthmadog: 01766 513402
24hr information line: 0870 321 2402

Internet address: *Web site:* www.whr.co.uk

Car park: Free — overflow car park opposite the railway; this is council owned, with the usual charges and includes accommodation for coaches

Catering facilities: 'Russells' supplying a range of adult/children's meals and light refreshments

Access by public transport: Central Trains to Porthmadog station. Bus Gwynedd service 1 and 3 to Porthmadog

On site facilities: Souvenir and railway book/video shop, disabled toilet facilities, information boards, footplate passes and extended shed tours. Steam Driver Experience courses available

Length of line: To Pen-y-Mount, Tremadog. Three-quarter-mile, 1ft 11.5in gauge

Passenger trains: Porthmadog-Pen-y-Mount. Return journey approx 40min incorporating works tours. Steam-hauled Bank Holidays, every weekend and daily from early July to end of August

Name	No	Builder	Type	Built
Katherine	9	M/Rail (605363)	4wDM	1968
—	4	M/Rail (605333)	4wDM	1963
—	5	Hunslet (6285)	4wDM	1968
—	3	R/Hornsby (370555)	4wDM	1953
Jonathon	6	M/Rail (11102)	4wDM	1959
—	7	Hunslet (7535)	4wDM	1977
—	10	R/Hornsby (481552)	4wDM	1962
—	11	Hunslet (3510)	4wDM	1947
Beddgelert*	NG120	S. F. Belge	2-8-2	1950
Snowdonia/Eryri†	—	Buch (23389)	0-6-0DM	1977
—†	—	Buch (2405)	0-6-0DH	1980
—	—	Barclay (554)	4wDH	1970
—	—	Barclay (555)	4wDH	1970
—	—	M/Rail (22237)	4wDM	1965
Kathy	—	H/Barclay (LD 9350)	0-4-0DM	1994
Emma	—	H/Barclay (LD 9346)	0-4-0DM	1994

*ex-South African Railways Class NG15
†ex-Polish State Railways class LYD2

Locomotive notes: Newly refurbished *Gelert* will operate 2004 steam service. Ex World War 1 Baldwin locomotive currently on display will be reconstructed as the famous WHR No 590

Stock
Passengers will have the opportunity to travel in the historic 'Gladstone' coach; other replica Welsh Highland coaches in the course of construction. Rebuilt 1923 Hudson 'Toastrack' coach will be in service from Easter 2004

(all other trains are diesel hauled)
Family tickets: Available, 2 adults + 2 children
Tickets: Your ticket enables you to travel all day. Rover tickets avaiable covering both WHR (Porthmadog) and WHR (Caernarfon) together with the Ffestiniog Railway
Period of public operation: 3-25 April; 1-3, 8/9, 15/16, 22/23, 29-31 May; daily 1 June-2 September; 4/5, 7-9, 11-16, 18-23, 25-27 September; 2/3, 8-10, 16/17, 23-31 October
Special events: Easter Bunnies — 11 April; Teddy Bears' Picnic —

15/16 May; Anniversary Gala — 19/20 June; Snowdonia Transport Festival — 9-11 October
Facilities for disabled: Toilets, plus ramp to facilitate access to shed for guided tour. Disabled passengers can be accommodated without prior notice
Membership details: Membership Secretaries, R. & P. Hughes, 2 Clos Sulien, Llanbadarn, Aberystwyth, Ceredigion SY23 3GF. Instant membership available at the shop
Membership journal: *The Journal* — quarterly

Member: HRA
There is a decidedly foreign atmosphere to the trains over this line. The steam locomotive collection embraces examples from three continents, and the coaches are turn-of-the-century balcony saloons from Austria or 1960s bogies from

Africa. The line follows a steeply graded route (maximum 1 in 24) through very attractive rolling countryside, and is rather a gem in an area too often missed by the traveller heading for further shores
General Manager: Terry Turner
Headquarters: Welshpool &

Llanfair Light Railway Preservation Co Ltd, The Station, Llanfair Caereinion SY21 0SF
Telephone: Llanfair Caereinion (01938) 810441
Fax: (01938) 810861
Internet address: *Web site:* www.wllr.org.uk

Main station: Welshpool (Raven Square)

Other public stations: Castle Caereinion, Sylfaen, Llanfair Caereinion

OS reference: SJ 107069

Car parks: Llanfair Caereinion, Welshpool (both free)

Access by public transport: Main line station at Welshpool, one mile from Raven Square. Arriva buses from Shrewsbury, Oswestry and Newtown to Welshpool

Refreshment facilities: Light refreshments at Llanfair Caereinion. Picnic areas at Welshpool and Llanfair

Souvenir shops: Welshpool, Llanfair Caereinion

Depot: Llanfair Caereinion

Length of line: 8 miles, 2ft 6in gauge

Passenger trains: Welshpool-Llanfair Caereinion

Period of public operation: Easter to October. Daily in school holidays

Special events: Steam Gala — 4/5 September; Santa trains — 11/12, 18/19 December

Facilities for disabled: Specially adapted coaches for wheelchairs.

Locomotives

Name	No	Builder	Type	Built
The Earl	1	B/Peacock (3496)	0-6-0T	1902
The Countess	2	B/Peacock (3497)	0-6-0T	1902
Monarch	6	Bagnall (3024)	0-4-4-0T	1953
Chattenden	7	Drewry (2263)	0-6-0DM	1949
Dougal	8	Barclay (2207)	0-4-0T	1946
Sir Drefaldwyn	10	S. F. Belge (2855)	0-8-0T	1944
Ferret	11	Hunslet (2251)	0-4-0DM	1940
Joan	12	K/Stuart (4404)	0-6-2T	1927
SLR No 85	14	Hunslet (3815)	2-6-2T	1954
Orion	15	Tubize (2369)	2-6-2T	1948
Scooby	16	Hunslet (2400)	0-4-0DM	1941

Locomotive notes: Locomotives expected in service 2004 — *The Earl, The Countess, Orion, SLR No 85*. The remainder can be seen at Llanfair station, No 12 is displayed with access to the footplate

Stock

1 Wickham trolley; 6 W&LLR wagons; 8 ex-Admiralty wagons; 2 ex-Bowater wagons; 6 ex-Zillertalbahn coaches; 4 ex-Sierra Leone coaches, 2 Hungarian State Railway coaches

Please phone in advance. Easy access to shops. Disabled toilet facility at Welshpool and Llanfair

Membership details: David Barker, 458 Oxford Road, Gomersal, Cleckheaton, West Yorks BD19 4LB

Membership journal: *The Journal*

— quarterly

Marketing name: Llanfair Railway

Special notes: Open balcony coaches — travel right next to the engine at the front of the train. Or see the line rolling away behind the back end!

The driver of *Countess* awaits the right away from the guard at Sylfaen station during the line's Gala Weekend. *ACB*

Wales

Channel Islands & Isle of Man

In 1997 the Alderney Railway was 150 years old, having opened on 14 July 1847. Queen Victoria was the only passenger until 1980
Location: Alderney, Channel Islands
Operating society/organisation: Alderney Railway Society, PO Box 75, Alderney, Channel Islands
Telephone: (01481) 822978
Car park: Yes
Access by public transport: Aurigny Air Services from Southampton
On site facilities: Station at Braye Road (tickets & souvenirs)
Public opening: Weekends and Bank Holidays, Easter to end of September
Special events: Alderney Week August. Easter Egg Specials on

Industrial locomotives

Name	No	Builder	Type	Built
Elizabeth	—	Vulcan (D2271)	0-4-0DM	1949
Molly 2	—	R/Hornsby	0-4-0DM	1958

Stock
4 Wickham cars
2 Goods wagons
2 ex-London Underground 1956 Stock tube cars (locomotive-hauled)
2 Wickham flats

Easter Sunday. Santa Specials, Saturday before Christmas
On site facilities: Miniature railway (7.25in gauge), quarter-mile circuit operates at Mannez in connection with standard gauge line
Length of line: 2 miles
Facilities for disabled: No, but train crew will always help

wherever possible
President: Frank Eggleston
Chairman: Anthony le Blanc (tel: 01481 822978)
Hon Sec: Mike Taylor
Notes: Engine shed at Quarry. Wickham 'train' operates in low season; *Elizabeth* and tube cars in high season and Easter

Location: Groudle Glen Railway, Isle of Man
Officer in charge: Tony Beard
Operating company: Groudle Glen Railway Ltd (managed by the Isle of Man Steam Railway Supporters' Association) of 29 Hawarden Avenue, Douglas, Isle of Man IM1 4BP
Telephone: (01624) 622138 (evenings); (01624) 670453

Locomotives

Name	No	Builder	Type	Built
Dolphin	1	H/Hunslet (4394)	4wDM	1952
Walrus	2	H/Hunslet (4395)	4wDM	1952
Sea Lion	—	Bagnall (1484)	2-4-0T	1896
Annie	—	Booth/GGR	0-4-2T	1998
Polar Bear	—	BEV (556801)	2-B-2	1988

(weekends)
Car park: Yes

Access by public transport: Manx Electric Railway (Groudle Hotel)

On site facilities: Sales shop
Length of line: 0.75-mile, 2ft gauge
Public opening: Easter Sunday and Monday, Sundays May to September (11.00-16.30); Tuesday evening services August (19.00-21.00); Wednesday evening services July/August (19.00-21.00); Santa Trains — December (11.00-15.30)
Facilities for disabled: Due to the line's location, those who are disabled will have some difficulty. It is suggested that they telephone for advice

Further information and membership details: From above address
Membership journal: *Manx Steam Railway News* — quarterly

| Timetable Service | Isle of Man Railway | Isle of Man |

The 3ft gauge Isle of Man Railway is a survivor of a system which previously also operated from Douglas to Peel and Ramsey. Almost continuous operation since 1873 makes it one of the oldest operating railways in the British Isles. The railway has changed little since the turn of the 19th century. It runs for over 15 miles between Douglas and Port Erin through the island's rolling southern countryside.

The line is owned and operated by the Isle of Man Government
Director of Public Transport: David R. Howard
Head of Railways: M. P. Ogden
Railway Engineer: G. F. Lawson
Headquarters: Isle of Man Transport, Transport Headquarters, Banks Circus, Douglas, Isle of Man IM1 5PT
Telephone: Douglas (01624) 663366
Fax: (01624) 663637
Main station: Douglas
Other public stations: Port Soderick, Santon, Castletown, Ballasalla, Port St Mary and Port Erin
Car parks: Douglas, Ballasalla, Castletown, Port Erin
Access by public transport: Isle of Man Transport bus to main

Locomotives

Name	No	Builder	Type	Built
Loch	4	B/Peacock (1416)	2-4-0T	1874
Fenella	8	B/Peacock (3610)	2-4-0T	1894
G. H. Wood	10	B/Peacock (4662)	2-4-0T	1905
Maitland	11	B/Peacock (4663)	2-4-0T	1905
Hutchinson	12	B/Peacock (5126)	2-4-0T	1908
Caledonia	15	Dubs & Co (2178)	0-6-0T	1885
Viking	17	Schottler (2175)	0-4-0DH	1958
—	—	M/Rail (22021)	4wDM	1959
—	—	M/Rail (485280)	4wDM	1966
—	—	Wickham	4wPM	1961

Locomotive note: All operational, all other rolling stock stored off the line

On display in museum at Port Erin

Name	No	Builder	Type	Built
Peveril	6	B/Peacock (1524)	2-4-0T	1875
Mannin	16	B/Peacock (6296)	2-4-0T	1926

Rolling stock
Gibbons crane (on display at the former Union Mills station/owned by private company), 20 coaches, 20 runners, 3 vans, 2 open wagons, 1 well wagon

centres
Refreshment facilities: Port Erin and Douglas
Souvenir shops: None
Museum: Port Erin
Depot: Douglas
Length of line: 15.5 miles, 3ft gauge
Passenger trains: Douglas-Port Erin

Period of public operation: Daily 3 May-31 October 2004
Facilities for disabled: Level access throughout Douglas and Port Erin stations including refreshment area. Carriages able to carry wheelchairs, ramps provided. Advance notice helpful

| Timetable Service | Manx Electric Railway | Isle of Man |

The 3ft gauge Manx Electric Railway is a unique survivor of Victorian high technology. A mixture of railway and tramway practice, it was built in 1893 and was a pioneer in the use of electric traction. It illustrates an example of a true electric interurban line. Two of the original cars are still in service making them the oldest tramcars still in operation on their original route in the British Isles.

158   **Channel Islands & Isle of Man**

After leaving Douglas, the railway passes the Groudle Glen Railway before reaching the charming village of Laxey, for the Snaefell Mountain Railway. The line continues over some of the most breathtaking coastal scenery in the island before reaching its terminus at Ramsey nearly 18 miles from Douglas.

The line is owned and operated by the Isle of Man Government
Director of Public Transport: David R. Howard
Head of Railways: M. P. Ogden
Railway Engineer: G. F. Lawson
Headquarters: Isle of Man Transport, Transport Headquarters, Banks Circus, Douglas, Isle of Man IM1 5PT
Telephone: Douglas (01624) 663366
Fax: (01624) 663637
Main stations: Douglas (Derby Castle), Laxey and Ramsey
Other public stations: Groudle, Dhoon Glen, Ballaglass and numerous wayside stops
Car parks: Douglas, Laxey, Ramsey (nearby)
Access by public transport: Isle of Man Transport buses to main centres. Douglas Corporation Horse Tramway to Derby Castle in summer
Depots: Douglas, Laxey, Ramsey
Refreshment facilities: Laxey in summer
Length of line: 17.5 miles, 3ft gauge
Passenger service: Douglas-Ramsey

Period of public operations: Daily all year round
Special notes: Folded wheelchairs can be carried. Please notify in advance. One trailer with disabled access used on request

Motor cars

Nos	Type	Seats	Body	Built
1, 2	Unvestibuled saloon	34	Milnes	1893
5, 6, 7, 9	Vestibuled saloon	32	Milnes	1894
16	Cross-bench open	56	Milnes	1898
19-22*	Winter saloon	48	Milnes	1899
25	Cross-bench open	56	Milnes	1898
32, 33	Cross-bench open	56	UEC	1906

*22 rebodied 1991, McArd/MER

Trailers

Nos	Type	Seats	Body	Built
36, 37	Cross-bench open	44	Milnes	1894
40, 41, 44	Cross-bench open	44	EE Co	1930
42, 43	Cross-bench open	44	Milnes	1903
45-48	Cross-bench open	44	Milnes	1899
49-51, 53, 54	Cross-bench open	44	Milnes	1893
56*	Cross-bench open	44	ERTCW	1904
57, 58	Saloon	32	ERTCW	1904
59	Special Saloon	18	Milnes	1895
60	Cross-bench open	44	Milnes	1896
61, 62	Cross-bench open	44	UEC	1906

*rebuilt as disabled access trailer in 1993

Note: Other rolling stock stored off the line

Snaefell Mountain Railway

The 3ft 6in gauge Snaefell Mountain Railway is unique. It is the only electric mountain railway in the British Isles. Almost all the rolling stock is original and dates back to 1895. The railway begins its journey at the picturesque village of Laxey where its station is shared with the Manx Electric Railway. The climb to the summit of Snaefell (2,036ft) is a steep one and the cars travel unassisted up gradients as steep as 1 in 12. From the summit, the views extend to Wales, Scotland, England and Ireland.

The line is owned and operated by the Isle of Man Government
Director of Public Transport: David R. Howard
Head of Railways: M. P. Ogden
Railway Engineer: G. F. Lawson
Headquarters: Isle of Man Transport, Transport Headquarters, Banks Circus, Douglas, Isle of Man IM1 5PT
Telephone: Douglas (01624) 663366
Fax: (01624) 663637
Main station: Laxey
Other public stations: Bungalow, Summit
Car parks: Laxey, Bungalow (nearby)
Access by public transport: Manx Electric Railway or Isle of Man Transport bus to Laxey
Depot: Laxey
Refreshment facilities: Laxey, Summit
Souvenirs shops: Summit
Length of line: 4.5 miles, 3ft 6in gauge
Passenger service: Laxey-Snaefell summit
Period of public operation: Daily 5 April-3 October 2004

Trams

Nos	Type	Seats	Body	Built
1-4, 6	Vestibuled saloon	48	Milnes	1895
5 (rebuild)	Vestibuled saloon	48	MER/ Kinnin	1971

159

Northern Ireland

Downpatrick Railway Museum

Member: HRA
Location: The Railway Station, Market Street, Downpatrick, Co Down BT30 6LZ
OS reference: J483444
Operating society/organisation: Downpatrick & Ardglass Railway Co Ltd, with the support of the Downpatrick Railway Society
Telephone: (028) 4461 5779
Internet address: *Web site:* www.downpatricksteamrailway.co.uk
Car park: Free parking adjacent to station
Access by public transport: A regular service is operated by Ulsterbus from Belfast Europa bus centre (next to Great Victoria Street railway station). Tel: (028) 9032 0011
Refreshment facilities: Buffet carriage open on operating days
On site facilities: Souvenir shop, toilets
Length of line: 4 miles open to public traffic. Current terminus: King Magnus's Halt. Track was extended southwards to Balldugan and north to a new station at Inch Abbey
Public opening: Operating days:
—17 March (St Patrick's Day); Easter Sunday, Monday; Saturdays and Sundays in July and August; first two Saturdays and Sundays in September. 14.00-17.00
Station tours — Monday-Friday June-August (static) 11.00-14.00
Journey time: 45min return journey from Downpatrick town to Downpatrick Loop Platform and King Magnus's Halt and Inch Abbey
Special events: Ghost Trains — Halloween weekend, travel to the Loop Platform and visit Merlin the

Diesel locomotives and multiple-unit

Name	No	Origin	Class	Type	Built
W. F. Gillespie OBE	E421	CIE	421	C	1962
—	E432	CIE	421	C	1962
—	G611	CIE	611	B	1962
—	G613	CIE	611	B	1962
—	G617	CIE	611	B	1962
—	RB3	BRE-Leyland	—	4wDM	1981

Name	No	Origin	Class	Manufacturer	Type	Built
—	712	CIE	–	Wickham (8919)	4wDH	1962

Steam locomotives

Name	No	Builder	Type	Built
—	1	O&K (12475)	0-4-0T	1934
—	3	O&K (12662)	0-4-0T	1935

Rolling stock

2 CIE Brake open standards (Nos 1918 & 1944); CIE Travelling Post Office (No 2978); 1 CIE Brake open standard generating steam van (No 3223); CIE Buffet open standard (No 2419); NIR '70' class railcar brake open standard intermediate (No 728); B&CDR 'Royal Saloon' (No 153); B&CDR 1st/2nd composite (No 152); B&CDR 3rd open (ex-railmotor); B&CDR 6-wheeled 2nd (No 154); B&CDR 6-wheeled brake 3rd (No 39); GS&WR 3rd open (No 836); GSWR 6-wheeled brake first (No 69); Ulster Railway Family Saloon (No 33); GNR 6-wheeled third, M&GW full brake c1900; 4 LMS (NCC) parcels vans; 2 LMS (NCC) open wagon; LMS (NCC) brake van; CIE closed van; 2 GNR closed vans; GNR brake van; GSWR ballast hopper; GSWR ballast plough; LMS (NCC) steam crane; 2 private oil company tankers, CIE track inspection vehicle No 712; selection of carriage and wagon underframes for internal use

Owners

1 and 3 the Irish Sugar Locomotive Group
712, G611 and G617 the Irish Traction Group
G613 and M&GW full brake privately owned
RB3 is owned by Translink
E421 and E432 the Downpatrick & Ardglass Railway Co Ltd

Magician on board his own Grotto Train. Children receive a present; Santa Specials — December weekends, travel to the Loop Platform and visit Santa Claus on board his own Grotto Train. Children receive a present. Footplate experience courses

available on summer Saturdays
Facilities for disabled: Toilets, shop, platform and trains accessible for disabled
Membership details: The Secretary, Downpatrick Railway Society, The Railway Station, Downpatrick, Co Down BT30 6LZ

Museum — Foyle Valley Railway Museum — County Londonderry

Member: HRA

The Foyle Valley Railway Museum is a centre of narrow gauge railways in the north-west of Ireland. The museum houses a number of items and rolling stock from the former County Donegal and Lough Swilly railways. The centre is housed in a modern building in an attractive, newly developing, riverside park.

Location: Foyle Valley Railway Museum, Foyle Road, Londonderry BT48 6AQ

Car park: Adjacent to the museum

Access by public transport: By NI Railways to Londonderry station (half-mile). By Ulsterbus from various centres (quarter-mile)

Facilities for disabled: Yes

Refreshment facilities: None on site but city centre quarter-mile away

Locomotives and railcars

Name	No	Origin	Class	Type	Built
Meenglas	4	CDRJC	5	2-6-4T	1907
Columbkille	6	CDRJC	5	2-6-4T	1907
—	12	CDRJC	—	Diesel railcar	1934

Industrial locomotive

Name	No	Origin	Type	Built
—	—	M/Rail (11039)	0-4-0DH	1956

Rolling stock

L&LSR carriage No 18 (Oldbury 1885), 2 ex-CDR carriage Nos 14 and 13 (Oldburt 1893/1901) — all restored.
1 ex-Clogher Valley (& CDR) Railway Box wagon No 19, 3 ex-CDRJC goods wagons, 1 ex-L&LSR hand crane (1902)

On site facilities: Souvenir shop, toilets

Note: At the time of going to press the museum is currently closed. Prospective visitors are advised to contact the museum (028 7126 5234) to ascertain the current situation, alternatively Derry City Council Museum Service can be contacted on 028 7137 2411

Timetable Service — Giant's Causeway & Bushmills Railway — Co Antrim

The GC&BR was opened in 2002 using the stock of the former Shane's Castle Railway on the last two miles of the site of the Portrush to Giant's Causeway electric tramway closed in 1949

Location: The railway links the distillery (open to visitors) village of Bushmills to the entrance of the Giant's Causeway. Follow the signs to either Bushmills or the Giant's Causeway and the railway is clearly signposted. Car parking is free at Bushmills station and expensive at the Causeway Visitor Centre

Operating organisation: Giant's Causeway & Bushmills Railway, Giant's Causeway Station, Runkerry Road, Bushmills, Co Antrim, Northern Ireland BT57 8SZ

Telephone: (028) 2073 2594 (information line)

Telephone/Fax: (028) 2073 2844

Industrial locomotives

Name	No	Builder	Type	Built
Tyrone	1	Peckett (2264)	0-4-0T	1904
Rory	2	Simplex (102T016)	4wDH	1976
Shane	3	Barclay(2281)	0-4-0T	1949

Internet address: *e-mail:* info@giantscausewayrailway.org
Web site: www.giantscausewayrailway.org

OS reference: 943437 (Irish Grid)

Access by public transport: Nearest Northern Ireland Railway stations are Portrush (5 miles), Coleraine (7 miles). Various bus routes (including an open topped vehicle on fine days in the summer) operate from either or both, depending on the route. For timetables either telephone Translink enquiries on (028) 9066 6630 or www.translink.co.uk

Length of line: 2 miles, 3ft gauge

On site facilities: Souvenir shop, also light refreshments, toilets and picnic tables at Giant's Causeway station. Free parking at both stations

Passenger trains: Bushmills-Giant's Causeway

Public opening Usually St Patricks Day (17 March) and weekends until end of October; daily for two weeks over Easter; daily from mid-May until the end of September, but please check information line for 2004 details (028) 2073 2594

Special notes: 2004 marks the centenary of locomotive No 1. It is hoped to announce a programme of commemorative events presently

Members: HRA, TT

The RPSI was formed in 1964, making it one of the older preservation societies in these islands. It has always specialised in main line steam operations, and runs an intensive summer programme of trips out of both Belfast and Dublin. The main maintenance base is situated at Whitehead, 15 miles north of Belfast on the NIR route to Larne Harbour. Here not only are the traffic locomotives shedded but the locomotive shed is also used for heavy maintenance; currently the society is completing the full rebuilding of its sixth boiler 'in-house'. A large engineering workshop has just been constructed for the Locomotive Department, with the 100-year-old overhead crane which was originally in the Belfast & County Down Railway Locomotive Erecting Shop at Queen's Quay in Belfast. This workshop which will undertake all heavy engineering for the Society is currently being fitted out. A large carriage shed is also on site where traffic vehicles are maintained and coaches are fully rebuilt. There are also heavy lifting facilities on site, and access may occasionally be limited for safety reasons when these are in use. Annual operations commence with 'Easter Bunny' trains out of Belfast, usually on Easter Monday. In May the 'International Railtour' is the main event, a three day steam extravaganza, which in 2004 will visit Waterford. During June there are main line trips out of both Belfast and Dublin, including a Midsummer Barbecue train and a Musical Special. July and August see the 'Portrush Flyers' from Belfast to Portrush and back, around 180 miles of main line steam, as well as the 'Sea Breeze' excursions from Dublin to Rosslare and back, covering 205 miles. During June, July and August there are steam train rides on site at Whitehead on Sunday afternoons, and at the end of July there will be

Locomotives

Name	No	Origin	Class	Type	Built
Merlin	85*	GNR(I)	V	4-4-0	1932
Slieve Gullion	171†	GNR(I)	S	4-4-0	1913
—	4	LMS (NCC)	WT	2-6-4T	1947
—	184†	GS&WR	J15	0-6-0	1880
—	186††	GS&WR	J15	0-6-0	1879
—	461†	D&SER	K2	2-6-0	1922
Lough Erne	27	SL&NCR	Z	0-6-4T	1949

Industrial locomotives

Name	No	Builder	Type	Built
Guinness	3	H/Clarke (1152)	0-4-0ST	1919
R. H. Smyth	3	Avonside (2021)	0-6-0ST	1928
—	23	Planet (3509)	0-4-0DM	1951
—	1	R/Hornsby	0-4-0DM	1954

*on loan from Ulster Folk & Transport Museum
†awaiting restoration
††returning to traffic in 2004

Stock

The Society also owns some 20 operational coaches, normally divided between Whitehead and Dublin. Further coaches are awaiting restoration and a small number of freight wagons are also preserved, as well as a steam crane. A serious fire due to vandalism a couple of years ago destroyed several vehicles, and any rebuilding is likely to be some years in the future at best. The Society has purchased a variety of Mk 2 coaches which are undergoing major overhaul for return to traffic in 2004. The Society's secondary maintenance base is at Mullingar, Co Westmeath, but there is **no** access to the public.

an Open Day in conjunction with the Whitehead Community Association when not only will there be train rides but also at least two locomotives will be in steam and there will be access to the workshop areas. The season usually ends with further excursions in September to Rosslare and Whitehead, and Halloween shuttles between Belfast and Whitehead. November sees the operation of a Santa Special to Derry out of Belfast, before the Santa Specials out of both capital cities

Location: Whitehead Excursion Station, Co Antrim, Northern Ireland

Operating society: Railway Preservation Society of Ireland, Castleview Road, Whitehead, Carrickfergus, Co Antrim BT38 9NA

Telephone/fax:
From UK (028) 2826 0803.

From Eire (01) 280 9147

Internet address: *e-mail:* rpsitrains@hotmail.com
Web site: http://www.rpsi-online.org

Car park: Public car parking is readily available adjacent to the Society premises, with a further large car park less than 5min walk away on the sea front. Both car parks are normally free

Access by public transport: Northern Ireland Railways or Ulsterbus to Whitehead

On site facilities: Souvenir shop (operating days only)

Public opening: Visitors welcome most weekends. Site not open during the week (except public holidays) or when main line trains are operating from Whitehead or Belfast. Special opening for parties, or in the evening, may be arranged by telephoning in advance

Special notes: The RPSI is noted

for its main line excursions and traditional rolling stock. For details: RPSI Railtours, Box 171 Larne BT40 1UU (9x4 SAE please).

Facilities for disabled: Please note that wheelchair facilities can be provided on trains, with advance notice if possible. A dedicated coach for carrying wheelchairs operates out of Whitehead on Belfast-based trains. Wheelchair access around the workshops at Whitehead is possible, but difficult, and advanced warning is requested of any visitors who may need special facilities

Membership details: Membership Secretary, 148 Church Road, Newtownabbey, Co Antrim BT36 6HJ

Future developments: Completion of a new heavy engineering workshop is planned, as well as a projected extension to the Carriage Shed and additional stores and maintenance areas, and there are further developments in the pipeline which will hopefully improve access. Additional locomotive and coach restoration is proposed

---

Museum — Ulster Folk & Transport Museum — County Down

Member: HRA

Forty-five acres are devoted to the Transport Galleries. Permanent exhibitions include the earliest forms of transport, horse-drawn vehicles, bicycles, motor cars and the Museum's *Titanic* exhibition.

The Irish Railway Collection is displayed in an award-winning purpose-built gallery — the largest Transport Museum gallery in Ireland.

The collection features *Maedb* — the largest locomotive run in Ireland. The display includes narrow gauge and standard gauge rolling stock, locomotives, carriages, goods wagons, railcars and railbuses along with memorabilia

Location: Ulster Folk & Transport Museum, Cultra, Holywood

Operating organisation: Ulster Folk & Transport Museum, Cultra, Holywood BT18 0EU

Telephone: (028) 9042 8428

Fax: (028) 9042 8728

Internet address: *Web site:* www.magni.org.uk

Access: By car or bus the museum is about 7 miles from Belfast city centre on the A2 Belfast-Bangor road. You can also reach the museum by train

Car park: Extensive free parking

On site facilities: Shops, toilets, tea room

Opening times: All year round; opening times vary with season, check with the Museum for details

Locomotives (5ft 3in)

Name	No	Origin	Class	Type	Built
—	93	GNR(I)	JT	2-4-2T	1895
—	30	BCDR	I	4-4-2T	1901
Dunluce Castle	74	LMS(NCC)	U2	4-4-0	1924
Maedb	800	GSR	B1A	4-6-0	1939
—	1	R/Stephenson (2738)	—	0-6-0ST	1891
Merlin*	85	GNR(I)	V	4-4-0	1932
—	1	GNR(I)	—	Railbus	1932

*on loan to Railway Preservation Society of Ireland at Whitehead

Locomotives (narrow gauge)

Name	No	Origin	Class	Type	Built
Blanche	2	CDRJC	5A	2-6-4T	1912
Kathleen	2	CLR	—	4-4-0T	1887
Phoenix	11	CVR	—	4wD	1928
—	20	Industrial	—	0-4-0	1905
—	2	Industrial	—	0-4-0	1907

Stock

1 Dublin, Wicklow & Wexford Railway coach; 1 Dundalk, Newry & Greenore Railway coach; 1 Midland & Great Western Railway director's saloon (ex-private vehicle); 1 Electric tramcar of Bessbrook-Newry Tramway; 2 trams from Giant's Causeway Tramway, Great Northern Railway Ireland Fintona tram, Great Northern Railway Ireland Hill of Howth electric tramcar, 1 Cavan-Leitrim Railway coach; 2 County Donegal Railway railcars; 1 County Donegal Railway director's coach; 1 County Donegal Railway trailer coach (bodywork ex-Dublin & Lucan Railway coach); 1 Giant's Causeway (P&BVR) saloon trailer; 1 Castlederg & Victoria Bridge Tramway 1st/3rd coach; 1 County Donegal Railway 7-ton open wagon, 3 Belfast trams, 1 Belfast trolleybus, 1 Belfast double-deck bus. Extensive collection of cars, motorcycles, bicycles, commercial vehicles, horse-drawn vehicles, fire-fighting equipment and industrial railway vehicles

Eire

Steam Centre — Cavan & Leitrim Railway — County Leitrim

Restoration work commenced in June 1993 and to date some half-mile of line has been rebuilt, water tower and engine shed refurbished and new workshops and carriage shed constructed. The ultimate objective is to rebuild a further 5.75 miles of line to Mohill

Location/headquarters: The Narrow Gauge Station, Dromod, Co Leitrim, adjacent to the Irish Rail station

General Manager: Michael Kennedy

Telephone: 0035 7196 38599 (from UK)

Internet address: *Web site:* www.irish-railway.com *e-mail:* dromod@eircom.net

Main station: Dromod

Car park: At Dromod terminus

Access by public transport: Rail service to Dromod (Irish Rail) on the Dublin/Sligo line. Bus Eireann and Ulsterbus routes also call at Dromod

Refreshment facilities: Tea room open by arrangement. Full meals available at nearby bars

Souvenir shop: Dromod

Length of line: Half-mile (3ft gauge)

Museum: Large collection of locomotives, rolling stock, road vehicles and aircraft, many still awaiting restoration

Period of public operation: Daily all year round. Steam trains Sundays April to September or by special arrangement

Special events: Annual Vintage Day — 2 May; Hollowe'en Ghost Trains — 31 October; Santa Steam Trains — 5, 12, 19 December

Contact address: The Cavan & Leitrim Railway Co Ltd, Station Road, Dromod, Co Leitrim, Republic of Ireland

Locomotives

3ft gauge

Name	No	Builder	Type	Built
Dromod	1	K/Stuart (3024)	0-4-2ST	1916
Nancy*	1	Avonside (3024)	0-6-0T	1908
Dinmor	F511	Fowler (3900011)	4wDM	1947
—	LM11	Ruhrthaler (1082)	4wDM	1936
—	9	M/Rail (115U093)	4wDH	1970
—	LM350	Simplex (60SL748)	4wDM	1980
—	LM91	R/Hornsby (371962)	4wDM	1952
—	LM131	R/Hornsby (379086)	4wDM	1955
—	LM87	R/Hornsby (329696)	4wDM	1952
—	LM131	R/Hornsby (382809)	4wDM	1955
—	LM260	Deutz (57841)	0-4-0DM	1965
—	LM180	Deutz (57122)	0-4-0DM	1960
—	LM186	Deutz (57132)	0-4-0DM	1960
—	—	Hunslet (6075)	4wDM	1961

*Nancy under restoration at Alan Keef Ltd, Ross on Wye

5ft 3in gauge

Name	No	Builder	Type	Built
—	SZA 979	Scammel lorry	2-2wDM	1959

2ft gauge

Name	No	Builder	Type	Built
—	D5	H/Hunslet (2659)	4wDM	1942
—	1	H/Hunslet (7340)	4wDM	1940
—	2	H/Hunslet (7341)	4wDM	1940
—	3	H/Hunslet (7341)	4wDM	1943
—	LM198	R/Hornsby (398076)	4wDM	1954

1ft 10in gauge (Ex Guinness locomotives)

Name	No	Builder	Type	Built
—	22	Spence	0-4-0T	1912
—	31	Planet (3446)	4wDM	1950
—	36	Planet (3447)	4wDM	1950
—	26	Planet (3255)	4wDM	1948

Railcars

Name	No	Builder	Type	Built
—	*5	Drewry Car (1945)	4wDMR	1927
—	C11	Bord na Móna	4wDMR	
—	C42	Wickham (7129)	4wPMR	1955
—	C47	Bord na Móna	4wPMR	1958
—	C56	Wickham (7681)	4wPMR	1957
—	W6/11-4	Wickham (9673)	2-2-0PM	1964

*built as 5ft 3in gauge inspection car for Great Southern Railway, regauged in 1994

C42 used as unpowered p-way trolley

Rolling stock
Tralee & Dingle coaches 47C (6T), 45C (7T), 48C (8T) and 44C (10T) (all built 1890) ; Great Northern Railway (Ireland) AU345 (built 1955) and Alan Keef-built No 13 (built 1997)
GNR Gardiner 389 (built Dundalk 1951) bus

Museum | County Donegal Railway Restoration Society | County Donegal

Member: HRA
Old Station House opened as a permanent Railway Museum & Heritage Centre from Easter 1995
Location/Headquarters: Old Station House, Tyrconnell Street, Donegal Town, Co Donegal, Ireland
Telephone: (00353-7497 [from UK]) (07497 [from Ireland]) 22655
Fax: (00353-7497 [from UK]) (07497 [from Ireland]) 23843
Internet address: *e-mail:* rrailway@gofree.indigo.ie
Web site: http://cdrrs.future.easyspace.com/
Contacts: Anne Temple
Public opening: October-May Monday-Friday 09.00-16.00 (closed weekends). June-September

Locomotives

Name	No	Origin	Class	Type	Built
Drumboe*	5	CDR	5	2-6-4T	1907

*on loan from the Foyle Valley Railway

Stock
1 CDR brake/third coach No 28
1 CDR railcar No 14
1 CDR trailer No 5
1 CDR combined goods/cattle and horse van (247 of 1893)
1 goods van

Viewing of all rolling stock is by arrangement only

Monday-Saturday 09.00-17.00, Sunday 14.00-17.00
Membership details: From above address
Membership journal: *The Phoenix*

Special notes: Outline planning permission has been received for a 3/4-mile long line from the station to Gorrelks crossing

Steam Centre | Cumann Traenach na Gaeltacht Láir | County Donegal

This stretch of track has been laid on the formation of the Fintown-Glenties line. The railway runs along the shore of Lough Finn and it is planned to have a dual ride, out by rail and return by boat. The rolling stock presently used consists of an ex-mining Simplex locomotive with three turn of the century (19th/20th) passenger tramcars from Charleroi (Belgium)
Location/headquarters: Fintown Railway Station, Fintown, Co Donegal, Eire
Main station: Fintown Station
Car park: Located at station area
Access by public transport: Local buses
Refreshment facilities: Local café

Locomotives

Name	No	Builder	Type	Built
—	LM77	R/Hornsby (329680)	4wDM	1952
—	—	M/Rail (102T007)	4wDM	1974

Railcar

Name	No	Origin	Class	Type	Built
—	18	CDRJC	—	Diesel railcar	1940

Rolling stock
3 Belgian tramcars

at top of station lane
Souvenir shop: Located at station area
Length of line: 2.5 miles (3ft gauge)

Museum: Not in operation but a collection of antiquated farm machinery is being restored
Period of public operation: June — Monday/Friday 13.00-16.00,

Eire

Sunday 13.00-17.00; July-September Monday/Friday 11.00-17.00, weekends 1.00-18.00. Departures from Fintown every half hour

Special events: Easter Specials, Halloween Train, Santa Specials in December
On site facilities: Toilet, it is also hoped to have a playground in

operation
Membership details: Membership Secretary, c/o above address
Membership journal: *An Mhuc Dhubh* — annually

Steam Centre — Irish Steam Preservation Society — County Laois

Member: HRA, NTET
Location: Stradbally Hall, eight miles from Athy, six miles from Portlaoise (on N80 road).
Telephone: 00353 502 25444 (from UK)
Internet address: *Web site:* www.irishsteam.ie
Access by public transport: Irish Rail train to Athy or Portlaoise. Kavanagh's Bus Portlaoise-Stradbally-Athy-Carlow (Monday-Saturday), also Bus Eireann Waterford-Kilkenny-Stradbally-Portlaoise-Athlone (one daily service including Sunday)
On site facilities: 3ft gauge railway
Catering facilities: None on site but town centre quarter-mile away
Length of line: 1km
Public opening: Easter Sunday and Stradbally Point-to-Point Races* — 11 April; Easter Monday — 12 April; May Bank Holiday weekend Sunday & Monday — 2/3 May; Stradbally Point-to-Point Races* —

Industrial locomotives

Name	No	Builder	Type	Built
—	2	Barclay (2264)	0-4-0WT	1949
—	—	Hunslet (2281)	4wDM	1941
Nippy	—	Planet (2014)	4wDM	1936
—	4	R/Hornsby (326052)	4wDM	1952

Stock
1 passenger coach; 2 ballast wagons; 1 brake van

9 May; June Bank Holiday weekend Sunday & Monday — 6/7 June; 40th National Steam Rally* and August Bank Holiday weekend Sunday & Monday — 1/2 August; October Bank Holiday weekend Sunday & Monday — 26/27 October.
Trains run as required 1430-17.00 on all dates except 1/2 August when 12.00-18.30
*On these dates admission charge in addition to train fare.
Any additional operating dates which may be arranged will be

shown on the web site
Special notes: This is the longest established heritage railway in Ireland, now in its 36th year. It is hoped to reopen the Steam Museum in Stradbally in 2004. Please contact Rally Secretary, ISPS, Bunnacrannagh, Timahoe Road, Stradbally, Co Laois for further details or telephone above number or visit web site. All trains will be operated by a veteran diesel locomotive, pending repairs to the steam locomotive

---

Museum — Irish Traction Group — County Tipperary

Member: HRA
Location: The former goods store adjacent to Carrick-on-Suir railway station
Operating society/organisation: Irish Traction Group, 31 Hayfield Road, Bredbury, Stockport, Cheshire SK6 1DE, England
Telephone: 07713 159869 (Mon-Sat 09.00-18.00 only)
Car park: Available in station goods yard
Access by public transport: Infrequent train service. Services operated by Bus Eireann from

Locomotives/Railcar

Name	No	Origin	Class	Manufacturer	Type	Built
—	1	NIR	DH	E/Electric (D1266)	6wDH	1969
—	2	NIR	DH	E/Electric (D1267)	6wDH	1969
—	3	NIR	DH	E/Electric (D1268)	6wDH	1969
—	A3R	CIE	001/A	M/Vickers (889)	Co-Co	1955
—	A39	CIE	001/A	M/Vickers (925)	Co-Co	1956
—	B103	CIE	101/B	BRCW (DEL22)	A1A-A1A	1956
—	226	CIE	201/C	M/Vickers (972)	Bo-Bo	1957
—	C231	CIE	201/C	M/Vickers (977)	Bo-Bo	1957
—	G601	CIE	601/G	Deutz (56119)	4wDH	1956
—	G611	CIE	611/G	Deutz (57225)	4wDH	1962
—	G616	CIE	611/G	Deutz (57227)	4wDH	1962
—	G617	CIE	611/G	Deutz (57229)	4wDH	1962
—	712	CIE	–	Wickham (8919)	4wDH	1962

166

Eire

Dublin, Limerick and Waterford
Facilities: Toilets on IE station. Site is located quarter-mile from town centre
Special events: Operation of railtours over IE/NIR systems
Opening times: Premises not open to the public, although most locomotives are stabled outside.

Notes:
A3R and A39 are stored at IE Inchicore Works
G611 and G617 currently on loan to Downpatrick Steam Railway
C231 is stored at IE Inchicore Works
712 is currently on loan to Downpatrick Steam Railway

| Timetable Service | Waterford & Suir Valley Railway | Co Waterford |

This heritage narrow gauge railway follows over 6km of the route of the abandoned Waterford-Dungarvan line. The line runs mostly along the picturesque banks of the River Suir between Kilmeaden and Waterford offering panoramic views of the River Suir, rolling farmland and mountains
Location: Kilmeaden station, Kilmeaden, Co Waterford on the R680.
Contact: Maria Kyte, Business Development Manager, Waterford & Suir Valley Railway Co, Chamber of Commerce, George's Street, Waterford
Telephone: 00353 (0) 51 311137
Fax: 00353 (0) 51 876002
Internet address: *E-mail:* wsvr@waterfordchamber.ie
Web site: www.wsvrailway.ie
Access by public transport: Suirway bus service to Kilmeaden (schedule can vary)
Length of line: 6km, 3ft gauge railway. The line is currently being extended to 10km but will not be open for 2004 season
Catering facilities: Plans are in hand for cafeteria at Kilmeaden for 2004 season
Souvenir shop: Kilmeaden
Car parking: On site
Public opening: Provisional schedule for 2004 is April to September — Tuesday to Friday 11.00-16.00, Saturdays and Sundays 12.00-17.00
Special events: Halloween Ghost Trips — October; Santa Trips — December
Facilities for disabled: Wheelchairs accessible to train carriages, ticket office, shop and toilets

Industrial locomotives

Name	No	Builder	Type	Built
—	LM179	Deutz (57121)	0-4-0DM	1960
—	LM183	Deutz (57127)	0-4-0DM	1960
—	—	M/Rail (60SP382)	4wDM	1969

Stock
Two carriages built specially for the railway. The steel coaches have approximately two thirds of the accommodation in open toastrack seating, the remainder being an enclosed saloon, accessed from an end veranda

Visitors enjoy a trip on the Waterford & Suir Valley Railway, a Deutz-built diesel hauls the line's passenger coaches under Whela's Bridge. *W&SVR*

Originally closed in 1961, the West Clare Railway is being recreated at the triangular Moyasta Junction station where only the original station house survives. The line was made famous (or infamous) by the Percy French song called 'Are ye right there, Michael'

Location/headquarters: West Clare Railway, Moyasta Junction, Kilrush, Co Clare, Republic of Ireland
Telephone: 065 9051284
Internet address: *Web site:* www.westclarerailway.com
Chief Executive: Jackie Whelan
Access by public transport: On National Route N67 between Kilrush and Kilkee

Locomotives

Name	No	Builder	Type	Built
Slieve Callan	5*	Dübs (2890)	0-6-2T	1892
—	—	RFS (101L)	4wDH	1989

*an original West Clare Railway locomotive undergoing restoration in England

Rolling stock
2 carriages

Main station: Moyasta Junction
Car park: Located beside station
Length of line: 1.25 miles (3ft gauge), ongoing construction
On site facilities: Refreshments located in carriage beside station, Souvenir Shop and Museum located in Station House. The main depot is also located at Moyasta Junction
Period of public operation: Daily all year round, 10.00-18.00
Facilities for disabled: Yes, including wheelchair
Membership details: Membership Secretary, c/o above address

Miniature Railways

Audley End Railway, Essex

Audley End, Saffron Walden, Essex. Tel: (01799) 541354 or 541956
Internet address: e-mail — aee@farming.co.uk   web site: —www.audley-end-railway.co.uk
General Manager: H. T. White
Opening details: 20/21, 27/28 March; 1-6, 12/13, 19/20, 26/27 June; 3/4, 10/11, 17-31 July; 1-31 August; 1-5, 11/12, 18/19, 25/16 September; 2/3, 9/10, 16/17, 23-31 October. Trains run from 14.00, except on Bank Holidays and in December which is from 11.00
Special events: 40th Anniversary Celebrations — 16 May; Children's Special Event Day — 29 June; Steam Gala 12 September; Santa Specials 4/5, 11, 23 December
10.25in gauge; 1.5 miles long; 5 steam, 3 diesel locomotives
Public access: Rail to Audley End (1 mile), free car park
Site facilities: Ticket office, shop and light refreshments, toilets, large picnic area
Facilities for disabled: New carriage built in 2002 to enable wheelchair access
Note: (Postal address) Audley End Estate Office, Brunketts, Wendens Ambo, Saffron Walden, Essex CB11 4JL

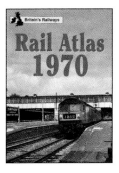
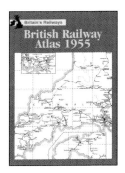

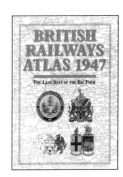
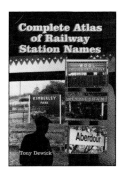

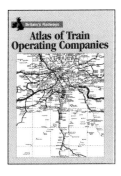
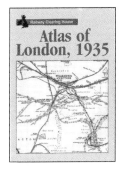

Dobwalls Family Adventure Park

Dobwalls, Nr Liskeard, Cornwall PL14 6HB. Tel: (01579) 320325/321129. Fax: (01579) 321345
General Manager: Lyn Southern
Opening details: Daily Easter-end of October. 10.30-17.00. Closed some days in early/late season
7.25in gauge; two 1-mile long routes; 6 steam and 4 diesel locomotives
Public access: By train to Liskeard — 3 miles; by bus — National Express coaches to/from Cornwall via
Plymouth stop in Dobwalls village; By car — signposted off A38
Site facilities: Refreshments, picnic areas, souvenirs and gift shop, children's indoor and outdoor adventure
playground, wildlife art gallery, steam back in time. Toilets inc disabled, mother & baby facilities
Facilities for disabled: Wheelchair access throughout (free loan, subject to availability), toilets

Great Cockcrow Railway, Surrey

Hardwick Lane, Lyne, Chertsey, Surrey. Tel: Mon-Fri (01932) 255514; Sun (01932) 565474
Opening details: Every Sunday Easter to October inclusive, 14.00-17.30
7.25in gauge; choice of two routes, each approx 2 miles; 20 steam locomotives, 1 electric, 3 petrol (6 normally in
service). Journey time about 15-20min. Unique signalling system worked from 4 signalboxes
Public access: Chertsey railway station (1.25 miles); London Buslines 561, 586 Holloway Hill (half-mile), free
car park
Site facilities: Toilet, light refreshments, picnic area. Disabled facilities and access
Special note: Sponsored by Ian Allan Group. Send 20p SAE for brochure. Fare £2.50

Kerr's Miniature Railway

West Links Park, Arbroath, Angus. Tel: (01241) 879249
(Along the sea front to the west of town)
General Manager: Mathew B. Kerr
Internet addresses: e-mail: kmr@kerr12.f9.co.uk   *Web site:* www.geocities.com/kerr_scotland
Opening details: Easter-end of September — weekends (14.00-17.00). All of July and first half of August —
daily 11.30-14.00-17.00, but trains usually run from noon onwards. All times weather permitting
10.25 in gauge; 400yd (alongside ScotRail line); 3 steam, 2 diesel, 2 petrol
Public access: ScotRail Arbroath station 1.5 miles; Strathtay Buses route A92
Site facilities: None, but park has toilets, snack bar, etc

Lightwater Valley Theme Park, North Yorkshire

North Stainley, Nr Ripon, North Yorkshire. Tel: 0870 458 0070 (24 hours), 0870 458 0040 (administration/party
bookings)
Opening details: Easter-October (daily in June/July/August). Telephone for details
Operations & Maintenance Dept: P. Walker
15in gauge; 1 mile long; 1 diesel
Public access: Main line station Harrogate (12 miles) and Thirsk (9 miles), free car park
Site facilities: 125 acres of country park featuring unique white knuckle rides including the world's longest
rollercoaster, family attractions, go-karting. Wide range of catering facilities and themed shopping malls

Moors Valley Railway, Dorset

Moors Valley Country Park, Horton Road, Ashley Heath, Nr Ringwood, Dorset. Tel: (01425) 471415
General Manager: Mr J. A. W. Haylock
Internet address: e-mail: info@moorsvalley.co.uk web site: www.moorsvalleyrailway.co.uk
Opening details: Weekends all year; daily all school holidays and Spring Bank Holiday to mid-September. Santa
Specials in December.
Special events: Tank Engine Day — 14 March; Railway Open Day — 28 March; Grand Summer Gala — 5/6
June; American Weekend — 3/4 July; Hornby/LGB Railways Weekend — 24/25 July; Wessex Narrow Gauge
Exhibition — 20 September; Tinkerbell Rally — 2/3 October; Santa Specials — 5, 12 December
7.25 in gauge; 1 mile long; 10 steam locomotives
Public access: Wilts & Dorset bus X34, from Bournemouth/Ringwood to Ashley Heath
Site facilities: Picnic areas, lakeside walks, adventure playground, railway shop and refreshments all set in the
beautiful Moors Valley Country Park. Car park and toilets (including disabled)

Heritage Railway Association

Company Limited by Guarantee and not having a share capital.
Registered in England No 2226245
(Registered Office: 2 Littlestone Road, New Romney, Kent TN28 8PL)
President: Dame Margaret Weston DBE
Vice Presidents: Ian Allan OBE, Allan Garraway MBE, Brian Simpson MEP

Friends of HRA Membership Secretary:
Ian Leigh, 206B Crowfield House, North Row, Milton Keynes, MK9 3LQ.
E-mail: ileigh@dialstart.net

Corporate Membership Secretary:
Steve Wood, 15 Croftlands Drive, Ravenglass, Cumbria CA18 1SJ
Tel: 01229 717080 (weekends)
E-mail: woodsysteve@hotmail.com

Members of the Heritage Railway Association

UK Affiliate Members (not in the main part of the book)

Association of Community Rail Partnerships: Dr P. Salvenson, Brian Jackson Centre, New North Parade, Huddersfield HD1 5JP

Brookes No 1 Locomotive Co: Mr D. R. C. Moncton, 10 Blenheim Terrace, Woodhouse Lane, Leeds LS2 9HX

Edmondson Ticket Printing Co: Pat & Andrea Geall, Proprietors, 1 Winchester Drive, Muxton, Telford, Shropshire TF2 8SJ

English Welsh & Scottish Railways: Mr P Johnson, Loco Engineer, Toton TNMD, Toton Sidings, Long Eaton, Nottingham NG10 1HA

Europe Railway Heritage Trust: Mr M. Pease, 52 Marian Street, Blaengarw, Bridgend CF32 8AG

Guild of Railway Artists: Mr F. Hodges, Chief Executive Officer, 45 Dickins Road, Warwick CV34 5NS

Gullane Entertainment plc: Mathew Way, Live Events Manager, Stoneham Gate, Stoneham Lane, Eastleigh, Hants SO50 9PB

Lloyd's Railway Society: Mr P. E. Wood, 30 Beechwood Road, Caterham, Surrey CR3 6NA

Locomotive Club of Great Britain: Mr R. L. Patrick, 8 Wolviston Ave, Bishopgate, York YO1 3DD

LocoRH200 DE No 424839: Mr B Cunningham, 20 Ladybrook, Chapel Park, Newcastle upon Tyne

Marsh (UK) Ltd: Mr A. J. C. Brown, No 1, The Marsh Centre, London EC1 8DX

Transport Trust: Mr D. Muirhead, 202 Lambeth Road, London SE1 7JW

Westinghouse Signals Ltd: Helen Webb, PO Box 79, Pew Hill, Chippenham, Wiltshire SN15 1ND

Overseas Affiliate Members

Australian Railway Historical Society: Mr R. Jowett, New South Wales Division, 67 Renwick St, Redfern, NSW 2016, Australia*Puffing Billy Railway:* Mr

Mel Elliot, PO Box 451, Belgrave, Victoria 3160, Australia

Stoomscentrum Maldegem: Rik Degruyter, De Streep 19, B-8340 Damme-Sysele, Belgium

Stoompoorlijn Dendermonde-Puurs: Mr Jaak Serckx, Station Baasrode Noord, Fabrieksstraat 118, B-9200, Baasrode, Belgium

Additional Corporate Members not listed in the main part of the book

Aln Valley Railway Society: Mr S. Manley, Alnwick Station, Alnwick, Northumberland NE66 2NP

Altrincham Electric Railway Preservation Society: Mr A. D. Macfarlane, 25 Prestbury Avenue, Timperley, Altrincham, Cheshire WA15 8HY

Battle of Britain Locomotive Preservation Society:
Mr J. Gartside, 66 Hawthorn Hill, Letchworth, Herts SG6 4HQ

171

Bridgend Valleys Railway:
Mr J. Leach, 10 Y-Wern, Bettws, Bridgend, Mid Glamorgan CF32 8RR

Britain's Great Little Railways: Mr M. B. Beevers, 64 Bullar Road, Southampton SO18 1GS

Britannia Locomotive Society:
Mr A. Sixsmith, 6 Vermont Grove, Peterborough PE3 6BN

Bulleid Society Ltd:
Mr A. J. Fry, 28 Houndean Rise, Lewes, Sussex BN7 1EQ

Caerphilly Railway Society Ltd: Mr A. Smith, 51 Worcester Crescent, Newport NP9 7NX

Camelot Locomotive Society: Mr P. W. Gibbs, 13 Clarendon Road, High Wycombe, Bucks HP13 7AW

Class 45/1 Preservation Society: Mr N. Burden, 97 Richmond Park Crescent, Handsworth, Sheffield S13 8HF

Class 56 Group: Tim Dawe, 1 Stanley Avenue, Sutton Coldfield B75 7EQ

Cornish Steam Locomotive Preservation Society Ltd:
Mr M. Orme, 3 Jubilee Terrace, Goonhavern, Truro, Cornwall TR4 9JY

Cravens Heritage Trains:
Mr G. Thorp, The Thatched Cottage, High Wych Lane, Sawbridgeworth, Herts CM2 0JN

Darlington Railway Preservation Society: Mr M. Bentley, 64 Dimsdale View East, Porthill, Newcastle under Lyme, ST5 8HL

Dean Forest Locomotive Group:
Mr J. S. Metherall, 15 Sudbrook Way, Gloucester GL4 4AP

Darjeeling Himalayan Railway Society:
Mr P. K. Jordan, Lime Tree Lodge, Thorpe Road, Mattersley, Doncaster DN10 5ED

Devon Diesel Society Ltd: Mr D. Martin, 89 Osprey Park, Thornbury, Bristol BS35 1LZ

Diesel and Electric Group:
Mr J. E. Cronin, The Old Goods Shed, Williton Station, Williton, Somerset TA4 4RQ

Diesel Unit Preservation Associates Ltd: Mr M. Cornell, 24 Ashbury Drive, Marks Tey, Colchester, Essex CO6 1XW

Dolgarrog Railway Society:
Mr P. Smith, 84 Gorlan, Conwy LL32 8RR

East Essex Locomotive Preservation Society: Mr R. Moore 7 Woodbine Grove, Enfield, Middx EN2 0EA

Eastleigh Railway Preservation Society Ltd:
Michael Bragg, 7 Wheatears Drive, West Wellow, Romsey, Hants SO51 6RA

Eden Valley Railway Trust:
Ms G. Boyd, 1 Victoria Road, Barnard Castle, Co Durham DL12 8HW

EPB Preservation Group: Mr R. Baines, 73 Woodhurst Avenue, Petts Wood, Orpington, Kent BR5 1AT

Firefly Trust: Mr S. Bee, 9 Shenstone, Lindfield, West Sussex RH16 2PU

Foxcote Manor Society:
Mr G. Heddon, 31 Lordsmill Road, Shavington, Crewe, Cheshire CW2 5HB

Galatea Locomotive Trust Ltd: Mrs H. I. Evans, Far Cockcroft Farm, Rishworth, Sowerby Bridge, West Yorkshire HX6 4RE

Gloucester Railcars Trust Ltd:
Mr M. Hancocks, 19 Abbots Road, Abbots Langley, Herts WD5 0AY

Glyn Valley Tramway Group:
David Norman, 4 Yew Tree Court, Gresford, Wrexham LL12 8ET

Great Western Heritage Trust:
Stephen Atkins, Dowsers Cottage, 25 High Street, Meysey Hampton, Glos GL7 5JT

GWR 813 Preservation Fund:
Mr P. Goss, 23 Hatchmere, Thornbury, Bristol BS35 2EU

Hampshire & Sussex Units Preservation Society: Mr C. Dann, 48 Hollybrook Park, Bordon, Hants GU35 0DL

Hastings Diesels Ltd:
Mr J. White, The Rail Engineering Centre, Bridgeway, St Leonards on Sea, East Sussex TN38 8AP

Hull & Barnsley Railway Stock Fund: Mr A. E. Hallman, 6 Chequerfield Court, Pontefract, West Yorkshire WF8 2TQ

Kingdom of Fife Railway Association (The):
Mr A. Sawson, 54 Townend Place, Kirkcaldy, Fife KY1 1HB

Lambton No 29 Syndicate:
Mr J. M. Richardson, 509 Westgate Apartments, York YO26 4ZF

Lancashire & Yorkshire Railway Preservation Society: Mr E. Ring, 111 Huddersfield Road, Elland, West Yorkshire HX5 0EE

Lincolnshire Coast Light Railway Historical Vehicles Trust:
Mr H. L. Goy, 12 Giles Street, Cleethorpes DN35 8AE

Locomotive Owners Group (Scotland) Ltd: Mr H. Stevenson, 28 Hazeldean Avenue, Bo'ness, West Lothian EH51 0NJ

London & North Western Society:
Mr S. C. Fountain, 4 Ferrers Way, Darley Abbey, Derby DE22 2AA

Lynton & Barnstaple Light Railway:
Mr D. Hill, 8 Long Lakes, Williton, Taunton, Somerset TA4 4SR

Maid Marian Locomotive Fund: Mr H. Johns, 139 Stoops Lane, Doncaster DN4 7RG

Market Drayton Railway Preservation Society:
Mr R. Pitt, 1 Queens Drive, Newport, Shropshire TF10 7EU

Maunsell Locomotive Society:
Mr J. S. Pilcher, 312 Riverside Mansions, Garnett Street, Wapping, London E1 9SZ

Merchant Navy Locomotive Preservation Society Ltd:
Mr R. Abercrombie, 12 Inglewood Avenue, Heatherside, Camberley, Surrey GU15 1RJ

Midsomer Norton Station Project:
John Baxter, 12 Huxley Close,
Shrewsbury SY2 6JR

Modern Railway Society of Ireland:
Mr D. Brian King, 4 York Avenue,
Whitehead, Co Antrim, N. Ireland
BT38 9QT

Moseley Railway Trust: Dr John
Rowlands, 10 Braxfield Court, St
Annes Road West, St Annes on Sea,
Lancs FY8 1LQ

*North Eastern Locomotive
Preservation Group:*
Mr C. Hatton, 20 Sorrell Court,
Marton, Middlesbrough TS7 8RZ

*North Gloucestershire Railway Co
Ltd:* Mr R. H. Wales,
'Wellesbourne', Oakfield Street,
Tivoli, Cheltenham, Gloucestershire
GL33 8HR

North Somerset Railway Co Ltd:
Mr D. G. Edwards, 40 Belvedere,
Lansdown Road, Bath, Somerset
BA1 5HR

Ongar Railway Preservation Society:
Mr B. Ayton, 75 Highland Road,
Nazeing, Essex EN9 2PU

*Princess Royal Locomotive Trust
Ltd:*
Mr H. Routledge, 29 Crown Way,
Chellaston, Derby DE73 1NU

Red Rose Society:
Mr G. Jones, Astley Green Colliery
Museum, Higher Green Lane, Astley,
Tyldesley, Manchester M29 7JB

*Salisbury Steam Locomotive
Preservation Trust:* Mr E. J. Roper,
33 Victoria Road, Wilton, Salisbury,
Wiltshire SP2 0OZ

*Scottish Locomotive Preservation
Trust Fund:* Mr F. Landrey, 45
Sycamore Drive, Hamilton ML3 7HF

*Sir Nigel Gresley Locomotive
Preservation Trust Ltd:* Mr A. Pitt,
30 Barham Road, Stevenage, Herts
SG2 9HX

South Wales Pannier Group:
Mr J. Melhuish, 74 Coychurch Road,
Bridgend, Mid Glamorgan
CF31 2AP

Southern Electric Group:
Mr B. Cakebread, 41 The Drive,
Shoreham by Sea, West Sussex
BN43 5GD

Southern Locomotives Ltd:
Mr S. Troy, 16 Arcadia Road, Istead
Rise, Meopham, Kent DA13 9EH

Southwold Railway Society (The):
Mr J. Bennett, 1 Barnaby Green,
Southwold, Suffolk IP15 6AP

Stanier 8F Locomotive Society Ltd:
Mr G. Moon, 5 Orchid Fields, St
Christopher's Way, Burnham on Sea,
Somerset TA8 2NU

Steam Power Trust '65:
Mr A. R. Thompson, The Station
House, Penshaw, Houghton le Spring
DH4 7PQ

Stephenson Locomotive Society: Mr
B. F. Gilliam, 25 Regency Close,
Chigwell, Essex IG7 5NY

*Stratford on Avon, Broadway
Railway Society:*
Mr G. Turner, Manor Lodge,
Penelope Gardens, Manor Road,
Wickhamford, Evesham, Worcs
WR11 6SG

*Suburban Electric Railway
Association:*
Mr R. Davidson, 6 Coombfield
Drive, Darenth, Dartford, Kent
DA2 7LQ

*Timothy Hackworth Victorian &
Railway Museum:* Mr A. Pearce,
Soho Cottages, Shildon, Co Durham
DL4 1PQ

*Underground Railway Rolling Stock
Trust:* Mr D. C. Alexander, 13 Irvine
Drive, Stoke Mandeville, Aylesbury
HP22 5UN

Urie Locomotive Society:
Mr A. Ball, 'Lavenham', Adams
Lane, Selborne, Alton, Hants GU34
3LJ

*Wainwright 'C' Preservation
Society:* Mr N. W. DeMaid, Flat 2,
The Old Stable House, Bromley,
Kent BR1 3JF

Weardale Railway Trust:
Mr G. Chatsfield, Stanhope Station,
Bondisle, Bishop Auckland, Co
Durham DL13 2YS

Western Locomotive Association: Mr
D. H. Tompkins, 23 Haytor Drive,
Newton Abbot, Devon TQ12 4DR

Worcester Locomotive Society Ltd:
Mr A. T. Dowling, 9 Queens Court,
Ledbury, Herefordshire HR4 9DN

1857 Society: Mr G. West, 21A
Broad Street, Brigtown, Cannock,
West Midlands WS11 3DA

4247 Ltd: Mr N. Powles, Station
House, Station Road, Lower
Heyford, Oxon OX6 3PD

48624 Locomotive Soc: G. Robb, 26
Old Gardens Close, Tunbridge
Wells, Kent TN2 5ND

6201 Princess Elizabeth Society Ltd:
Mr A. Harries, 1 Ormerod Close,
Sandbach, Cheshire CW11 4HA

35006 Locomotive Co Ltd: Mr G.
Chidley, 102 Anfield Court, Russell
Terrace, Leamington Spa, CV31
1HD

*71000 Duke of Gloucester Steam
Locomotive Trust Ltd:* Mr F. Reid,
2 Bodmin Avenue, Marthside,
Southport PR4 9TU

8E Railway Association: Mr A.
Ashurst, 149 St Mary Street,
Latchford, Warrington, Cheshire
WA4 1EL

LM2MT 46464 Trust: Mr I. Hopley,
The Carmyllie Pilot Co Ltd, 6 Ninian
Place, Portlethen AB12 4QW

*44871 Sovereign Preservation
Society:* Mr D. Buchan, Clickham,
Milnab Terrace, Crieff, Perthshire
PH7 4ED

Applicant Organisations

Amman Valley Railway Society

*Bolton Derelict Railway
Preservation Society*

*Bury Port & Gwendraeth Railway
Co Ltd*

*Colne Valley Railway Preservation
Society*

*Derwent Valley Railway (see main
section)*

Gwendraeth Valley Railways Co Ltd

Haig Colliery Mining Museum

Heaton Park Electric Tramway

Holden F5 Steam Locomotive Trust

*Llanelli & Mynydd Mawr Railway
Co Ltd*

Railway Vehicle Preservations Ltd

*Rhondda & Cynon Valleys Railway
Society*

South Eastern & Chatham Railway Preservation Society

Stainmore Railway Co Ltd

Waltham Abbey Gunpowder Mills

Waverley Route Heritage Association

Britain's Great Little Railways

Brookside Miniature Railway: Mr C. Halsall, Brookside Garden Centre, Macclesfield Road, Poynton, Cheshire SK12 1BY

Dragon Miniature Railway: Mr B. Lomas, Wyevale Garden Centre, Otterspool, Marple, Cheshire SK6 7HG

Eastleigh Lakeside Railway:

Lakeside Country Park, Wide Lane, Eastleigh, Hants

Exmoor Steam Railway: (see main section)

Fairbourne Railway (see main section)

Haigh Hall Railway: Mr T. Sharratt, Haigh Hall Country Park, Haigh, Wigan, Lancs WN2 1PE

Little Giant Railways: Merton Hill Railway, Merton Abbey Mills, London SW19 2RD

Moors Valley Railway (see miniature section)

Mull Rail (see main section)

Perrygrove Railway: Mr M. Crofts, Perrygrove Farm,

Coleford, Glos GL16 8QB

Road, Rail & Waterway: Mr J. Shackell, 27 Witney Road, Duckington, Witney, Oxon OX8 7TX

Rudyard Lake Railway: Mr P. Hanson, Rudyard Old Station, Rudyard, Leek, Staffs ST13 8PF

Shibden Miniature Railway: Shibden Park, Listers Road, Halifax, W. Yorks HX3 6XG

Swanley New Barn Railway: Mr P. Jackson, New Barn Lane, Swanley, Kent

Weston Miniature Railway: Mr R. Bullock, Marine Parade, Weston-super-Mare, Somerset

With some spectacular scenery to be seen, Giant's Causeway & Bushmill Railway No 1 *Tyrone* heads towards the Giant's Causeway. *GC&BR*

INDEX

175

Heritage Railway Association

Anyone interested in nationwide railway preservation can become a Friend of the Heritage Railway Association. Benefits include receiving a copy of the *Heritage Railway Journal,* published three times a year, and a copy of the Annual Report, which details the work of the Association during the year. There is the opportunity of attending various business meetings, weekend meetings, which include visits to member railways, and seminars. This gives an opportunity to learn more about the preservation movement.

There is the opportunity to purchase *Railways Restored* at a reduced price and to purchase an Inter-Rail pass which allows visits to member railways at a concessionary price.

Current annual subscription is
£15 (non UK £20),
Life Membership is £200 (non UK £250).

For further information, please contact the Private Membership Secretary, or send this form (or a photcopy) to:
Ian Leigh, 206B Crowfield House, North Row, Milton Keynes, MK9 3LQ.

Application Form to become a Friend of the Heritage Railway Association

Name
....

Address
....

....

....

Post Code
....

Telephone
....

Subscription enclosed
....

Donation enclosed
....

Price £1.50

HERITAGE RAILWAYS
2004

NATIONAL TIMETABLE OF SCHEDULED SERVICES

61572

32
A

Railways
ILLUSTRATED

Heritage Railways Timetable 2004

This timetable has been produced by *Railways Illustrated* and Ian Allan Publishing Ltd and was printed by Ian Allan Printing Ltd of Hersham, Surrey.

NOTES TO THE TIMETABLE

Throughout the Timetable, the 24 hour clock is used.

Days of operation are shown on the grid at the head of most entries. The letter, or in some cases number, contained in each square denotes the service pattern for that day, and the appropriate letter or number is shown against 'service' in the timetable columns below.

Many trains have refreshment facilities. These are not shown herein as availability may vary according to staffing conditions and seasons of the year.

For details of Wine and Dine, Thomas the Tank Engine, Santa Specials and other out-of-the-ordinary facilities, please enquire of the appropriate railway company for details. Operating days for these are shown by the letter X on the grids.

The telephone number and postal address of each railway operator is shown at the head of each entry so that specific enquiries can be made direct.

The entries are mostly in alphabetical order but in some cases there has been a slight variation to meet space requirements.

It would be helpful if this timetable was read in conjunction with the annual publication *Railways Restored,* obtained from booksellers or direct from Ian Allan Publishing Ltd.

DISCLAIMER

This timetable has been compiled from information received from operating companies and is believed to be accurate. However, neither the publisher nor HRA accept any responsibility for any loss, damage or delay which may be caused by variances between this brochure and actual operations or any other cause.

© Ian Allan Publishing Ltd 2004

MARKS OF QUALITY

Some railways excel in certain fields, and in this timetable special merit markings are applied as has been thought appropriate. The symbols represent individual quality; a double symbol represents excellence. Winners in the 2002 Ian Allan Independent Railway of the Year Awards are highlighted.

	Award winner 2003		Interesting Rolling Stock		On-board catering
	On-shore catering		Interesting Engines		Interesting Stations and Signals
	Big Engines	**WC**	Loos		Views from the train

INDEX TO TIMETABLES

Front cover: Ex-LNER Class B12 No 61572 on the North Norfolk Railway. *Alan Barnes*

AVON VALLEY RAILWAY

Bitton Station, Bath Road, Bitton, Bristol BS30 6HD
Fax: 0117 932 5935   E-mail: enquiries@avonvalleyrailway.co.uk

0117 932 5538 (General Enquiries)
0117 932 7296 (Talking Timetable)
Web: www.avonvalleyrailway.co.uk

2004	1	2	3	4	5	6	7	8	9	10	11	12	13	14	15	16	17	18	19	20	21	22	23	24	25	26	27	28	29	30	31
Jan	A																														
Mar																				A											
Apr								A	A	A	A	A	A	A				B	A						A						
May	A	A	A					T	T							A				B	A							A	A	A	A
June	A	A	A			A							B	A						A					B	A					
July			A						B	A							A		A	A	A		B	A		A	A	A			B
Aug	A		A	A	A		B	A		A	A	A		B	A		A	A	A		B	A		A	A	A		A	A	A	
Sept			B	A						A							A			A					A						
Oct		T	T						A							B	A						A			A	A	A		B	A
Dec			S	S	S					S	S	S					S	S			S	S	S					A			

T denotes Thomas events, S denotes Santa Specials, see local announcements.   *No service in February and November.*

A denotes steam operation.
B denotes diesel operation.

Bitton	dep	11.00	12.15	13.30	14.45	16.00
River Boyd		No alighting or boarding				
Bitton	dep	11.25	12.40	13.55	15.10	16.25
Oldland	dep	11.45	13.00	14.15	15.30	16.45
Bitton	arr	11.50	13.05	14.20	15.35	16.50

BALA LAKE RAILWAY

The Station, Llanuwchllyn, Bala, Gwynedd LL38 2NX
Fax: 01678 540535   E-mail: balalake@freenetname.co.uk

01678 540666

2004	1	2	3	4	5	6	7	8	9	10	11	12	13	14	15	16	17	18	19	20	21	22	23	24	25	26	27	28	29	30	31
Apr			A	A			A	A	A	A	A	A	A	A	A	A	A	A		A	A	A		A	A		A	A	A		
May	A	A	A	A	A		A	A		A	A		A	A		A	A		A	A		A	A		A	A		A	A	A	A
June	A	A	A	A		A	A		A	A			A	A		A	A		A	A		A	A		A	A		A	A	A	
July	A	A		A	A		A	A	A		A	A		A	A	A		A	A		A	A	A		A	A		A	A	A	
Aug	A	A		A	A	A		A	A		A	A	A		A	A		A	A	A		A	A		A	A	A		A	A	
Sept	A	A			A	A		A	A			A	A		A	A			A	A		A	A			A	A		A	A	
Oct		A	A																												
Dec				S	S																										

S denotes Santa Specials.   *No service in January, February, March, November and December (except Santa weekend).*

Service A

Llanuwchllyn	dep	11.15	12.50	14.25	16.00
Bala	dep	11.50	13.25	15.00	16.35

Journey times:
Llanuwchllyn–Bala: Return trip 1 hour; single trip 25 minutes. Break of journey allowed at any station.
Bala–Llanuwchllyn: Return trip 1 hour 30 minutes as train stops at Llanuwchllyn to take on coal and water etc. Single journey 25 minutes.

All trains arrive at and depart from Llangower 10 minutes after leaving Llanuwchllyn and 15 minutes after leaving Bala. Trains also call by request at Pentrepiod and Bryn Hynod halts. To join the train please signal clearly to the Driver. To alight, inform the Guard when you board the train.

BRECON MOUNTAIN RAILWAY

Pant Station, Merthyr Tydfil CF48 2UP
Fax: 01685 384854   Web: www.breconmountainrailway.co.uk

01685 722988

2004	1	2	3	4	5	6	7	8	9	10	11	12	13	14	15	16	17	18	19	20	21	22	23	24	25	26	27	28	29	30	31
Mar																											A	A		A	A
Apr	A		A	A	A	A	A	A	A	A	A	A	B	A	A	A	A	A	A		A	A	A		A	A	A	A	A		
May	A	B	B	A	A	A	A	A	A		A	A		A	A		A	A		A	A	A		A	A		A	A	A	A	
June	A	A	A	A	A	A	A	A	A	A	A	A	A	A	A	A	A	A	A	A	A	A	A	A	A	A	A	A	A	A	
July	A	A	A	A	A	A	A	A	A	A	A	A	A	A	A	A	A	A	A	A	A	A	A	A	A	A	A	A	A	A	A
Aug	A	A	A	A	A	A	A	A	A	A	A	A	A	A	A	A	A	A	A	A	A	A	A	A	A	A	A	A	B	B	B
Sept	A	A		A	A		A	A		A	A		A	A		A	A		A	A		A	A		A	A		A	A	A	
Oct		A	A					A	A		A	A																			
Nov																											S	S	S	S	
Dec	S	S	S	S	S	S	S	S	S	S	S	S	S	S	S	S	S	S	S	S	S	S	S	S							

S denotes Santa Specials, see local announcements.   *No service in January and February.*

Service A

Pant	dep	11.00	12.15	13.30	14.45	16.00

Service B

11.00	12.15	13.30	14.45	16.00	17.15

BATTLEFIELD LINE

Shackerstone Station, Shackerstone, Leicestershire CV13 6NW   01827 880754

Fax: 01827 881050   Web: www.battlefield-line.railway.co.uk

2004	1	2	3	4	5	6	7	8	9	10	11	12	13	14	15	16	17	18	19	20	21	22	23	24	25	26	27	28	29	30	31
Apr									C	B	A	A	C				C	B						C	B						
May	C	B					X	X							X	X		C	B										C	B	
June					X	X							B	A						A						X	X				
July			B	A						X	X						X	X						B	A						B
Aug	A						B	A						B	A						B	A						B	A		
Sept					X	X					B	A						B	A						B	A					
Oct			C	B						X	X						C	B						C	B					X	B
Nov																											S	S			
Dec			S	S							S	S						S	S							S					

X denotes special events, S denotes Santa Specials, see local announcements.   *No service in January, February and March.*

Service A

Shackerstone	dep	11.15	12.30	13.45	15.00	16.15
Shenton	arr	11.35	12.50	14.05	15.20	16.35
Shenton	dep	11.50	13.05	14.20	15.35	16.50
Shackerstone	arr	12.10	13.25	14.40	15.55	17.10

Service B

12.30	13.45	15.00	16.15
12.50	14.05	15.20	16.35
13.05	14.20	15.35	16.50
13.25	14.40	15.55	17.10

Service C (Diesel Railcar)

12.30	13.30	14.30	15.30
12.50	13.50	14.50	15.50
13.00	14.00	15.00	16.00
13.20	14.20	15.20	16.20

BLUEBELL RAILWAY

Sheffield Park, Uckfield, East Sussex TN22 3QL

01825 720800

Fax: 01825 720804   E-mail: info@bluebell-railway.co.uk

2004	1	2	3	4	5	6	7	8	9	10	11	12	13	14	15	16	17	18	19	20	21	22	23	24	25	26	27	28	29	30	31
Jan	B	B	B	B						C	C						C	C						C	C						B
Feb	B						B	B						B	B	C	C	C	C	C	B	B						X	X		
Mar						B	B						B	B				B	B								X	B			
Apr			B	B	C	C	C	C	A	A	A	A	C	C	C	C	B	B						A	A						
May	A	A	A	C	C	C	C	X	X	C	C	C	C	C	B	B	C	C	C	C	C	B	B	C	C	C	C	C	A	A	A
June	B	B	B	B	B	B	C	C	C	C	C	A	A	C	C	C	C	C	X	X	C	C	C	C	X	X	C	C	C		
July	C	C	A	A	C	C	C	C	A	A	C	C	C	C	A	A	C	C	C	C	A	A	A	A	A	A	A	A	A	A	A
Aug	A	A	A	A	A	A	A	A	A	A	A	A	A	A	A	A	A	A	A	A	A	A	A	A	A	A	A	A	A	A	A
Sept	A	A	A	A	A	C	C	C	C	C	B	B	C	C	C	C	C	B	B	C	C	C	C	C	B	B	C	C	C	C	
Oct	C	B	B				B	B					B	B									X	X	B	B	B	B	B	X	X
Nov						B	B						B	B				B	B						B	B					
Dec			S	S						S	S						S	S					S	S		C	B	B	B	B	B

S denotes Santa Specials, X denotes special events, see local announcements.

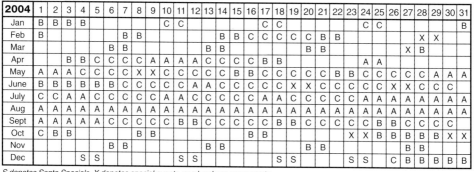

Service A

Shefield Park	dep	–	11.00	12.00	13.00	14.00	15.00	16.00	16.47
Horsted Keynes	arr	–	11.15	12.15	13.16	14.15	15.16	16.15	17.02
Horsted Keynes	dep	–	11.20	12.20	13.19	14.20	15.19	16.20	–
Kingscote	arr	–	11.33	12.33	13.32	14.33	15.32	16.33	–
Kingscote	dep	–	11.55	13.00	13.55	15.00	15.55	16.59	–
Horsted Keynes	arr	–	12.08	13.13	14.08	15.13	16.08	17.12	–
Horsted Keynes	dep	11.17	12.16	13.21	14.16	15.21	16.16	–	17.17
Shefield Park	arr	11.30	12.29	13.34	14.29	15.34	16.29	–	17.30

Service B

Shefield Park	dep	–	11.00	12.00	13.00	14.00	15.00	16.00	16.47
Horsted Keynes	arr	–	11.15	12.15	13.16	14.15	15.16	16.15	17.02
Horsted Keynes	dep	–	11.20	12.20	13.19	14.20	15.19	16.20	–
Kingscote	arr	–	11.33	12.33	13.32	14.33	15.32	16.33	–
Kingscote	dep	–	11.55	13.00	13.55	15.00	15.55	16.59	–
Horsted Keynes	arr	–	12.08	13.13	14.08	15.13	16.08	17.12	–
Horsted Keynes	dep	11.17	12.16	13.21	14.16	15.21	16.16	–	17.17
Shefield Park	arr	11.30	12.29	13.34	14.29	15.34	16.29	–	17.30

Service C

11.00	12.45	14.15	15.50
11.15	13.00	14.30	16.05
11.17	13.02	14.32	16.07
11.30	13.15	14.45	16.20
11.52	13.30	15.00	16.35
12.05	13.43	15.13	16.48
12.07	13.47	15.18	16.50
12.20	14.00	15.31	17.03

BODMIN & WENFORD RAILWAY
Bodmin General Station, Bodmin, Cornwall PL31 1AQ   **01208 73666**

Fax: 01208 77963   E-mail: manager@bodminandwenfordrailway.co.uk

2004	1	2	3	4	5	6	7	8	9	10	11	12	13	14	15	16	17	18	19	20	21	22	23	24	25	26	27	28	29	30	31
Mar										A							A			X	X				A				A		· A
Apr			X	X	A	A	A	A	C	C	C	C	A	A	A	A	A	A		A	A			A			A	A	A		
May	X	X	X	A	A					A		A	A				A		A	A			A		A	A			X	X	X
June	A	A	A	A	A	A	A	A	A	A	A	A	A	A	A	A	A	A	A	A	A	A	A	A	A	A	A	A	A	A	
July	A	A	A	A	A	A	A	A	A	A	B	B	B	B	B	B	A	A	B	B	B	B	C	C	C	C	C	C	C	C	C
Aug	C	C	B	B	B	B	A	A	B	B	B	B	B	A	A	B	B	B	B	B	A	A	B	B	B	B	B	A	A	B	B
Sept	B	B	B	X	X	A	A	A	A	A	A	A	A	A	A	A	A	X	X	A	A	A	A	A	A	A	A	A	A	A	
Oct		A		A	A				A		A	A			A		A	A				A	A	A	A	A	A	A	A	A	A
Nov				A					A																						
Dec			S	S						S	S						S	S				S	S	S		A	A	A	A	A	A

X denotes special events, S denotes Santa Specials, see local announcements.   No service in January and February.

Service A

Bodmin General	dep	10.40	11.30	12.35	14.20	15.25
Bodmin Parkway	arr	10.52	–	12.52	–	15.42
Boscarne Junction	arr	–	11.45	–	14.35	–
		D				
Boscarne Junction	dep	–	11.55	–	14.45	–
Bodmin Parkway	dep	10.55	–	13.05	–	15.53
Bodmin General	arr	11.07	12.12	13.27	15.02	16.15

Service B

	10.40	11.30	12.35	13.45	14.40	15.45	16.40
	10.52	–	12.52	–	14.57	–	16.57
	–	11.45	–	14.00	–	16.00	–
	–	11.55	–	14.08	–	16.08	–
	10.55	–	13.05	–	15.05	–	17.05
	11.07	12.12	13.27	14.25	15.27	16.25	17.25

Service C

Bodmin General	dep	10.45	11.45	12.35	13.35	14.25	15.25	16.15
Bodmin Parkway	arr	11.02	–	12.52	–	14.42	–	16.32
Boscarne Junction	arr	–	11.58	–	13.48	–	15.38	–
Boscarne Junction	dep	–	12.05	–	13.55	–	15.45	–
Bodmin Parkway	dep	11.15	–	13.05	–	14.50	–	16.40
Bodmin General	arr	11.35	12.20	13.25	14.10	15.10	16.00	17.00

Some trains call on request at Colesloggett Halt.
D   Diesel Train (only runs on certain days).

BO'NESS & KINNEIL RAILWAY
Union Street, Bo'ness, West Lothian EH51 9AQ   **01506 822298**

Web: www.srps.org.uk

Please phone or write for timetable details.

BURE VALLEY RAILWAY
Aylsham Station, Norwich Road, Aylsham, Norfolk NR11 6BW   **01263 733858**

Fax: 01263 733814   E-mail: info@bvrw.co.uk

2004	1	2	3	4	5	6	7	8	9	10	11	12	13	14	15	16	17	18	19	20	21	22	23	24	25	26	27	28	29	30	31
Jan	M																														
Feb															A	A	A	A	A	A	A	A									
Apr				A	A	A	A	A	B	B	B	B	A	A	A	A	A	A	A	A	A	A	A	A	A	A	A	A	A	A	
May	A	B	B	A	A	A	A	A	A	A	A	A	A	A	A	A	A	A	A	A	A	A	A	A	A	A	A	A	T	T	T
June	B	B	B	A	A	B	B	B	B	B	B	A	A	B	B	B	A	A	B	B	B	A	A	B	B	B	B	B	A	A	
July	B	B	B	B	B	B	B	B	B	B	B	B	B	B	B	B	B	B	B	B	B	B	B	B	B	B	B	B	B	B	B
Aug	B	B	B	B	B	B	B	B	B	B	B	B	B	B	B	B	B	B	B	B	B	B	B	B	B	B	B	B	B	B	B
Sept	B	B	B	B	B	B	B	B	B	B	B	B	A	A	A	A	A	A	A	A	A	A	A	A	T	T					
Oct																		A	A	A	A	A	A	A	A	A	A	A			
Nov																											S	S			
Dec	S	S		S	S			S	S		S	S			S	S		S	S	S	S	S	S	S	S			M	M	M	M

T denotes Thomas events, S denotes Santa Specials, M denotes Mince Pie Specials, see local announcements.   No service in March.

Service A

Aylsham	dep	10.15	12.45	15.15
Wroxham	arr	11 00	13.30	16.00
Wroxham	dep	11.30	14.00	16.30
Aylsham	arr	12.15	14.45	17.15

Service B

	10.15	11.30	12.45	14.00	15.15	16.30
	11.00	12.15	13.30	14.45	16.00	17.15
	10.15	11.30	12.45	14.00	15.15	16.30
	11.00	12.15	13.30	14.45	16.00	17.15

All trains call at intermediate stations:
Brampton (12), Buxton (17) and
Coltishall (32) minutes after leaving
Aylsham and at Coltishall (13),
Buxton (28) and Brampton (33)
minutes after leaving Wroxham.

CHASEWATER RAILWAY

Chasewater Country Park, Pool Road, Nr Brownhills, Staffs WS8 7NL 01543 452623

Fax: 01543 452623   E-mail: info@chasewaterrailway.co.uk

2004	1	2	3	4	5	6	7	8	9	10	11	12	13	14	15	16	17	18	19	20	21	22	23	24	25	26	27	28	29	30	31
Jan				C							C							C							C						
Feb	C						C							C							C							C			
Mar						C							C							C							C				
Apr				B						C	A	A						A						A							
May	C	A	A						B							B	X						A						C	A	A
June							A						B							X							A				
July			C	A							C	A						C	A						C	A					C
Aug	A						C	B						C	A						C	A						C	A	A	
Sept				C	A						C	X						C	A						C	A					
Oct			X							B							B							B							B
Nov						C							C							C							C				
Dec				S							S							S							C						

X denotes special events, S denotes Santa Specials, see local announcements.

Service A (Steam Service) and **Service B** (Diesel)

Brownhills West	dep	11.00	12.00	then every 60 minutes until	17.00
Chasetown (Church Street)	arr	11.20	12.20		17.20
Chasetown (Church Street)	dep	11.30	12.30		17.30
Brownhills West	arr	11.45	12.45		17.45

Service C (Diesel)

12.00	13.00	then every 60 minutes until	16.00
12.20	13.20		16.20
12.30	13.30		16.30
12.45	13.45		16.45

CHINNOR & PRINCES RISBOROUGH RAILWAY

Chinnor Station, Station Road, Chinnor, Oxon OX39 4ER   01844 353535

Fax: 01844 354117   E-mail: info@cprra.co.uk

2004	1	2	3	4	5	6	7	8	9	10	11	12	13	14	15	16	17	18	19	20	21	22	23	24	25	26	27	28	29	30	31
March																					X				X						
Apr				A						X	X	X	X						A						A						
May	T	T	T						A								A							A					B	X	X
June					B	A						B	A						B	A						B	A				
July			B	A						B	A						B	A						B	A						B
Aug	A						T	T						B	A						X	X						B	A	A	
Sept				A									X						A						A						
Oct			A							A								A						A							X
Dec			S	S							S	S						S	S						X	X					

X denotes special events, T denotes Thomas events, S denotes Santa Specials, M denotes Mince Pie Specials, see local announcements.   *No service in January, February and November.*

Service A

Chinnor	dep	10.00	11.00	12.15	13.30	15.00	16.30	17.30*

Service B

12.00	13.00	14.00	15.00	16.00

*This time July and August only. Journey time about 50 minutes.

CHOLSEY & WALLINGFORD RAILWAY

PO Box 16, Wallingford OX10 9YN   01491 835067

E-mail: cwrail@yahoo.co.uk   Web: www.cholsey-wallingford-railway.com

Services operate March 20th & 21st – April 10th, 11th, 12th, 24th & 25th – May 2nd, 3rd, 30th & 31st – June 20th – July 25th – August 29th & 30th – September 3rd, 4th, 5th & 26th – December 5th, 11th, 12th, 18th & 19th.

Service X

Wallingford	dep	11.10	12.10	13.10	14.10	15.10	16.10
Cholsey	dep	11.35	12.35	13.35	14.35	15.35	16.35

CLEETHORPES COAST LIGHT RAILWAY

Lakeside Station, Kings Road, Cleethorpes, Lincs DN35 0AG   01472 604657

E-mail: genoff@cclrltd.freeserve.co.uk

Trains run weekends (except November) and daily in the peak summer season.

CHURNET VALLEY RAILWAY
Cheddleton Station, Cheddleton, Staffordshire ST13 7EE   01538 360522
Fax: 01538 361848   E-mail: mgt@cheddcur.freeserve.co.uk

2004	1	2	3	4	5	6	7	8	9	10	11	12	13	14	15	16	17	18	19	20	21	22	23	24	25	26	27	28	29	30	31
Jan				A																											
Feb													T	T	T			T													
Mar				A										A					A							A					
Apr			X	X				A	A	A	A								A					X	X						
May		A	A						A							A				A										A	A
June					A								A						A							A					
July			A	A			A				A	A			A				A	A				T	T	T		T			A
Aug	A		A	A	A		A	A			A	A	A		A	A		A	A	A		A	A		A	A	A		A	A	A
Sept				A									A						A					D	D						
Oct			A									A						A												X	
Nov						X																									
Dec			S	S							S	S							S	S			S	S	S						

X denotes special events, S denotes Santa Specials, see local announcements.

Please phone or write for timetable details.

COLNE VALLEY RAILWAY
Castle Hedingham, Halstead, Essex CO9 3DZ   01787 461174
Web: www.colnevalleyrailway.co.uk

2004	1	2	3	4	5	6	7	8	9	10	11	12	13	14	15	16	17	18	19	20	21	22	23	24	25	26	27	28	29	30	31
Mar																					S							S			
Apr			S		D	S	D	S	S	S	S	D	S	D				S						S							
May	D	S	S						S							S					S								D	S	S
June	D	S	D			S									E	E	E		T	T		E	E	E		T	T				
July			S						S									S			D	D	D	S	D	D	D	S	S	D	D
Aug	S	D	D	S	S	D	D	S	D	D	S	S	D	D	S	D	D	S	S	D	D	S	D	D	S	S	D	D	S	S	D
Sept					S							S							S						S						
Oct		T	T		V	V	V		T	T							S							S		D	S	D			S
Dec					SS						SS	SS						SS	SS												

Please phone for timetable details.   *No service in January, February and November.*

Service S – Steam
Service D – Diesel
Service V – Victorian
Service T – Thomas
Service SS – Santa Specials
Service E – Educational School Days

DEAN FOREST RAILWAY
Forest Road, Lydney, Gloucestershire GL15 4ET   01594 843423
Fax: 01594 845840   E-mail: subscribe@deanforestrailway.co.uk   Web: www.deanforestrailway.co.uk

2004	1	2	3	4	5	6	7	8	9	10	11	12	13	14	15	16	17	18	19	20	21	22	23	24	25	26	27	28	29	30	31
Mar																					A								A			
Apr			A					A	A	A	A				X	X	X	X						A	A						
May	A	A	A					A								A						A							A	A	A
June		D	X	X	X	X		D			D	A			D			D	A		D			D	A			D			
July		D	A			A			D	A			A			D	A			A			D	A			A				D
Aug	A		A	A		A	X			A	A		A	A		A	A		A	A		A	A		A	A		A	A	A	
Sept	A			X	X			A			X	X				A			D	A			A			X	X		A		A
Oct			A								A							A						A							A
Dec				S							S	S						S	S				S	S							

X denotes special events, S denotes Santa Specials, see local announcements.   *No service in January, February and November.*

Service A – Steam with DMU shuttle to Whitecroft.   **Service D** – DMU Service.   *Please phone for timetable details.*

DARTMOOR RAILWAY

Okehampton Station, Okehampton, Devon EX20 1EJ

01837 55637
FAX: 01837 54588

2004	1	2	3	4	5	6	7	8	9	10	11	12	13	14	15	16	17	18	19	20	21	22	23	24	25	26	27	28	29	30	31
Jan	M	M	M	M						C	C						C	C						C	C/E						C
Feb	C						C	C						C/E	C				C	C								C	C		
Mar						B	B					B	B					B	B/E								B	B			
Apr			B	B					B	B	B	B	B				B	B						B	B						
May	B	B	B					B	B						B	B						B	A						B	A	B
June				B	B	A					B	B	A					B	B	A					B	B	A				
July		B	B	A					B	B	A						B	A	B	B	B	B	B	B	A	B	B	B	B	B	B
Aug	A	B	B	B	B	B	B	A	B	B	B	B	B	B	A	B	B	B	B	B	B	A	B	B	B	B	B	B	A	B	B
Sept	B	B	B	B	A	B	B	B	B	B	B	A	B	B	B	B	B	B	A						B	A					
Oct		B	B							B	B					B	B													B	B
Nov						C	C						C	C					C	C							C	C			
Dec				S	S						S	S						S	S								M	M	M	M	M

E denotes special events, S denotes Santa Specials, M denotes Mince Pie specials, see local announcements.

Service A

Okehampton	dep	10.20	11.20	12.20	13.20	14.20	15.20	16.20	17.20
Meldon Viaduct	arr	10.30	11.30	12.30	13.30	14.30	15.30	16.30	17.30
Meldon Viaduct	dep	10.45	11.45	12.45	13.45	14.45	15.45	16.45	17.45
Okehampton	arr	10.55	11.55	12.55	13.55	14.55	15.55	16.55	17.55

Service B

Sampford Courtenay	dep	–	12.05	13.35	15.05	–
Okehampton	dep	11.00	12.30	14.00	15.30	16.30
Meldon Viaduct	arr	11.10	12.40	14.10	15.40	16.40
Meldon Viaduct	dep	11.30	13.00	14.30	16.00	17.00
Okehampton	dep	11.45	13.15	14.45	–	–
Sampford Courtenay	arr	12.00	13.30	15.00	–	–

Service C

–	12.05	13.35	15.05	–
11.00	12.30	14.00	15.30	16.30
11.10	12.40	14.10	15.40	16.40
11.30	13.00	14.30	16.00	17.00
11.45	13.15	14.45	–	–
12.00	13.30	15.00	–	–

DIDCOT RAILWAY CENTRE

Great Western Society, Didcot, Oxfordshire OX11 7NJ

01235 817200

Fax: 01235 510621   E-mail: didrlyc@globalnet.co.uk   Web: www.didcotrailwaycentre.org.uk

2004	1	2	3	4	5	6	7	8	9	10	11	12	13	14	15	16	17	18	19	20	21	22	23	24	25	26	27	28	29	30	31
Jan	A	O	O	O						O	O						O	O						O	O						O
Feb	O						O	O						A	A	O	O	A	O	X	X	A						O	O		
Mar						O	O					T	T	T				O	A						O	A					
Apr			O	A	O	O	O	O	A	A	A	A	O	O	O	O	O	O						X	X						
May	A	A	A					O	O						O	O						O	O						A	A	A
June	O	O	O	O	O	A	O	O	O	O	O	O	A	O	O	O	O	O	O	O	O	O	O	A	A	O	O	O			
July	O	O	O	A	O	O	O	O	O	O	A	O	O	A	O	O	O	A	O	O	O	A	O	O	A	O	O	A	O	O	O
Aug	A	O	O	A	O	O	A	A	O	O	A	O	O	A	A	O	O	A	O	O	A	A	O	O	A	O	O	A	A	A	O
Sept	A	O	O	O	A					O	O						O	O						X	X						
Oct		O	A				T	T	T								O	O	O	O	O	O	O	O	O	O	O	O	O	O	A
Nov						O	O						O	O					O	O							O	O			
Dec			O	O					S	S	S						S	S	S							O	O	O	O	O	

Service A – Steam Day.   **Service O** – Open.   **Service S** – Thomas Santa Special.   **Service T** – Thomas Event.
Service X – Special Event.

EAST LANCASHIRE RAILWAY

Bolton Street Station, Bolton Street, Bury, Lancs BL9 0EY   **0161 764 7790**

Fax: 0161 763 4408   E-mail: admin@east-lancs-rly.co.uk

2004	1	2	3	4	5	6	7	8	9	10	11	12	13	14	15	16	17	18	19	20	21	22	23	24	25	26	27	28	29	30	31
Jan	X		A	A						A	A						A	A						A	A				X	X	A
Feb	A					A	A						A	A						X	X						A	A			
Mar					A	A						A	A						X	A						A	A				
Apr			A	A						A	A						A	A						A	A						
May	X	X	X		B	B	B	A	A		B	B	B	A	A		B	B	B	A	A			B	B	B	X	X	X		
June		B	B	B	X	X		B	B	B	A	A		B	B	B	A	A			B	B	B	A	A			B			
July	B	B	A	A			X	X	X	X	X						A	A						A	A						A
Aug	A			B	B	X	X	X			B	B	B	A	A		B	B	B	A	A			B	B	B	A	A	X		
Sept	B	B	B	A	A		B	B	B	X	X	X			B	B	B	A	A			B	B	B	A	A					
Oct		X	X							A	A					A	A						A	A						X	X
Nov						A	A						A	A						X	A						S	S			
Dec				S	S						S	S						S	S												

X denotes special services, S denotes Santa Specials, please enquire for details.

Service A – Bury to Rawtenstall

Bury	dep	09.00	10.00	11.00	12.00	13.00	14.00	15.00	16.00	17.00
Rawtenstall	arr	09.41	10.41	11.41	12.41	13.41	14.41	15.41	16.41	17.41
Rawtenstall	dep	10.00	11.00	12.00	13.00	14.00	15.00	16.00	17.00	18.00
Bury	arr	10.38	11.38	12.38	13.38	14.38	15.38	16.38	17.38	18.38

Service A – Bury to Heywood

Bury	dep	09.30	10.45	11.45	12.45	13.55	14.45	15.45	16.45
Heywood	arr	09.45	11.00	12.00	13.00	14.10	15.00	16.00	17.00
Heywood	dep	10.00	11.15	12.15	13.30	14.25	15.15	16.15	17.15
Bury	arr	10.15	11.30	12.30	13.45	14.40	15.30	16.30	17.30

Service B – Bury to Rawtenstall midweek running

Bury	dep	10.00	11.40	13.20	15.00	16.40
Rawtenstall	arr	10.35	12.15	13.55	15.35	17.15
Rawtenstall	dep	10.50	12.30	14.10	15.50	17.30
Bury	arr	11.21	13.01	14.41	16.21	18.01

No through train service Rawtenstall to Heywood and vice versa.

EAST SOMERSET RAILWAY

Cranmore Station, Cranmore, Shepton Mallet, Somerset BA4 4QP   01749 880417

Fax: 01749 880764   E-mail: info@eastsomerset.org

2004	1	2	3	4	5	6	7	8	9	10	11	12	13	14	15	16	17	18	19	20	21	22	23	24	25	26	27	28	29	30	31
Jan				A							A							A							A						
Feb	A							A							A							A							A		
Mar							A							A							A							A			
Apr			B	C					D	D	D	D					B	C						X	X						
May	X	X	X					B	C						B	C						B	C						D	D	D
June		B				C	D					C	D					B					C	D				B		X	
July			C	D				B				C	D					B					C	D				B			X
Aug	X				X	X		C	D			B	B				C	D				B	B				C	D	X	X	X
Sept	B					C	D					X	X					X	X				B			C	D			B	
Oct		B	C						B	C						B	C						B	C						B	C
Nov							A							A							A							S	S		
Dec				S	S						S	S						S	S	S	S	S	S	S	S						

X denotes special events, S denotes Santa Specials, please phone for timetable details.

Service A

Cranmore	dep	12.00	13.30	15.00

Service B

12.00	14.00	15.30

Service C

Cranmore	dep	11.00	12.30	14.00	16.00

Service D

11.00	12.30	14.00	15.00	16.00

EMBSAY & BOLTON ABBEY RAILWAY

Bolton Abbey Station, Bolton Abbey, Skipton, N. Yorks BD23 6AF   01756 710614

Fax: 01756 710720   E-mail: embsay.steam@btinternet.com

2004	1	2	3	4	5	6	7	8	9	10	11	12	13	14	15	16	17	18	19	20	21	22	23	24	25	26	27	28	29	30	31
Jan	X			A							A							A							A						
Feb	A							A						A	A	A	A	A	A	A	A	A							A		
Mar							A							A				A										A			
Apr			A	A					T	T	T	T						A	A					A	A						
May	X	X	X					A	A					A	A						A	A							T	T	T
June	A							A						A				A							A						
July			A	A		A			A	A		A	A	A	A	A	A	A	A	A	A	A	X	X	A	A	A	A	A	A	A
Aug	A	A	A	A	A	A	A	A	A	A	A	A	A	A	A	A	A	A	A	A	A	A	A	A	A	A	A	T	T	T	A
Sept			A	A		A				A	A		A					X	X		A				A	A		A			
Oct		A	A						A	A						X	X				A	A	A	A	A	A	A	A	A	A	X
Nov							A									A			S									S			
Dec			S	S							S	S						S	S												

A denotes operating day, X denotes special events, S denotes Santa Specials.   Telephone/email for timetable information.

FAIRBOURNE & BARMOUTH STEAM RAILWAY

Beach Road, Fairbourne, Gwynedd LL38 2PZ   **01341 250362**

Fax: 01341 250240   E-mail: enquiries@fairbourne-railway.co.uk

2004	1	2	3	4	5	6	7	8	9	10	11	12	13	14	15	16	17	18	19	20	21	22	23	24	25	26	27	28	29	30	31
Apr								A	A	B	B	B	B	A	A	A	A														
May	A	B	B	A	A	A	A	A	A	A	A	A	A	A	A	A	A	A	A	A	A	A	A	A	A	A	A	A	B	B	B
June	B	B	B	B	B	B	A	A	A	A	A	B	B	A	A	A	A	A	A	A	A	A	A	A	A	A	A	A	A	A	
July	A	A	A	A	A	A	A	A	A	A	A	A	A	A	A	A	A	B	B	B	B	B	B	B	B	B	B	B	B	B	B
Aug	B	B	B	B	B	B	B	B	B	B	B	B	B	B	B	B	B	B	B	B	B	B	B	B	B	B	B	B	B	B	B
Sept	B	A	A	A	A	A	A	A	A	A	A	A	A	A	A	A	A	A	A						A	A	A	A	A	A	A
Oct																									A	A	A	A	A	A	A
Dec								S	S																						

S denotes Santa Specials, see local announcements.   *No service in January, February, March and November.*

Service A

Fairbourne	dep	11.00	12.30	14.15	15.45
Penrhyn Point	dep	11.45	13.15	15.00	16.30

Journey time lasts 20 minutes.

Service B

10.40	11.20	12.00	12.40	13.40	14.20	15.00	15.40	16.20
11.20	12.00	12.40	13.40	14.20	15.00	15.40	16.20	17.00

FOXFIELD STEAM RAILWAY

PO Box 1967, Stoke-on-Trent ST4 8YT   **01782 396210**

Fax: 01782 396210   E-mail: enquiries@foxfieldrailway.co.uk

2004	1	2	3	4	5	6	7	8	9	10	11	12	13	14	15	16	17	18	19	20	21	22	23	24	25	26	27	28	29	30	31
Apr				A					A	A	A	A						A							A						
May	A	A	A						A							A							A						A	A	A
June						A							A						A	A							A				
July				A							A						X	X							A						
Aug	A							A							A							A							A	A	A
Sept					A							A							A							A					
Oct			A							A							A							A					A	A	A
Dec			S	S							S	S						S	S	S											

X denotes special events, S denotes Santa Specials, see local announcements.   *No service in January and February.*

Services A

Cavershall Road	dep	11.30	13.00	14.00	15.00	16.00
Dilhorne Park	arr	11.43	13.18	14.10	15.18	16.10
Dilhorne Park	dep	11.55	13.25	14.25	15.25	16.25
Cavershall Road	arr	12.13	13.43	14.43	15.43	16.43

March opening: March 21st & 28th.
November opening: 27th & 28th.

FFESTINIOG RAILWAY
Harbour Station, Porthmadog, Gwynedd LL49 9NF

01766 516073
Fax: **01766 516005**   E-mail: **info@festrail.co.uk**

2004	1	2	3	4	5	6	7	8	9	10	11	12	13	14	15	16	17	18	19	20	21	22	23	24	25	26	27	28	29	30	31
Jan	A	A	A	A			B							B							B							B			B
Feb	B			B	B		B	B			B	B		C	C	C	C	C	C	C	C	C	C	C	C	C	C	C	C		
Mar			C	C		D	D			C	E		B	B			F	E		B	B			F	C		H	H	C	C	H
Apr	H	C	H	H	H	H	H	H	H	H	I	I	I	I	I	H	H	H	H	H	C	H	H	H	C	H	H	H	C	H	
May	X	X	X	H	H	H	C	H	H	C	H	H	H	C	H	H	H	C	H	H	H	C	H	H	H	H	H	H	H	I	I
June	J	J	J	I	H	H	H	H	H	H	H	H	H	H	H	H	H	H	H	H	H	H	H	H	H	H	H	H	K	H	
July	K	H	H	H	H	K	H	K	H	H	H	H	K	H	K	H	H	H	K	H	K	H	H	H	K	K	K	H	K	H	K
Aug	K	K	L	L	L	K	K	K	K	L	L	L	K	K	K	K	L	L	L	K	K	K	K	L	L	L	K	K	K	K	L
Sept	L	L	K	K	H	K	H	K	H	K	H	H	H	K	H	K	H	H	H	K	H	K	H	H	K	H	X	X	H	H	
Oct	C	H	H	C	H	H	H	C	H	H	H	C	H	H	H	C	H	H	C	H	H	H	C	H	H	H	H	H	C	C	C
Nov			C	C		P	P			P	P		P	P			P	P		P	P			P	P		P	P			
Dec	P	P		P	P		P	P		S	S		P	P		S	S					C	C	C	C	C	C				

X denotes special events, S denotes Santa Specials, see local announcements.

Service A
Porthmadog	dep	10.20	13.40
Blaenau Ffestiniog	arr	11.30	14.55
Blaenau Ffestiniog	dep	11.45	15.10
Porthmadog	arr	12.50	16.20

Service C
10.20	13.40
11.35	14.55
11.50	15.15
12.55	16.20

Service E
10.20	13.40
11.30	14.55
11.45	–
12.50	–

Service B
Blaenau Ffestiniog	dep	11.45	13.45
Tan-y-Bwlch	arr	12.15	14.15
Tan-y-Bwlch	dep	12.30	14.30
Blaenau Ffestiniog	arr	13.00	15.00

Service D
11.30	13.40
12.10	14.20
12.20	14.30
12.55	15.00

Service F
Porthmadog	dep	–	13.40
Blaenau Ffestiniog	arr	–	14.55
Blaenau Ffestiniog	dep	11.45	15.10
Porthmadog	arr	12.50	16.20

Service H
Porthmadog	dep	10.20	11.30	13.40	16.00
Blaenau Ffestiniog	arr	11.35	12.50	14.55	17.10
Blaenau Ffestiniog	dep	11.50	13.35	15.15	17.30
Porthmadog	arr	13.00	14.55	16.20	18.35

Service I
Porthmadog	dep	10.20	11.30	12.40	13.40	14.50	16.00
Blaenau Ffestiniog	arr	11.35	12.50	13.55	14.55	15.40	17.15
Blaenau Ffestiniog	dep	11.50	13.00	14.00	15.15	16.20	17.30
Porthmadog	arr	13.00	14.10	15.10	16.35	17.30	18.35

Service J
Porthmadog	dep	09.10	10.20	11.30	12.40	13.40	14.50	16.00	18.15
Blaenau Ffestiniog	arr	10.15	11.35	12.50	13.55	14.55	15.40	17.15	19.20
Blaenau Ffestiniog	dep	10.30	11.50	13.00	14.00	15.15	16.20	17.30	19.50
Porthmadog	arr	11.50	13.00	14.10	15.10	16.35	17.30	18.35	20.55

Service K
10.20	11.30	12.40	13.40	14.30	16.00
11.35	12.50	14.00	14.55	15.40	17.15
11.50	13.00	14.35	15.15	16.05	17.30
13.00	14.10	15.45	16.35	17.20	18.35

Service L
Porthmadog	dep	09.10	10.20	11.30	12.40	13.40	14.30	16.00	18.15
Blaenau Ffestiniog	arr	10.15	11.35	12.50	14.00	14.55	15.40	17.15	19.25
Blaenau Ffestiniog	dep	10.30	11.50	13.00	14.35	15.20	16.05	17.30	19.50
Porthmadog	arr	11.50	13.00	14.10	15.45	16.35	17.20	18.35	21.00

GLOUCESTERSHIRE WARWICKSHIRE RAILWAY
The Railway Station, Toddington, Glos GL54 5DT   **01242 621405**

E-mail: enquiries@gwsr.plc.uk

2004	1	2	3	4	5	6	7	8	9	10	11	12	13	14	15	16	17	18	19	20	21	22	23	24	25	26	27	28	29	30	31
Jan	C																														
Mar											A	B	B						A	A						A	A				
Apr			A	A				A	A	B	B	C	C	C	C		A	B				X	X								
May	A	B	B			A	B	B				A	A						A	A					A	B	B				
June	C	C	C	C	A	A			A	A					A	A				A	B										
July		A	A		C		A	A		C		A	A			C		A	B		C	C	C		A						
Aug	B		C	C	C	B	B		C	C	C	B	B		C	C	C	B	B		C	C	C	B	B	B	C				
Sept	C	C		A	B			A	A			A	A					A	A												
Oct		A	A			X	X				B	B						C	C		C	C	C			C	C				
Nov			C	C												C	C			B	B										
Dec			S	S				S	S					S	S				S	S	S	C	A	C	C	C					

X denotes special event, S denotes Santa Specials, see local announcements.   *No service in February.*

Service A

Toddington	dep	10.20	11.30	12.40	13.50	15.00	16.10
Winchcombe	arr	10.29	11.39	12.49	13.59	15.09	16.19
Cheltenham	arr	10.52	12.02	13.12	14.22	15.32	16.42
Cheltenham	dep	11.10	12.20	13.30	14.40	15.50	17.00
Winchcombe	dep	11.41	12.51	14.01	15.11	16.21	17.24
Toddington	arr	11.50	13.00	14.10	15.20	16.40	17.33

Service C

Toddington	dep	11.00	13.30	15.30
Winchcombe	arr	11.09	13.39	15.39
Cheltenham	arr	11.32	14.02	16.02
Cheltenham	dep	11.50	14.20	16.20
Winchcombe	dep	12.14	14.44	16.44
Toddington	arr	12.23	14.53	16.53

Service B

Toddington	dep	10.20	10.40	11.30	11.55	12.40	13.05	13.50	14.15	15.00	15.25	16.10
Winchcombe	arr	10.29	10.50	11.39	12.05	12.49	13.15	13.59	14.25	15.09	15.35	16.19
Cheltenham	arr	10.52	–	12.02	–	13.12	–	14.22	–	15.32	–	16.42
Cheltenham	dep	11.10	–	12.20	–	13.30	–	14.40	–	15.50	–	17.00
Winchcombe	dep	11.41	11.10	12.51	12.25	14.01	13.35	15.11	14.45	16.21	15.55	17.24
Toddington	arr	11.50	11.20	13.00	12.35	14.10	13.45	15.20	14.55	16.40	16.05	17.33

GOLDEN VALLEY LIGHT RAILWAY
Butterley Station, Ripley, Derbyshire DE5 3QZ **01773 747674**
Fax: 01773 570721   E-mail: mac@rapidial.co.uk

2004	1	2	3	4	5	6	7	8	9	10	11	12	13	14	15	16	17	18	19	20	21	22	23	24	25	26	27	28	29	30	31
Mar						X	X						X	X																	
Apr									A	A	A	A	A	A	A	A	A	A													
May	A	A	A				A	A								A	A					A	A						A	A	A
June	A	A	A	A	A	A						A	A						A	A						A	A				
July			A	A					A	A						A	A					A	A	A	A	A	A	A	A	A	A
Aug	A	A	A	A	A	A	A	A	A	A	A	A	A	A	X	X	A	A	A	A	A	A	A	A	A	A	A	A	A	A	A
Sept				A	A								A	A					A	A									A		
Oct		A	A						A	A						X	X						A	A						X	
Nov						X																									

X denotes special events, see local announcements.   No service in January, February and December.

Service A   ★

Butterley Park	dep	12.30	13.15	14.00	14.45	15.30	16.15
Newlands Inn	arr	12.40	13.25	14.10	14.55	15.40	16.25

Newlands Inn	dep	12.45	13.30	14.15	15.00	15.45	16.30
Butterley Park	arr	12.55	13.40	14.25	15.10	15.55	16.40

All trains call at Brands Crossing 5 minutes after leaving Newlands Inn.

★ Runs as required.

Steam hauled services will operate on certain dates. Ring for details.

GREAT CENTRAL RAILWAY
Great Central Road, Loughborough, Leicestershire LE11 1RW   **01509 230726**
Fax: 01509 239791   E-mail: sales@gcrailway.co.uk

2004	1	2	3	4	5	6	7	8	9	10	11	12	13	14	15	16	17	18	19	20	21	22	23	24	25	26	27	28	29	30	31
Jan	X	X	X	X						W	W						W	W						X	X						W
Feb	W						W	W						X	X	X	X	C	C	C	C	W	W					W	W		
Mar							W	W						W	W					W	W							X	X	X	
Apr			S	S	C	C	C	C	X	X	X	C	C	C	C	S	S							S	S						
May	X	X	X				S	S						S	S			S	S										X	X	X
June	X	C	C	C	S	S	C	C	C	C	X	X	X	C	C	C	C	C	S	S	C	C	C	C	C	S	S	C	C	C	
July	C	C	S	S	C	C	C	C	C	S	S	C	C	C	C	C	S	S	C	C	C	C	C	X	X	C	C	C	C	C	S
Aug	S	C	C	C	C	C	S	S	C	C	C	C	C	S	S	C	C	C	C	C	X	X	X	X	X	X	X	X	X	X	X
Sept			S	S						S	S			X	X	X								S	S						
Oct		S	S						X	X							S	S	C	C	C	C	X	X	X	X			S	W	
Nov				X	W	W						W	W						W	W							X	X			
Dec			X	X						X	X						X	X	X	X	X	X	X	X	X	X	X	X	X	X	X

Trains run on days shown above, please phone for timetable details.
W = Winter timetable, S = Summer timetable, C = Midweek timetable, X = Gala or Special timetable.

GREAT ORME TRAMWAY
Conwy Tourism Services, 1-2 Chapel Street, Llandudno LL30 2SY   **01492 575275**
Web: www.greatormetramway.com

Open:	20th March – 31st October 2004, 10.00 to 18.00 every day.
Frequency:	Every 20 minutes – on the hour, twenty past and twenty to the hour (trams are able to run every 10 minutes during the peak season).
Journey time:	The journey is split into two sections: each section takes approximately 8-10 minutes to complete. Passengers change at the Halfway Station, where there is a tramway exhibition and a chance to view into the Winding House, before boarding the tram to the summit.
System:	The technical term for the operating system is a double reversible funicular with passing loops. 800m of track lead from Victoria Station to Halfway Station (lower section), with a further 750m taking you to the Summit Station (upper section). The track is single, except for the interlaced section at the two passing loops.

GROUDLE GLEN RAILWAY
29 Hawarden Avenue, Douglas, Isle of Man IM1 4BP

01624 622138 (evenings)
01624 670453 (weekends)
E-mail: tbeard@manx.net

2004	1	2	3	4	5	6	7	8	9	10	11	12	13	14	15	16	17	18	19	20	21	22	23	24	25	26	27	28	29	30	31
Apr											A	A																			
May		A							A							A							A							A	
June						A							A							A							A				
July				A				B						A				B				A						B			
Aug	A		B	B						A		B	B				A			B	B			A		B	B				A
Sept								A									A									A					
Dec												S						S	S							M					

No services in January, February, March, October and November.

Service A – From 11.00 to 16.30 weekends (every ½ hour).
Service B – From 19.00 to 21.00 mid-week (every ½ hour).
Service S – Santa Specials from 11.00 to 15.30.
Service M – Mince Pie trains from 12.00 to 15.30.

GWILI STEAM RAILWAY
Bronwydd Arms Station, Bronwydd Arms, Carmarthen SA33 6HT　01267 230666

Web: www.gwili-railway.co.uk

2004	1	2	3	4	5	6	7	8	9	10	11	12	13	14	15	16	17	18	19	20	21	22	23	24	25	26	27	28	29	30	31
Apr									X	X	X	X	X																		
May		A	A						A							A							A							A	A
June	A	A	A			A			A				A			A				A			A				A			A	
July				A			A				A			A				A				A			A				A		A
Aug	A	A	A	A	A	A	A	A	A	A	A	A	A	A	A	A	A	A	A	A	A	A	A	A	A	A	A	A	A	A	A
Sept				A								A							A							A					
Oct																													X	X	X
Dec									S	S						S	S					S	S	S							

X denotes special events, S denotes Santa Specials, see local announcements.　No service in January, February, March and November.

Service A

Gwili	dep	11.15	12.30	14.00	15.15	16.30

ISLE OF MAN STEAM RAILWAY
Banks Circus, Douglas, Isle of Man IM1 5PT

01624 663366

Fax: 01624 663637 E-mail: info@busandrail.dtl.gov.im

Daily Service – Monday 3rd May to Sunday 31st October 2004.

Douglas	dep	10.10	11.50	13.50	15.20	16.40
Port Erin	arr	11.07	12.47	14.47	16.17	17.37

Port Erin	dep	10.10	11.50	13.50	15.20	16.40
Douglas	arr	11.07	12.47	14.47	16.17	17.37

ISLE OF WIGHT RAILWAY
The Station, Havenstreet, Ryde, IOW PO33 4DS

01983 882204

Fax: 01983 884515

2004	1	2	3	4	5	6	7	8	9	10	11	12	13	14	15	16	17	18	19	20	21	22	23	24	25	26	27	28	29	30	31
Mar																									C			S			
Apr	C			C		C	C	C	B	B	B	B	C	C	C		C			C		C			B	B			A	A	A
May		C	C		B	B			C			B	B			C			B	B			C			B	B		A	A	A
June	B	B	B	C	C	C	C	B	B	B	C	C	C	C	C	B	B	B	C	C	C	C	B	B	B	C	C	C	B	B	
July	A	B	S	S	B	B	B	A	B	S	S	B	B	B	A	B	B	B	B	B	B	A	T	T	T	T	A	A	A	A	A
Aug	A	A	A	A	A	A	A	A	A	A	A	A	A	A	A	A	A	A	A	A	A	A	A	A	A	X	X	X	X	X	A
Sept	A	A	A	A	A	B	B	B	B	B	B	B	B	B	B	B	C	C	C		B	B		C	C			B	B		
Oct			C			B		C				B			C			B				C	C	B	B	B	C				C

T denotes Thomas Events, X denotes special events, please phone for details.   No service in January, February, November and December.

Service A

Havenstreet	dep	10.35	11.36	12.36	14.15	15.15	16.15
Smallbrook Jct	arr	10.47	11.47	12.47	14.26	15.26	16.26

Smallbrook Jct	dep	10.53	11.53	12.53	14.35	15.35	16.35
Havenstreet	arr	11.04	12.04	13.04	14.46	15.46	16.46

Havenstreet	dep	11.08	12.08	13.08	14.48	15.48	16.48
Wootton	arr	11.14	12.14	13.14	14.54	15.54	16.54

Wootton	dep	11.20	12.20	13.20	15.00	16.00	17.00
Havenstreet	arr	11.25	12.25	13.25	15.05	16.05	17.05

Service B

10.35	11.36	12.36	14.15	15.15
10.47	11.47	12.47	14.26	15.26

10.53	11.53	12.53	14.35	15.35
11.04	12.04	13.04	14.46	15.46

11.08	12.08	13.08	14.48	15.48
11.14	12.14	13.14	14.54	15.54

11.20	12.20	13.20	15.00	16.00
11.25	12.25	13.25	15.05	16.05

Service C

Havenstreet	dep	10.35	11.52	14.00	15.15
Smallbrook Jct	arr	10.48	12.05	14.13	15.28

Smallbrook Jct	dep	10.56	12.13	14.21	15.36
Havenstreet	arr	11.09	12.26	14.34	15.49

Havenstreet	dep	11.12	12.29	14.37	15.52
Wootton	arr	11.19	12.36	14.44	15.59

Wootton	dep	11.27	12.44	14.52	16.07
Havenstreet	arr	11.33	12.50	14.58	16.13

KEITH & DUFFTOWN RAILWAY
Dufftown Station, Dufftown, Banffshire AB55 4BA

01340 821181

Services operate on Saturdays and Sundays only from 10th April to 26th September; Sundays only during October; Santa Specials on December 4th, 5th, 11th, 12th, 18th and 19th.
Departures from Dufftown are at 10.00, 11.50, 14.30 and 15.50. And from Keith at 10.50, 12.40, 14.50 and 16.40. Journey time 38 minutes.

KEIGHLEY & WORTH VALLEY RAILWAY

01535 645214

Haworth Station, Keighley, West Yorkshire BD22 8NJ

Fax: 01535 647317

2004	1	2	3	4	5	6	7	8	9	10	11	12	13	14	15	16	17	18	19	20	21	22	23	24	25	26	27	28	29	30	31
Jan	X	X	B	B						B	B						B	B						B	B						B
Feb	B						B	B					B	B	C	C	C	C	C	X	X							B	B		
Mar					B	B							B	B					B	B							T	T			
Apr			B	B					A	A	A	A	B	C	C	C	B	X						B	B						
May	B	A	A						B	B					B	X				B	B								B	A	A
June	C	C	C	C	B	X						B	A		X	X	X		X	X		X	X	X		B	A		X	X	
July	X		B	A	C	C	C	C	C	C	B	A	C	C	C	C	C	C	B	A	C	C	C	C	C	B	A	C	C	C	C
Aug	A	C	C	C	C	C	B	A	C	C	C	C	C	B	A	C	C	C	C	C	B	A	C	C	C	C	C	B	A	A	C
Sept	C	C	C	B	A							B	A						T	T								B	A		
Oct		B	B					X	X								B	B						B	B					B	B
Nov				B	B								B	B					B	B							S	S			
Dec			S	S							S	S					S	S							X	X	X	X	X	X	X

X denotes special events, T denotes Thomas Events, S denotes Santa Specials, please phone for further details.

Service A

		D		D	‡		D		‡				‡				‡			
Oxenhope	dep	09.15	10.30	11.15	12.00	12.45	13.30	14.15	15.00	15.45	16.30	17.15
Keighley†	arr	09.40	10.50	11.40	12.25	13.10	13.55	14.40	15.25	16.10	16.55	17.40

Keighley†	dep	09.55	11.15	12.00	12.45	13.30	14.15	15.00	15.45	16.30	17.15	18.00
Oxenhope	arr	10.15	11.40	12.30	13.15	13.55	14.40	15.25	16.10	16.55	17.40	18.25

Service B

		D	D	‡	‡	‡	‡	★
Oxenhope	dep	09.15	10.30	11.15	12.45	14.15	15.45	17.15
Keighley*	arr	09.40	10.50	11.40	13.10	14.40	16.10	17.40

Keighley*	dep	09.55	11.15	12.00	13.30	15.00	16.30	18.00
Oxenhope	arr	10.15	11.40	12.25	13.55	15.25	16.55	18.25

Service C

D	‡	‡	‡	‡
10.10	11.25	13.00	14.35	16.10
10.30	11.50	13.25	15.00	16.35
10.40	12.10	13.45	15.20	16.55
11.00	12.35	14.10	15.45	17.20

† Direct connections to the National Rail network.

D Heritage diesel train.

‡ Real-Ale Buffet Car, available from March to October.

★ Does not run in January, February and November.

All trains call at Haworth (5), Oakworth (8), Damems (13) and Ingrow (16) minutes after leaving Oxenhope and Ingrow (5), Damens (8), Oakworth (10) and Haworth (15) minutes after leaving Keighley.

KENT & EAST SUSSEX RAILWAY

Tenterden Town Station, Station Road, Tenterden, Kent TN30 6HE   **01580 765155**

E-mail: enquiries@kesr.org.uk   Web: www.kesr.org.uk

2004	1	2	3	4	5	6	7	8	9	10	11	12	13	14	15	16	17	18	19	20	21	22	23	24	25	26	27	28	29	30	31
Jan	A																														
Feb														X	X						T	T	A	A	A	T	T	T	T		
Mar																								X	X						
Apr			X	X				A	A	A	C	C	A	A	A	A	A	A	A	A	A	A	A	A	A	A					
May	A	B	B	A	A	A		X	X		A	A	A		X	X		A	A	A		X	X		A	A	A		A	B	B
June	A	A	A	A	X	X		A	A	A		X	X		A	A	A		T	T		A	A	A		T	T		A	A	
July	A		X	X		A	A	A		X	X		A	A	A		X	X	B	B	B	B	B	B	B	B	B	B	B	B	B
Aug	B	B	B	B	B	B	B	B	B	B	B	B	B	B	B	B	B	B	B	B	B	B	B	B	B	B	B	B	C	C	B
Sept	B	B	B	B	B		A	A	A		X	X		A	A	A		T	T		A	A	A		T	T		A	A	A	
Oct		X	X					X	X								X	X				X	X	A	A	A	A	A	A	A	A
Dec			S	S							S	S					S	S				S	S	S							

X denotes special events, T denotes Thomas events, S denotes Santa Specials, see local announcements.   *No service in November.*

Train Times

Tenterden Town	dep	10.40	11.45	13.15	14.20	15.30
Northiam	dep	11.15	12.20	13.50	14.55	16.05
Bodiam	arr	11.29	12.37	14.04	15.12	16.22
Bodiam	dep	11.40	12.50	14.15	15.25	16.30
Northiam	dep	11.55	13.00	14.30	15.40	16.45
Tenterden Town	arr	12.27	13.38	15.02	16.12	17.16

Service A – One steam/one diesel (off peak service)

Service B – Two steam (regular service)

Service C – Peak Service (additional trains)

KIRKLEES LIGHT RAILWAY
Park Mill Way, Clayton West, Near Huddersfield HD8 9XJ **01484 865727**

2004	1	2	3	4	5	6	7	8	9	10	11	12	13	14	15	16	17	18	19	20	21	22	23	24	25	26	27	28	29	30	31
Jan	A		A	A						A	A						A	A						A	A						A
Feb	A						A	A						A	A	A	A	A	A	A	A	A						A	A		
Mar					A	A								A	A									A	A						
Apr				B	B	B	B	B	B	B	B	B	B	B	B	B	B	B	B	B				B	B						
May	B	B	B					B	B							B	B						B	B					B	B	B
June	B	B	B	B	B	B	B	B	B	B	B	B	X	X	B	B	B	B	B	B	B	B	B	B	B	B	B	B	B	B	
July	B	B	B	B	B	B	B	B	B	B	B	B	B	B	B	B	B	B	B	B	B	B	B	X	X	B	B	B	B	B	B
Aug	B	B	B	B	B	B	B	B	B	B	B	B	B	B	B	B	B	B	B	B	B	B	B	B	B	B	B	B	B	B	B
Sept				B	B						B	B					B	B						B	B						
Oct		B	B						B	B						B	B						B	B	B	B	B			C	C
Nov					A	A								A	A						A	A						A	S		
Dec			S	S						S	S						S	S						S	S					A	A

S denotes Santa Specials, C Evening Halloween Ghost Trains, see local announcements.

Service A – Hourly trains from 11.00 to 15.00. **Service B** – Hourly trains from 11.00 to 16.00. **X** – Special Events from 10.00 to 16.00.

LAKESIDE & HAVERTHWAITE RAILWAY
Haverthwaite Station, Ulverston, Cumbria LA12 8AL **01539 531594**

Daily Service – Saturday 3rd April to Sunday 31st October 2004
Santa Specials operate on 4th, 5th, 11th, 12th, 18th, and 19th December.

LEIGHTON BUZZARD RAILWAY
Page's Park Station, Billington Road, Leighton Buzzard LU7 4TN 01525 373888
Fax: 01525 377814   E-mail: info@buzzrail.co.uk

2004	1	2	3	4	5	6	7	8	9	10	11	12	13	14	15	16	17	18	19	20	21	22	23	24	25	26	27	28	29	30	31
Mar														A							A							A			
Apr			A						A	A	B	B		A					A							A					
May	A	B	B						A							A							A						A	B	B
June		A	A			A	A		C				A			C				B			C				B			C	
July			B				C				A			C				A			A				B			A			
Aug	B		A	A	A		A	B		A	A	A		A	B		A	A	A		A	B		A	A	A		A	B	B	A
Sept	A	A		A	B						X	X						A								A		A		B	
Oct		A	A							A						A								A		A				S	S
Dec			S	S			S				S	S					S			S	S					S	S				

X denotes special services, S denotes Santa Specials, see local announcements.   No service in January, February and November.

Service A ★

Page's Park	dep	10.40	12.20	14.00	15.40*
Stonehenge Wks	arr	11.05	12.45	14.25	16.05
Stonehenge Wks	dep	11.25	13.05	14.45	16.25
Page's Park	arr	11.50	13.30	15.10	16.50

★ 15.40 trains do not run on 24th, 27th and 31st October.

Service C

Page's Park	dep	10.30	12.00	13.30
Stonehenge Wks	arr	10.55	12.25	13.55
Stonehenge Wks	dep	11.10	12.40	14.10
Page's Park	arr	11.35	13.05	14.35

Service B ★ †

10.40	11.30	12.20	13.10	14.00	14.50	15.40	16.30
11.05	11.55	12.45	13.35	14.25	15.15	16.05	16.55
11.25	12.15	13.05	13.55	14.45	15.35	16.25	17.15
11.50	12.40	13.30	14.20	15.10	16.00	16.50	17.40

† 16.30 train does not run on 31st October and runs subject to demand on all other days.

Trains run only if school parties have pre-booked, although other passengers may also travel, subject to seat availability. Phone or email in advance to check status.

LAUNCESTON STEAM RAILWAY
St Thomas Road, Launceston, Cornwall PL15 8DA 01566 775665

2004	1	2	3	4	5	6	7	8	9	10	11	12	13	14	15	16	17	18	19	20	21	22	23	24	25	26	27	28	29	30	31
Apr									A	A	A	A	A	A	A	A		A		A					A		A				
May		A		A					A		A					A		A					A		A					A	A
June	A	A	A	A		A	A	A	A				A	A	A	A				A	A	A	A				A	A	A	A	
July	A	A		A	A	A	A	A	A		A	A	A	A	A	A		A	A	A	A	A	A		A	A	A	A	A	A	
Aug	A	A	A	A	A	A		A	A	A	A	A	A		A	A	A	A	A	A		A	A	A	A	A	A		A	A	A
Sept	A	A	A		A	A	A	A	A		A	A	A	A	A	A		A	A	A	A	A	A		A	A	A	A	A	A	

No service in January, February, March, October, November and December.

Service A

Launceston	dep	11.00	11.50	12.45	14.00	14.45	15.35	16.30
Newmills	dep	11.20	12.10	13.05	14.20	15.05	15.55	16.50

Trains also run during the October half term week. Trains stop by request at Hunts Crossing for walkers and picnic parties.

LLANGOLLEN RAILWAY

The Station, Abbey Road, Llangollen, Denbighshire LL20 8SN

01978 860951 (Talking Timetable)
01978 860979

Fax: 01978 869247   E-mail: office@llangollen-railway.co.uk   Web: www.llangollen-railway.co.uk

2004	1	2	3	4	5	6	7	8	9	10	11	12	13	14	15	16	17	18	19	20	21	22	23	24	25	26	27	28	29	30	31
Jan	A	A	A	A							A							A							A						
Feb	A					A	A						T	T	T	T	T	T	T	T	T							X	X		
Mar						A	A						A	A						A	A						X	X			
Apr								B	C	C	C	A	A	A	A	B	B	A	A	A	A	A	B	B	A	A	A	A			
May	B	C	C	A	A	A	A	A	A	A	A	A	A	A	A	A	A	A	A	A	A	A	A	A	A	A	A	A	X	X	X
June	A	A	A	A	A	A	A	A	A	A	A	C	C	A	A	A	A	A	A	A	A	C	C	A	A	A	A	A	A	A	
July	A	A	X	X	A	A	A	A	C	C	A	A	A	A	C	C	A	A	A	A	A	T	T	T	T	T	T	T	T	T	T
Aug	T	B	B	B	B	B	C	C	B	B	B	B	B	C	C	B	B	B	B	B	C	C	B	B	B	B	B	C	C	C	B
Sept	B	B	B	C	C	A	A	A	A	A	A	A	A	A	A	A	A	X	X	A	A	A	A	A	A	A	A	A	A	A	
Oct	A	A	A	A	A	A	A	X	X	X	A	A	A		A	A		A	A	A		T	T	T	T	T	T	T	T	T	T
Nov				A	A																							S	S		
Dec				S	S				S	S								S	S	S	S	S	S	S		A	A	A	A	A	A

X denotes special events, S denotes Santa Specials, T denotes Thomas events, see local announcements.

Service A

Llangollen	dep	11.00	13.00	15.00
Berwyn	dep	11.09	13.09	15.09
Carrog	arr	11.31	13.31	15.31
Carrog	dep	11.50	13.50	15.50
Berwyn	dep	12.12	14.12	16.12
Llangollen	arr	12.20	14.20	16.20

Service B

10.45	12.30	14.15	16.00
10.54	12.39	14.24	16.09
11.15	13.00	14.45	16.30
11.35	13.20	15.05	16.50
11.42	13.27	15.12	16.57
12.03	13.48	15.33	17.18

All trains call at Glyndyfrdwy 24 minutes after leaving Llangollen and 8 minutes after leaving Carrog.

Service C

Llangollen	dep	–	11.00	12.00	13.00	14.00	15.00	16.00	16.45
Berwyn	dep	–	11.09	12.09	13.09	14.09	15.09	16.09	16.53
Carrog	arr	–	11.32	12.32	13.32	14.32	15.32	16.32	17.15
Carrog	dep	11.15	12.00	13.00	14.00	15.00	16.00	17.00	–
Berwyn	dep	11.40	12.26	13.26	14.26	15.26	16.26	17.26	–
Llangollen	arr	11.46	12.33	13.33	14.33	15.33	16.33	17.33	–

LLANBERIS LAKE RAILWAY
Padarn Country Park, Llanberis, Gywnedd LL55 4TY

01286 870549

Fax: 01286 870549 E-mail: info@lake-railway.co.uk Web: www.lake-railway.co.uk

2004	1	2	3	4	5	6	7	8	9	10	11	12	13	14	15	16	17	18	19	20	21	22	23	24	25	26	27	28	29	30	31
Mar															A	A	A					A	A	A	A				A	A	A
Apr	A			A	A	A	A	A	A	A	A	A	A	A	A	A		A	A	A	A	A			A	A	A	A	A	A	
May	A	A	A	A	A	A	A		A	A	A	A	A	A		A	A	A	A	A	A		A	A	A	A	A	A	A	B	B
June	B	B	B	A		A	A	A	A	A	A		A	A	A	A	A	A		A	A	A	A	A		A	A	A	A		
July	A	A	A	A	B	B	B	B	A	A	A	B	B	B	B	A	A	A	B	B	B	B	A	A	A	B	B	B	B	A	A
Aug	A	B	B	B	B	A	A	A	B	B	B	B	A	A	A	B	B	B	B	A	A	A	B	B	B	B	A	A	A	B	B
Sept	B	B	A	A	A	A	A	A	A	A	A		A	A	A	A	A	A		A	A	A	A	A		A	A	A	A	A	
Oct		A	A	A	A	A	A	A	A	A	A	A	A	A			A	A	A	A	A			A	A	A	A	A	A	A	

No service in January, February, November and December.

Service A

Gilfach Ddu	dep	11.00*	12.15	13.30	14.45	16.00†

* Not Saturdays or Sundays.
† Does not run in March or late October.

Service B

Gilfach Ddu	dep	10.45	11.30	12.15	13.00	14.30	15.15	16.00

MANX ELECTRIC RAILWAY
Banks Circus, Douglas, Isle of Man IM1 5PT

01624 663366

Fax: 01624 663637 E-mail: info@busandrail.dti.gov.im

Daily 5th April to 26th September 2004.

Services			A		B		C				B	A		Daily Winter Service C	C
Douglas Derby Castle	dep	09.40	10.10	10.40	11.10	11.40	12.40	13.40	14.10	15.10	15.40	16.10	16.40	09.40	13.40
Laxey	dep	10.10	10.40	11.10	11.40	12.10	13.10	14.10	14.40	15.40	16.10	16.40	17.10	10.10	14.10
Ramsey Tram Station	arr	10.55	11.25	11.55	12.25	12.55	13.55	14.55	15.25	16.25	16.55	–	17.55	10.55	14.55
				A		B				A		A		C	C
Ramsey Tram Station	dep	10.10	11.10	11.40	12.10	12.40	13.40	14.40	15.10	15.40	–	16.40	17.10	11.40	15.10
Laxey	dep	10.55	11.55	12.25	12.55	13.25	14.25	15.25	15.55	16.25	16.55	17.25	17.55	12.25	15.55
Douglas Derby Castle	arr	11.25	12.25	12.55	13.25	13.55	14.55	15.55	16.25	16.55	17.25	17.55	18.25	12.55	16.25

A – Runs daily between 26th April to 26th September.
B – Runs Monday to Friday between 31st May to 3rd September.
C – Runs daily 5th January to 4th April 2004.

Intermediate stops are BY REQUEST except Groudle and Laxey.
TO ALIGHT inform conductor on boarding.
TO BOARD give a clear signal to driver.

MID-NORFOLK RAILWAY
The Railway Station, Station Road, Dereham, Norfolk NR19 1DF **01362 690633**

Fax: 01362 698487 E-mail: info@mnr.org.uk

2004	1	2	3	4	5	6	7	8	9	10	11	12	13	14	15	16	17	18	19	20	21	22	23	24	25	26	27	28	29	30	31
Feb																												X	B		
Mar							B							B						X	X						B	B			
Apr			B	B					B	B	B	B					B	B				B	B								
May	B	B	B					B	B						B	B			B				B	B			B			B	B
June		B				B	B					B				B	B			B	B				B		B	X		B	
July			B	B			B			B	B			B				B	B			C	C		B	B			C	C	B
Aug	B			C	C			B	B			C	C		B	B			C	C		B	B			C	C		B	B	B
Sept	B				B	B			B				X	X			B			B	B			B			B	B			
Oct		B	B					B	B								D	D					B	B				B		B	B
Nov							A								A								A					A			
Dec					S						S	S						S	S						S						

X denotes special events, S denotes Santa Specials, see local announcements. *No service in January.*

Service A

Dereham	dep	11.00	14.00
Wymondham Abbey	arr	11.38	14.38
Wymondham Abbey	dep	11.45	14.45
Dereham	arr	12.22	15.22

Service B

11.00	13.45	15.45
11.38	14.23	16.23
11.45	14.30	16.30
12.22	15.07	17.07

Service C

10.00	11.45	14.00	15.45
10.38	12.23	14.38	16.23
10.45	12.30	14.45	16.30
11.22	13.07	15.22	17.07

All trains call at intermediate stations: Yaxham (8), Thuxton (16) minutes after leaving Dereham and Thuxton (18) and Yaxham (26) minutes after leaving Wymondham Abbey. Kimberley Park Station is due to open in 2004.

MID-HANTS RAILWAY (Watercress Line)

The Station, Alresford, Hampshire SO24 9JG

01952 733810

Fax: **01962 735448**   E-mail: **info@watercressline.co.uk**

2004	1	2	3	4	5	6	7	8	9	10	11	12	13	14	15	16	17	18	19	20	21	22	23	24	25	26	27	28	29	30	31
Jan	A																A	D						A	D						A
Feb	D				A	D								A	D	A	A	A	A	A	D							A	D		
Mar							B	B					X	X				B	B								B	B			
Apr									T	T	T	T	T	T	T	T	T	T	T					B	B						
May	B	C	B	A	A	A		B	C		A	A	A		B	C		A	A	A		X	X	X		A	A	A	B	C	B
June	A	A	A		B	C		A	A	A		B	C		A	A	A		X	X		A	A	A		B	C		A	A	
July	A		B	X		A	A	A		B	C		A	A	A		B	X		A	A	A		B	C		A	A	A		B
Aug	C	B	B	B	B	B	B	B	T	T	T	T	T	T	T	T	T	B	B	B	B	B	B	B	C	B	B	B	B	B	B
Sept	B	B	B	B	B		A	A	A		B	X		A	A	A		X	X	X		A	A	A		B	C		A	A	A
Oct		B	B						B	B						B	B						X	X	X	X	X	X	X	X	X
Nov						A	D																								
Dec				S	S						S	S					S	S		S	S	S	S			X	X				

X denotes special events, T denotes Thomas events, S denotes Santa Specials, see local announcements.

Services A & B (Steam/Diesel) – departures from Alresford every hour from 11.10 to 16.10 and from Alton hourly from 11.00 to 16.00.

Service C – departures from Alresford at 11.10 and hourly to 16.10 and from Alton at 11.20 and hourly to 16.20

Service D – departures from Alresford at 11.10 and hourly to 16.10 from Alton at 11.20 and hourly to 16.20.

All trains call at intermediate stations: Ropley (11 minutes) and Medstead (26 minutes) after leaving Alresford and at Medstead (13 minutes) and Ropley (23 minutes) after leaving Alton.
Some services are by DMU.

MIDLAND RAILWAY CENTRE

Butterley Station, Ripley, Derbyshire DE5 3QZ

01773 747674

Fax: **01773 570721**   E-mail: **mac@rapidial.co.uk**

2004	1	2	3	4	5	6	7	8	9	10	11	12	13	14	15	16	17	18	19	20	21	22	23	24	25	26	27	28	29	30	31
Jan	X	X	X	X																					A						
Feb	A								A					A	A	A	A	A	A	A	A	A							A		
Mar				C	C							C	C							B								B			
Apr			X	X				A	A	B	B	C	C	A	A	A	A	B	B							B					
May	C	C	C					B	B							B	B					X	X						C	C	C
June	B	B	B	B	C	C						B	C					A			B	B				A			B	B	
July	A		B	B				B		B	C					B		B	B		B	B	X	X	B	B	B	B	B	B	C
Aug	C	B	B	B	B	B	B	C	C	B	B	B	B	B	B	C	C	B	B	B	B	B	B	B	B	B	B	B	C	C	C
Sept				X	X					A		B	C					A			X	X							B		
Oct		B	C					X	X							C	C							B	B					X	A
Nov				X	A									A						S	S						S	S			
Dec				S	S				S			S	S				S			S	S		S	S	S	S	X	X	X	X	X

X denotes special events, S denotes Santa Specials, see local announcements.

Service A

Butterley	dep	10.30	11.30	12.30	14.00	15.15
Swanwick Jctn	arr	11.00	12.09	13.09	14.39	15.54

Swanwick Jctn	dep	11.05	12.15	13.15	14.45	16.00
Butterley	arr	11.09	12.19	13.19	14.49	16.15

Service B

		10.30	11.30	12.30	14.00	15.15	16.30
		11.00	12.09	13.09	14.39	15.54	16.45

		11.05	12.15	13.15	14.45	16.00	17.00
		11.09	12.19	13.19	14.49	16.04	17.15

Service C

Butterley	dep	10.30	11.00	11.30	12.00	12.30	13.00	14.00	14.45	15.30	16.30
Swanwick Jctn	arr	11.00	11.28	12.09	12.39	13.09	13.39	14.39	15.26	16.09	16.45

Swanwick Jctn	dep	11.05	11.45	12.15	12.45	13.15	14.15	15.00	15.45	16.15	17.00
Butterley	arr	11.09	11.49	12.19	12.49	13.19	14.19	15.04	16.00	16.19	17.15

MULL RAIL
Old Pier Station, Craignure, Isle of Mull, Argyll PA65 6AY 01680 812494
Fax: 01680 300595 E-mail: mullrail@dee-emm.co.uk

2004	1	2	3	4	5	6	7	8	9	10	11	12	13	14	15	16	17	18	19	20	21	22	23	24	25	26	27	28	29	30	31
Apr	A	A	B	A	A	A	A	A	A	B	A	A	A	A	A	A	A	B	A	A	A	A	A	A	B	A	A	A	A	A	
May	B	A	A	A	B	A	A	A	B	A	A	A	A	B	A	A	A	A	A	B	A	A	A	A	A	B	A	C	C	A	C
June	C	C	C	A	B	A	A	A	A	A	A	B	A	A	A	A	A	A	B	A	A	A	A	A	A	B	A	C	C	C	
July	C	A	B	A	C	C	C	C	A	B	A	C	C	C	C	A	B	A	C	C	C	C	B	A	C	C	C	C	C	B	A
Aug	A	C	C	C	C	C	B	A	C	C	C	C	C	B	A	C	C	C	C	C	B	A	C	C	C	C	C	B	A	A	A
Sept	A	A	A	B	A	A	A	A	A	A	B	A	A	A	A	A	A	B	A	A	A	A	A	A	B	A	A	A	A	A	
Oct	A	B	A	A	A	A	A	A	B	A	A	A	A	A	A	B	A	A	A	A	A	A	B	X	X	A	A	A	X	X	X

X denotes special events, see local announcements. No service in January, February, March, November and December.

Service A

Torosay	dep	10.40	12.10	14.10	14.50‡	16.10	17.30†
Craignure	dep	11.15	13.15	14.30‡	15.10	–	–

Service B

10.10	11.45	14.10	15.10¶	16.10
10.45	12.45	14.45	15.45	–

Service C

Torosay	dep	10.45	11.35	11.50	12.15	12.55	14.00	14.15	15.05	15.40	16.10	16.20*	17.30*
Craignure	dep	11.10	11.20	11.50	12.30	13.10	13.30	14.20	15.10	15.25	15.55	–	17.00*

‡ Trains run from 17th May to 12th September. † Commences on 4th July to 29th August (Sundays only).
¶ Trains run from 22nd May to 11th September. * Does not run on Fridays.

NORTH YORKSHIRE MOORS RAILWAY
Pickering Station, Pickering, North Yorkshire YO18 7AJ 01751 472508
Fax: 01751 476970 E-mail: admin@nymrpickering.fsnet.co.uk

2004	1	2	3	4	5	6	7	8	9	10	11	12	13	14	15	16	17	18	19	20	21	22	23	24	25	26	27	28	29	30	31
Jan	A	A	A	A	A																										
Feb														A	A	A	A	A	A	A	A	A									
Mar																											A	A	A	A	A
Apr	A	A	B	B	B	B	B	B	C	C	D	D	C	C	C	B	B	B	B	B	B	B	X	X	X	B	B	B	B	B	
May	B	D	D	B	B	B	B	B	B	B	B	B	B	B	B	X	X	B	B	B	B	B	B	B	B	B	B	B	D	D	D
June	D	D	D	C	C	C	B	B	B	B	B	B	B	B	B	X	X	B	B	B	B	B	B	B	B	B	B	B	D	D	
July	B	B	B	C	C	C	C	C	C	C	C	C	C	C	C	C	C	X	X	C	C	C	C	C	C	C	D	D	D	D	C
Aug	D	D	D	D	D	C	C	D	D	D	D	D	C	C	D	D	D	D	D	C	C	D	D	D	D	D	C	C	D	D	D
Sept	D	D	D	C	C	C	C	C	C	C	X	X	B	B	B	B	B	B	C	B	B	B	B	B	B	B	B	B	B	B	
Oct	X	X	X	B	B	B	B	B	B	B	B	B	B	B	B	X	X	X	B	B	B	B	B	B	C	C	C	C	C	X	X
Nov						A	A							A	A				A	A											
Dec				S	S						S	S							S	S	A	A	A	A			A	A	A	A	A

S denotes Santa Specials, X denotes Special Events, see local announcements.

Service A

Pickering	dep	10.20	11.20	13.20	14.20
Grosmont	arr	11.25	12.25	14.25	15.25
Grosmont	dep	09.50	11.50	12.50	14.50
Pickering	arr	11.00	13.00	14.00	16.00

Service B

10.20	11.20	13.20	15.20	16.20
11.25	12.25	14.25	16.25	17.25
09.50	11.50	13.50	14.50	16.50
11.00	13.00	15.00	16.00	18.00

Service C

Pickering	dep	10.20	11.20	12.20	13.20	14.20	15.20	16.20
Grosmont	arr	11.25	12.25	13.25	14.25	15.25	16.25	17.25
Grosmont	dep	09.50	10.50	11.50	12.50	13.50	14.50	16.50
Pickering	arr	11.00	12.00	13.00	14.00	15.00	16.00	18.00

All services stop at intermediate stations: Levisham, Newton Dale and Goathland. Overall journey time 65 minutes.

Service D

Pickering	dep	10.20	11.20	12.20	13.20	14.20	15.20	16.20	17.20
Grosmont	arr	11.25	12.25	13.25	14.25	15.25	16.25	17.25	18.25
Grosmont	dep	09.50	10.50	11.50	12.50	13.50	14.50	15.50	16.50
Pickering	arr	11.00	12.00	13.00	14.00	15.00	16.00	17.00	18.00

NORTH NORFOLK RAILWAY
The Station, Sheringham, Norfolk NR26 8RA

01263 820800

Fax: 01263 820801   E-mail: enquiries@nnrailway.com

2004	1	2	3	4	5	6	7	8	9	10	11	12	13	14	15	16	17	18	19	20	21	22	23	24	25	26	27	28	29	30	31
Jan	X	X	X	X																											
Feb							D	C						D	C	X	X	X	C	C	D	C						D	C		
Mar					D	C							D	C				D	X							D	C			C	C
Apr	C		B	C	C	C	B	B	A	A	A	A	B	B	B	B	B	C			C	C	C		B	C		C	C	C	
May	X	X	X	C	C	C	C	B	C	C	C	C	C	C	B	C	C	C	C	C	C	B	C	C	C	C	C	C	A	A	A
June	A	A	A	B	B	B	C	C	C	C	C	B	C	C	C	C	C	C	B	X	C	C	C	C	C	C	B	B	B	B	
July	B	B	X	X	B	B	B	B	B	B	B	B	B	B	B	B	X	X	X	B	B	A	A	A	X	X	A	A	A	A	A
Aug	A	A	A	A	A	A	A	A	A	A	A	A	A	A	A	A	A	A	A	A	A	A	A	A	A	A	A	A	A	A	B
Sept	B	B	X	X	X	B	B	B	B	B	B	B	B	B	B	B	B	X	X	C	C	C	C	C	B	C	C	C	C	C	
Oct		X	X						B							B							X	X	X	X				B	
Nov						D	D						D	D						D	D							D	D		
Dec			S	S						S	S			S			X	S	S			S	S	S	S	X	X	X	X	X	X

X denotes special events, S denotes Santa Specials, see local announcements.

Service A

			†		†		†		†			
Sheringham	dep	09.30	10.30	11.15	12.00	12.45	13.30	14.15	15.00	15.45	16.30	17.40
Weybourne	dep	09.41	10.44	11.29	12.14	12.59	13.44	14.29	15.14	15.59	16.44	17.51
Holt	arr	09.50	10.53	11.38	12.23	13.08	13.53	14.38	15.23	16.08	16.53	18.00

Holt	dep	10.00	11.15	12.00	12.45	13.30	14.15	15.00	15.45	16.30	17.10	18.10
Weybourne	dep	10.10	11.28	12.13	12.58	13.43	14.28	15.13	15.58	16.43	17.20	18.20
Sheringham	arr	10.20	11.38	12.23	13.08	13.53	14.38	15.23	16.08	16.53	17.30	18.30

★ Operates Saturdays only.

† Diesel hauled on Saturdays only.

Service B

			★								
Sheringham	dep	09.30	10.30	11.15	12.00	12.45	13.30	14.15	15.00	15.45	17.00
Weybourne	dep	09.41	10.44	11.29	12.14	12.59	13.44	14.29	15.14	15.59	17.10
Holt	arr	09.50	10.53	11.38	12.23	13.08	13.53	14.38	15.23	16.08	17.19

Holt	dep	10.00	11.15	12.00	12.45	13.30	14.15	15.00	15.45	16.30	17.30
Weybourne	dep	10.10	11.28	12.13	12.58	13.43	14.28	15.13	15.58	16.43	17.40
Sheringham	arr	10.20	11.38	12.23	13.08	13.53	14.38	15.23	16.08	16.53	17.48

Service C

Sheringham	dep	10.30	12.00	13.30	15.00
Weybourne	dep	10.44	12.14	13.44	15.14
Holt	arr	10.53	12.23	13.53	15.23

Holt	dep	11.15	12.45	14.15	15.45
Weybourne	dep	11.28	12.58	14.28	15.58
Sheringham	arr	11.38	13.08	14.38	16.08

Service D

10.00	11.00	12.00	13.00	14.00	15.00	16.00
10.09	11.09	12.09	13.09	14.09	15.09	16.09
10.18	11.18	12.18	13.18	14.18	15.18	16.18

10.30	11.30	12.30	13.30	14.30	15.30	16.30
10.39	11.39	12.39	13.39	14.39	15.39	16.39
10.47	11.47	12.47	13.47	14.47	15.47	16.47

PAIGNTON & DARTMOUTH STEAM RAILWAY

Queens Park Station, Torbay Road, Paignton, Devon TQ4 6AF   01803 555872

Fax: 01803 664313   E-mail: pdsr@talk21.com

2004	1	2	3	4	5	6	7	8	9	10	11	12	13	14	15	16	17	18	19	20	21	22	23	24	25	26	27	28	29	30	31
Apr				A	A	A	A	A	A	A	A	A	A	A	A	A	A	A		A		A	A			A		A			
May	A	A	A	A		A		A	A		A		A		A	A		A		A		A	A	A	A	A	A	A	A	A	A
June	A	A	A	A	A	A	A	A	A	A	A	A	A	A	A	A	A	A	A	A	A	A	A	A	A	A	A	B	B	B	
July	B	A	A	A	B	B	B	B	A	A	A	B	B	B	B	A	A	A	C	C	C	C	B	A	A	C	C	C	C	B	A
Aug	A	C	C	C	C	B	A	A	C	C	C	C	B	A	A	C	C	C	C	B	A	A	C	C	C	C	B	B	A	B	B
Sept	B	B	A	A	A	A	A	A	A	A	A	A	A	A	A	A	A	A	A	A	A	A	A	A	A	A	A	A			
Oct		A	A		A		A	A		A		A	A		A		A		A	A	A	A	A	A	A	A	A	A	A	A	A
Dec											S	S						S	S			S	S	S							

A denotes Standard, B denotes Mid-season, C denotes Peak season, S denotes Santa Specials.   No service in January, February, March and November.

Service A

Paignton	dep	10.30	12.00	14.00	16.15
Kingswear	arr	11.00	12.30	14.30	16.45
Kingswear	dep	11.15	12.45	15.15	17.00
Paignton	arr	11.45	13.15	15.45	17.30

Service B

10.30	11.50	13.45	15.00	16.15
11.00	12.20	14.15	15.30	16.45
11.10	12.30	14.20	15.40	17.00
11.40	13.00	14.50	16.10	17.30

Note:
The Company operates a connecting ferry service to Dartmouth where passengers will arrive about 20 minutes after train arrival at Kingswear. Returning passengers should be ready to embark at Dartmouth at least 30 minutes before scheduled train departure from Kingswear.

Service C

Paignton	dep	09.45	10.30	11.15	12.00	12.45	14.00	14.45	15.30	16.15	17.00
Kingswear	arr	10.15	11.05	11.50	12.35	13.20	14.35	15.20	16.05	16.50	17.30
Kingswear	dep	10.30	11.15	12.00	12.45	14.00	14.45	15.30	16.15	17.00	17.45
Paignton	arr	11.05	11.50	12.35	13.20	14.35	15.20	16.05	16.50	17.30	18.15

All trains call at intermediate stations: Goodrington (5) and Churston (15) minutes after leaving Paignton and at Churston (20) and Goodrington (30) minutes after leaving Kingswear.

PEAK RAIL PLC

Matlock Station, Matlock, Derbyshire DE4 3NA   01629 580381

Fax: 01629 760645   E-mail: peakrail@peakrail.co.uk

2004	1	2	3	4	5	6	7	8	9	10	11	12	13	14	15	16	17	18	19	20	21	22	23	24	25	26	27	28	29	30	31
Jan				A							A							A							A						
Feb	A							A							A							A							A		
Mar							A							A							A							A			
Apr			A	A					A	A	A	A	A				A	A						X	X						
May	A	A	A				A	A						A	A			A	A										A	A	A
June		A			A	A		A					A	A			A	A		A	A				A	A		A			
July			A	A		B	A			A	A		B	A			A	A		B	A			A	A		B	A			A
Aug	A		B	A	A		X	X		B	A	A		A	A		B	A		A	A		B	A		A	A		A	A	
Sept	A	A		A	A			A			A	A			A			X	X					A	A						
Oct		A	A				A	A					A	A				A	A					A	A		A	A		X	A
Nov					A									A				A							A						
Dec			X	X							X	X						X	X			X	X								

X denotes special events, see local announcements.

Service A (Steam operated) ¶

Matlock Riverside	dep	–	11.55	13.05	14.15	15.25	*16.35*
Rowsley South	arr	11.05*	12.15	13.25	14.35	15.45	*16.55*
							¶	¶
Rowsley South	dep	11.25	12.35	13.45	14.55	*16.05*	*17.15*
Matlock Riverside	arr	11.45	12.55	14.05	15.15	*16.25*	–

¶ Does not operate January, February, March, November and December and 26th, 27th & 31st October.

* Depart Darley Dale at 11.00.

Service B (DMU)

Matlock Riverside	dep	–	11.40	12.40	13.30	14.20	15.10	16.00	16.50
Rowsley South	arr	–	11.53	12.53	13.43	14.33	15.23	16.13	17.03
Rowsley South	dep	11.15	12.15	13.05	13.55	14.45	15.35	16.25	–
Matlock Riverside	arr	11.30	12.30	13.20	14.10	15.00	15.50	16.40	–

ROMNEY, HYTHE & DYMCHURCH RAILWAY

New Romney Station, New Romney, Kent TN28 8PL   **01797 362353**

Fax: 01797 363591   E-mail: danny.martin2@btinternet.com   Web: www.rhdr.org.uk

2004	1	2	3	4	5	6	7	8	9	10	11	12	13	14	15	16	17	18	19	20	21	22	23	24	25	26	27	28	29	30	31
Jan	A																														
Feb														A	A			A	A	A	A	A	A	A	A	A	A	A			
Mar				A	A									A	A					A	A						A	A			
Apr	C	C	B	B	B	B	B	B	B	D	D	D	D	B	B	B	B	B	B	B	C	C	C	C	C	A	A	C	C	C	C
May	D	D	D	A	A	A	A	B	B	A	A	A	A	A	X	X	A	A	A	A	A	B	B	A	A	A	A	A	D	D	D
June	D	D	D	D	D	B	B	B	B	B	B	B	B	B	B	B	B	B	B	B	B	B	B	B	B	B	B	B	B	B	
July	B	B	D	D	B	B	B	B	B	B	D	D	B	B	B	B	B	X	X	D	D	D	D	D	D	D	D	D	D	D	D
Aug	D	D	D	D	D	D	D	D	D	D	D	D	D	D	D	D	D	D	D	D	D	D	D	D	D	D	D	D	X	X	D
Sept	D	D	D	X	X	B	B	B	B	B	B	B	B	A	A	A	A	A	B	B	A	A	A	A	A	B	B	C	C	C	
Oct	C	X	X					A	A					A	A							A	A	A	A	A	A	A	A	A	A
Nov				A	A																										
Dec			S	S							S	S						S	S			S	S	S	S						

S denotes Santa Specials, T denotes Thomas events, X denotes special events, see local announcements.

Service A

Hythe	dep	–	10.30	11.30	12.30	13.30	14.30	15.30	16.30	17.30
New Romney	dep	10.25	11.08	12.08	13.08	14.05†	15.08	16.05	17.05	18.05
Dungeness	arr	10.52	11.35	12.35	13.35	–	15.35	–	–	–
Dungeness	dep	–	–	11.00	12.05	13.05	14.05	–	16.05	–
New Romney	dep	09.35	10.35	11.35	12.35	13.35	14.35	15.15	16.35	–
Hythe	arr	10.10	11.10	12.10	13.10	14.10	15.10	15.50	17.10	–

Service C

11.10	12.40	14.20	17.10
11.48	13.15	14.58	17.45
12.15	–	15.25	–
–	–	12.55	15.55
10.00	11.55	13.25	16.25
10.35	12.30	14.00	17.00

Service B

							D		**E**					
Hythe	dep	–	10.30	11.30	12.30	13.30	14.00	14.30	15.30	–	–	16.30	17.30	18.15
New Romney	dep	10.25	11.08	12.08	13.08	14.08	15.08†	15.08	16.08	–	–	17.08	18.05	18.50
Dungeness	arr	10.52	11.35	12.35	13.35	14.35	–	15.35	16.35	–	–	17.35	–	–
Dungeness	dep	–	–	11.00	12.05	13.05	14.05	–	15.05	–	16.05	17.05	17.37	–
New Romney	dep	09.35	10.35	11.35	12.35	13.35	14.35	–	15.35	16.10	16.35	17.35	18.05	–
Hythe	arr	10.10	11.10	12.10	13.10	14.10	15.10	–	16.10	16.40	17.10	18.10	–	–

† = Arrival

Service D

														E
Hythe	dep	–	10.20	11.05	11.50	12.35	13.20	14.05	14.50	15.35	16.20	17.05	17.30	18.15	18.55
New Romney	dep	09.43	10.58	11.43	12.28	13.13	13.58	14.43	15.28	16.13	16.58	17.43	18.05	18.50	19.25
Dungeness	arr	10.10	11.25	12.10	12.55	13.40	14.25	15.10	15.55	16.40	17.25	18.10	–	–	–
Dungeness	dep	–	–	10.25	–	11.40	12.25	13.10	13.55	14.40	15.25	16.10	16.55	17.40	18.15
New Romney	dep	09.25	10.10	10.55	11.40	12.10	12.55	13.40	14.25	15.10	15.55	16.40	17.25	18.10	18.45†
Hythe	arr	10.00	10.45	11.30	12.15	12.45	13.30	14.15	15.00	15.45	16.30	17.15	18.00	18.45	

Trains call at Romney Sands (15), St Mary's Bay (38) and Dymchurch (45) minutes after leaving Dungeness and at Dymchurch (18), St Mary's Bay (23) and Romney Sands (50) minutes after leaving Hythe.

D Kent Coast Express runs non stop to New Romney via Dungeness on 12th and 26th June and 11th September only.

E Kent Coast Express runs non-stop to Hythe on 12th and 26th June and 11th September only.

RAVENGLASS & ESKDALE RAILWAY
Ravenglass Station, Ravenglass, Cumbria CA18 1SW

01229 717171

Fax: 01229 717011   E-mail: rer@netcomuk.co.uk

2004	1	2	3	4	5	6	7	8	9	10	11	12	13	14	15	16	17	18	19	20	21	22	23	24	25	26	27	28	29	30	31
Jan	A	A	A	A																											
Feb											A	A	A	A	A	A	A	A	A	A	A	A	A	A	A	A	A	A	A		
Mar					A	A							A	A				B	B	B	B	B	B	B	B	B	B	B	B	B	B
Apr	B	B	B	B	B	B	B	B	B	C	C	C	C	C	C	C	C	B	B	B	B	B	B	B	B	B	B	B	B	B	
May	C	C	C	B	B	B	B	B	B	B	B	B	B	B	B	T	T	B	B	B	B	B	B	B	B	B	B	B	D	D	D
June	D	D	D	C	C	C	C	C	C	C	C	C	C	C	C	C	C	C	C	C	C	C	C	C	C	C	C	C	C	C	
July	C	C	C	C	C	C	C	C	C	C	C	C	C	C	C	C	C	D	D	D	D	D	D	D	D	D	D	D	D	D	D
Aug	D	D	D	D	D	D	D	D	D	D	D	D	D	D	D	D	D	D	D	D	D	D	D	D	D	D	D	D	D	D	D
Sept	D	D	C	C	C	C	C	C	C	C	C	C	C	C	C	C	C	C	C	B	B	B	B	B	B	B	B	B	B	B	
Oct	B	T	T	B	B	B	B	B	B	B	B	B	B	B	B	B	B	B	B	B	B	B	B	B	B	B	B	B	B	B	B
Nov					A	A							A	A																	
Dec			S	S						S	S							S	S						A	A	A	A	A	A	

T denotes Thomas weekends, S denotes Santa Specials, see local announcements.

Service A

Ravenglass	dep	–	11.55	13.55	15.55
Eskdale (Dalegarth)	arr	–	12.35	14.35	16.30
Eskdale (Dalegarth)	dep	10.55	13.05	15.00	–
Ravenglass	arr	11.30	13.40	15.35	–

Service B

10.30	11.30	12.10	12.50	13.50	14.50	15.50
11.10	12.10	12.50	13.30	14.30	15.30	16.25
11.30	12.30	13.10	13.50	14.50	15.50	16.35
12.10	13.10	13.50	14.30	15.30	16.30	17.05

Service C

Ravenglass	dep	09.00	–	10.30	11.30	12.10	12.50	13.50	14.50	15.50	16.50
Eskdale (Dalegarth)	arr	09.35	–	11.10	12.10	12.50	13.30	14.30	15.30	16.30	17.25
		x	†								
Eskdale (Dalegarth)	dep	09.40	10.10	11.30	12.30	13.10	13.50	14.50	15.50	16.50	17.30
Ravenglass	arr	10.15	10.50	12.10	13.10	13.50	14.30	15.30	16.30	17.30	18.05

x Runs Saturdays only.

† *Does not* run on Saturdays.

* *Does not* run on Friday, Saturday or Sunday.

Service D

				*		*				*			*			
Ravenglass	dep	09.00	–	10.30	11.10	11.30	11.50	12.10	12.50	13.30	13.50	14.10	14.30	14.50	15.30	15.50	16.30	17.30
Eskdale (Dalegarth)	arr	09.35	–	11.10	11.50	12.10	12.30	12.50	13.30	14.10	14.30	14.50	15.10	15.30	16.10	16.30	17.10	18.05
				*		*				*			*			
Eskdale (Dalegarth)	dep	09.40	10.10	11.30	12.10	12.30	13.10	13.30	13.50	14.30	14.50	15.10	15.30	15.50	16.30	16.50	17.30	18.15
Ravenglass	arr	10.15	10.50	12.10	12.50	13.10	13.50	14.10	14.30	15.10	15.30	15.50	16.10	16.30	17.10	17.30	18.05	18.50

All trains call at intermediate stations: Muncaster Mill (5), Irton Road (20), The Green (24), Fisherground (28) and Beckfoot – to set down only (33) minutes after leaving Ravenglass and at Beckfoot – to pick up only (2), Fisherground (6), The Green (10), Irton Road (14) and Muncaster Mill (28) minutes after leaving Eskdale.

SITTINGBOURNE AND KEMSLEY LIGHT RAILWAY
PO Box 300, Sittingbourne, Kent ME10 2DZ

07946 717217

E-mail: info@sklr.net

2004	1	2	3	4	5	6	7	8	9	10	11	12	13	14	15	16	17	18	19	20	21	22	23	24	25	26	27	28	29	30	31
Apr				A					B	A	B	B						A							A						
May	A	B	B						A							A					A					A	B	B			
June					A							A						A						A							
July			X	X					A							A				A					A						
Aug	B			A				B		A				B			A				B			A			A	B	B		
Sept					A						A					A					B				X	X					
Dec			S	S					S	S							S	S							S						

X denotes special events, S denotes Santa Specials, see local announcements.

No service in January, February, March, October and November.

Service A

Sittingbourne Viaduct	dep	13.00	14.00	15.00	16.00
Kemsley Down	arr	13.15	14.15	15.15	16.15
Kemsley Down	dep	13.35	14.35	15.35	16.45
Sittingbourne Viaduct	arr	13.50	14.50	15.50	17.00

Service B

11.00	12.00	13.00	14.00	15.00	16.00
11.15	12.15	13.15	14.15	15.15	16.15
11.35	12.35	13.35	14.35	15.35	16.45
11.50	12.50	13.50	14.50	15.50	17.00

Trains call at Milton Regis Halt on request.

SEATON TRAMWAY
Harbour Road, Seaton, Devon EX12 2NQ

01297 20375

Fax: 01297 625626   E-mail: info@tram.co.uk

2004	1	2	3	4	5	6	7	8	9	10	11	12	13	14	15	16	17	18	19	20	21	22	23	24	25	26	27	28	29	30	31
Jan										X								X						X							
Feb	X													C	C				X				C	C				C	C		
Mar						C	C							C	C					C	C						C	C			
Apr		A	A	A	A	A	A	A	A	A	A	A	A	A	A	A	A	A	A	A	A	A	A	A	A	A	A	A	A	A	A
May	A	A	A	A	A	A	A	A	A	A	A	A	A	A	A	A	A	A	A	A	A	A	A	A	A	A	A	A	A	A	A
June	A	A	A	A	A	A	A	A	A	A	A	A	A	A	A	A	A	A	A	A	A	A	A	A	A	A	A	A	A	A	
July	A	A	A	A	A	A	A	A	A	A	A	A	A	A	A	A	A	A	A	A	A	A	A	B	B	B	B	B	B	B	B
Aug	B	B	B	B	B	B	B	B	B	B	B	B	B	B	B	B	B	B	B	B	B	B	B	B	B	B	B	B	B	B	B
Sept	A	A	A	A	A	A	A	A	A	A	A	A	A	A	A	A	A	A	A	A	A	A	A	A	A	A	A	A	A	A	
Oct	A	A	A	A	A	A	A	A	A	A	A	A	A	A	A	A	A	A	A	A	A	A	A	A	A	A	A	A	A	A	A
Nov						C	C							C	C					C	C						C	C			
Dec				C	S						C	S						C	S							S					

X denotes special services, S denotes Santa Specials, see local announcements.

Service A

Seaton	dep	10.00	then at these minutes past each hour	20	40	00	until	17.00
Colyton	arr	10.23		43	03	23		17.23

Colyton	dep	10.30	then at these minutes past each hour	50	10	30	until	17.30
Seaton	arr	10.54		14	34	54		17.54

Service B

	10.00	then at these minutes past each hour	40	00	20	until	20.40
	10.23		03	23	43		21.03

	10.30	then at these minutes past each hour	10	30	50	until	21.10
	10.54		34	54	14		21.34

Service C

Seaton	dep	10.00	then at these minutes past each hour	40	00	20	until	16.00
Colyton	arr	10.23		03	23	43		16.23

Colyton	dep	10.30	then at these minutes past each hour	10	30	50	until	16.30
Seaton	arr	10.54		34	54	14		16.54

All trams call at Colyford 13 minutes after leaving Seaton and 10 minutes after leaving Colyton.

Pre-booked groups welcomed all year round.

Extra departures run according to demand at peak periods.

Normal fares structure suspended on Santa Special dates. Pre-booking essential for bird watching specials.

STRATHSPEY RAILWAY
Aviemore Station, Dalfaber Road, Aviemore PH22 1PY

01479 810725

Fax: 01479 812220   E-mail: information@strathspeyrailway.co.uk

2004	1	2	3	4	5	6	7	8	9	10	11	12	13	14	15	16	17	18	19	20	21	22	23	24	25	26	27	28	29	30	31
Mar																												A			A
Apr				A			A	A	A	A	A	A	A					A			A				A			A			
May	A	A	A		A	A		A	A			A	A		A	A			A	A		A	A			A	A		X	X	X
June	A	A	A	A	A	A	A	A	A	A	A	A	A	A	A	A	A	A	A	A	A	A	A	A	A	A	A	A	A	A	
July	A	A	A	A	A	A	A	A	A	A	A	A	A	A	A	A	A	A	A	A	A	A	A	A	A	A	A	A	A	A	A
Aug	A	A	A	A	A	A	A	A	A	A	A	A	X	X	X	X	X	X	X	X	A	A	A	A	A	A	A	A	A	A	A
Sept	A	A	A	A	X	A	A	A	A	A	A	A	A	A	A	A	A	A	A	A	A	A	A	A	A	A	A	A	A	A	
Oct		A	A		A	A		A	A			A	A		A	A			A	A		A	A			A	A			A	A
Dec				S					S									S	S			S	S			X	X				X

X denotes special events, S denotes Santa Specials, see local announcements.   *No service in January, February and November.*

Additional trains run on 14th, 15th, 21st and 22nd August.

Service A

Aviemore	dep	–	10.30	12.20	14.45	16.25
Boat of Garten	arr	–	10.45	12.35	15.00	16.40
Boat of Garten	dep		10.50	12.40	15.05	16.45
Broomhill	arr	–	11.15	13.05	15.30	17.00
						★
Broomhill	dep	–	11.30	13.20	15.40	17.30
Boat of Garten	arr	–	11.45	13.35	15.55	17.45
Boat of Garten	dep	10.00	11.50	13.40	16.00	17.50
Aviemore	arr	10.15	12.05	13.55	16.15	18.05

★ Runs 5th September only.

SEVERN VALLEY RAILWAY

01299 403816

The Railway Station, Bewdley, Worcs DY12 1BG

Fax: 01299 400839

2004	1	2	3	4	5	6	7	8	9	10	11	12	13	14	15	16	17	18	19	20	21	22	23	24	25	26	27	28	29	30	31
Jan			A	A						A	A						A	A						A	A						A
Feb	A						A	A						A	A	A	A	A	A	A	X	A						X	X		
Mar					X	X								X	X										X	X					
Apr			B	B	B	B	B	B	B	B	B	D	D	D	B	B	B	B	B	B	B			B	B						
May	B	D	D					X	X	B	B	C	C	C	X	X	B	C	C	C	C	C	B	B	C	C	C	C	B	C	D
June	B	B	B	B	X	X	B	B	B	B	B	C	B	B	B	B	B	B	B	C	B	B	B	B	B	B	X	X	B	B	
July	B	B	X	X	B	B	B	B	B	C	B	B	B	B	B	B	B	C	B	B	B	B	B	B	C	B	B	B	B	B	C
Aug	B	B	B	B	B	B	B	C	B	B	B	B	B	B	C	B	B	B	B	B	B	C	B	B	B	B	B	B	C	D	D
Sept	B	B	B	X	X	A	A	A	A	A	X	X	A	A	A	A	A	A	B	B	A	A	A	A	X	X	X				
Oct	X	X	X					B	X					X	X	X					B	B	A	A	A	A	A	A	B	B	
Nov					A	A					A	A					A	A								A	A				
Dec			S	S						S	S					S	S			S	S	S	S			X	X	X	X	X	X

X denotes special events, S denotes Santa Specials, see local announcements.

Service A

Kidderminster	dep	10.45	12.00	13.15	14.30	16.25
Bridgnorth	arr	11.54	13.09	14.24	15.36	17.27
Bridgnorth	dep	11.15	12.30	13.45	15.00	16.15
Kidderminster	arr	12.26	13.42	14.57	16.03	17.18

Service B ★

10.25	11.45	12.15	13.05	14.20	15.35	16.50
11.39	12.54	13.28	14.13	15.31	16.42	18.01
			★			
11.00	12.15	13.35	14.20	14.50	16.05	17.25
12.13	13.27	14.44	15.20	16.00	17.13	18.30

Service C ¶

Kidderminster	dep	10.00	10.35	11.15	12.45	13.30	14.15	15.00	16.30	19.00
Bridgnorth	arr	11.00	11.45	12.30	13.59	14.44	15.29	16.14	17.44	20.05
Bridgnorth	dep	11.05	11.50	12.35	13.20	14.50	15.35	16.20	17.05	21.10
Kidderminster	arr	12.22	13.07	13.52	14.37	16.07	16.52	17.37	18.18	22.07

★ Sundays only. Restaurant car service.
¶ Certain Saturdays only.

Service D

Kidderminster	dep	09.55	10.30	11.15	12.00	12.45	13.30	14.15	15.00	15.45	16.30	–
Bridgnorth	arr	11.00	11.45	12.30	13.14	13.59	14.44	15.29	16.14	16.59	17.44	–
Bridgnorth	dep	–	11.05	11.50	12.35	13.20	14.05	14.50	15.35	16.20	17.05	17.50
Kidderminster	arr	–	12.22	13.07	13.52	14.37	15.22	16.07	16.52	17.37	18.18	18.56

All trains call at intermediate stations: Bewdley (20), Arley (38), Highley (47) and Hampton Loade (58) minutes after leaving Kidderminster and at Hampton Loade (22), Highley (34), Arley (47) and Bewdley (66) minutes after leaving Bridgnorth.

SOUTH DEVON RAILWAY

0845 345 1427

The Station, Buckfastleigh, Devon TQ11 0DZ

Fax: 01364 642170   E-mail: info@southdevonrailway.org

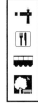

2004	1	2	3	4	5	6	7	8	9	10	11	12	13	14	15	16	17	18	19	20	21	22	23	24	25	26	27	28	29	30	31
Mar																											B	B			
Apr		A	A	A	A	A	A	A	A	A	X	X	A	A	A	A	A	A	A	A	A	A	A	A	A	A	A	A	A	A	
May	X	X	X	A	A	A	A	A	A	A	A	A	A	A	X	X	A	A	A	A	A	A	A	A	A	A	A	A	A	B	B
June	B	B	B	A	A	A	A	A	A	A	A	X	X	A	A	A	A	A	A	A	A	A	A	A	A	A	A	A	A	A	
July	A	A	A	B	A	A	A	A	A	A	A	A	A	A	A	A	A	A	A	A	A	A	B	B	B	B	A	A			
Aug	B	B	B	B	B	A	A	A	B	B	B	B	A	A	B	B	B	B	A	A	A	B	B	B	B	A	A	B	B	B	
Sept	B	B	A	A	B	A	A	A	A	X	X	A	A	A	A	A	A	A	A	A	A	A	A	A	A	A	A	A			
Oct	A	A	B	A	A	A	A	A	A	A	A	A	A	A	A	A	A	A	A	A	A	A	A	A	A	A	A	A	A	B	
Dec			S							S	S					S	S		S	S	S								A	A	

X denotes special events, S denotes Santa Specials, see local announcements.   *No service in January, February and November.*

Service A

Buckfastleigh	dep	10.45	12.15	14.15	15.45
Totnes	arr	11.15	12.45	14.45	16.15
Totnes	dep	11.30	13.00	15.00	16.30
Buckfastleigh	arr	12.00	13.30	15.30	17.00

Service B

10.00	10.45	11.30	12.15	13.00	14.15	15.00	15.45	17.15
10.30	11.15	12.00	12.45	13.30	14.45	15.30	16.15	17.45
10.45	11.30	12.15	13.00	14.15	15.00	15.45	16.30	18.00
11.15	12.00	12.45	13.30	14.45	15.30	16.15	17.00	18.30

All trains call at intermediate station: Staverton (15) minutes after leaving Buckfastleigh and (10) minutes after leaving Totnes.

SNAEFELL MOUNTAIN RAILWAY
Banks Circus, Douglas, Isle of Man IM1 5PT

01624 663366
Fax: 01624 663637   E-mail: info@busandrail.dtl.gov.im

Daily Service – Monday 26th April to Sunday 26th September 2004 (subject to weather conditions), between 10.15 and 15.45 (last guaranteed ascent).

SNOWDON MOUNTAIN RAILWAY
Llanberis, Caernarfon, Gwynedd LL55 4TY

0870 458 0033
Fax: 01286 872518   E-mail: info@snowdonrailway.co.uk

Daily Service – Mid March to the first week of November 2004 (subject to weather conditions). From mid-March to early May trains terminate at Clogwyn or Rocky Valley.

SOUTH TYNEDALE RAILWAY
The Railway Station, Alston, Cumbria CA9 3JB

01434 381696
Talking Timetable: 01434 382828   Web: www.strps.org.uk

2004	1	2	3	4	5	6	7	8	9	10	11	12	13	14	15	16	17	18	19	20	21	22	23	24	25	26	27	28	29	30	31
Apr									A	A	A	A	A	A	A	A	A	A						A	A						
May	X	X	X					A	A						A	A						A	A						A	A	A
June	A	A	A	A	X	X							A	A					A	A						X	X		A	A	
July	A		A	A			A	A	A		A	A		A	A	A		A	A	A	A	A	A	A	A	A	A	A	A	A	A
Aug	A	A	A	A	A	A	A	A	A	A	A	A	A	A	A	A	A	A	A	A	A	A	A	A	A	A	A	A	A	A	A
Sept			A	A							A	A					A	A						A	A						
Oct			B							B							B							B		B	B	B		X	X
Dec				S	S						S	S						S	S												

X denotes special service, S denotes Santa Specials, see local announcements.   No service in January, February, March and November.

Service A

Alston	dep	11.00	12.00	13.45	15.00	16.15
Kirkhaugh	dep	11.30	12.30	14.15	15.30	16.45

Service B

11.00	12.00	13.45	15.00
11.30	12.30	14.15	15.30

Trains may leave Kirkhaugh up to 10 minutes later than times shown.
Journey run about 15 minutes in each direction.

SPA VALLEY RAILWAY
West Station, Tunbridge Wells, Kent TN2 5QY

01892 537715
Web: www.spavalleyrailway.co.uk

2004	1	2	3	4	5	6	7	8	9	10	11	12	13	14	15	16	17	18	19	20	21	22	23	24	25	26	27	28	29	30	31
Jan	B	B	B	B																											
Mar														X						B							X	X			
Apr			X	X					A	A	A	A	A	B	B	B	B	A	A					A	A						
May	A	A	A					A	A						A	A						A	A						A	A	A
June	B	B	B	B	A	A						A	A						A	A						A	A				
July			X	X						A	A						A	A			B	B	B	A	A			B	B	B	A
Aug	A			B	B	B	X	X		B	B	B	B	A	A			B	B	B	A	A			B	B	B	A	A	A	B
Sept	B	B	B	A	A						A	A						X	X						A	A					
Oct		X	X						X	X						A	A						A	A			B	B	B	B	B
Dec			S	S							S	S						S	S	S	S	S	S	S			B	B	B	B	B

X denotes special events, S denotes Santa Specials, see local announcements.   No service in February and November.

Service A

Tunbridge Wells West	dep	10.30	11.45	12.50	14.00	15.15	16.30	18.00 (D)	19.30 (★D)
Groombridge	arr	10.46	12.01	13.06	14.16	15.31	16.46	18.16	19.46
Groombridge	dep	11.05	12.20	13.25	14.35	15.50	17.05	18.35	20.05
Tunbridge Wells West	arr	11.23	12.38	13.43	14.53	16.08	17.23	18.53	20.23

Service B

11.00	12.15	14.00	15.15
11.16	12.31	14.16	15.31
11.35	12.50	14.35	15.50
11.53	13.08	14.53	16.08

All trains call at High Rocks 8 minutes after leaving Tunbridge Wells and 10 minutes after leaving Groombridge.

D Heritage Diesel hauled service.
★ Runs only on Saturdays 31st July, 14th, 21st and 28th August.

SWANAGE RAILWAY
Station House, Swanage, Dorset BH19 1HB

01929 425800
Fax: 01929 426680   E-mail: davidagreen@orange.net

2004	1	2	3	4	5	6	7	8	9	10	11	12	13	14	15	16	17	18	19	20	21	22	23	24	25	26	27	28	29	30	31
Jan	A	A	A	A																											
Feb													X	X	X	X	X	X	X	X	X										
Mar					A	A							A	A					A	A							X	X			
Apr	B	B	B	B	B	B	B	B	B	X	X	X	X	B	B	B	B	B	B	B	B	B	B	B	B	B	B	B	B	B	
May	C	C	C	B	B	B	B	B	B	X	B	B	B	B	B	B	B	B	B	B	B	B	B	B	B	B	B	B	C	C	C
June	B	B	B	B	X	X	B	B	B	B	B	X	X	B	B	B	B	B	B	B	B	B	B	B	B	B	B	B	B	B	
July	B	B	C	C	B	B	B	B	B	B	B	B	B	B	B	B	C	C	C	C	C	C	C	C	C	C	C	C	C	C	C
Aug	C	C	C	C	C	C	C	C	C	C	C	C	C	C	C	C	C	C	C	C	C	C	C	C	C	C	C	C	C	C	C
Sept	C	C	C	C	C	B	B	B	B	B	X	X	B	B	B	B	B	B	B	B	B	B	B	B	A	A	A	A	A	A	
Oct	A	A	A	A	A	A	A	A	A	A	A	A	A	A	A	A	A	A	A	A	A	X	X	X	X	X	X	X	X	X	X
Nov					A	A							A	A					A	A									A	X	
Dec			S	S					S	S									S	S		S	S	S		A	A	A	A	A	A

Service A

Swanage	dep	09.50	11.05	12.15	13.25	14.35	15.45
Norden Park & Ride	arr	10.15	11.30	12.40	13.50	15.00	16.10
Norden Park & Ride	dep	10.30	11.40	12.50	14.00	15.10	16.20
Swanage	arr	10.53	12.03	13.13	14.23	15.33	16.43

X denotes special events, S denotes Santa Specials, see local announcements.

Service B

Swanage	dep	09.50	11.05	12.15	13.25	14.35	15.45	16.55	★ 19.10	★ 20.20	★ 22.00	★ 23.00
Norden Park & Ride	arr	10.15	11.30	12.40	13.50	15.00	16.10	17.20	–	–	–	–
Norden Park & Ride	dep	10.30	11.40	12.50	14.00	15.10	16.20	17.30	–	–	–	–
Swanage	arr	10.53	12.03	13.13	14.23	15.33	16.43	17.53	20.03	21.28	22.48	23.42

Service C

Swanage	dep	09.50	10.30	11.05	11.40	12.15	12.50	13.25	14.00	14.35	15.10	15.45	16.20
Norden Park & Ride	arr	10.15	10.55	11.30	12.05	12.40	13.15	13.50	14.25	15.00	15.35	16.10	16.45
Norden Park & Ride	dep	10.30	11.05	11.40	12.15	12.50	13.25	14.00	14.35	15.10	15.45	16.20	16.55
Swanage	arr	10.53	11.28	12.03	12.38	13.13	13.48	14.23	14.58	15.33	16.08	16.43	17.18

Swanage	dep	16.55	17.30	D 18.05	D 19.10	D 20.20	D 22.00	D 23.00
Norden Park & Ride	arr	17.20	17.55	18.30	–	–	–	–
Norden Park & Ride	dep	17.30	18.05	18.35	–	–	–	–
Swanage	arr	17.53	18.28	18.57	20.03	21.28	22.48	23.42

D Diesel train to and from Corfe Castle only.
★ Runs Fridays and Saturdays only to and from Corfe Castle.

All trains call at Harmans Cross (10) and Corfe Castle (20) minutes after leaving Swanage. And at Corfe Castle (2) and Harmans Cross (11) minutes after leaving Norden.

TEIFI VALLEY RAILWAY
Henllan Station, Henllan, Newcastle Emlyn, Ceredigion SA44 5ST

01559 371077
Fax: 01559 371077   E-mail: lizperry@paperwork.sagehost.co.uk

2004	1	2	3	4	5	6	7	8	9	10	11	12	13	14	15	16	17	18	19	20	21	22	23	24	25	26	27	28	29	30	31
Apr		A	A	A	A	A	A	A	A	A	A	A	A	A	A	A	A	A	A	A	A			A	A	A	A				
May	A	A	A	A	A			A	A	A	A			A	A	A	A	A			A	A	A	A	A				A	A	A
June	A	A	A	A	A	A	A	A	A	A		A	A	A	A	A		A	A	A	A	A	A		A	A	A	A	A		
July	A		A	A	A	A	A		A	A	A	A	A	A	X	X	B	B	B	B	B	B	B	B	B	B	B	B	B	B	B
Aug	B	B	B	B	B	B	B	B	B	B	B	B	B	B	B	B	B	B	B	B	B	B	B	B	B	B	B	B	B	B	B
Sept	A	A	A	A	A	A		A	A	A	A	A			A	A	A	A	A			A	A	A	A	A			A	A	
Oct		A	A	A	A			A	A	A	A			A	A	A	A	A			A	A	A	A	A					A	X
Dec								S	S	S										S	S	S	S	S							

X denotes special events, S denotes Santa Specials, see local announcements.   No service in January, February, March and November.

Service A

Henllan	dep	11.00	12.00	13.30	14.30	15.30

Service B

		11.00	12.00	13.30	14.30	15.30	16.30

Journey: From Henllan to Llandyfriog and return. Journey time: 30-40 minutes including stop to visit waterfalls en route. Extension in progress – completion uncertain.

TALYLLYN RAILWAY
Wharf Station, Tywyn, Gwynedd LL36 9EY

01654 710472

Fax: 01654 711755   E-mail: enquiries@talyllyn.co.uk

2004	1	2	3	4	5	6	7	8	9	10	11	12	13	14	15	16	17	18	19	20	21	22	23	24	25	26	27	28	29	30	31
Jan	A	A	A																												
Feb								A						A	A	A	A	A	A	A	A	A							A		
Mar						A								A						A								A	A	A	A
Apr	A	A	A	B	B	B	B	B	B	B	B	B	B	B	B	B	B	B	B	B	B	B	B	B	B	B	B	B	B	B	
May	B	B	B	B	B	B	B	B	B	B	B	B	B	B	B	B	B	B	B	B	B	B	B	B	B	B	B	B	D	D	D
June	D	D	D	D	B	B	B	B	B	B	B	B	B	B	B	B	B	B	B	B	B	B	B	B	B	B	B	B	B	B	
July	B	B	B	B	B	B	B	B	B	B	B	B	B	B	X	X	X	X	D	D	D	D	D	C	C	D	D	D	D	D	C
Aug	C	D	D	D	D	D	D	C	C	D	D	D	D	D	D	C	C	D	D	D	D	D	X	C	D	D	D	D	D	D	D
Sept	C	C	C	C	C	B	B	B	B	B	B	B	B	B	B	B	B	B	B	B	B	B	B	B	B	B	B	B	B	B	
Oct	B	B	B	B	B	B	B	B	B	B	B	B	B	B	B	B	B	B	B	B	B	B	B	B	B	B	B	B	B	B	A
Nov	A	A	A	A	A	A																									
Dec																		S	S				S	S		A	A	A	A	A	A

X denotes special services, S denotes Santa Specials, see local announcements.

Service A

Tywyn (Wharf)	dep	11.00	14.00
Abergynolwyn	arr	11.45	14.45
Abergynolwyn	dep	11.46	14.46
Nant Gwernol	arr	11.52	14.52
Nant Gwernol	dep	12.02	15.02
Abergynolwyn	arr	12.07	15.07
Abergynolwyn	dep	12.35	15.30
Tywyn (Wharf)	arr	13.20	16.15

Service B

10.30	11.40	13.55	15.00
11.15	12.25	14.40	15.45
11.19	12.26	14.41	16.06
11.25	12.32	14.47	16.12
11.35	12.45	15.00	16.22
11.40	12.50	15.05	16.27
12.10	13.20	15.30	16.30
12.55	14.05	16.15	17.15

Service C

10.30	11.40	13.25	14.30	16.10
11.15	12.25	14.10	15.15	16.55
11.19	12.26	14.11	15.16	17.11
11.25	12.32	14.17	15.22	17.17
11.35	12.45	14.30	15.35	17.27
11.40	12.50	14.35	15.40	17.32
12.10	13.20	15.00	16.05	17.35
12.55	14.05	15.45	16.50	18.20

Service D

Tywyn (Wharf)	dep	10.10	10.50	11.40	12.35	13.30	14.20	15.15	16.10
Abergynolwyn	arr	10.55	11.35	12.25	13.20	14.15	15.05	16.00	16.55
Abergynolwyn	dep	10.59	11.36	12.26	13.21	14.16	15.06	16.01	17.11
Nant Gwernol	arr	11.05	11.42	12.32	13.27	14.22	15.12	16.07	17.17
Nant Gwernol	dep	11.15	11.55	12.50	13.40	14.35	15.30	16.20	17.27
Abergynolwyn	arr	11.20	12.00	12.55	13.45	14.40	15.35	16.25	17.32
Abergynolwyn	dep	11.40	12.35	13.30	14.20	15.15	16.10	17.00	17.35
Tywyn (Wharf)	arr	12.21	13.16	14.11	15.01	15.56	16.51	17.45	18.20

All trains call at intermediate stations: Rhydyronen (12) and Dolgoch Falls (31) minutes after leaving Tywyn and at Dolgoch Falls (10) and Rhydyronen (25) minutes after leaving Abergynolwyn.

VALE OF RHEIDOL RAILWAY
Park Avenue, Aberystwyth, Ceredigion SY23 1PG

01970 625819

Fax: 01970 623769   E-mail: info@rheidolrailway.co.uk   Web: www.rheidolrailway.co.uk

2004	1	2	3	4	5	6	7	8	9	10	11	12	13	14	15	16	17	18	19	20	21	22	23	24	25	26	27	28	29	30	31
Apr			A		A	A	A	A	A	A	A	A	A	A	A		A		A	A	A	A		A		A	A	A	A	A	
May	A	A	A	A	A	A		A		A	A	A	A		A		A	A	A	A		A	A	A	A		A	A		A	B
June	B	B	B	A	A	A	A	A	A	A	A	A	A	A	A	A	A	A	A	A	A	A	A	A	A	A	A	A	A	A	
July	A	A	A	A	A	A	A	A	A	A	A	A	A	A	A	A	A	A	A	A	A	A	A	A	A	B	B	B	B	A	A
Aug	A	B	B	B	B	A	A	A	B	B	B	B	A	A	A	B	B	B	B	A	A	A	B	B	B	B	A	A	A	B	B
Sept	B	B	A	A	A	A	A	A	A	A		A	A	A	A	A		A	A	A	A	A		A	A	A	A	A	A	A	
Oct		A		A	A	A	A		A		A	A	A	A		A		A	A	A	A		A		A	A	A	A		A	

No service in January, February, March, November and December.

Service A

Aberystwyth	dep	10.30	14.00
Devils Bridge	arr	11.30	15.00
Devils Bridge	dep	12.30	16.00
Aberystwyth	arr	13.30	17.00

Service B

10.30	12.15	14.00	15.45
11.30	13.15	15.00	16.45
12.30	14.15	16.00	17.45
13.30	15.15	17.00	18.45

WELSH HIGHLAND RAILWAY (CAERNARFON)

c/o Ffestiniog Railway, Harbour Station, Porthmadog, Gwynedd LL49 9NF

Tel: 01766 516073   Fax: 01766 516005   E-mail: info@festrail.co.uk

2004	1	2	3	4	5	6	7	8	9	10	11	12	13	14	15	16	17	18	19	20	21	22	23	24	25	26	27	28	29	30	31
Jan	A	A	A	A																											
Feb														A	A	A	A	A	A	A	A	A	A	A	A	A					
Mar					A	A								A	A				A	A		A	A	A			A	A		A	A
Apr	A	A	B	B	A	B	B	B	B	C	D	D	C	C	C	C	A	B	B	A	B	B	B	A	B	B	B	A	B	B	
May	X	X	X	B	B	B	A	B	B	A	B	B	B	A	B	B	A	B	B	B	A	B	B	A	B	B	B	A	C	D	D
June	D	D	D	C	C	C	A	B	B	B	A	B	B	A	B	B	A	B	B	A	B	B	B	A	B	B	A	B	B	B	
July	B	A	C	C	A	B	B	B	A	C	C	A	B	B	B	B	C	C	B	B	B	B	B	C	C	B	B	B	B	B	C
Aug	C	C	D	D	D	D	C	C	C	C	D	D	D	C	C	C	C	D	D	D	C	C	C	C	D	D	D	C	C	D	D
Sept	D	D	C	C	C	B	B	B	B	A	X	X	A	A	A	A	A	A	B	B	A	A	A	A	A	A	B	B	B	A	
Oct	A	B	B	A	A	A	A	A	B	B	A	A	A	A	A	A	B	B	A	A	A	A	A	B	B	A	B	B	B	A	A
Nov					A	A								A	A				A	A							A	A			
Dec				A	A						S	S							S	S						A	A	A	A	A	A

X denotes special events, S denotes Santa Specials, see local announcements.

Service A

Caernarfon	dep	10.30	13.30
Rhyd Ddu	arr	11.40	14.35
Rhyd Ddu	dep	12.00	15.00
Caernarfon	arr	13.05	16.05

Service B

	10.30	12.00	13.30	15.00
	11.40	13.10	14.40	16.10
	12.00	13.30	15.00	16.30
	13.10	14.45	16.15	17.45

Service C

–	10.30	12.00	13.30	15.00
–	11.40	13.10	14.40	16.10
–	12.00	13.30	15.00	16.30
11.45	13.10	14.45	16.15	17.45

Service D

Caernarfon	dep	–	10.30	12.00	13.30	15.00	16.30
Rhyd Ddu	arr	10.10	11.40	13.10	14.40	16.10	17.40
Rhyd Ddu	dep	10.35	12.00	13.30	15.00	16.30	18.00
Caernarfon	arr	11.45	13.10	14.45	16.15	17.45	19.10

WELSHPOOL & LLANFAIR LIGHT RAILWAY

The Station, Llanfair Caereinion, Welshpool, Powys SY21 0SF   01938 810441

Fax: 01938 810861   E-mail: info@wllr.org.uk

2004	1	2	3	4	5	6	7	8	9	10	11	12	13	14	15	16	17	18	19	20	21	22	23	24	25	26	27	28	29	30	31
Apr			A	A	A	A	A	A	A	B	B	B	A	A	A	A	A							A	A						
May	B	B	B				A	A						A	A					A	A								B	B	B
June	A	A	A	A	A	A		A	A	A		A	A		A	A	A		A	A		A	A	A		A	A		A	A	
July	A		A	A		A	A		A	A		A	A		A	A	A	A	A	A	A	A	A	A	A	A	A	A	A	A	A
Aug	A	A	A	A	A	A	A	A	A	A	A	A	A	A	A	A	A	A	A	A	A	A	A	A	A	A	A	B	B	B	A
Sept	A	A	A	X	X		A	A	A		A	A		A	A	A		A	A					A	A						
Oct		A	A				A	A						A	A				A	A				A	A	A	A	A	A	A	A
Dec											S	S							S	S											

X denotes special events, S denotes Santa Specials, please phone for details.   No service in January, February, March and November.

Service A

Welshpool	dep	–	11.15	14.15	17.00
Llanfair	arr	–	12.05	15.05	17.50
Llanfair	dep	10.00	13.00	15.45	–
Welshpool	arr	10.50	13.50	16.35	–

Service B

–	–	10.05	11.15	12.40	14.15	15.40	17.00
–	–	10.55	12.05	13.30	15.05	16.30	17.50
09.00	10.00	11.30	13.00	14.30	15.45	–	–
09.50	10.50	12.20	13.50	15.20	16.40	–	–

WELLS & WALSINGHAM LIGHT RAILWAY
Wells-next-the-Sea, Norfolk NR23 1QB

01328 710630

Talking Timetable: 01328 710631

2004	1	2	3	4	5	6	7	8	9	10	11	12	13	14	15	16	17	18	19	20	21	22	23	24	25	26	27	28	29	30	31
Apr									B	B	B	B	B	B	B	B	B	B	B	B	B	B	B	B	B	B	B	B	B	B	B
May	B	B	B	B	B	B	B	B	B	B	B	B	B	B	B	B	B	B	B	B	B	B	B	B	B	B	B	B	B	B	B
June	B	B	B	B	B	B	B	B	B	B	B	B	B	B	B	B	B	B	B	B	B	B	B	B	B	B	B	B	B	B	
July	B	B	B	B	B	B	B	B	B	B	B	B	B	B	A	A	A	A	A	A	A	A	A	A	A	A	A	A	A	A	A
Aug	A	A	A	A	A	A	A	A	A	A	A	A	A	A	A	A	A	A	A	A	A	A	A	A	A	A	A	A	A	A	A
Sept	B	B	B	B	B	B	B	B	B	B	B	B	B	B	B	B	B	B	B	B	B	B	B	B	B	B	B	B	B	B	
Oct	C	C	C	C	C	C	C	C	C	C	C	C	C	C	C	C	C	C	C	C	C	C	C	B	B	B	B	B	B	B	B

No service in January, February, March, November and December.

Service A

Wells	dep	10.15	11.45	13.30	15.00	16.30
Walsingham	dep	11.05	12.30	14.15	15.45	17.15

Service B

10.30	12.00	14.00	15.30
11.15	12.45	14.45	16.15

Service C

11.00	12.30	14.00
11.45	13.15	14.45

Journey time 30 minutes in each direction.

WEST SOMERSET RAILWAY
The Railway Station, Minehead, Somerset TA24 5BG

01643 704996

Fax: 01643 706349   E-mail: info@West-Somerset-Railway.co.uk

2004	1	2	3	4	5	6	7	8	9	10	11	12	13	14	15	16	17	18	19	20	21	22	23	24	25	26	27	28	29	30	31
Jan	A		A	A																											
Feb														E	E		E	E	E		E	E			E	E			E		
Mar							E						A	A						A	A				X	X	X	X			
Apr	A		A	A		C	C	C	C	D	D	D	C	C	C	C	C	C		A	A	A		A	A		A	A	A		
May	C	D	D	B	B	B	X	X	X		B	B	B		B	B		B	B	B		B	B		B	B	B	B	D	D	D
June	D	D	D	C	D	C	C	C	C	C	C	C	C	C	C	C	C	C	C	C	C	C	C	C	C	C	C	C	C	C	C
July	C	C	X	X	C	C	C	C	C	C	C	C	C	C	C	C	C	C	C	C	D	D	C	C	C	C	D	D	D	C	C
Aug	C	D	D	D	D	C	D	D	D	D	D	D	C	X	X	D	D	D	D	C	C	C	D	D	D	D	C	C	C	D	D
Sept	D	D	C	C	C	C	C	C	C	C	C	C	C	C	C	B	B	B	B	B	B	B		B	B		B	B	B		
Oct	X	X	X		A	A	A		A	A		A	A	A		A	A		A	A	A		X	X		C	C	C		C	C
Nov																											S	S			
Dec		X	X	S	X	X				S	S	X				S	S				S	S					A	A	X	A	A

X denotes special services, S denotes Santa Specials, please phone for details.

Service A

Minehead	dep	10.15	12.15 (D)	14.20	16.00 (D)
Bishops Lydeard	arr	11.29	13.26	15.32	17.06
Bishops Lydeard	dep	10.25 (D)	12.25	14.30 (D)	16.05
Minehead	arr	11.32	13.34	15.37	17.13

Service B

10.15	12.15	14.00	15.55
11.29	13.30	15.17	17.11
10.25	12.25	14.10	16.05
11.38	13.36	15.21	17.15

All services are steam hauled except those marked D.

D = Diesel Train

Service C

Minehead	dep	10.15	11.10	12.15 (D)	14.00	14.50	15.55 (D)	17.35 (D)
Williton	arr	10.58	11.54	12.58	14.45	15.34	16.39	18.09
Bishops Lydeard	arr	11.29	–	13.30	15.17	–	17.11	18.36
Bishops Lydeard	dep	09.40 (D)	10.25	–	12.25 (D)	14.10	– (D)	16.05
Williton	arr	10.08	11.00	12.05	12.59	14.45	15.45	16.39
Minehead	arr	10.44	11.38	12.46	13.36	15.21	16.24	17.15

All trains call at intermediate stations: Dunster (6), Blue Anchor (14), Washford (23), Watchet (32), Williton (43), Stogumber (54) and Crowcombe (64) minutes after leaving Minehead and at Crowcombe (15), Stogumber (23), Williton (35), Watchet (44), Washford (52), Blue Anchor (60) and Dunster (67) minutes after leaving Bishops Lydeard.

Service D

Minehead	dep	10.15	11.10	12.15 (D)	14.00	14.55	15.55	16.45	17.35 (D)
Williton	dep	11.02	12.07	12.58	14.48	15.40	16.34	17.27	18.18
Bishops Lydeard	arr	11.50	12.50	13.30	15.20	16.15	17.06	17.55	18.49
Bishops Lydeard	dep	09.40 (D)	10.25	11.25	12.25	14.10	14.55	15.50	16.40
Williton	dep	10.08	11.00	12.05	12.59	14.50	15.42	16.36	17.30
Minehead	arr	10.44	11.39	12.46	13.36	15.27	16.23	17.15	18.05

Service E

Minehead	dep	11.15	14.00
Williton	arr	11.53	14.36
Williton	dep	12.15	14.50
Minehead	arr	12.51	15.28